THE WORLD REFUGEES MADE

THE WORLD REFUGEES MADE

Decolonization and the Foundation of Postwar Italy

PAMELA BALLINGER

CORNELL UNIVERSITY PRESS
Ithaca and London

Open access edition funded by the National Endowment for the Humanities.

Copyright © 2020 by Cornell University

The text of this book is licensed under a Creative Commons Attribution-NonCommercial-NoDerivatives 4.0 International License: https://creativecommons.org/licenses/by-nc-nd/4.0/. To use this book, or parts of this book, in any way not covered by the license, please contact Cornell University Press, Sage House, 512 East State Street, Ithaca, New York 14850. Visit our website at cornellpress.cornell.edu.

First published 2020 by Cornell University Press

Library of Congress Cataloging-in-Publication Data

Names: Ballinger, Pamela, 1968– author.
Title: The world refugees made : decolonization and the foundations of postwar Italy / Pamela Ballinger.
Description: Ithaca : Cornell University Press, 2020. | Includes bibliographical references and index.
Identifiers: LCCN 2019020923 (print) | LCCN 2019981505 (ebook) | ISBN 9781501747588 (cloth) | ISBN 9781501747601 (pdf) | ISBN 9781501747595 (epub)
Subjects: LCSH: Refugees—Italy—History—20th century. | Repatriation—Italy—History—20th century. | Italians—Africa—History—20th century. | Italians—Balkan Peninsula—History—20th century. | Decolonization—Africa. | Decolonization—Balkan Peninsula. | Italy—Politics and government—1945–1976.
Classification: LCC HV640.5.I8 B35 2020 (print) | LCC HV640.5.I8 (ebook) | DDC 308.9/069140945—dc23
LC record available at https://lccn.loc.gov/2019020923
LC ebook record available at https://lccn.loc.gov/2019981505

Cover photograph courtesy of Archive Mario Schifano. “When I remember Giacomo Balla, New York City 1964.” 1964 enamel and graphite on paper mounted on canvas; 180x126 cm diptych.

For John
My port of refuge

Contents

List of Illustrations *ix*
Preface *xi*
Acknowledgments *xv*
List of Abbreviations *xix*
Note on Names *xxiii*

Introduction: Mobile Histories 1

1. Empire as Prelude 28
2. Wartime Repatriations and the Beginnings of Decolonization 43
3. Italy's Long Decolonization in the Era of Intergovernmentalism 77
4. Displaced Persons and the Borders of Citizenship 134
5. Reclaiming Fascism, Housing the Nation 175

Conclusion: "We Will Return" 206

Notes *215*
Archives and Collections Consulted *291*
Index *293*

Illustrations

1. Map of Italy in 1961 at the close of formal decolonization 19
2. Detail from wall maps at former IsIAO site 22
3. Map of Italian Empire, 1940 41
4. Italian Red Cross sisters assisting Italian civilians, Berbera 50
5. Italian civilians from Ethiopia in transit to repatriation ships, Berbera 51
6. "Torneremo," 1943 56
7. *Guida del rimpatriato d'Africa* 57
8. Eritreans welcome UN commission, 1950 127
9. The road to decolonization: Italia Oltremare in 1952 133
10. Casa Doria, Fertilia, Sardinia 185
11. Wives of HELP refugees, Simaxis, Italy, 2015 200
12. "Ritorneremo": Political poster in Monteverde neighborhood of Rome, 2011 213

Preface

Like the processes by which citizens "came home" from the various possessions Italy lost after the Second World War, researching and writing this study has extended over many years. The seeds for this project were laid in the 1990s during my doctoral research with Italians who had migrated to Trieste from those eastern Adriatic territories of Istria, Kvarner, and Dalmatia that Italy ceded to Yugoslavia between 1947 and 1954. As I recuperated and analyzed memories of this mass migration, "exiles" (*esuli*) and their descendants I interviewed often mentioned living in refugee camps alongside Italians similarly displaced from Libya or Eritrea or the Dodecanese Islands, all territories Italy lost in the wake of fascism's defeat. Likewise, *esuli* who resettled outside Trieste in other parts of Italy in state-built housing often shared their neighborhoods with these fellow Italians repatriated from the former colonies. Nonetheless, these individual memories of common experiences of displacement as "national refugees" (*profughi nazionali*) found no resonance in either the scholarly literature or the political debates about the eastern border that took off in Italy in the late 1990s. Nor did discussions of Italy's own refugees in the postwar period make reference to those foreign displaced persons who continued to make their way to the Italian peninsula in significant numbers from the end of World War II into the 1960s. This study is the result of my attempt to fill those academic and political lacunae, as well as to understand the reasons for those silences.

When I began my research, apart from the extensive literature on the Istrian exodus, I had few signposts or secondary literature on the specific Italian case to guide me, a situation that has begun to change in recent years. As a result, the research stretched over years—and soon, continents. Although agreements between the Italian state and the intergovernmental bodies tasked with assisting refugees in the wake of World War II made these Italian displacees the responsibility of the Italian state with a few key exceptions, the international organizations nonetheless played an important role in this story. These agencies included the United Nations Relief and Rehabilitation

Administration (UNRRA), the International Refugee Organization (IRO), and the United Nations High Commissioner on Refugees (UNHCR). Indeed, the very understandings of national refugees and international bona fide refugees and their respective assistance regimes that emerged in the postwar period developed through a dialogic relationship, as this study demonstrates. I soon realized that the story of Italy's rebirth after World War II was deeply entangled with the genesis of the postwar international refugee regime. Beginning my research with the archives of the relevant intergovernmental bodies (located, respectively, in New York, Paris, and Geneva), I then identified relevant archives in Italy, as well as in former Italian possessions such as Rhodes (Greece) and Tirana (Albania). I conducted the most concentrated phase of research during the academic year of 2010–2011, while living in Rome.

During that period, preparations for commemoration of the 150th anniversary of Italian unification played out in the press, on the streets, and even at the annual San Remo Song Festival, where comedian Roberto Benigni exclaimed "Viva l'Italia!" and sang Italy's national anthem, "Inno di Mameli" (also known as "Il canto degli Italiani") in a pointed message to those who contended that Italy's unification was something to mourn, rather than celebrate. In a quivering voice, Benigni sang the hymn, which begins with the call to *fratelli d'Italia*, or "brothers of Italy." At issue was how to understand Italy's past, present, and future, as well as just who rightfully belonged to the community of Italian brothers and sisters. Since the nation's founding, the question of "making" Italy and Italians has preoccupied politicians and scholars alike.

Important initiatives to recuperate Italy's complex history of emigration and frequent return migration, such as the Museo Nazionale Emigrazione Italiana opened in 2009 in advance of the 150th anniversary, occasioned controversy. Located in the Vittoriano, the monument to Italy's first monarch, Vittorio Emanuele II—"altar of the Patria" and the symbolic heart of national Italian Rome—the museum provoked criticism. Critics particularly objected to the museum's final room, whose exhibit compared immigrants to contemporary Italy to Italian emigrants in the past. In addition, some voices called for the dismantling of the museum after the unification celebrations; despite an extended life, the museum shuttered its doors in 2016, though it lives on in virtual space and is slated to find a new physical home in Genoa. These debates occurred in a climate of ongoing fiscal crisis and increasingly charged political discussions about immigration to Italy. At a deeper level, however, they pointed to the long-standing ambivalence of Italian society and scholars toward the experience of mass emigration abroad, as well as still largely unacknowledged histories of encounters with immigrants of various types in the immediate aftermath of World War II.

On the evening of 17 March 2011, I walked down to central Rome from the Janiculum Hill, where crowds thronged the streets in the rain and damp cold. Despite the show of flags and the requisite fireworks, the celebrations for the 150th anniversary were understated, given their significance. No consensus existed on two key questions: What did it mean to be Italian in the twenty-first century? And how were Italians to understand the arrival of newcomers to their shores? As the residents of places like Lampedusa struggled to offer humanitarian relief to migrants arriving on their island, some Italians on the peninsula argued against sending these migrants on to camps hastily constructed in mainland Italy. Just a month before the anniversary celebration, I had caught a news transmission on a television monitor in the Rome airport as I awaited a plane to Tirana to finish up archival work there. The news featured a makeshift refugee camp somewhere in the north of Italy and captured an ugly confrontation between locals and the Africans at the barbed wire dividing them. One of the African men, speaking broken Italian, appealed to his Italian counterpart, "Siamo tutti fratelli . . . siamo tutti uguali" (We are all brothers . . . we are all equal), he pleaded. "No, non è vero, non siamo tutti uguali," shot back the older Italian, denying any common ground. In that disavowal of brotherhood, the Italian man also unwittingly denied an extensive history of encounters on Italian soil with refugees and migrants, both foreign and Italian. Marked by forms of solidarity, as well as indifference, these encounters continue to shape Italian legal and social responses to the contemporary migrations that have become only more pressing in the wake of the refugee crises that have made the Mediterranean the central site of dangerous passage to Europe. Contrary to all the claims that Italians in the twenty-first century face an unprecedented refugee crisis, this book demonstrates how in the first decade and a half after the Second World War both the Italian state and everyday Italians confronted a large and complicated refugee "problem"—a refugee population that included Italian citizens displaced with the defeat of fascism.

Acknowledgments

Henry Miller famously wrote, "One's destination is never a place but rather a new way of looking at things."[1] This book represents the end point of a long journey, one that has led me to a new way of seeing Italy and what I call its "long decolonization." In making my way to that destination, I have been given much assistance and support along the way by colleagues to whom I owe sincerest thanks for their inspiration, good humor, and invaluable directions. The process of conceptualizing and researching this study began while I was teaching in the Department of Anthropology and Sociology at Bowdoin College. A semester-long fellowship in 2006 at the Italian Academy at Columbia University allowed me to begin digging into the United Nations archives. Monies from Bowdoin's Faculty Resources Committee made possible various short research stints in Italy, as well as consultation of the IRO documentation at the Archives Nationales in Paris. Sabbatical funds from Bowdoin supplemented a fellowship at the Center for Advanced Study in the Behavioral Sciences at Stanford University (CASBS) in 2009–2010. Many thanks to my colleagues at Bowdoin, CASBS, Stanford, and Columbia who helped me begin to think through the place of the refugee in Italian history: Kanchan Chandra, J. P. Daughton, Victoria de Grazia, Barbara Faedda, Estelle Freedman, Pekka Hämäläinen, Simon Levis Sullam, Saba Mahmood, Gregory Mann, Devin Naar, Marilyn Reizbaum, Tanya Richardson, Cabeiri deBergh Robinson, Aron Rodrigue, Arielle Saiber, and Margaret (Peggy) Somers. I am also appreciative of the help provided by librarians and archivists at the Hoover Institution.

I am deeply grateful for a National Endowment for the Humanities Fellowship and an ACLS Frederick Burkhardt Residential Fellowship for Recently Tenured Scholars, which made possible an intensive year of research (2010–2011) based in Italy at the American Academy in Rome. Kind thanks to academy directors Carmela Franklin and Christopher Celenza for their sponsorship of my residence there. Among my many interlocutors during my time in Italy I cannot fail to acknowledge Federico Cresti, Valeria Deplano, Stephanie Malia Hom, Nicola Labanca, Daniela Melfa, Antonio Morone,

Alessandro Pes, David Rifkind, Rovena Sakja, Silvia Salvatici, Joshua Samuels, Matteo Sanfilippo, Jennifer Scappettone, Franco Tagliarini, Anna Teodorani, Saskia Maria van Genugten, and Joseph Viscomi. Deepest gratitude as well to the Istituto Regionale per la Storia del Movimento di Liberazione nel Friuli–Venezia Giulia—especially to colleagues Riccardo Bottoni, Gloria Nemec, Raoul Pupo, Roberto Spazzali, and Sergio Zucca—for a stay there as an Insmli Visiting Scholar. Thanks as well to Marisa Ferrara, Orietta Moscarda, Giovanni Radossi, and Nicolò Sponza for their help during my many visits to the Centro Ricerche Storiche di Rovigno in Croatia.

During my research sojourn in Italy I frequented many archives. *Tante grazie* to the staffs of the Archivio Centrale dello Stato (particularly Erminia Ciccozzi and Giulia Barrera), Archivio di Stato di Trieste, Archivio Storico Società Dante Alighieri, Archivio Storico Diplomatico del Ministero degli Affari Esteri (especially Stefania Ruggeri and Michele Abbate), Centro Studi Emigrazione Roma, INPS (with particular shout-outs to Marianna Frustaci, Marco Matini, Antonella Uselli, and my cappuccino companions Barbara de Iudicibus, Francesca Ciafardoni, and Francesca Paola Sica), Istituto Agronomico per l'Oltremare (in particular Antonella Bigazzi), and the Presidenza del Consiglio dei Ministri (above all, Bruna Colarossi and Stefania Mariotti). Elidor Mëhilli graciously facilitated my initial contacts with the Central State Archives in Tirana, Albania, where I worked with Italian-era materials. Sabina Donati, Valerie McGuire, and Mia Fuller likewise provided valuable information about the State Archives of the Dodecanese, whose director Eirini Toliou patiently worked with me translating between English, Italian, and Greek to locate relevant documents.

The archival trail did not end there, however. I made multiple visits to Geneva to pore through papers at the archives of the UNHCR, the ICRC, and the ICEM/IOM. Archivists Fabrizio Bensi, Montserrat Canela, Kerstin Lau, and Patricia Fluckiger-Livingstone all helped me cover extensive ground in a short period. In my off hours from the archives, Jane Cowan, Sabina Donati, Jérôme Elie, Francesca Piana, and Davide Rodogno offered stimulating discussions about refugees, humanitarianism, and more. Peter Gatrell drew my attention to the Don Murray / HELP project with his suggestion to consult the Papers of the United Nations Career Records Project held at the Bodleian Library in Oxford. This eventually led me to Belden and Lisa Paulson, who graciously welcomed me to their home in the mountains of Vermont for an interview one long summer day. Ken Grossi at Oberlin College provided guidance to the Paulson papers there.

Belden Paulson offered me a virtual introduction to Vlada Pavcic, one of the descendants of the refugees settled by HELP in Sardinia. Vlada, her mother, and their neighbors and relatives hosted me at the Pavcic home in Simaxis and shared their experiences with me. Thanks to them for the wonderful conversation and the traditional cake! Multiple visits to the refugee resettlement town of Fertilia also relied on similar generosity and openness. Particular thanks are owed to Marisa Brugna, Dario Manni, Marina Nardozzi, Agata Ortel, Barbara Sbisà, and Franca Venier. Similarly, Roberta Cafà kindly arranged interviews with residents of Gebelia / SACIDA near Anzio. Thank you, as well, to Giovanna Ortu at AIRL for a helpful encounter when this project was still just a vague idea.

Like the research, the writing of the book stretched over many years and benefited from countless conversations and readings of drafts. My wonderful colleagues at the University of Michigan continually impress and inspire me. Research funds and assistance from the Associate Professor Support Fund at Michigan, together with monies from UM's Publication Subvention Fund, made a critical difference in the later stages of this project. A new vista of human rights thinking was opened up for me by the Fred Cuny Chair in the History of Human Rights and my colleague Robert (Bob) Donia, whose vision informs the Donia Human Rights Center at Michigan. Although my debts there are too numerous, I must single out for their suggestions my colleagues Giorgio Bertellini, Howard Brick, Kathleen Canning, Max Cherem (from Kalamazoo College), Rita Chin, Joshua Cole, Jay Cook, Geoff Eley, Dario Gaggio, Mary Kelley, Karla Malette, Brian Porter-Szücs, Rebecca Scott, Minnie Sinha, Peggy Somers, Scott Spector, Paolo Squatriti, Melanie Tanielian, Kiyo Tsutsui, Jeff Veidlinger, Penny Von Eschen, and Geneviève Zubrzycki. My former and present students Cristian Capotescu, Nevila Pahumi, Ashley Rockenbach, Lediona Shahollari, and Joseph Viscomi also offered valuable feedback, as did Giulio Salvati and Noelle Turtur. Likewise, the fellows and colleagues at the Shelby Cullom Davis Center at Princeton with whom I shared dinners and seminars during the 2014–2015 year commented on and enriched draft chapters: Jeremy Adelman, Nicole Archambeau, David Barnes, Matthew Carp, Jennifer Foray, Pierre Force, Sheldon Garon, Molly Greene, Atina Grossman, Harold James, Michael Laffan, Rebecca Nedostup, and M'hamed Oualdi. Director Phil Nord's uncanny ability to grasp the heart of my argument even when I could still barely discern its outlines provided a clear road map on several key occasions.

On my winding journey there are many, many others who have offered me feedback or incentives to travel onward by presenting a paper or attending a conference. Most notable in this regard are Patrizia Audenino, Daniela (Gia) Caglioti, Ruth Ben-Ghiat, Mark Choate, Olindo Di Napoli, Ronald Eyerman, Katherine Fleming, Mia Fuller, Peter Gatrell, Emily Greble, Anna Holian,

Alison Frank Johnson, Pieter Judson, Borut Klabjan, Manoela Patti, Roberta Pergher, Dominique Reill, Jessica Reinisch, Giuseppe Sciortino, Glenda Sluga, Marla Stone, Annalisa Urbano, Marta Verginella, Larry Wolff, and Tara Zahra. Thanks as well to Jordanna Bailkin, Paul Bijl, Elizabeth Buettner, Christoph Kalter, Andrea Smith, and Lori Watt for their inspirational conversations regarding colonial repatriation.

This book includes a small amount of previously published material from the following articles and chapter by the author: "Borders of the Nation, Borders of Citizenship: Italian Repatriation and the Redefinition of National Identity after World War II," *Comparative Studies in Society and History* 49, no. 3 (2007); "Entangled Histories or 'Extruded' Histories? Displacement, Refugees, and Repatriation after World War II," *Journal of Refugee Studies* 25, no. 3 (2012); "History's Illegibles: National Indeterminacy in Istria," *Austrian History Yearbook* 43 (2012); "Beyond the Italies? Italy as a Mobile Subject," in *Italian Mobilities*, edited by Ruth Ben-Ghiat and Stephanie Malia Hom (New York: Routledge University Press, 2016); "Colonial Twilight: Italian Settlers and the Long Decolonization of Libya," *Journal of Contemporary History* 51, no. 4 (2016); and "A Sea of Difference, A History of Gaps: Migrations between Italy and Albania, 1939–1992," *Comparative Studies in Society and History* 60, no. 1 (2018). I thank the respective publishers for this reuse permission.

I am grateful to the three anonymous reviewers of this manuscript and to Cornell Press for the care given to this study. Especial thanks are due to Mike Bechthold (cartography), Glenn Novak (copy editor), Sandy Sadow (indexer), and Susan Specter (senior production editor). Particular gratitude to the Archivio Mario Schifano for permission to reproduce the image "When I Remember Giacomo Balla," on the book's cover. Above all, it has been a pleasure to work with my editor Emily Andrew—I appreciate her responsiveness, professionalism, and keen interest in questions of Italian decolonization.

My deepest thanks go to my family members who lived this project—and endured the long absences it entailed—for far too many years. My mother, Sandra Ballinger, fretted over my many travels but always cheered me on. B. and Z. offered their unconditional love and found ways to maneuver around piles of papers and books. Finally, my husband John Henshaw shared this journey with me. I can never thank him enough for his unending support, patience, and faith that the destination was in sight.

List of Abbreviations

AAI	Amministrazione per gli Aiuti Internazionali / Amministrazione per le Attività Assistenziali Italiane ed Internazionali
ACC	Allied Control Commission
ACS	Archivio Centrale dello Stato
AFHQ	Allied Force Headquarters
AFIS	Amministrazione Fiduciaria Italiana della Somalia
AIRL	Associazione Italiani Rimpatriati dalla Libia
AMG	Allied Military Government
AMGOT	Allied Military Government of Occupied Territories
ANCIFRA	Associazione Nazionale Cittadini Italiani e Familiari Rimpatriati dall'Albania
ANCIS	Associazione Nazionale Comunità Italo-Somala
ANVGD	Associazione Nazionale Venezia Giulia e Dalmazia
AOI	Africa Orientale Italiana
AQSH	Arkivi Qendror Shtetëror
ASDMAE	Archivio Storico Diplomatico del Ministero degli Affari Esteri
ASMAI	Archivio Storico del Ministero dell'Africa Italiana
BMA	British Military Administration
CASAS	Comitato Amministrativo Soccorso ai Senzatetto
CLN	Comitato di Liberazione Nazionale
CLNI	Comitato di Liberazione Nazionale dell'Istria
CNRI	Comitato Nazionale per i Rifugiati Italiani
CORI	Commissione permanente per il rimpatrio degli italiani all'estero
CRI	Croce Rossa Italiana
CRS	Catholic Relief Services
CTIID	Commissione per la tutela degli interessi italiani nel Dodecaneso
DC	Democrazia Cristiana

DELASEM	Delegazione per l'Assistenza degli Emigranti Ebrei
DP	displaced person
ECA	Ente comunale di assistenza
ECL	Ente per la Colonizzazione della Libia
EFC	Ente Ferrarese di Colonizzazione
EFTAS	Ente di Trasformazione Fondiaria e Agraria in Sardegna
E.GI.S.	Ente Giuliano di Sardegna "Don Francesco Dapiran"
ENDSI	Ente Nazionale per la Distribuzione dei Soccorsi in Italia
ERLAAS	Ente Regionale per la Lotta Anti Anofelica in Sardegna
ERP	European Recovery Plan (Marshall Plan)
EUR	Esposizione Universale di Roma
FAO	Food and Agriculture Organization
FeNPIA	Federazione Nazionale dei Profughi Italiani d'Africa
FTT	Free Territory of Trieste (Territorio Libero di Trieste)
GSAD	Greek State Archives of the Dodecanese
HELP	Homeless European Land Program
IAO	Istituto Agronomico per l'Oltremare
ICEM/IOM	Intergovernmental Committee for European Migration / International Organization for Migration
ICRC	International Committee of the Red Cross
IGCR	Intergovernmental Committee on Refugees
ILO	International Labor Organization
INA	Istituto Nazionale delle Assicurazioni
INFPS	Istituto Nazionale Fascista della Previdenza Sociale
INPS	Istituto Nazionale della Previdenza Sociale
IRC	International Rescue Committee
IRO	International Refugee Organization
IsIAO	Istituto Italiano per l'Africa e l'Oriente
MAE	Ministero degli Affari Esteri
MAI	Ministero dell'Africa Italiana
NCWC	National Catholic War Council / National Catholic Welfare Council
NGO	nongovernmental organization
OAPGD	Opera per l'Assistenza ai Profughi Giuliani e Dalmati
OETA	Occupied Enemy Territory Administration
ONARMO	Opera Nazionale per l'Assistenza Religiosa e Morale degli Operai
ONC	Opera Nazionale Combattenti
PAI	Polizia Africa Italiana
PCA	Pontificia Commissione di Assistenza

PCAP	Pontificia Commissione di Assistenza ai Profughi
PCI	Partito Comunista Italiano
PCM	Presidenza del Consiglio dei Ministri
POA	Pontificia Opera di Assistenza
RSI	Repubblica Sociale Italiana
SACIDA	Società Agricola Cooperativa fra i Colonizzatori Italiani d'Africa
SAIS	Società Agricola Italo-Somala
SHAEF	Supreme Headquarters Allied Expeditionary Force
TNA	The National Archives of the United Kingdom
UDHR	Universal Declaration of Human Rights
UNA	United Nations Archives, New York, United States
UNHCR	United Nations High Commissioner for Refugees
UNRRA	United Nations Relief and Rehabilitation Administration
UNRRA-CASAS	Comitato Amministrativo Soccorso ai Senzatetto
UZC	Ufficio per le Zone di Confine
WCC	World Council of Churches
WRY	World Refugee Year

Note on Names

This study deals with toponyms that often have multiple variants. When using a name, I have generally used the common English form—for example, Mogadishu—where appropriate. At other times, I give both the Italian version commonly used during the period of the Oltremare d'Italia and the name in official use today. I put the prevalent contemporary name first; for example, Pula/Pola to refer to the city in the southern Istrian peninsula under Italian control from 1920 to 1947, Yugoslav sovereignty from 1947 to 1991, and part of Croatia since 1991. This usage does not imply any political commentary about the "rightful" belonging of such a territory.

For the period under study, one also encounters multiple spellings for the same place. Both Italian and English language speakers alike in the 1940s and 1950s, for example, commonly spelled Ethiopia's capital city as either Addis Ababa or Addis Abeba. Unless the spelling "Addis Abeba" is specifically used in a document, however, I employ the prevalent spelling today of "Ababa." Likewise, Italian documents from the twentieth century alternatively refer to the Aegean Islands as the Dodecanneso or Dodecaneso. When citing documents, I use the variant they employ. Otherwise, I use the English spelling of Dodecanese, as well as "Aegean Islands" or the Italian alternative of Isole Egeo. When referring in English to individuals coming from the lost territories of Venezia Giulia (in English, the Julian March), I use "Julian." When employing the Italian place name in reference to the region's inhabitants, I instead write of Venezia Giulians.

In the variety of documents consulted, personal names also exhibit multiple spellings and misspellings. Spurgeon Milton Keeny of UNRRA sometimes makes appearances as "Keeney." Similarly, Myer Cohen of UNRRA sometimes figures as Mayer Cohen. Likewise, the UNRRA representative Wankowicz in Rhodes appears in certain documents as "Wancowica." When referring to such figures myself, I use the correct version. Nonetheless, I have left the spelling in the documents as is. Testifying to the transnational work of assisting refugees, such alternative namings highlight the diverse actors interacting in the postwar humanitarian arena.

THE WORLD REFUGEES MADE

Introduction
Mobile Histories

In 1958, Italian officials puzzled over letters received from the Unione Coloni Italiani d'Africa demanding a resolution of the outstanding problems of Italian "refugees" displaced from the region of Cyrenaica in former Italian Libya. The prefect of Verona, for example, requested information about this association in a telegram to the Ministero degli Affari Esteri (MAE). Bergamo's prefect Antonino Celona sent the ministry a similar wire, noting "Unione Coloni Italiani Africa is unknown here. We beg you to furnish relevant details with which to identify this organization."[1] Answering Celona's query, this study uses the experiences of Italians repatriated "home" in the wake of decolonization to trace both the genesis of the postwar international refugee regime and the consequences of one of its key omissions: the ineligibility from international refugee status and protection of those migrants scholars have labeled "national refugees" or, in contemporary parlance, internally displaced persons. Many historians have shared the prefect of Bergamo's seeming ignorance about these colonists displaced by the end of empire. This has prompted one observer to characterize such repatriates as "Europe's invisible migrants," contrasting their relative scholarly invisibility to the intense interest in the immigration to the metropole by former colonial *subjects*.[2] The irony is that, at the time of the events, many of these population movements were highly—if selectively—visible at the level of diplomatic negotiations, in the press, and in the local communities that housed camps for such migrants.

Those prefects charged with matters of public security who sought information about the Unione Coloni Italiani d'Africa proved all too aware of the pressing need to resettle Italians from the former possessions. The officials' incomprehension centered instead on the identity of this specific association precisely because a large and confusing array of advocacy groups for national refugees and repatriates already existed. Contrary to a popular belief that the presence and experiences of such migrants were erased or repressed in Italy, then, "what emerges is the sense that they were displaced."[3] In place of an assumed amnesia about Italian imperialism and its ending, *The World Refugees Made* focuses on a literal displacement and re-emplacement of that colonial past: the return of Italian settlers from the colonies and other *possedimenti* or possessions lost after World War II and their insertion into a series of political, classificatory/taxonomic, and built environments.

By the time Celona sent his telegram in 1958, Italian authorities and international actors had spent over a decade and a half debating the identity and refugee status of migrants from former Italian lands in Africa and the Balkans. These individuals came from the wide range of territories Italy lost with the defeat of fascism: Eritrea, Ethiopia, and Somalia (after 1936 collectively known as Africa Orientale Italiana or Italian East Africa), Libya (first a colony and after 1938 incorporated directly into the Italian state), the Dodecanese Islands (a province or department rather than a colony), and Albania (a protectorate). With the 1947 Peace Treaty, Italy renounced its claims to its African colonies and Albania. It also ceded the Dodecanese Islands to Greece; the Tenda-Briga District of Piedmont, parts of Little Saint Bernard Pass in the Valle d'Aosta, and parts of the Val Roja in Liguria to France; the small concession of Tientsin or Tianjin to China; and the southern portion of Venezia Giulia to Yugoslavia. Another area of the contested Venezia Giulia region—which had been an integral part of the Italian state—was awarded to Yugoslavia in 1954. Finally, Italian supervision of a UN trusteeship over Somalia ended in 1960, effectively bringing Italy's colonial era to a close. As a result of the transfer of sovereignty over these territories, as many as 425,000 Italians migrated to the Italian peninsula from the African possessions, over 50,000 from Albania, some 16,000 from the Aegean Islands, and up to 200,000 from Italy's eastern Adriatic lands.[4] Though modest in comparison to the approximately 6.2 million Japanese citizens repatriated from the former Japanese Empire or the some 11 to 12 million ethnic Germans expelled from Central and Eastern Europe in the immediate postwar, these flows out of former Italian possessions had a significant impact at the local, national, and international levels. They stimulated extensive debate over what it meant to be Italian, to be a refugee, and what sort of Italy would house these national refugees.

As this study demonstrates, Italy served as a crucial laboratory in which categorizations differentiating foreign or international refugees from national refugees were worked out in practice, with consequences that resonated far beyond the particular time and place. Despite this, in histories of both refugee flows and decolonization Italy has represented an anomalous or peripheral case, at best. Even accounts dedicated to modern Italian history tend to treat these population flows as footnotes to the main events of the war and early postwar period: the 1943 deposition of Mussolini and subsequent armistice that divided the country into two governments and sparked a civil war that ended only in 1945; the 1946 institutional referendum that abolished the monarchy and established the Constituent Assembly that drafted the constitution for the new Italian Republic; the Peace Treaty of 1947 that delimited Italy's new borders; the decisive electoral defeat of the Partito Comunista Italiano (PCI) by Democrazia Cristiana (DC) in the general election of 1948; the extension of the Marshall Plan to revive Italy's economy (1948–1952); the beginning of the "economic miracle" in the 1950s that transformed Italy into a mass consumer society; and Italy's admission into the United Nations in 1955. All of these critical milestones, however, remained entangled with the protracted dismantling of Italian empire. The rhythm and tempo of repatriation from Italy's lost possessions, for example, were conditioned by both international events and the exigencies of Italian domestic politics, even as these flows created urgent humanitarian emergencies on the Italian peninsula. A focus on refugees reframes the history of Italy's emergence as a postfascist republic in the early Cold War era.

The presence of displaced persons posed the complex question of who belonged—culturally and legally—in this territorially and politically reconfigured Italy. In the years immediately following the war, Italy housed a varied population of migrants from Eastern Europe, notably Yugoslavia, Poland, Bulgaria, and the Soviet Union. Many of these individuals met the requirements for assistance as international refugees from the intergovernmental United Nations bodies: first the United Nations Relief and Rehabilitation Administration, or UNRRA, in operation between 1943 and 1947; the International Refugee Organization, or IRO, that ran from 1946 to 1952; and finally the United Nations High Commissioner on Refugees, or UNHCR, which began its work in 1950.[5] A variety of "voluntary agencies" (many of them faith-based NGOs) collaborated with the UN agencies in aiding these refugees. For those who did not satisfy those requirements, the Italian state was often the only hope for assistance. Italy thus assumed care of those foreigners deemed ineligible as international refugees or labeled as "undesirables," with many of these migrants housed in camps that after 1947 came under the aegis of the Amministrazione per gli Aiuti Internazionali (AAI) or the Direzione di Pubblica Sicurezza and, later, the Ministero dell'Interno.[6] Italy also remained responsible for those considered its "own" refugees, that is, Italian nationals displaced from any part of Italy's prewar territory. This reflected a broader division of labor that emerged out of the postwar encounter with displaced persons in Europe: national governments became responsible for their own displacees who remained within national borders, whereas those individuals who crossed an international border and met other criteria (notably persecution or well-founded fear of it) came under the care and maintenance of the UN agencies. In existence from 1938 to 1947, the Intergovernmental Committee on Refugees (IGCR) also cared for some displaced persons who could not return to their home countries; from 1952 on, the Intergovernmental Committee on European Migration (ICEM) played an important role in aiding "post-hostility" refugees, notably those from Hungary in 1956. This divvying up, in both practical and conceptual terms, of the task of assistance assumed that individuals who could claim Italian citizenship and had left a territory like Somalia or the Dodecanese Islands—even if owing to intimidation or fear—had not crossed an international border when they migrated to the Italian peninsula.

The 1951 Geneva Convention on Refugees, the guiding legal document for the work of the Office of the UN High Commissioner on Refugees created the previous year, codified the concept of the international refugee. In its origins, the convention was anything but a universal instrument of protection, for the most part covering pre-1951 European refugees. Article 1 of the convention defined as a refugee anyone who

> as a result of events occurring before 1 January 1951 and owing to well-founded fear of being persecuted for reasons of race, religion, nationality, membership of a particular social group or political opinion, is outside the country of his nationality and is unable or, owing to such fear, is unwilling to avail himself of the protection of that country; or who, not having a nationality and being outside the country of his former habitual residence as a result of such events, is unable or, owing to such fear, is unwilling to return to it.[7]

A subsection further clarified,

For the purposes of this Convention, the words "events occurring before 1 January 1951" in article 1, section A, shall be understood to mean either:

a) "events occurring in Europe before 1 January 1951"; or
b) "events occurring in Europe or elsewhere before 1 January 1951," and each Contracting State shall make a declaration at the time of signature, ratification or accession, specifying which of these meanings it applies for the purpose of its obligations under this Convention.[8]

The Geneva Convention on Refugees thus placed temporal and geographic limits on who qualified as a refugee. In addition, individual states had the right to adopt the "geographic reservation"—clause (a) of the subsection—that restricted the refugees they would admit to those from Europe. Among the states initially exercising the reservation was Italy, which only abolished the reservation with the 1990 Martelli Law.[9] Article 40 of the convention, the "territorial clause" (sometimes referred to as the colonial clause), also permitted signatory states to either extend or exclude the convention's applications to their colonial possessions and overseas dependencies.[10]

Notably, the Geneva Convention excluded from its remit national refugees. Most German expellees, as well as Italian repatriates, technically fell under this category, defined by Article 1 Section E of the convention as an individual "recognized by the competent authorities of the country in which he has taken residence as having the rights and obligations which are attached to the possession of the nationality of that country."[11] This clause built upon, even if it did not prove synonymous with, understandings of the refugee enshrined in the constitution of the International Refugee Organization, whose work concluded as the convention and UNHCR came into existence.[12]

While various regional and national regimes of refugee management arose in the decade after World War II to cope with the problems of displacement occurring on a global scale, only the highly particularistic European one embodied by the convention became normative as international law.[13] Together with European national refugees like Italian repatriates and ethnic German expellees from Central and Eastern Europe, the convention's refugee definition omitted from eligibility a whole range of non-European refugees. These included those produced by decolonization in South Asia (the partition of India and Pakistan in 1947), the end of the British mandate in Palestine and the creation of Israel in 1948, and the influx of persons fleeing communist China in 1949 into the British colony of Hong Kong. In addition, the *hikiagesha*, Japanese colonial repatriates who arrived in the homeland as refugees from Manchuria, Korea, and Taiwan as the consequence of mandatory repatriation carried out by Allied forces, had been excluded prima facie from this UN assistance regime.[14] Later colonial repatriates, notably the European settlers from Algeria known as the *pieds-noirs*, also fell outside the terms of eligibility laid down by the convention. Only with the 1967 Protocol Relating to the Status of Refugees did the convention remove geographic and temporal restrictions on displacement. Nevertheless, the criteria of persecution and movement across an international border remained central to the definition of the refugee, thereby excluding so-called "economic" migrants as well as subsequent colonial repatriates like the Portuguese *retornados*. However imperfect, many of the international legal frameworks for assisting and managing refugees still in place today developed out of Europe's extended refugee crisis in the 1940s and 1950s.

The parceling out of responsibility for the displaced and the construction of legal frameworks like that of the Geneva Convention on Refugees were achieved only through painstaking debates over how to classify the millions of people displaced by the Second World War and its aftermaths. This book reconstructs that story. Whereas much of the critical analysis of the convention has focused on the Eurocentric nature of its exclusions,[15] the Italian case points up how the refugee definition also excluded many European displaced persons from recognition. As one of the premier scholars of international refugee law notes, after World War II "a consensus emerged that such national refugees were not 'an international problem,' and did not require international protection."[16] Yet achieving such consensus did not prove easy in practice, nor was it a foregone conclusion. In fact, "nothing in historical practice precluded bringing IDPS [internally displaced persons] within the scope of the [1951] Convention."[17] Not surprisingly, then, the question of how to classify displacees from Italy's lost territories arose repeatedly and preoccupied a wide range of actors, including personnel with UNRRA, the IRO, the Italian government, the Vatican, and the British Military Administrations that governed former Italian territories in Africa and the Dodecanese Islands until their final disposition could be determined. Unpacking the Italian case thus highlights how laborious was the work at the foundational moment of the international refugee system to exclude from the international refugee category individuals such as those migrating from former Italian possessions, an exclusion rooted in the "turbulent days" of the war's conclusion and aftermaths but also in the continuing postwar commitment of many European powers to colonialism.[18] Heeding the call of legal scholars to take historical and "real account" of the refugee convention's context, this study offers deep context and a critical prehistory.[19] Doing so reveals how the displaced themselves—like those petitioning under the banner of the Unione Coloni Italiani d'Africa—often challenged the categorizations applied to them as they navigated an emerging world of relief, assistance, and rights.

At the same time, as an Italian state defeated in war sought to regulate the movements of both "national" and "foreign" refugees into its territory, management of the displaced became a critical arena through which to reconstitute sovereignty and its instruments (notably citizenship). In the run-up to the 1947 Peace Treaty, for example, Italian officials insisted on the need to slow entry of Italian nationals from its former possessions, contrary to the recommendations and desire of the British who administered these territories. In 1947, the Italian government conducted a census and registration of aliens in its territory aimed at increased monitoring and control.[20] This occurred in the same year as the treaty that many Italians saw as a humiliation imposed by the Great Powers but which also symbolized, paradoxically, the full restoration of Italian sovereignty after the war. In negotiations over the transition from UNRRA to the IRO, Italian authorities even threatened to pull out; this would have required, however, Italy to assume full logistical and, even more problematic, *financial* commitment for all foreign refugees in the country. By the time the IRO concluded its work in 1952, a joint committee composed of representatives of both the UNHCR and the Italian Ministry of Foreign Affairs and Ministry of the Interior had begun to determine eligibility of international refugees, signaling Italy's growing assertiveness in the management of foreigners on its soil.[21] Simultaneously, assisting and integrating Italy's own refugees of empire became part of a broader process to reclaim a sense of nation contaminated by fascism.

Decolonization and Refugeedom: The View from Italy

Throughout the nearly two decades in which Italian decolonization unfolded, Italian authorities uniformly insisted that Italy could barely absorb its own citizen refugees, let alone those coming from other states. At the same moment in 1958 that Italians from Cyrenaica were demanding from the Italian state the *qualifica di profugo* or rights as national refugees that had been codified legislatively in 1949 and 1952 (Law n. 51 of 1 March 1949 and Law n. 137 of 4 March 1952, respectively),[22] the Italian state was engaged in a delicate dance with the UNHCR over the possibilities for foreign refugees to acquire citizenship. To this point, Italy had served merely as a transit country for foreign refugees awaiting permanent homes elsewhere. Italian authorities continued to insist that those seeking Italian citizenship provide "a certificate to the effect that they are freed from their nationality of origin issued by the competent authorities of that country." Not surprisingly, very few refugees could meet this requirement. Although for the UNHCR the issue appeared to be a small technicality that could be easily overcome, the relevant Italian authorities continued to drag their feet over the question until 1970.[23] A strategy of bureaucratic inertia served as cover for Italy's general unwillingness to become permanent home to foreign displaced persons.

The UNHCR had begun to press the question with the Italian government in the late 1950s in light of what one agency official, Ernest Schlatter, deemed the challenge posed by "those refugees who, for various reasons, cannot emigrate to other countries."[24] The UNHCR called for a campaign of "camp clearance" and integration to resolve the long-standing problem of all of Europe's "hard core" or "hard to settle" refugees—those whose age, health, or political or ethnic identity rendered them undesirable to those countries accepting refugees as migrants. In 1959–1960, the United Nations sponsored the World Refugee Year (WRY) in recognition of the specific and enduring problems created by displacement in Europe during and after the Second World War, together with the broader challenges of displacement at a global level. In the preparations leading up to the WRY, Italian representatives on the ICEM's planning committee continued to stress—as Italian officials had done since the waning days of the war—that Italy's perennial problems of overpopulation and economic underdevelopment, together with the needs of Italy's own displacees, limited the country's ability to provide long-term refuge to the hard core.[25] Ignoring the changed possibilities wrought by the growing postwar economic boom in Italy, these assertions repackaged older claims about Italian surplus population that had justified empire in the name of a "demographic colonization."

Although the number of Italian nationals coming from Italy's former possessions had tapered off by the time of the WRY discussions in the late 1950s, flows of Italian migrants to the peninsula increased from the newly decolonized states (especially Algeria, Tunisia, and Egypt) of other European powers. These individuals left for the same combination of reasons that had motivated the national refugees from former Italian territories who preceded them: economic and social dislocation, legal difficulties created by the passport regimes of the new states, intimidation, expropriation, and even violence. In light of the continued needs of a wide range of Italian refugees excluded from the convention, Italian officials were no doubt pleased that the UN resolution establishing the parameters for the WRY offered a broad definition of refugee—one that went well beyond the legal requirements for UNHCR recognition—in order to highlight the staggering global dimensions and human costs of displacement.[26] WRY organizers thus employed a capacious understanding of refugee that dovetailed with the category of "displaced persons" (DPs) that became prominent during and after the Second World War.[27]

Employing now familiar tactics of humanitarian initiatives such as celebrity appeals, local grassroots fund-raising, and public information campaigns, the World Refugee Year raised awareness of the struggles of those denied international refugee status in places like Hong Kong, as well as the protracted nature of Europe's post-1945 "displaced persons question" embodied by the hard-core refugees.[28] The UNHCR, for example, commissioned booklets like Kaye Webb and Ronald Searle's *Refugees 1960: A Report in Words and Drawings*, which offered brief portraits of the displaced individuals the authors met on their visits to refugee camps in Italy, Austria, and Greece. The pamphlet included a sketch of a little girl encountered in the transit camp of Risiera di San Sabba in Trieste. Singled out by the authors for its precarious living conditions and its large population of difficult-to-settle refugees (particularly those suffering from tuberculosis), this camp housed both foreign and national displaced persons who had made their way to Italy from the areas of Venezia Giulia ceded to Yugoslavia, as well as from Eastern Europe.

Like many refugee camps in Italy and beyond, San Sabba possessed a dark history during the war as a Nazi-fascist concentration camp. In the text accompanying their drawing of the young girl, Webb and Searle noted the irony of the camp's postwar repurposing: "This child is one of many who wander about the cinder playground which was once the floor of a gas chamber."[29] Those cinderblocks at the Risiera di San Sabba became a literal meeting point of Italy's national refugees and foreign displaced persons, revealing how in practice two populations and histories often treated as running in parallel actually converged in both time and space. San Sabba thus stands as a chronotope of the intertwined historical processes of Italian defeat, decolonization, and European forced migration(s).

Choosing the image of the child in San Sabba to grace the UN report's cover, Webb and Searle drew upon a well-established iconography featuring children and women as quintessential refugees and objects of compassion.[30] Yet even as they literally provided a face to that young refugee, the authors effaced her voice and individuality, noting, "When we tried to identify her after the drawing was made, no one knew her name and she never re-appeared. She was just another stateless child, a number on a card but having no individual existence."[31] In this book, I aim to reconstruct both the stories of those who became "a number on a card"—or a question mark on an official telegram to a ministry—and the processes (legal, organizational, and political) by which displaced persons were counted, evaluated, and sorted into categories such as international refugee, national refugee, (colonial) repatriate, and (mere) migrant, as well as citizen.

The World Refugees Made thus charts the emergence of what Peter Gatrell has deemed "refugeedom," focusing on a critical historical moment and geographic space where the modern international refugee regime coalesced. Representing "a capacious and also an insistent term," the notion of refugeedom highlights mobilities together with a "specific category of humanity," as well as "the changing manifestations of a 'refugee regime,' taken to mean the principles, rules and practices adopted by government officials and others in order to manage refugees, and the protection gaps in the system."[32] Gatrell and other scholars of displacement have noted how the conceptual and classificatory boundaries employed in managing displacement have created persistent lacunae in our scholarly understandings of refugees, with refugees' frequent social marginality mirrored in their marginality within mainstream historiography. Within accounts of modern Italy, not only refugee histories but even the much broader experiences of migration have remained surprisingly peripheral. This remains true despite the formative role played by outmigration in Italian history.

The last decade has, however, witnessed the growth of a specialized historical literature on displacement, particularly European population flows during and in the aftermath of World War II. Once-peripheral questions now sit at the center of both national and international histories. "Nonetheless, the emerging canon still has some notable and fundamental blind spots," acknowledge Matthew Frank and Jessica Reinisch. These two key contributors to critical debates in refugee history admit, "Overall, there is still no consistent historiography that locates the many different kinds of refugees, migrants and uprooted people within a common framework."[33] One of this study's many aims includes putting together categories of migrants—foreign and national refugees—usually kept apart in order to probe both the processes and consequences in theory and practice of such conceptual differentiations. Doing this directs attention to those persistent "blind spots" that characterize relevant scholarly literatures, notably the entangled histories of foreign and national refugees (including colonial repatriates) and the longevity of Italian decolonization and its visibility at the time of events.

Making Refugees: Critical Entanglements, Categorical Ambiguities

Although the modern refugee was largely a product of the First World War, it was in the aftermath of the twentieth century's second global conflict that the international regime of protection, relief, and regulation familiar to us today consolidated. This system differed in key respects from the first international refugee system centered on the League of Nations. Though the League did begin to codify refugee rights, these remained far from widely accepted; only eight states, for example, ratified the 1933 Convention on Refugees. As the League's first High Commissioner for Refugees, the Norwegian polar explorer and scientist Fridtjof Nansen lent his moniker to the travel document known as the "Nansen passport" that facilitated travel for stateless people. The League's work with refugees focused on Russians displaced by the events of the Revolution and survivors of the Armenian genocide, together with the Greek and Turkish populations compulsorily exchanged by the terms of the 1923 Treaty of Lausanne. In these instances, membership in a group (rather than having crossed a political border) determined refugee status prima facie.[34] In the aftermath of the Second World War, by contrast, refugee recognition was accorded to individuals, rather than groups. This created time-intensive eligibility procedures in which "the individual evaluation of personal narratives became a predominant aspect of refugee selection."[35]

The events of World War II also produced a displacement crisis on a much greater scale than had the Great War, prompting organized assistance on a scale not seen in the interwar period. In 1945, Europe was a continent in ruins, literally and figuratively. By VE Day in May 1945, an estimated eleven million civilians in Europe had become refugees. This figure does not include the millions of prisoners of war, as well as the significant numbers of European refugees in other parts of the world, such as China. Displaced persons in Europe included Jewish survivors, individuals deported to the Third Reich as forced laborers, persons fleeing occupying armies or civil wars, and those whose homes had been destroyed by warfare. Within six months of the conclusion of the conflict, Allied military authorities (SHAEF, Supreme Headquarters Allied Expeditionary Force) and the Displaced Persons section of the United Nations Relief and Rehabilitation Administration had repatriated the majority of Europe's refugees.

There remained, however, at least a million or so persons who would not or could not be returned home because they feared persecution.[36] These displaced persons were soon joined by new refugees coming from Eastern Europe, including Jewish survivors fleeing pogroms in Poland, between eleven and twelve million ethnic German expellees, and those whom the US State Department would come to deem Cold War "escapees" from state socialism.[37] In the face of these new refugee flows and the realization that Europe's displaced persons problem had not disappeared, the International

Refugee Organization came into being in 1946, with the aim of finding new homes for those who could not return safely to their countries of origin. The IRO had a fixed term of five years, reflecting the misplaced optimism that the refugee crisis produced by the war and its aftermath was exceptional and finite. Likewise, the UNHCR that succeeded the IRO initially had a five-year mandate. The UNHCR, of course, ultimately became permanent, in recognition that refugees had become an all too regular feature of international politics.

Debates between 1945 and 1960 over just who constituted a bona fide refugee eligible for international protection point to a complex story, one that is as much about exclusions as it is about inclusions. This characterization challenges many broader histories of human rights, often depicted along a fairly linear path or in terms of circles of ever-widening inclusion. While the history of refugee relief and law should not and *cannot* stand in for all of human rights history, it does prove representative in many ways. Historian Daniel Cohen even goes so far as to characterize Europe's DP crisis as a central moment in the post-1945 "human rights revolution."[38] In the case of refugee protections, though, we find a narrowing circle of eligibility worked out in practice through the successive efforts of UNRRA, the IRO, and the UNHCR, rather than the "history of progressive inclusion in the rights protection system through a series of successful struggles"[39] usually ascribed to human rights genealogies. After initial reluctance to help Italians as an "ex-enemy," UNRRA provided critical relief to the peninsula and assistance in repatriating Italians to their homes. By contrast, the IRO generally excluded from its remit Italians displaced to the peninsula. By the time the UNHCR came into existence, the distinction between international refugees and national refugees had hardened—as seen by its consolidation in the 1951 Geneva Convention on Refugees. The refinement of these eligibility procedures required a new bureaucratic apparatus of experts (translators, interviewers, placement officials), one largely filled by Anglo-American personnel, many of them women, in the first decade and a half after the war. At the same time, this management regime demanded local expertise, as well as cooperation with officials of the host countries.

The shift away from collective definitions and rights for refugees that underwrote these new regimes of expertise and management reflects the broader post-1945 redefinition of human rights as inhering in the individual rather than groups. The degree to which postwar human rights rested on this individualistic basis, however, should not be overstated, as collective categories such as gender and family remained inextricably built into what is usually taken as the quintessential expression of the individual focus of human rights after the Second World War: the United Nations Universal Declaration of Human Rights (UDHR). As we shall see, in both philosophy and practice, humanitarianism also reinscribed collective categories such as gender, ethnicity, and nationality.[40] The very notion of a refugee implies a certain inescapable degree of groupness. Status as a Jew in/from the former Nazi occupation zones, for instance, quickly became the grounds for automatic refugee status and a key exception to the requirement of individual determination of eligibility.[41]

For those ultimately left out of the category of international refugee, like the displaced Italians at the center of this book, the classifications applied to them actually reinscribed notions of groupness—that is, belonging to a national community, however tenuous that nation might appear in the wake of catastrophic defeat. Yet the displaced in postwar Italy bore many labels and statuses beyond those of international and national. The term *sinistrati* typically referred to so-called "bomb-damaged" Italians internally displaced within the peninsula, "those persons whose homes were partially or completely destroyed by enemy action who lost most or all of their belongings, who did not leave their town of residence either voluntarily or through evacuation. In general they are crowded in with friends and relatives or are billeted in homes or shelters in their own community by local authorities."[42] Italian authorities and international agencies alike sometimes distinguished these internally displaced Italians from *sfollati* or *profughi*—Italians displaced into the peninsula from territories no longer under Italian control, like Libya or Ethiopia. *Sfollati* and *profughi* alike might also qualify as *profughi di guerra* (war refugees) displaced by German occupation on the peninsula or in Italy's Balkan territories. Such displacees were contrasted with *rifugiati stranieri* (foreign refugees), a broad term covering both those recognized as eligible for UN assistance and "undesirables"; the latter category included war criminals and collaborators. Before 1948, Jews transiting through Italy for clandestine passage to Palestine formed a significant portion of those foreign refugees. Yugoslavs, including supporters of the Chetnik leader Draža Mihailović and the Ustaša head Ante Pavelić, also crowded into the peninsula along with demobilized soldiers from the Polish army in exile. Many of these displaced populations were already present in large numbers on the Italian peninsula by 1943–1944, fleeing the German zones in the north and the Balkans. With its proximity to Yugoslavia and Albania by sea, the region of Puglia, in particular, hosted many foreigners.[43]

The diverse personnel in charge of processing these arrivals often applied such labels in an inconsistent manner. Italians who had left their homes within the peninsula were sometimes deemed *sfollati* alongside their fellow citizens who had come from beyond Italy's peninsular borders. Foreign and national refugees alike might be labeled either *profughi* or *rifugiati*. Indeed, in 1947 the parastatal Comitato Nazionale per i Rifugiati Italiani (CNRI) came into existence to aid Italians from the lost territories; this committee would give rise to the Opera per l'Assistenza ai Profughi Giuliani e Dalmati (OAPGD), dedicated to helping Italian displacees from the eastern Adriatic. These entities thus used the terms *profugo* and *rifugiato* interchangeably for Italians from lost possessions. And both words—*profugo* and *rifugiato*—translate into English as refugee, though in certain contexts their Italian versions possess more technical or precise juridical meanings. *Rifugiato*, for example, typically denotes those who have fled or been expelled from their country. The relevant Italian laws of 1949 and 1952 instead defined *profugo* to include displaced Italian citizens with demonstrated need from Libya and Africa Orientale Italiana (AOI), from those territories over which Italy ceded sovereignty by the terms of the Peace Treaty of 1947, from foreign territories, and from parts of Italy impacted by war. Nonetheless, usage of these terms outside the legal realm remained labile. Furthermore, migrants from Italy's lost Adriatic territories (technically *profughi* in legal terms) often referred to themselves as *esuli* or exiles, reflecting their hope for an eventual return to their homes.

The imprecision inherent in the vocabulary of repatriation further complicates our understanding of just what kind of migrants officials in postwar Italy were dealing with. Intergovernmental agencies like UNRRA, whose work with displaced persons focused on repatriation—return to countries of origin—employed a category that stressed the *voluntary* nature of this return migration.[44] This contrasted with those who could not go home owing to persecution and therefore became classified as refugees. Both classifications ignored the troubling question of just what "home" or "country of origin" consisted in (the former colony? the metropole?) for repatriate settlers. Further confusing matters, Italian settlers who had been displaced out of areas like Libya or the Aegean Islands during the war often requested to repatriate *back* to the possessions at conflict's end, a complicated situation of multidirectional migration. When humanitarian organizations like the International Red Cross (ICRC) offered impoverished Italians from Cyrenaica clothing and other assistance in the late 1950s, however, they did not classify these individuals as refugees but rather as repatriates, revealing that such organizations viewed mainland Italy as these migrants' rightful homes.[45]

In Italian, the category of *rimpatriato* translates to "return migrant." This may refer either to individuals from the former colonies who "returned" to Italy or to those voluntary or "economic" migrants who came back to the peninsula in the return migrations that typified Italy's nineteenth- and twentieth-century mass migrations.[46] The Italian concept *rimpatriato* thus overlaps with, even as it proves more expansive than, scholarly terminology that describes flows of colonial settlers to the metropole as "population refluxes" or mere "reverse migrations."[47] Such labels sidestep the contentious issue of whether such colonial migrations constitute something akin to the refugee experience. In the Italian case, then, the *rimpatriato* designation contrasts with that of populations like the *pieds-noirs*, European settlers who fled Algeria in the early 1960s and whose particular bureaucratic classification as *rapatrié* within France served to mark out their difference from other migrants, on the one hand, and metropolitan French citizens, on the other.

Whether in France or Italy or elsewhere in Europe, the migration of colonial settlers to the metropole provoked humanitarian and political crises similar to and often intimately bound up with the "emergencies" prompted by the arrival of foreign refugees. Skinner and Lester have underlined the need for research that captures the intersections of imperialism and humanitarianism, given "that the two phenomena are ultimately bound together in a series of mutually constituting histories, in which the ideas and practices associated with imperial politics and administration have both been shaped by and have in themselves informed developing notions of humanitarianism."[48] In heeding this call, this study examines a foundational moment in which imperial and humanitarian histories collided and proved mutually constitutive in the making of the modern refugee system. This challenges the common view that refugees became a global concern only in the 1960s *after* the resolution of Europe's refugee question.

Precisely because 1960 stands as a key temporal marker in many accounts of refugee history, this study takes it as its ending point in order to problematize what has often seemed like a sharp transition. In a review of the history of the international refugee system, for example, Dennis Gallagher contends, "By 1960 the European refugee problem was greatly reduced in scale." He adds, "However, refugee problems were burgeoning in other parts of the globe and new approaches were needed to address them."[49] One reason for the expanding refugee question beyond Europe, implies Gallagher, were the displacements attendant to decolonization. Of course, 1960 marked not only a World Refugee Year that celebrated the achievement of closing many of Europe's camps, but also the "Year of Africa" in which seventeen African countries attained independence and the UN issued its "Declaration on the Granting of Independence to Colonial Countries and Peoples." Somalia numbered among those attaining independence that year, after a decade of an Italian-administered United Nations trusteeship. This actually marked the *end* of formal Italian decolonization. The Italian case thus evidences how the displacements produced by the Second World War and by decolonization not only run on parallel tracks but also cross and entangle at many points, in contrast to a periodization that treats these as successive moments in a history of refugees. Nor does the simultaneity of such entangled displacements prove unique in the Italian case.

Decolonization processes in Dutch possessions began during World War II, as the Netherlands confronted the dual displacements created by Nazi occupation in the metropole and Japanese occupation in the Dutch East Indies. The defeat of the Japanese, in turn, resulted in rapid decolonization and the mandatory repatriation by Allied personnel of imperial settlers from Taiwan, Korea, and Manchuria to the metropole. Lori Watt has detailed the clear linkages in Allied planning for handling displaced persons in Europe and Asia, noting that the US Special Committee on Migration and Displacement commissioned by President Roosevelt and in existence from June 1943 to November 1944 took operations in Italy in 1943 as its template or "prototype" for assistance to displaced persons elsewhere in Europe and Asia. In particular, the Inter-Divisional Area Committee on the Far East in the US State Department "suggested that the repatriation of Italians from East Africa might serve the U.S. military as a model for the Japanese."[50]

Some scholars have nonetheless dismissed the temporally inconvenient examples of Italy and Japan by deeming them "precocious" or "third-party" decolonizations.[51] Such labels replicate the teleological narrative of decolonization that underwrites many histories of the "rise" of the global refugee and thereby obscure how the end of the Second World War already constituted a refugee crisis of global dimensions and one in which, as Watt demonstrates, "the American military became involved in facilitating the migrations of decolonization."[52] In many ways, too, the territorial and geographic clauses of the 1951 Refugee Convention represented "relics of the world of European colonialism."[53] Yet all too often in accounts that wrongly position the era of decolonization and the globalization of refugee crises as subsequent to Europe's displaced persons crisis colonial repatriates disappear from the refugee story altogether.

Whereas refugees are by definition liminal (betwixt and between home and host country), colonial repatriates possess an *additional* classificatory ambiguity, placing them somewhere between metropolitan citizen and foreign displaced person. Repatriates fit uneasily into a whole range of conceptual paradigms: those of refugees and displacement, forced migration, and diaspora. The Italian case was further complicated by the ambiguous citizenship status of a number of these repatriates. While my discussion so far has emphasized the conceptual dilemmas that produced scholarly blind spots around national refugees, the political dimensions of these populations' reception in their putative homelands must not be overlooked. At the time of events, colonial settlers displaced to the metropole were not erased from view but rather served as uncomfortable reminders of repudiated pasts, what I deem "extruded" histories in recognition of the ways they can erupt painfully into public debate.[54]

Unlike their Dutch or French counterparts, Italian repatriates bore the burden not only of a problematic history of colonialism but also that of fascism.[55] Rightly or wrongly, both non-Italian populations in the former possessions and metropolitan Italians tended to portray repatriates as enthusiastic agents of fascism. In this, the Italian repatriates proved most similar to the Japanese (as the Allied planners had recognized) and the Portuguese *retornados* from Angola and Mozambique who migrated after 1974 to a "homeland" only just emerging from decades of authoritarianism under Salazar. Many Italian repatriates also shared with their Portuguese counterparts a relatively low socioeconomic status, one reflective of an "emigrant nation" whose poor had hoped that the colonies would facilitate social mobility.[56] As these comments suggest, Italian experiences of decolonization and refugeedom possess many analogues with other cases. This contrasts with the frequent claim by both scholars and Italian popular media that both Italy's colonial engagements and their conclusion prove exceptional in the annals of European imperialism. In such a telling, Italian colonialism figures as belated and brief, its legacies limited by comparison with those of its European counterparts. The protracted migrations of Italian national refugees put paid to the myth of either a quick or easy decolonization.

A Long Decolonization? Presences and Silences in the Archives and Beyond

> This nonevent is, precisely, the cultural effects of decolonization in Italy. The term nonevent suggests, indeed, that the lack of any traumatic severing of Italy's colonial appendages has contributed to the lack of a full-scale national reevaluation of the country's colonial past.
>
> Karen Pinkus, "Empty Spaces: Decolonization in Italy" (2003)

The characterization of Italian decolonization as quick, relatively unproblematic, and lacking the trauma associated with events like the Algerian or Indochina wars that marked the French experience proves widespread among

Italian and foreign scholars alike. Nonetheless, while the diagnosis of a mild "imperial hangover" for Italy suggests a benign process,[57] such language hints at another pervasive bias that views returning colonists as undigestible bits of an unpalatable past. Gastric imagery of hangovers or refluxes suggests that with its regurgitation of settlers into the homeland, decolonization left a bilious aftertaste. Regurgitative images thus reveal a "conceptual anguish" that highlights "memory's importance in self-definition."[58] Certainly, the arrival of over a half of million national refugees in Italy between 1943 and 1960 left multiple traces, as this study evidences. How to conceptualize this history in light of the frequent assertion that the "uneventful" nature of Italian decolonization (epitomized by the work of scholars like Pinkus) resulted in collective amnesia?

First, we need to examine critically the notion of an abrupt and "precocious" process of decolonization in the Italian case. This notion of "precocity" refers to the fact that well before formal renunciation of these territories after World War II, during the conflict Italy had already lost effective control over its overseas colonies: East Africa in 1941, Libya between 1942 and 1943, the Dodecanese Islands in 1943, and Albania between 1943 and 1944. In the Dodecanese, Libya, and much of East Africa, the British Military Administration (BMA) temporarily governed the territories until their fate could be determined after the war. Article 23 of the 1947 Peace Treaty with Italy renounced Italian claims to its colonies but did not provide for their final disposition. This led many settlers and metropolitan Italians alike to hope that Italy might retain special relationships with, or even trusteeships over, several of the African territories. In particular, it led to protracted negotiations over Libya. Even after Libyan independence in 1951, it took another five years for the new state and Italy to conclude bilateral accords settling a wide range of contentious issues, including the properties in agricultural villages created for Italian settlers under fascism.[59] In Eritrea, the BMA ended only in 1952 with the advent of federation with Ethiopia. Somalia, by contrast, would remain under a UN trusteeship administered by Italy until 1960. In reality, then, Italy's African territories did not attain independence (de jure) during or even in the immediate aftermath of World War II. Contrary to claims about its "precocious" nature, Italian decolonization actually does not prove an exception within the general chronology of European colonial exit.[60] In light of these extended engagements, Italian decolonization—whether understood in the more conventional terms of diplomatic history or the decentered histories of Italian outmigration from the former territories—appears as anything but quick, easy, or *early*. It was also highly uneven, a reality highlighted by this study's very structure. Rather than aim for uniform chapters, I have embraced units of varying length in recognition of the distinctly irregular tempos and rhythms of repatriation attendant to Italian decolonization.[61]

Reframing and reperiodizing Italy's contraction not as precocious but rather as a "long decolonization" thus proves productive here. Drawing on recent historical reevaluations of decolonization, this phrasing takes its specific cues both from Vazira Fazila-Yacoobali Zamindar's argument that scholars have failed to adequately account for the spatial and temporal processes involved in India's "long partition" and Nicola Labanca's discussion

FIGURE 1. Italian territory in 1961 at the close of formal decolonization. Map designed by Mike Bechthold.

of the challenges in (and multiple possibilities for) defining Italian decolonization. In his pioneering work on Italian colonialism, Labanca has argued that "decolonization is never finished, especially on the cultural level." Elsewhere, though, Labanca deems the Italian experience a "strange decolonization," a phrasing that I reject, given its implication of the deviation from a standard or normative decolonization.[62] This wording repeats the trope of anomaly or exceptionalism prevalent in other scholarship on Italian colonialism. One might instead view the Italian case as another instantiation of what Akiko Hashimoto has called "the long defeat." Though focusing on Japan, Hashimoto calls for understanding such protracted defeat in a global comparative context.[63]

Scholars' tendency to focus on the formal, diplomatic aspects of empire's end in Italy has reinforced a reductive or even dismissive view of Italian decolonization, ignoring the many cultural and social reverberations of colonialism's end. The myth of a *decolonizazzione mancata* has thus joined those of the *rivoluzione mancata* and the *conquista mancata*. Yet Jordanna Bailkin's reasoning for recasting decolonization in broad terms for Britain proves equally valid for Italy. "I am not arguing that Britons were especially knowledgeable about the end of empire," writes Bailkin. "Rather, the consequences of imperial collapse were built into the structures of their world. Decolonization changed how people in Britain lived whether they knew it or not."[64] In Italy, decolonization manifested itself in everything from rearticulations of citizenship to a diffidence toward foreign refugees and migrants to the remaking of the built environment—whether Italians knew it or not.

Framing decolonization in this way emphasizes a politics of selective recognition, as well as nonrecognition, rather than either an active erasure or a wholesale forgetting. The anxious tendency of "looking and looking away at the same time" characteristic of postwar Germany proves true for postfascist and decolonizing Italy as well.[65] The tight control exercised by the Italian state and a colonial lobby over colonial archives for several decades after World War II is often invoked as evidence for both the amnesia and imposed forgetting theses.[66] A 1952 interministerial decree established the Comitato per la Documentazione dell'Opera dell'Italia in Africa. Restricting access to the materials of the Ministero dell'Africa Italiana (Ministry of Italian Africa or MAI, closed definitively in 1953) and seeking to control the narrative of Italy's colonial experience, this committee—in existence until 1984 and functioning as the "'custodian' of official memory"[67]—produced forty volumes of dubious scholarly quality.[68] Without a doubt, the efforts to regulate access slowed, but did not halt, the development of a critical historiography on Italian colonialism in Africa. Nor did this committee prevent former settlers and national refugees from Africa from making their own claims, publishing memoirs, or organizing themselves in associations like the Unione Coloni Italiani d'Africa. As far as I know, no similar *archival* custodians of memory existed to police and discipline study of Italy's other possessions in the Balkans, though the geopolitics of the Cold War weighed heavily on the remembrance and analysis of such experiences.

In any case, the dispersal of documentation continues to pose logistical challenges to scholars studying Italian colonialism and its afterlives. This remains true even with the opening up of access to MAI's documentation on deposit at the Archivio Storico Diplomatico del Ministero degli Affari Esteri (ASDMAE) and the recent availability of the records of the Istituto Nazionale della Previdenza Sociale (INPS) for its colonial entities in Libya and the files of the Presidenza del Consiglio dei Ministri (PCM) for the Ufficio per le Zone di Confine.[69] Access to relevant documentation in the former possessions was sometimes impossible, as in the case of the Italian materials at the Albanian Central State Archive in Tirana that became available only after the end of state socialism there. The fifty-year embargoes placed on most archival documents in Italy (with a seventy-year ban for materials containing sensitive personal information, such as medical records) have further slowed historiographic undertakings, as have pressing resource questions (particularly funding for archivists to catalog material and to staff consultation rooms).[70] Staff in several specialized institutions in Italy where I consulted documents urged me to hurry my efforts, since they did not know whether their contracts would be renewed (with subsequent temporary closure of the archive). The most dramatic example occurred with the 2011 closure and liquidation of the Italian Institute for Africa and the Orient (IsIAO).[71] When I worked in the State Archive of the Dodecanese in 2010, I likewise found Italian-era materials that had suffered from water damage and mold, a consequence of Greece's severe austerity crisis and cuts to cultural institutions.[72] In a very real sense, then, the decolonization of the archives in and of Italy has proven as long and complex as the broader political and cultural processes of decolonization, and it is still under way. As Bailkin has urged, "Conceiving of decolonization as an archival event can enrich our understanding of its diverse histories and give it a new multidimensionality."[73] Such a perspective recognizes greater nuance than that of mere forgetting / enforced forgetting.

The so-called "archival turn" has encouraged scholars to think ethnographically about archives, treating them as both event and *process*. Ann Laura Stoler, in particular, reminded scholars that archives prove important repositories not only of content but also of form—as sites where "colonial sense and reason conjoined social kinds with the political order of colonial things."[74] In tracking down evidence of the complex intertwining of displacement, decolonization, and the emergence of the postwar international refugee regime in Italy, I have considered archive-as-subject, as well as archive-as source. Thus, I have seen the archive in both ethnographic and "extractive" terms. When working in institutes with their origins in colonial-era collections, such as the Istituto Agronomico per l'Oltremare (IAO, the Overseas Agronomy Institute, formerly the Istituto Agricolo Coloniale Italiano) in Florence and the now defunct IsIAO in Rome, I was struck by literal questions of form—that is, how the architecture and physical organization of these institutions gave clear expression to their colonial logics.

Dusty botanic and zoological specimens from long-ago colonial expeditions line the halls of the IAO, evidence of old colonial taxonomies that live on in the mission of this branch of the Ministry of Foreign Affairs today dedicated to agricultural development abroad. The tropical plants raised at IAO bring to mind Kew and all those other imperial botanical gardens that blended questions of beauty with utility, science with sovereignty, pleasure with power. The former IsIAO's building instead featured colorful, wall-size colonial-era maps with airplanes and naval liner routes marking out the

FIGURE 2. Detail from wall maps at site of former IsIAO, now closed permanently.

distance between the Italian peninsula and its colonial cities. Symbols of a lost imperium, these maps were relegated to a storage area near the bathrooms. For a country that is supposedly amnesiac about its colonial past, then, such spaces resemble nothing more than museums to Italy's lost empire, even as they encode considerable ambivalence toward that past.

Italy does not possess a central archival repository specifically for the colonial possessions akin to France's Archives nationales d'outre-mer, an issue of form that reveals much about the selective visibility of Italy's imperial legacy. Nonetheless, the Archivio Centrale dello Stato (ACS) and the Archivio Storico Diplomatico del Ministero degli Affari Esteri house many relevant collections essential to the study of Italian colonialism and decolonization. These two archives reside in buildings built in the fascist monumental style. The ASDMAE is found in the Ministry of Foreign Affairs complex adjacent to the Foro Italico, built by the fascist regime and repurposed for the 1960 Rome Olympics. The ACS instead occupies a prominent place in Rome's EUR quarter, begun in celebration of fascism's achievements but completed only after the war (and a site of resettlement for national refugees). Mia Fuller has wryly noted that after fascism, the EUR neighborhood "became the repository for yet another 'end' of history: the state archives, where scholars have tried to make historical fragments into smooth, new narratives."[75] In a very real sense, then, Italy's imperial past hides in plain sight, its archival traces assembled in structures that owe their existence to fascism's expansionist project.

As these comments about Italy's most prominent state archives remind us, Stoler's prescriptions to treat archives ethnographically go well beyond the colonial realm and alert us to both the epistemological assumptions and workings of power inscribed in all archives, as well as the production of historical knowledge more generally. Yet whereas all histories therefore necessarily encode silences and prove inevitably fragmentary, histories of both decolonization and refugees/displacement arguably pose greater methodological challenges because of the frequent silences and wide gaps in the making of both sources and archives. Certainly, these archival gaps have contributed to the mistaken belief that Italian decolonization and the arrival of national refugees in the metropole went largely unnoticed or possessed little reverberation at the time of events.

In many instances of decolonization, departing colonizers deliberately destroyed archival documents, or archival documents perished as collateral damage.[76] In the Italian case, decolonization's beginnings within the context of the Second World War meant that bombings or occupation destroyed or reduced any number of documentary repositories. In 1955, for example, a search for relevant materials from the Amministrazione Governativa Centrale di Tripoli was made. The archive was said to have been definitively lost, having been sent to the recycling mill (*macero*) in the summer of 1944 during the British occupation.[77] Filiberto Sabbadin claims that most of the other relevant documentation of the communal administration of Italian Tripolitania was likewise destroyed or lost through neglect.[78] Similarly, the central archive of the Società Dante Alighieri in Rome—a cultural organization that sponsored branches in both Italian territories and diasporic communities alike—proves highly uneven, the building having been occupied by German forces during the war and some files lost or gutted. The fate of some Italian-era materials left behind in former colonies that have experienced civil war like Libya or Somalia likewise remains unknown. A number of collaborative Italo-Libyan projects had been launched before the events of 2011 disrupted communications.[79] In Eritrea and Somalia, the destruction of archives in war has complicated efforts by mixed-race children to attain Italian citizenship; in many instances, too, records of birth were not registered in the first place, a silence encoded at "the moment of fact creation (the making of *sources*)."[80]

The precarity of archives in both Italy and the former possessions has also meant that once-available documentation has actually become *less* accessible. For example, large chunks of the archive of the Ente per la Colonizzazione della Libia (ECL), one of two parastatal entities that administered rural settlements in Libya, remained unavailable until recently. Historian Federico Cresti made a detailed study of the ECL documentation before its transfer to the Central State Archive in Rome. He also published an inventory of that documentation, an inventory that drew on the original categories and classification system of the ECL itself. Inventory in hand, in March 2011 I approached the archivists at the Central State Archive, who seemed puzzled by what sounded like well-ordered files, including ones explicitly labeled "Repatriation." Venturing into the depths of the ACS basement, an archivist and I disappointingly found only a few dust-caked boxes containing accounting books (*contabilità*) and some dossiers from the settlement at Baracca. Most of the documentation has now become available, though bearing classificatory logics different from those used by the ECL or in Cresti's pioneering study of the ECL.[81]

Similarly, when I made the first of two visits to the State Archives of the Dodecanese in Rhodes I came armed with information from a colleague who had worked there that a catalog in Italian existed and could be easily consulted on the computer. Since my colleague's visit, however, the Italian-language and Italian-era records had undergone recataloging in Greek. This exercise in rearchiving appeared to have followed out of a careful reordering and study of the documentation to ascertain whether Italy had exercised sovereignty over the islets of Imia / Kardak (contested between Greece and Turkey since 1996) and thus had transferred it to Greece by the 1947 Peace Treaty.[82] The Italian documentation had thus become caught up in postcolonial projects of Greek and Turkish nation-building and sovereignty. In searching for documents on movements in and out of the islands, the archive's director Eirini Toliou patiently translated key terms ("repatriation," "citizenship," "migration") into Greek after I had translated them from Italian into English (our language of communication at the time; she has since learned Italian). All this made for a much slower and opaque process of archival digging.

In my exploration of the interregnum in the Dodecanese between Italian rule and union with Greece, much of the relevant documentation came from records of the International Red Cross, which had visited the islands during the famine winter of 1945 and again after the war's conclusion. UNRRA also sent a mission to the Dodecanese, and that material—housed primarily in the UN archives in New York—proved invaluable in reconstructing the story of Italian repatriation out of the Isole Egeo, as well as out of Albania.[83] In fact, the records of international organizations like the ICRC and the UN intergovernmental organizations yielded critical data on Italian nationals and the process of Italy's departure from its overseas possessions. Tacking between the archives of state institutions (Italian, as well as those of the British who administered these former territories and of the now independent states themselves) and international organizations helped me fill critical gaps in the story. In this, I followed the example of scholars like Bailkin, who has demonstrated the value in turning to sources not typically associated with decolonization, such as welfare records or debates over foster parenting in Britain.[84] Going against archival and historiographic convention in order to discover "'information out of place'"—such as the insistent demands by and about Italian repatriates and national refugees in the files of UNRRA and the IRO—reminds us that "the failure of some kinds of practices, perceptions, and populations to fit into a . . . ready-made system of classification—may tell us as much or more"[85] than the consensual archival categories.

Indeed, by its nature, decolonization—like displacement—refers to processes or states of transition, ones that may not necessarily be legible within the logics of archival cataloging. Tony Kushner has argued forcefully that historians have generally failed to take account of refugees more for ontological than epistemological reasons—not because of source difficulties but because of an "enforced and absolute absence coming out of discrimination, exclusion and expulsion."[86] While seconding Kushner's verdict regarding historians' relative lack of engagement with refugee questions until recently,

Gatrell nonetheless points ways forward that underline challenges precisely with sources. In offering solutions, Gatrell reminds us, "there is also a conversation to be had between historians and refugees themselves,"[87] something I have taken to heart in my own ethnographic research in this book and elsewhere. The ethnographic research for this study centered on communities in Italy designated for refugee resettlement.

Returning to the question of written sources, refugee histories often don't present themselves neatly as such in terms of the archival classifications common to state institutions. Furthermore, tracking migrants frequently requires following them through multiple archives—in those moments when their tracks actually became traces. Because the sites of refugee camps are usually transient, the literal infrastructures of many refugee histories were typically dismantled soon after the time of events. In postwar Italy, as in much of Europe, authorities frequently repurposed military structures, internment camps, or even concentration camps (like the Risiera di San Sabba) to house displaced persons. Memorials at those sites may recall their earlier usages, privileging wartime histories of violence over refugee stories. When the Italian state declared the Risiera di San Sabba a national monument in 1965, for example, the refugee camp that had existed there for nearly two decades was disassembled and the Nazi camp carefully reconstructed. I visited the Risiera in 2002 with a former national refugee from Pula/Pola who had not returned there since her family immigrated to the United States in 1958. She marveled at how different the space looked, particularly as sites of sociability where she had played as a child like the dining hall had been returned to their role as wartime cells. Similarly, the notorious concentration camp at Fossoli—from which departed the train deporting Primo Levi to Auschwitz—later became a camp housing first foreign and then national refugees. Refugees from Italy's lost lands in the eastern Adriatic succeeded in 2011, after years of lobbying, in having a small plaque placed within the confines of the camp to acknowledge their experiences in nearby Carpi and the Villaggio San Marco.[88] Nonetheless, Fossoli remains best known for its role as a fascist-Nazi camp, highlighting once again the selective and shifting visibilities of Italy's postwar refugee histories. The museum at the former refugee camp at Padriciano on the Triestine Karst, by contrast, instead focuses on the histories of Istrian-Julian-Dalmatian refugees who lived there to the exclusion of the foreign displacees who replaced them as camp residents in the 1970s.

In light of their fragmentary and processual natures, refugee and decolonization histories alike may thus pose particularly acute, if not necessarily unique, methodological challenges. In considering the displacements of

Italian decolonization as gap-ridden, it is useful to reconceptualize gaps as not just erasures or absences but as generative spaces that may encode surfeits of meaning.[89] *The World Refugees Made* makes a case for the generative nature of refugee studies in general and histories of the displacements of decolonizing settlers and national refugees in particular. Heeding the admonitions of Stoler and others, this book draws on an archive of my own synthesis and creation, fashioned out of many documents and accounts and traversing many gaps—one that involves "attention to new kinds of sources, but also to different ways of approaching those we already have, different ways of reading than we have yet done."[90] My hope is that this will inspire research into the many histories of national and foreign refugees in the era of Italy's long decolonization still waiting to be told.

Chapter 1

Empire as Prelude

> A specter haunted Italian nation building and the imperial histories entwined with it: the emigrant, emblem of a poor country's inability to provide for its citizens.
>
> —Ruth Ben-Ghiat, *Fascism's Empire Cinema* (2015)

Migration has proven paradoxically both central and peripheral to accounts of modern Italy, a state defined in many ways by its long experience as an "emigrant nation." Italians seeking opportunities abroad in the nineteenth and twentieth centuries participated in the largest single voluntary migration in global history, in which some twenty-seven million individuals departed between 1876 and 1976, often leaving and returning to the peninsula multiple times in a pattern of circular migration. From almost the beginning of its existence the Italian state had preoccupied itself with protecting its emigrants, on the one hand, and seeking to contain the potentially disruptive effects of migration, on the other. Italians who moved to Italy's overseas possessions numbered among these "voluntary" migrants, even if their return movements differed significantly from those of fellow citizens returning to Italy from countries like Argentina or the United States similarly classified as *rimpatriati*. The term *coloni* or colonist mirrors the linguistic imprecision of *rimpatriati*, discussed in the introduction, dissolving distinctions between Italian emigrants to third countries and settlers in Italian overseas territories, as well as Italian "pioneers" on fascist projects of land reclamation within the Italian nation-state.

Although they represented only 2 percent of Italians who left the peninsula,[1] Italians from former possessions who repatriated demanded a higher and more visible level of state intervention than other returning citizens.

Symbols of defeat, repatriates from the lost possessions also bore an ideological freight absent in the case of idiosyncratic return migrations made by individuals in non-Italian host countries. As life for Italians in former territories in Africa or the Balkans became untenable, the Italian state found itself tasked with humanitarian and political responsibilities defined in contradistinction to and in dialogue with those assumed by the postwar intergovernmental refugee regimes. At the same time, however, the Italian state's response to flows from the lost possessions involved nongovernmental and intergovernmental actors—often in novel ways.

The protracted and costly experience of dealing with its own refugees from the former territories also informed Italy's restrictive policies regarding resettlement and naturalization by foreign refugees until the end of the Cold War (see the introduction). This long-standing juridical diffidence to foreigners echoes in contemporary debates over today's newcomers to Italy. Many scholars have remarked on the connections between Italy's emigration past and immigration present, though they often treat the journeys of Italian emigrants as mere analogues to the dangerous Mediterranean crossings made by migrants who wash up on the shores of contemporary Italy. As Iain Chambers and Lidia Curti put it, "Although separated in time, yesterday's migrant who abandoned rural life in southern Italy for Buenos Aires, and today's migrant abandoned on a beach in Puglia or Lampedusa are part of the same historical constellation."[2] Invoking Walter Benjamin's concept of constellation, Chambers and Curti embrace an understanding of history that "does not necessarily favour the established notion of linearity. Nor does it favour the notion of processuality or chronology of history as such."[3] Unexpected juxtapositions thus work to illuminate and translate common experiences, in this case of migration, and provide the grounds for possible future solidarities and empathy. Teresa Fiore employs a similar method when, in her analysis of the "pre-occupied" spaces in which current migrants to Italy come to reside, she employs Italo Calvino's metaphor of an imaginary "one point" to foreground spatial linkages between past and present movements.

These literary scholars rightly question and complicate narratives of both outmigration and colonialism that operate "according to a temporal paradigm" that encodes an "apparent sense of historical completion,"[4] instead highlighting their open-ended legacies and potential for textual recombinations and remappings. In doing this, however, these scholars risk conflating Italian mass emigration and contemporary mass immigration to Italy without acknowledging a key historical moment of transition and connection between them: the migration out of the former Italian colonies of subjects who could make claims to both Italian citizenship and (national) refugeedom. This tendency to analogize Italian emigration and current immigration to Italy is encapsulated in the popular tagline, "Quando noi eravamo gli albanesi" or "When we were the Albanians"; the Albanians in question are those migrants whose boats overwhelmed the ports of Brindisi and Bari in 1991. Derived from the subtitle of journalist Gian Antonio Stella's best-selling account of Italian emigration *L'Orda*, this notion gestures to experiences of stigma, discrimination, and hardship uniting past and present migrants. Telescoping between "us" (Italians who left the peninsula, prototypically for *lamerica*) and "them" (Italy's new arrivals, many of them non-European), however, neglects the critical function played by colonial repatriates in mediating this "us" and "them" in both a legal and cultural sense. It also ignores the reality that in the aftermath of the Second World War, Italians not only confronted "immigrants" in the form of foreign refugees but also resolutely closed the door on large-scale naturalization. Fiore goes so far as to praise Calvino for anticipating the future with his story "All at One Point," penned in the mid-1960s when the country "was not yet affected by the arrival of immigrants."[5] Yet what Fiore posits as a future development—the flow of non-Italian migrants into the peninsula—was by the mid-1960s actually a very recent *past*. As this study evidences, the history of refugees—together with that of empire—thus constitutes a critical connective tissue linking Italy's emigration pasts and immigration presents both spatially and temporally.

The multidirectional flows of Italians between Libya and the Italian peninsula during the war and the early postwar period illustrate the explicit "preoccupation," to adopt Fiore's term, of contemporary spaces of migration by Italian settlers and repatriates. In June 1940, the fascist regime ordered a mandatory evacuation of Italian children from Libya. With the war's conclusion, some children began to rejoin family members who remained in Africa. By 1946, with an eye to the delicate question of the future territorial disposition of the country, the British Military Administration governing Libya suspended reentry of Italians. As a result, clandestine immigration to Tripolitania by Italians—particularly young people—became a persistent problem for the BMA. The Sicilian city of Syracuse served as a well-known departure point for these Italian migrants, who traveled in small boats to unmonitored points along the Libyan coastline and risked deportation if apprehended. Prefiguring the arrival of *clandestini* to Italy's shores from North Africa today, this history underscores the very recent reversal of flows across the Mediterranean in the Italian case. Few Italians are aware of, let alone appreciate, the irony that not so long ago *they* constituted the "illegals" in those very same

Libyan spaces where at the beginning of the twenty-first century potential migrants to the Italian peninsula were immobilized. Bilateral agreements with the Gadhafi regime had facilitated the removal of migrants from Italian locales such as Lampedusa to Libyan detention centers or, alternatively, the preventive detention of migrants in Libya before they ever reached Mediterranean shores. Here, then, the experience of Italian national refugees after World War II does not just prove analogous to that of today's immigrants ("when we were the Albanians") but rather constitutes a direct historical antecedent.

Recognizing and taking account of these deeper histories of migration—histories that intersect with the wider streams of population movements reshaping Europe and the globe in the aftermath of the Second World War—suggest the need for a notion of what I call *oltreitalie.*[6] In Italian, the prefix "oltre" means "beyond." Demographic studies of migratory flows from Italy frequently employ this label to differentiate those who emigrated beyond the sea (*oltremare*) from those who went beyond the mountains (*oltremontane*)—that is, within Europe.[7] Under fascism, the term *Oltremare d'Italia* or *L'Italia Oltremare* signified Italy's wide range of possessions and the imperial space within which movement no longer constituted emigration but rather internal or domestic movement. The notion of *oltreitalie* captures these associations—and many others. While in dialogue with the concept of *altre italie* (other Italies) that lends its name to a journal and research center,[8] *oltreitalie* nonetheless sidesteps the problematic ways in which *altreitalie* continues to define itself in relation to and as a kind of adjunct of a "standard" Italy. Leaving in place the notion of a normative Italy, the concept of "other Italies" risks reproducing the marginality of emigrants/migration within national historiographies and literatures. The vision of *oltreitalie* aims, then, not merely to pluralize an understanding of Italy but also destabilize and decenter it, just as the figure of the refugee decenters histories of the postwar period in Europe and beyond.

By reframing Italy in this way, I follow the lead of scholars like Donna Gabaccia, whose work demonstrates that Italian (nation-)state making—and, I would add, empire building—can only be comprehended through transnational perspectives that take into account global Italian migration. At the same time, Gabaccia cautions that "while their lives were transnational, the 'italiani nel mondo' did not form a 'nation unbound,' or a 'deterritorialized nation state.'"[9] Space and territory proved central to Italian visions of nation, empire, identity, and mobility. Indeed, *The World Refugees Made* builds on the insight of the "new imperial history" that the national/metropolitan must go beyond and be read through the imperial and vice versa.[10] At the same time, the study aims to go beyond (or *oltre*) historiographical conventions by bringing the insights of international history and recent findings on internationalisms to bear on understandings of Italian state-making in both its national and imperial forms. Putting refugees and colonial repatriates—by definition liminal and "out of place"—at the heart of this study thus provides the anchor from which to bring into dialogue disparate bodies of scholarship and to tack back and forth between varied scales: local, national, regional, imperial, transnational, international, and intergovernmental.

Expanding Italy, Migrating Italy: Competing and Entangled Models of Colonialism

Migration has preoccupied both the Italian state and students of Italy since Italian unification in 1861. With the achievement of statehood, the Direzione di Statistica (part of the Ministry of Agriculture, Industry, and Commerce) began to keep systematic statistics on movements out of the Italian peninsula. The Censimento degli Italiani all'estero, the first general census of Italians abroad, was carried out in 1871. Five years later, the Direzione began to compile and publish annual data on migrations.[11] These statistics testified to considerable outmigration, a phenomenon that figured prominently in the extensive political debates over whether the new Italian state should acquire formal colonies. The characterization of emigration as a debilitating drain necessitated by the Italian economy's deficiencies rhetorically underwrote Italy's nineteenth- and early twentieth-century colonial efforts in Africa, as well as fascism's more ambitious imperial expansionism. From the outset of Italy's colonial era, then, the emigration and colonization questions were inextricably entangled.

Within less than a decade after Italian unification, an Italian foothold on the Red Sea coast had been established with the lease from the local sultan of the port of Assab (in today's Eritrea) by the Compagnia Rubattino, which sought to exploit the opportunities created by the newly opened Suez Canal. The explorations of the Società Geografica Italiana, founded in 1867, had helped lay the groundwork for these commercial contacts.[12] In 1882, the Italian government assumed control over the area, followed by the military occupation of Massawa (Mits'iwa, Massaua) three years later. These acquisitions provided the basis for the creation of Italy's first formal colony: Eritrea. By 1884, Italians had also divvied up "Somaliland" with the French and British, the Compagnia Filonardi having obtained a lease over the Sultanates of Obbia and Majerteen by 1889. Within another four years, the Filonardi Company was also administering Barawa, Merca, Mogadishu, and Warsheikh, the latter a concession granted Italy by the sultan of Zanzibar. In the aftermath of a fatal 1896 attack on employees of Società Anonima Commerciale del Benadir, Filonardi's successor, the Italian state began to directly govern Somalia in 1905.[13] In the case of both Eritrea and Somalia, then, Italy followed a well-established European pattern in which private commercial concessions preceded formal colonization. In addition, the 1901 establishment of an Italian concession under a consul at Tientsin/Tianjin resulted from Italy's participation in the Eight-Nation Alliance responding to China's Boxer Rebellion. The Italian government undertook these actions in a context of rivalry and wrangling for position among European powers. The state (re)directed its energies to East Africa after the French created a protectorate over (formerly Ottoman) Tunis, home to a large population of Italian speakers.[14]

The Tunisian example highlights how, from the very beginning, demands for territories imagined as belonging to the *madrepatria* on cultural, linguistic, and/or historical grounds (the so called "unredeemed lands" or *terre irredente*) were bound up with the desire for the formal colonies that signified standing as a European Great Power. Indeed, Tunisia blurred the boundaries between such types of territories. Irredentists insisted on Italy's right to territories controlled by the Habsburgs (Veneto, Trento, Trieste), including the historically Venetian possessions along the Eastern Adriatic (Istria, Dalmatia), as well as other areas with large Italophone populations (e.g., Nice, Corsica). Although Italy's success in the 1866 war with Austria gave the fledgling state the Veneto, this did not still voices calling for the "redemption" of Italy's "lost" territories. Such activism would acquire greater organizational capacity in the 1890s, with the establishment of groups such as the Società Dante Alighieri in 1889 and the Lega Nazionale in 1891. Ostensibly cultural associations promoting Italian language and culture, these groups often proved overtly political in the actual work of advancing Italian interests.[15]

It is no coincidence that such irredentist networks flourished in the 1890s, the same decade in which Italy sought to both deepen and expand its colonial presence in East Africa. An 1890 parliamentary plan to transform Eritrea into a settler colony founded on small-scale agriculture (as well as an experiment in creating a textile industry there) was abandoned within five years, however, in the face of inadequate understanding of the environmental conditions and violent reactions by Eritreans to land expropriations.[16] Italian investment and retrenchment in Eritrea had followed the attack on Italian forces by Ethiopian soldiers at the battle of Dogali in 1887. This humiliating loss, however, did not quench Italian desires for Ethiopian territory, leading to the even more disastrous defeat of Italian soldiers at the hands of Emperor Menelik II's army at Adwa (alternatively Adowa, Adua) in 1896. Constituting the first major defeats of a modern European state army by an African one, these losses temporarily empowered critics of the colonial enterprise. In particular, Adwa led to the political downfall of Prime Minister Francesco Crispi, who had seen in African colonies the solution not only to Italy's problem of surplus population but also to its "Southern Question" constituted by the supposed developmental lag of the southern provinces. Crispi and other supporters of colonialism envisioned Eritrea and Ethiopia as future sites of large-scale settlement by Italian agriculturalists. Somalia, by contrast, was posited as the site for commercial interests and latifundia-style estates devoted to cotton and tobacco.[17]

In the aftermath of Adwa, liberals like Luigi Einaudi instead promoted an alternative "colonial" solution to the mass emigration that politicians like Crispi saw as both symptom and cause of national weakness. Einaudi argued that the informal or "expatriate" colonies formed by Italian migrants to countries like Brazil and the United States were better vehicles for promoting Italian interests abroad than costly formal colonies. Noting the semantic indistinguishability of the Italian term *colonie* to signify colonies of direct domination and concentrated migrant communities in other sovereign states, historian Mark Choate has described the latter as constituting "ethnographic colonies."[18] What Crispi and, later, Mussolini would see as a source of Italian weakness—mass emigration—Einaudi instead reconceived as a national asset. Einaudi's always minority vision of a colonialism formed by expatriate communities, however, would lose appeal after Italy acquired the former Ottoman territories of Libya and the Dodecanese Islands in 1912 as the result of the Italo-Turkish War.

The nationalist excitement over these territorial gains muted alternative models of colonialism, as formal colonies once again appeared a means for asserting Italian greatness and redirecting surplus labor. Still, an alternative form of "socialist" irredentism that rejected formal colonies persisted in the thought of figures like Cesare Battisti.[19] The 1911 speech by poet Giovanni Pascoli, delivered in honor of the Libyan campaign's dead and wounded, typified the belief that the existence of Italian colonies would erase the humiliations and discrimination suffered by Italians who went abroad to work. After condemning the indignities suffered by Italians in places like the United States, Pascoli praised the new colonial Italy in which these workers would instead labor for the greatness of the nation and retain their dignity as Italian citizens:

> There [in Italian Libya] they will be workers, not day laborers, poorly paid, poorly valued, and insulted; they will not be foreigners. They will be workers in the noblest sense of the word, and they will farm *their own property*, on the soil of the Motherland. They will not be forced to renounce allegiance to their Motherland, but instead will clear paths, cultivate new land, channel water, build houses, and open ports always seeing our tricolor flag flying high over the waves of our great sea.[20]

In reality, however, few Italian settlers made their way to these new territories before World War I. Italy's control over Libya remained nominal, confined to coastal areas of Tripolitania and Cyrenaica. Italy only formally acquired the Dodecanese Islands by the 1923 Treaty of Lausanne, having occupied them for the decade before that. Many more Italians continued to migrate to third countries, including the imperial possessions of other European powers (notably Algeria, Tunisia, and Egypt) than did to Italy's own colonial possessions. Indeed, Italy's peripheral status as a European power and the ever-growing diaspora of Italian workers had led nationalists like Enrico Corradini to describe Italy as a "proletarian nation." At the first congress of the Associazione Nazionalista Italiana, Corradini argued, "There are nations in a condition of inferiority in relation to others, just as there are classes that are in a condition of inferiority in relation to other classes."[21] For nationalists like Corradini, the means to overcome such national proletarian status were not those of international class struggle—the solution proposed by the Left—but, rather, colonial conquest.

With the advent of the Great War, Italy initially maintained a stance of neutrality despite its adherence since 1882 to the Triple Alliance with Austria-Hungary and Germany. Strident advocates of militarism like Corradini and the poet Gabriele D'Annunzio urged Italian intervention into the war. Italy then entered into secret negotiations first with the Central Powers and then the Allied Powers in pursuit of guarantees of the long-sought-after irredentist lands of Trieste, Trentino, Istria, parts of Dalmatia, and the port of Vlorë/Valona and the island of Sazan/Sanseno in Albania.[22] In May 1915, Italy joined the war on the side of the Allies, having signed the secret Treaty of London promising a range of territorial concessions. Despite Woodrow Wilson's insistence at the subsequent Paris Peace Conference that such secret pacts not be honored, Italy ultimately acquired the Alto Adige, Trentino, Trieste, Istria, the Dalmatian city of Zadar/Zara, and some islands in the Kvarner and Dalmatia in the aftermath of the Habsburg Empire's dissolution.

This did not satiate Italian territorial ambitions, however, and the Italian navy briefly occupied Vlorë/Valona. In 1919, the poet D'Annunzio also led a ragtag band of veterans, nationalists, and proto-fascists in seizing the city of Rijeka/Fiume desired by both the newly formed Kingdom of Serbs, Croats, and Slovenes and Italy. Italy would eventually annex Fiume in 1924, two years after the establishment of the fascist regime. Italy's military withdrawal from Albania in 1919 instead prompted schemes to bring Italian "colonists" (*coloni*) there.[23] This reflected the continued, if uneven, competition in Italy of two models: one stressing colonies of formal domination and another of expatriate or "ethnographic" colonies created by Italian migration to third countries. The regime headed by Benito Mussolini would embrace both of these, enfolding them into a third model: that of fascist empire.

When Mussolini and the fascist party took power in 1922, they inherited a fragmented set of possessions in Eritrea, Somalia, and the Aegean together with those newly "redeemed" northern and northeastern territories now incorporated into the Italian state. Mussolini had successfully exploited the economic and political crisis opened up by the war and the pervasive sense of disappointment that despite being among the Allied victors, Italy was in a position closer to that of a defeated power. Following the invalidation of the Treaty of London at the Paris peace negotiations, D'Annunzio captured this sense of betrayal in his denunciation of a "mutilated victory" (*la vittoria mutilata*). For D'Annunzio, Mussolini, and other nationalists, this betrayed victory figured as merely the latest in a chain of catastrophes that began with the Risorgimento's failure to forge unity through revolutionary means (later reformulated by Gramsci as *la rivoluzione mancata*) and was compounded by military fiasco in Africa (*la conquista mancata*). Mussolini positioned fascism as a revolutionary movement that would complete the work of forging the nation begun with the Risorgimento. In this vision, Italy and Italians would be (re)made through victory both at home and abroad, creating a hybrid "nation-empire."[24]

This remaking of Italy and Italians involved an ambitious transformation of the landscape through reclamation or *bonifica integrale*. Although technically referring to massive public works projects to render productive previously marginal areas like the malarial Pontine Marshes, *bonifica* also carried broader notions of spiritual, moral, and political regeneration. Ruth Ben-Ghiat argues, "The campaigns for agricultural reclamation (*bonifica agricola*), human reclamation (*bonifica umana*), and cultural reclamation (*bonifica della cultura*) . . . are different facets and phases of a comprehensive project to combat degeneration and radically renew Italian society by 'pulling up bad weeds and cleaning up the soil.'"[25] By the early 1930s, this process of regeneration explicitly included what Italian endocrinologist Nicola Pende deemed a "bonifica della razza" or racial reclamation.[26] In keeping with this, *bonifica* stood as a geographically comprehensive project that linked new settlements housing colonists on the Italian peninsula with those in the Italian possessions through the shared claim to conquer *terra nullius*.

This claim—common to settler colonialism—effaced the sometimes brutal displacements that made such reclamation possible. This was perhaps most evident in Libya, where the fascist regime waged a decade-long campaign between 1922 and 1932 aimed at "pacifying" the local population. Although termed a "reconquest" (*riconquista*), this repressive and at times genocidal military operation—which targeted Sanusi guerrilla fighters and civilians alike—actually consolidated Italian control for the first time over the three regions (Tripolitania, Cyrenaica, the Fezzan) composing Libya.[27] The internment of native populations and expropriation of land created the grounds of possibility for the subsequent projects of demographic colonization of Libya launched by Governor Italo Balbo, who had inherited the earlier projects of the Ente per la Colonizzazione della Libia (ECL) begun in 1932. Much propagandized by the regime, a contingent of state-sponsored settlers deemed the *Ventimila* arrived in 1938 to occupy agricultural villages quickly built in Tripolitania and Cyrenaica and overseen by the Istituto Nazionale Fascista della Previdenza Sociale (INFPS) and the ECL. In the space of four years, Libya's Italian population grew from 64,000 to 110,000.[28]

Fascism also entailed consolidation of Italian control over Somalia. When Cesare Maria De Vecchi became governor of Italian Somalia in 1923, he strengthened and reorganized the Somali Police Corps into the colonial Corpo Zaptié. De Vecchi put the corps to work disarming northern tribes long accustomed to indirect rule even as Italian Somalia grew through the incorporation of formerly British Jubaland into the territory. By the time De Vecchi left Somalia in 1928, Somalia's "pacification" was largely complete. The regime then began to pin its hopes on the sorts of agricultural settlement that later would assume pride of place in Libya. The Società Agricola Italo-Somala (SAIS, Society for Italian-Somalian Agriculture), in existence since 1920, held several agricultural concessions, with the largest one at Villaggio Duca degli Abruzzi (Villabruzzi). Government aid and land reclamation also revitalized the Azienda Agraria Governativa at Genale, founded in 1912. In contrast to the villages populated by Italian settlers constructed in Tripolitania and Cyrenaica in the late 1930s, however, Somalia's Villaggio Duca degli Abruzzi and Genale relied heavily on native labor and attracted relatively few Italians. In addition, agricultural outputs remained modest, and the high cost of certain products—such as bananas—made them uncompetitive on the world market.[29]

Following Italy's brutal invasion of Ethiopia, in which the military employed illegal chemical weapons, in May 1936 Mussolini triumphantly announced, "Italy finally has its empire." He did not hesitate to add, "A fascist empire." In this, Mussolini sought to distinguish Italian empire from what he saw as capitalist or bourgeois colonialism,[30] as well as from the ancient Roman example that fascism intended to exceed. The launch in December 1936 of construction on a "second Rome" on the outskirts of the capital gave concrete expression to this desire to both emulate and best ancient Rome. As the site for the Esposizione Universale di Roma (EUR) planned for the twentieth anniversary of the fascist revolution in 1942, the EUR neighborhood was to serve as "a parallel capital . . . [that] valorized the authority and prestige of Rome in a new, equally monumental but modern, setting."[31]

The declaration of empire brought other important shifts. Eritrea and Somalia were fused with Ethiopia in the newly established Africa Orientale Italiana (AOI). In keeping with the new conception of empire, the former Ministero delle Colonie became the Ministero dell'Africa Italiana (MAI) in 1937. Regime propaganda promoted AOI as an "impero di lavoro" (an empire of work or labor) for Italy's surplus laborers, as attested to by the influx of thirty-nine thousand Italian workers to Ethiopia's capital city within the space of three years.[32] In doing so, fascism furthered a process of "whitening" Italy's internal Others (southerners, rural poor) that had been under way since unification, deflecting stereotypes of "blackness" long associated with the *Meridione* or Italian south onto the native inhabitants of the colonies, above all those in the territories of AOI.[33] At the same time, the Italian state also sought to encourage return migration from expatriate communities to the new imperial acquisitions. This was just one initiative in a multipronged outreach to communities of Italian migrants; the Italian regime devoted considerable resources to sponsoring *fasci all'estero* with the intent of bringing Italians in the diaspora into the fascist fold. Asserting that Italy's territorial expansion had obviated the need for emigration, the regime claimed that those once labeled "emigrants" would now be known as "citizens" and part of an "army of workers."[34]

This reflected a much larger effort by the fascist regime to control and regulate migration within and beyond the peninsula. In 1927 the regime had abolished the Commissariato Generale dell'Emigrazione (created in 1901), signaling a key shift in governmental policy on emigration. In its place arose the Commissariato per le migrazioni e la colonizzazione interna, which explicitly fused the projects of external and internal colonization through settler-driven land reclamation. Through this entity the regime also sought to curb rural migration into Italian cities. Like so many fascist schemes, this one failed, and internal migration actually increased as a result of economic difficulties in the 1930s.[35]

The regime did succeed, however, in redefining the terms of migration and how some *coloni* conceived of their movements. As one settler bound for Libya put it, "We aren't emigrating though, are we? We're still going home, even more so; we were born here [in Italy] but there [in Libya] we will have land."[36] After 1938, Tripolitania and Cyrenaica (already administratively unified in 1934) were incorporated directly as a regional district or province of Italy, reinforcing this sense that a move to Libya entailed a move *within* Italy and not emigration abroad. As occurred in Libya with Balbo's much-publicized plan of demographic colonization, AOI also became the object of state-directed colonization schemes. Although technically these projects were administered by parastatal entities like the INFPS in Libya or the Ente Colonizzazione Puglia d'Etiopia in Ethiopia, they nonetheless remained top-down schemes in which settlers proved dependent on the state for their basic means of existence. In contrast, Somalia—perceived as unsuitable for large-scale European settlement—never received as many Italian settlers as Eritrea or Ethiopia. The top-down nature of these settlement efforts contradicted the stated aim of producing in the colonies a class of self-sufficient Italian agriculturalists who embodied the virtues of thrift, sobriety, and virility. While the regime exalted these agriculturalists as the model fascist settlers, Italian colonists also occupied a wide range of positions in the empire's cities: doctors, traders, businessmen, merchants, civil servants, mechanics, shopkeepers, and so on.

The establishment of empire also brought significant changes to the Dodecanese Islands, under Italian control since 1912 but only formally annexed in 1923. Unlike AOI, the Isole dell'Egeo held the status of *possedimento* or possession, rather than colony. The first civil governor of the islands, Mario Lago, pursued policies of Italianization and oversaw an ambitious program of infrastructural development. As in both Italy and other overseas territories, sites of land reclamation became home to Italian settlers, though in smaller numbers than in Libya. The regime established five such agricultural villages in the Dodecanese: three on Rhodes (Peveragno, San Marco, San Benedetto) and two at Kos (Fiorenza and Torre in Lambi).[37] Lago's successor, Cesare Maria De Vecchi (former governor of Somalia from 1923 to 1928), inaugurated a phase of harsher Italianization and fascistization that coincided with the proclamation of empire. When interviewed decades afterward, many Greek residents of the Dodecanese recalled the De Vecchi era as the time "when fascism came," even though technically the islands had been under fascist control since 1923.[38]

Italy acquired its final imperial possession in 1939, with the establishment of a protectorate over Albania. The fascist doctrine of *spazio vitale* or "vital space" envisioned concentric circles of influence and domination, with the *piccolo spazio* (or small space) reserved for ethnic Italians and the *grande spazio* (large space) encompassing southeastern Europe and much of the Mediterranean.[39] Within that larger sphere, Albania was to serve as a base for further expansion. As Dino Alfieri, head of the Ministero della Cultura Popolare, exulted on the day of the invasion, "Albania constitutes a bridgehead from which become possible further movements. One moves toward the restoration of the Roman Empire."[40] In that new Roman empire, Albania occupied an unusual position, conceptualized as a kind of "brotherly" union between Italians and Albanians but in which the king's lieutenant governor exercised executive power.[41] Like the ethnic Greeks of the Dodecanese, Albanians sat high in the imperial racial hierarchy owing to their status as fellow European subjects. One author in the journal *Difesa della Razza* (the most prominent of the journals embracing the racial line from 1938 on that Italians belonged to the Aryan race), for example, characterized the Albanian as belonging to one of the "piccole razze" (small, less important races) but nonetheless "a born warrior, valorous and generous, hospitable, sober, simple, but unrelenting in the vendetta."[42] In both the Aegean and Albania, intermarriage between Italians and locals was permitted. In contrast, the widespread practice of concubinage or *madamismo* with local women and the intimate contacts between officers and colonial soldiers (*ascari*) led Mussolini to impose anti-miscegenation laws and residential segregation in Italian Africa's colonial cities in a futile effort to avoid racial "promiscuity" in the empire.[43] The translation of these racial colonial hierarchies into legal and social practices of citizenship is discussed at length in chapter 4.

Given its importance in the fascist imperial imagination, Albania was projected to become Italy's *quinta sponda* or fifth shore. This followed on the proclamation of Libya as Italy's *quarta sponda*. The addition of Albania to the fascist empire attracted a number of Italian civilians to the country, as well as soldiers deployed there during the Greek campaign (1940–1941). Whereas the number of such civilians is estimated at no larger than fifty-eight thousand, it included state functionaries, employees in road construction and other public works projects, workers in various Italian companies

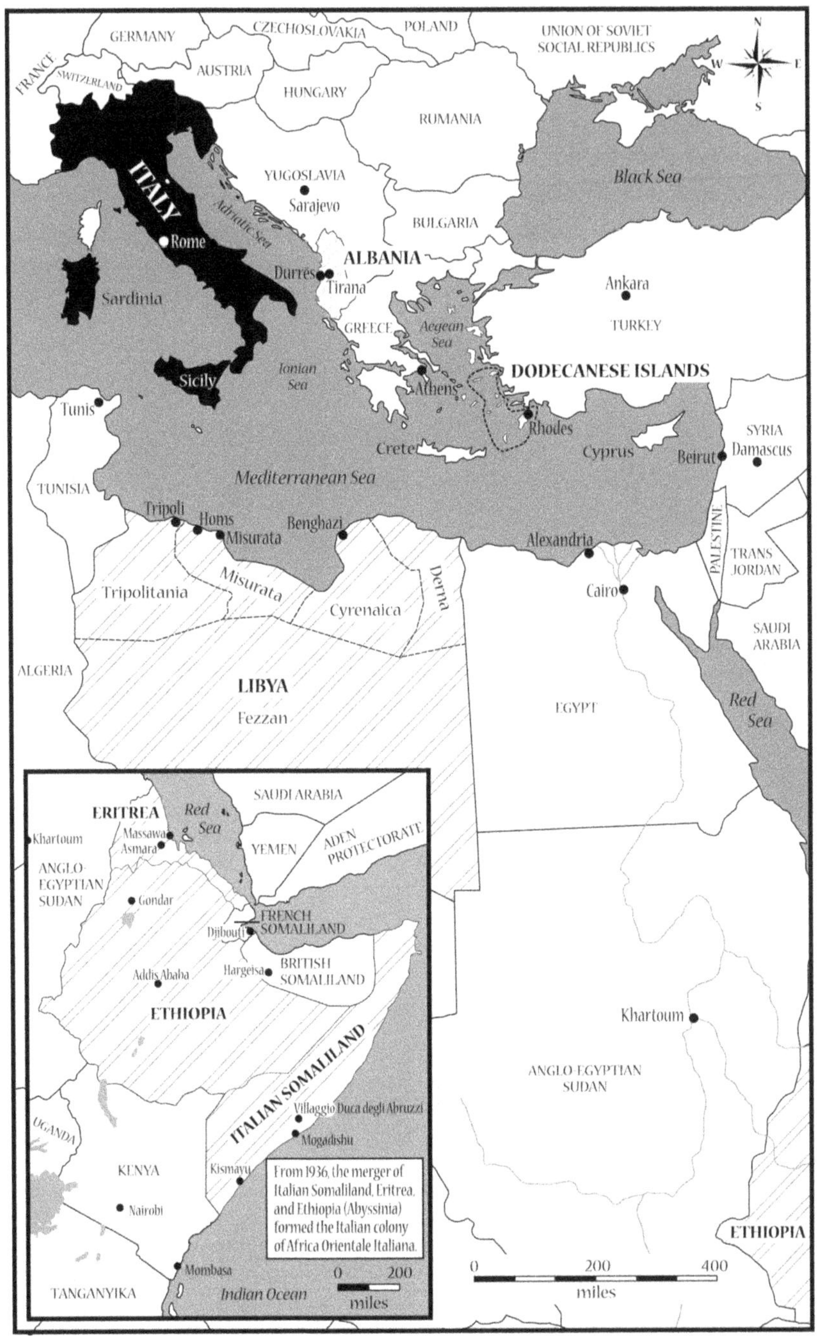

FIGURE 3. Map of Italian Empire, 1940. Map designed by Mike Bechthold.

with branches in Albania (such as Fiat), and teachers for Italian schools.[44] Italy's imperium—which incorporated territories with statuses ranging from colonies to possessions to protectorates—reached its maximum size, then, just a year before Italy entered the Second World War on 10 June 1940. In less than three years, Italy would lose military control over all its African and Balkan territories, precipitating the return of many (civilian) settlers. Exalted as the vanguard of Italian fascist empire, these settlers little suspected that they would instead serve as the vanguard of Italy's imminent (if protracted) decolonization.

CHAPTER 2

Wartime Repatriations and the Beginnings of Decolonization

> Today, when I'm asked where home is for me, I am struck by how far away it is; and yet, home is nowhere else but right here, at the edge of this body of mine. . . . Displacement takes on many faces and is our very everyday dwelling.
>
> *Elsewhere, within Here*, Trinh T. Minh-ha (2011)

On 2 June 1940, seven-year-old Grazia Arnese (Grimaldi) and her older brother Guerino hugged their parents goodbye and boarded the *Saturnia* bound from Tripoli to Marina di Ravenna on Italy's Adriatic coast. The Arnese children formed part of a contingent of an estimated thirteen thousand settler children (ages ranging from four to fifteen) sent from Libya to the Italian peninsula as a protective measure in advance of Italy's entry into the war eight days later. Parents knew why their children had been sent away but had little say in the matter, in contrast to the voluntary mass evacuations of children and other civilians taking place simultaneously in places like Britain. The children instead had been told they were embarking early on an exciting vacation to summer camps on the Italian mainland. This story would not necessarily have raised the suspicions even of older children, given the established practice of sending youngsters (including those in the colonies) to seaside and mountainside holiday camps sponsored by institutions of the fascist regime, notably the youth organization Gioventù Italiana del Littorio. Neither parents nor children, however, could have foreseen the long separations that awaited them.

Grazia Arnese would never again see her father or her older brother Antonio, victims of the war. Separated from her brother Guerino, Grazia reunited with both her sibling and their mother only after five years of hardship shuttling between various institutions on the peninsula.[1] Other families from Libya whose children were transferred to mainland Italy in 1940 endured even longer periods of separation. The diary entries for 1946 and 1947 of Giacomo Cason, an Italian colonist from the Oliveti settlement in Tripolitania under the aegis of the IN(F)PS, for example, center on his desire to see his three daughters. The girls finally returned to Libya in June 1947, after a seven-year separation from their parents.[2]

These large-scale repatriations of civilians from the "fourth shore" of Italy's empire would be among the first but certainly not the last of such mass, organized movements.[3] The Libyan repatriations occurred in tandem with evacuations from other Italian overseas territories on the eve of the war; five hundred women and children sent from the Isole Egeo on the *Oceania*, for instance, arrived in Bari on 9 June 1940.[4] From the very start, demographic colonization aimed at establishing sizable and permanent settler populations in various parts of the empire had necessitated policies of both voluntary and involuntary repatriation of individual colonists and settler families. Nonetheless, in contrast to the migrations of the *bimbi libici* ("Libyan children"), these earlier prewar repatriations had proven largely ad hoc.[5]

Reasons for such individual repatriations ranged from illness, to inability to work, to "immoral" behavior that could damage fascist prestige in the colonies and encourage insubordination on the part of fellow colonists. "The potential and actual presence of impoverished and 'unfit' whites informed social policies in many colonial contexts,"[6] notes Ann Laura Stoler, an observation that proves as true for Italy's African colonies as for the Dutch East Indies she studies. Administrators of colonial settlements in Ethiopia complained, rather unsurprisingly, about the tendency of colonists to "drink, dance and party" (*si beve si balla e si fa festa*); forcible repatriations from Ethiopia occurred for reasons that included "incapacity to work the land."[7] In the Libyan villages administered by the INFPS, offenses resulting in involuntary repatriation included theft, arson, family discord, and illegitimate pregnancies. In the case of an unmarried pregnant woman who requested a temporary return to Italy in 1938, INFPS officials agreed on the necessity of her removal from the village given that "women of the settlement engage in their usual gossiping." Just as importantly, the woman's condition prevented her from doing any "useful work."[8] Alberto Stern, the director of the INFPS's Tripoli section for "Demographic Colonization," treated the pregnancy—like other examples of work indiscipline—as the sign of a poor moral character. In Italy, he noted, this woman had worked as a maid, and from the beginning of her time in the colony she had displayed undisciplined behavior and antipathy toward life in the village. He characterized her as suffering from "tendencies that were scarcely colonial," which in Stern's reasoning had led her to slip off to Tripoli where she had a relationship with a man who abandoned her upon learning of the pregnancy.[9]

In contrast to such individual movements, the removal of Italian civilians from Italy's African territories carried out between 1940 and 1943 took place under the banner of state-sponsored humanitarianism. Once Italy joined the conflict, a number of repatriations occurred on so-called hospital ships—including the *Saturnia* on which the Arnese children had previously voyaged—and received considerable press coverage. The three missions from AOI to Italian ports carried out between 1942 and 1943 on the "white ships" or *navi bianche*—four transatlantic cruise ships painted white with the red cross—remain the best known of such efforts and brought approximately 27,778 citizens back to the peninsula.[10] These voyages required cooperation with the enemy British navy, as well as collaboration with humanitarian organizations such as the International Committee of the Red Cross (ICRC) and its Italian counterpart (Croce Rossa Italiana, or CRI). In several key aspects—notably the involvement of multiple actors, including members of the Allied governments and international humanitarian organizations—these migrations established a template for movements by Italians out of the former possessions and delivery of post-migration assistance after the armistice of 8 September 1943 and, in particular, after 1945. In other respects, however, these initial repatriations proved exceptional, thereby creating a mistaken impression that the end of Italian military control in much of Africa signaled the end of its imperial presence. As discussed in the introduction, the question of just when and how decolonization occurred in Italy's former possessions remains open to debate. If we consider decolonization from the point of view of the out-migrations of settler populations, the end of Italian empire proved protracted rather than abrupt and expeditious. In addition, repatriation proved anything but the definitive and one-way return "home" to the Italian peninsula usually implied by the term.

Organized Mass Repatriation and Rehabilitation Schemes: The *Navi Bianche*

Wartime schemes to evacuate Italian women, children, and elderly from the colonies of Eritrea, Ethiopia, and Somalia that made up AOI developed as a response to Italy's rapid military defeat in East Africa. Within just a year of entering the conflict, the Italians had lost control over their formal colonies in East Africa. Describing these dramatic losses, one author gives voice to a common view that Italy's colonial moment not only was brief but ended abruptly and decisively: "The Italian military machine, so overwhelmingly victorious five years earlier [in Ethiopia], literally crumbled, and Italy precipitously withdrew from Somalia. On February 25, 1941, only weeks after the British crossed the Jubaland border, Mogadishu was occupied and the colonial government ceased to function. . . . The last Italian flag in the horn of Africa was lowered at Gondar in northwestern Ethiopia on November 27, 1941."[11]

Armed with the benefit of hindsight, such an account takes for granted the irreversibility of Italian military collapse in East Africa. Likewise, when viewed in retrospect, the evacuations from AOI would become symbolic of the consequences of empire's end for civilians. At the time, however, the regime promoted these measures (like those of the Libyan children sent to Italy) as merely temporary, until the fortunes of war turned again in favor of Italy. Italian Cyrenaica became a battleground for much of 1941 and 1942, as Allied (largely British but also Australian) forces captured and occupied it, retreated, and took it again. In light of such dramatic reversals, Italians could continue to hope that their displacement and repatriation was merely temporary. Furthermore, Italians in AOI faced with the decision of whether or not to repatriate to Italy followed the events of the North African front closely, and "enthusiasm for the voyage to Italy ebbed and flowed with the tide of battle in Libya."[12]

By the time of the third and final British occupation of Cyrenaica in November 1942, however, very few Italians remained in that territory. On 29 November 1942, Cardinal Celso Costantini wrote in his diary that he had received word from Monsignor Moro in Benghazi/Bengasi that "no Italians remain in the vicariate except missionaries and the sisters."[13] Most Italians had either repatriated to the Italian peninsula (where many of them received financial assistance from the Ministry of Italian Africa) or been evacuated by the Italian military to Italian Tripolitania.[14] In 1942 Tripoli's bishop, Camillo Vittorino Facchinetti, organized a *casa dell'assistenza* to provide aid to the Cyrenaican evacuees in Tripolitania.[15] As late as 1958, as we have seen, the Italian Ministry of Foreign Affairs grappled with the issue of "refugees from Cyrenaica" living in and around Tripoli (*profughi della Cirenaica residenti Tripoli*), indicating that these individuals still remained in limbo over a decade after their initial displacement. These, no doubt, formed the core of the Unione Coloni Italiani d'Africa bombarding local prefects with requests for assistance. This highlights the protracted and multidirectional process by which populations left Italy's overseas possessions, beginning on a large scale in 1940 and 1941.

Like the fascist regime, the British military had not anticipated the rapid collapse of the Italian military and developed ad hoc responses to the humanitarian exigencies it created. As a 1944 publication on the British Military Administration in Eritrea and Somalia put it, "Even in January 1941, when the state of Italian morale was becoming apparent, General Cunningham believed that he could do no more by May than clear Kenya's Northern Frontier Province and capture Kismayu."[16] In reality, by April of that year all of AOI had fallen under British control. The British found themselves unprepared and shorthanded to deal with such a vast territory. The chief political officer of what was then known as the Occupied Enemy Territories Administration (OETA, subsequently the BMA) underlined the logistical difficulties when he noted drily, "By the end of June 1941 the total number of officers employed under me, in occupied enemy territories and at my headquarters, amounted only to 268, which is almost the exact strength of the European Italian staff of the Post Office at Asmara."[17]

Although OETA took as its model the military government exercised by the British over Palestine during the previous global conflict, Lord Rennell of Rodd—who worked under OETA's chief political officer for North and East Africa, Sir Philip Mitchell, and later wrote a detailed account—claimed, "We had no precedent to work on and builded [*sic*] empirically."[18] The BMA in East Africa thus developed, in part, as an ad hoc response to the emergencies created by the war. Rennell, in particular, possessed a pragmatic bent that allowed him to "thrive in a fluid wartime situation" even as "his thinking had its origins in a network of colonial administrators well versed in the traditions of indirect rule."[19] Like many of his fellow administrators in the BMA, Rennell favored leaving considerable control to local authorities (in this case, to Italian officials and police, as well as Italian courts). This reflected not only British traditions of indirect rule in many of its own imperial possessions but also the laws of war, as well as purely practical considerations.[20] Chief Political Officer Mitchell, for instance, stressed that a whole range of questions about the Italian territories "are likely to be raised at the Peace Conference which must follow the war . . . but at this stage it is impracticable to go beyond study and preparation."[21]

Confronted with sizable numbers of Italian military and civilians in East Africa, British authorities settled on a multipronged policy of internment, co-optation, and repatriation.[22] The British employed a category "E" to denote "an Italian Male Civilian over the age 16 who is able-bodied and medically fit, and therefore in the 'Evacuee' category and non-repatriable."

One Italian civilian male from Addis interned first in AOI and then Kenya claimed that there existed three subcategories of "evacuees." On the initial days of the occupation of AOI, the British sorted Italian men and gave them a red, green, or black card (*tessera*), depending on their status. Those with black cards were sent immediately to Berbera, those with red cards were considered civilian POWs and confined to the "Case Incis" that had previously housed Italian state employees, and those with green found accommodation in the camp of Dire Daua under British surveillance.[23] An unknown number of Italian males eluded the British net, either operating as guerrillas against the Allies or disappearing into the local population.[24] Postcards produced by the Fascist Party (PNF) celebrated this rearguard battle, featuring an Italian soldier astride a pile of corpses, a tattered British flag, and the vow "We will return!" (Ritorneremo). Nonetheless, the majority of Italian military men and other males over the age of sixteen remained confined to prisoner of war and "evacuation" camps scattered throughout the British Empire, rendering wives and children of these Italians particularly vulnerable.

Many of these remaining women, children, and elderly ultimately went to "transit camps" like those established at Ghinda, Harar, Sembel, Mandera, and the former Italian airport of Dire Daua until the diplomatic agreements and logistical arrangements necessary for their repatriation could be effected.[25] Prior to their internment, some families—such as that constituted by Maria Carelli and her two children, Luisella and Piero—had sought shelter in the Circolo Ufficiali in Addis Ababa or religious institutions such as the Missione della Consolata, fearing reprisals and violence by local populations. Carelli's husband, the *vice comandante* of the XIV Brigata Coloniale, had been imprisoned in Kenya in July 1941. Red Cross documents from September 1941 speak of four "safe zones" within Addis Ababa in which Italian civilians lived but which offered merely "temporary solutions," likely referencing the provisional accommodations initially occupied by families like that of the Carelli.[26]

Former settlers recall organizing local defense units, in which adolescents and older men served to protect Italian civilians and their property.[27] Whether fears about the safety of civilians proved exaggerated or not, they were shared at the time by Italian civilians themselves, some British officials, and members of the International Red Cross. As Alfredo Romiti, the former head of the AOI's Ufficio Commerciale Centrale dell'Ente Approvvigionamenti (Commercial Supply Agency) and a protagonist in providing food assistance to civilians and POWs in AOI, put it, "The predictions of the defeat and the specter of Abyssinian retaliation danced before the eyes of the authorities and fathers/heads of families." As a result, "One planned and discussed extensively a mass evacuation from Addis Ababa to Asmara of all women and children."[28] Eventually, this planned mass evacuation would instead carry many civilians to the Italian peninsula.

The primary and extended negotiations for carrying out this mass evacuation by sea involved the Italian and British governments, with the additional services of Swiss and American diplomacy. The Red Cross played an important role in the scheme's execution, less in its genesis. Upon visiting occupied AOI in 1941, the ICRC honorary delegate Henri-Philippe Junod—a Swiss citizen, missionary, anthropologist, and resident of Pretoria who worked with the South African Red Cross—highlighted the precarious position of Italian women and children, abandoned to a "hostile" climate and population.[29] Although he had not been charged with making a recommendation about repatriation,[30] Junod urged the necessity of returning these civilians to Italy as soon as possible. Junod noted that the situation in Eritrea proved less dire than in Ethiopia or Somalia, in part owing to the deeper roots of Italian settlement in the former. Nonetheless, Junod distinguished between colonists in Eritrea "who have been long established and more or less consider the country as their patrie and whose children consider it as their native soil" and "the others who were newly arrived" after the conquest of Ethiopia in 1935. Furthermore, a number of colonists had been evacuated from Ethiopia to Eritrea, and these colonists found themselves in "difficult, even desperate" circumstances. Junod further argued that while Italian Somalia, in contrast to Ethiopia and Eritrea, never proved home to sizable European populations, as many as seven thousand civilians remained there. He recommended that, among these civilians, women who suffered the additional burden of "the continuous and debilitating influence of a trying climate" should receive priority for repatriation.[31] Finally, Junod deemed the situation in Ethiopia "the most urgent and grave," contending that "it is absolutely certain that the Italian population, on a whole, is in danger and that only the presence of the occupation troops protects them." The Red Cross delegate attributed this to the hatred fomented by the 1935 war and occupation. Junod recommended, "I repeat that this [repatriation] should be done without delay."[32]

In her diary, Maria Carelli recounts the uncertainty and fear that prevailed among Italians themselves as the preparations for repatriation dragged on (eventually taking over eleven months). The British informed civilians that they would conduct a population census in preparation for eventual repatriation by ship to Italy. In compliance, the members of the Carelli family presented themselves in Addis Ababa's central piazza on 28 December 1941 and were assigned to the Dire Daua camp until their departure for Italy became possible. Carelli's diary, published in 2014 together with her daughter's recollections and embellishments on the events, details the key role in camp administration played by Italian carabinieri and colonial police (Polizia Africa Italiana, PAI), together with volunteers from the Italian Red Cross or CRI. In rereading her mother's words, Luisella Carosio (née Carelli) remarks, "The Red Cross: how frequently it is cited as a basic reference point, as a refuge, as a source of reassurance!"[33] The employment of Italian police in the camps and later on the *navi bianche* reflected the shortage of British personnel (particularly those with the requisite language skills), as well as the continuance of certain forms of Italian governance such as Italian law and courts.[34] In former AOI, the British thus kept on some Italian police despite pronouncements that "the Italian police organisation proved as incompetent as it was corrupt."[35]

Although civilian residents of these camps did not confront hunger or violence, they struggled with uncertainty and suspicion regarding the intentions of the British. In addition to complaints about lack of privacy and hygiene and her worries over the measles and malaria outbreaks that claimed the

Figure 4. Italian Red Cross sisters assisting Italian civilians, Berbera. Published with the permission of the ICRC Visual Archives. "War 1939–1945. Berbera, British Somalia. Italian [Red Cross] sisters give drinks to civilians aboard the transport barges." May 1942. V-P-HIST-E-01313, SOMALIA. Copyright ICRC.

lives of many children in the camp, Maria Carelli mistrusted British promises about repatriation. Even the reassurance of Red Cross representative André Evalet, who visited the camp in January 1942,[36] could not extinguish her fear that once aboard the ships the civilians would instead be sent to camps within the British Empire.

Although Carosio attributes her mother's fears to indoctrination with fascist propaganda about "perfidious Albion" (*perfida Albione*), as well as the silence of Vatican radio on this subject, such worries appear less fantastical when considered in light of the experience of civilians like Alfredo Romiti. After cooperating with the British authorities in the supply of emergency food to Italian civilians and internees in Ethiopia, Romiti was arrested in April 1942 for carrying a letter from a CRI worker intended for that volunteer's mother in the Dire Daua camp. Reassured by the support of some British officials who recognized the humanitarian relief he had carried out, Romiti learned he would be sent to the civilian camp at Mandera. Relieved at this prospect, in particular because his family was scheduled to depart for Italy from Mandera on the 10 May 1942 transport of the *Saturnia*, Romiti instead found himself sent to a POW camp in Kenya.[37] Despite his entreaties

FIGURE 5. Italian civilians from Ethiopia in transit to repatriation ships, Berbera. Published with the permission of the ICRC Visual Archives. May 1942. V-P-HIST-03222–03, SOMALIA. "War 1939–1945. Berbera, British Somalia. Embarkation of Italian civilians coming from Ethiopia." Copyright ICRC.

that he be treated as a civilian internee, as he had been previously, Romiti remained in a POW camp until war's end. Romiti's experience points to both the fluidity and definitional fuzziness of categories applied to Italians in the former possessions, a dilemma that would become only more pronounced after the war as the BMA and new international actors (notably personnel of UNRRA, the IRO, and the UNHCR) sought to sort out displaced persons and determine eligibility for assistance. The complexities of this process form the subject of the next chapter.

As would occur after the Second World War, other actors offering humanitarian assistance to these Italian civilians in Africa displaced by the events of war frequently disagreed with the relevant state powers as to the scope of their activities. The British, for instance, considered the Vatican—another sovereign power—as having overstepped its role when it began to intervene in 1943 on the question of repatriation of six hundred sick and wounded Italian POWs. As a British official testily put it, "With regard to the suggested reply to the request for their repatriation, we should explain that although we fully appreciate the valuable work done by the Holy See among prisoners of war we regard the question of repatriation as one which falls outside the scope of their activities and as one which should be dealt with through the Protecting Power."[38] A few months earlier, the BMA officers had complained about the Vatican advancing "personal" requests and asking for favors. The Vatican, for example, requested that the British grant permission to repatriate to one Gualtiero Agrati, employed in an oil company in Massawa and future son-in-law of the head of the Vatican Telegraph Office. As the official forwarding this request to Major Taylor of the BMA put it, "We are getting rather tired of these individual requests and should not wish to impose ourselves further on your exemplary patience by passing this one on to you if there were not the possibility that it may be as convenient as not to get rid of Signor Agrati. In that case we should acquire merit in the Vatican (for what that may be worth) without inconvenience to ourselves. We leave it to you to take action or not as you think fit."[39] After the war, the Vatican would play an important, if often underacknowledged, role in assisting Italian repatriates and foreign refugees alike in the Italian peninsula. The lack of access to much of the Vatican's documentation on these activities has contributed to this gap in understanding.[40]

Members of the Red Cross also came under attack for partiality or inappropriate activities. The ICRC representative to Ethiopia André Evalet, for instance, would ultimately be expelled by Haile Selassie. This occurred in the context of the bad feeling created in the aftermath of Italy's 1935 attack on Ethiopia, during which the organization had remained silent regarding evidence of Italy's use of chemical weapons and found itself accused by the Ethiopians of being pro-Italian.[41] According to a 1941 telegram from the ICRC delegate Junod, Evalet—a Swiss citizen born in Ethiopia and married to a German woman who ran a small *pensione* in Addis Ababa—initially met with general goodwill: "Evalet is persona grata to British, Italians and Ethiopians. . . . Evalet is about to take over responsibility for work of National Red Cross in Addis-Abeba. Everyone praises the work of this young intelligent and tactful man who pleases everybody."[42] By 1942, however, there existed growing doubts within the ICRC about whether Evalet had overstepped his role. In particular, Evalet was accused of siding with Italian civilians over the British authorities, having delivered personal Italian letters that also supposedly contained contraband material. Like Alfredo Romiti, who claimed that each time he visited an internment camp in his humanitarian role Italian women and young persons "assailed" him with letters and requests to send these missives to relatives in POW camps and on the peninsula, Evalet ran afoul of the occupying power over the issue of the post.[43] By 1945, things had taken a dramatic turn. Evalet had left Ethiopia for Eritrea, apparently expelled on the pretext of his wife's dealings with opponents of Emperor Selassie. One internal document within the ICRC suggests that the real reason had more to do with jealousy over properties held by Evalet's wife and stepmother in Ethiopia.[44]

At times, however, the BMA asked members of the Red Cross to engage in activities that those representatives themselves deemed inappropriate. In the early days of occupation in Eritrea, for example, the BMA requested that the American Red Cross carry out the distribution to European civilians of food supplies diverted to AOI from Greece. As the United States remained at this point neutral (prior to its entry into the war in December 1941), "this proved to be contrary to the principles of the American Red Cross administration which desired to limit its scope to handing over the supplies to the Administration on the spot."[45] Ultimately, members of the South African Red Cross took up this task of providing relief to Italians in the former colony. The fluidity and rapid transformation of events meant that states and international organizations like the ICRC and its national chapters often puzzled over the best and most appropriate ways to proceed.

Not surprisingly, controversies also embroiled members of the Italian Red Cross assisting civilians in AOI. Some of these CRI personnel were explicit fascist supporters, as evidenced by the testimony left by Clotilde del Balzo, who was repatriated to Italy on the *Giulio Cesare* in January 1943 (the *navi bianche*'s second mission). Del Balzo's detailed statement to PAI officials on board the ship testified to dissent within the CRI, as well as between the CRI and the BMA. In September 1941, del Balzo had transferred from the CRI offices in Addis Ababa to Asmara. She claimed that at that time, the CRI was in disarray, with a lawyer named Ostini heading it up. Del Balzo lauded the local Red Cross women there for carrying out difficult and heroic work (unsuited for women, in her opinion) among civilian prisoners. Soon, however, the British prohibited even this work, denying the CRI volunteers the necessary pass to enter the fort that housed the prisoners. According to del Balzo, various unpleasant incidents occurred with the aim of forcing all the CRI volunteers to abandon their posts. In February 1942, the British interned Ostini, the provisional head of the unit; an extraordinary commissioner, Latilla, then took over the work.

In del Balzo's opinion, the British sought to establish antifascist organizations among the Italian population, beginning with the CRI. The British instead likely saw their task as merely removing the most compromised individuals.[46] Asked whether she would join the newly reconstituted CRI, del Balzo sought the advice of Asmara's bishop, who encouraged her to fulfill her duties. Del Balzo thus reorganized her volunteers, and they set about putting together care packages for POWs. Del Balzo began to worry, however, when her request to meet with the CRI's newest extraordinary commissioner, Barile, met with silence. The final straw came when ICRC delegate Thiebaud arrived and there began negotiations with the BMA to establish a new committee to assist Italians, with discussions reaching an impasse on the question of del Balzo's participation. As she put it, "I remained sad and amazed and I confess that I didn't understand at all for what reason I was considered 'the black beast' [*la bestia nera*]." Despite reassurances to Thiebaud that del Balzo would continue her mission, once the ICRC delegate departed, Barile requested del Balzo's resignation. According to the Red Cross sister, Barile explained that del Balzo should never have agreed to take part in the newly constituted CRI, and that while "he approved of my gesture of fascist discipline he hoped that with my resignation the CRI would dissolve." Barile added that the British had already fingered her "as a person with strong fascist sentiments." In the end, del Balzo remained on in an unofficial capacity for another two months, after an unknown assailant shot and killed Latilla. At the time of her departure from Africa, Clotilde del Balzo took satisfaction in the fact that the CRI had weathered the storm and that thirty-five workers remained behind, providing assistance.[47]

Although thrilled at the prospect of leaving behind the internment camps, many other repatriates from the AOI on the *navi bianche* like Maria Carelli left the continent with heavy hearts, knowing that their husbands and other loved ones remained behind in Africa. The ambivalence felt by many of the departing repatriates was shared by Italian officials themselves, as Emanuele Ertola has demonstrated in his analysis of the documentation on the *navi bianche* contained in the archives of the Italian Ministry of Foreign Affairs (ASDMAE). Despite official pronouncements regarding the temporary nature of these evacuations, those within the government worried that such removals might ultimately become prelude to Italy's definitive loss of the territories. Nonetheless, many children of Africa ("i ragazzi di Africa") like Massimo Zamorani, who later penned a memoir of his experience on the *navi bianche*'s second mission, returned to Italy convinced that their country would ultimately emerge victorious. Zamorani thus shared the sentiments captured by a 1943 propaganda poster that featured a young boy and an elderly man (presumably repatriates) that declared: "I know, I know that millions and millions of Italians suffer that indefinable bug that we call 'mal d'Africa' [nostalgia for Africa]. There is only one cure: to return. And we will return." An alternative version of the same image bore the caption, "There where we were, there where our dead await us, there where we left powerful and indestructible traces of our civilization, there we will return."

In the same year, the Istituto Fascista dell'Africa Italiana published a *Guida del rimpatriato d'Africa* (Guide for the repatriate from Africa) that sought to put a positive spin on what might otherwise be read as a sign of defeat: "Besides its high humanitarian mission, the 'white fleet' represents for Italy an affirmation of prestige that is particularly dear to the hearts of those Italians constrained to make a temporary return from the Empire."[48] The guide facilitated assistance claims paid out by the Ministry of Italian Africa for the "profugo dell'Africa Orientale" or refugee from Italian East Africa, a bureaucratic category already in existence by 1942, suggesting that at least some in the government were aware of the possibility that such returns might become permanent.[49]

Contrary to the stalwart and heroic image of hardy pioneers eagerly awaiting a victorious return to Africa, internal documentation reveals the ambivalence of Italian officials toward the repatriates themselves. As Ertola details, the Italian officials in charge of the ships—notably Saverio Caroselli, former governor of Italian Somalia, and his official Bernardo Vecchi—perceived many of the Italian civilians as having degenerated as a result of their time in the internment camps, noting problems of both political and moral impropriety. Women who purportedly had sexual relationships with British officials were singled out, including those suffering from venereal disease or who "forgot" their imprisoned husbands and "trod upon any tradition of family." Particular note was made of a thirteen-year-old who gave birth during the second mission to a child sired by a British soldier; absent was any

FIGURE 6. "Torneremo," 1943. Reproduced with the permission of the Wolfsonian-Florida International University, Miami Beach, Florida. The Mitchell Wolfson Jr. Collection, XB1992.2392. Photo by David Almeida. Display card, "Io so, io sento che milioni e milioni di Italiani soffrono di un indefinibile male che si chiama il male d'Africa. Per guarirne non c'è che un mezzo: tornare. E torneremo" (I know, I feel that millions and millions of Italians suffer from an indefinable malady, known as the Africa sickness. There is only one means of recovering: to return. And we will return), 1943. Designed by Giulio Bertoletti (Italian, 1919–1976); published by Studio Tecnico Editoriale Italiano, Rome; and printed by Ind. Grafiche N. Moneta, Milan.

FIGURE 7. *Guida del rimpatriato d'Africa.* Istituto Fascista dell'Africa Italiana, Rome: Arti Grafiche G. Menaglia, 1943. Publication contained in collections of Istituto Agronomico per l'Oltremare, Florence.

sympathy for this minor or sensitivity regarding the potential circumstances of the pregnancy.[50] Likewise, a repatriate on board informed the crew of the moral laxity of a mother and her daughter traveling to Italy. According to the source, the daughter was "well known [in Asmara] for her sexual relationships with English, Americans, etc. Lately she was an '*entraîneuse*' [woman who attracted men into bars] at the Kit Kat, an evening club frequented exclusively by Englishmen." The woman was said to be infected with syphilis and to have borne an illegitimate child by an Allied serviceman.[51] Other criticisms targeted excessive drinking and smoking by women and minors, as well as the breakdown of class hierarchies.[52]

At the same time, the women of the Fasci Femminile or Women's Fascio assigned to assist the repatriates on board also came under fire for their unsuitability and lack of tact. Although officers highlighted the need to reinstate (fascist) hierarchy, they complained about one Alma Farnesi, sister of the vice secretary of the fascist party, who presumably obtained her post "not so much as a reflection of her individual qualities, but above all as a function of her kinship with a bigwig [*gerarca*]."[53] The impact of both *parentela* and *conoscenza* (kinship and connections) in the assignments aboard the ships pleased some repatriates—like Maria Carelli—and irritated others. After the "indignities" of having to mix with the lower classes in the camps, for instance, the officer's wife Carelli breathed a sigh of relief when she boarded the *Duilio*. Almost immediately, she made the acquaintance of the ship's doctor, who knew Carelli's brothers from medical school, and a pharmacist from her hometown. As a result, the family received a comfortable cabin, rather than merely beds in a room. Carelli's daughter Luisella remarks, "I have to smile at the thought that, having touched, so to speak, the soil of Italy [i.e., the ship], the mechanism of influential acquaintances and recommendations immediately kicked in!"[54]

As Luisella Carosio's comments indicate, the *navi bianche* were considered Italian ships under the command of Italian officers but with an English escort in the conduct of a humanitarian operation. As one of the special editions of Italian newspapers printed expressly for the *navi bianche* put it, "This comfortable steamer is a piece of your, our, Patria, it is a symbol of the Patria."[55] In spite of the fact that these ships symbolized Italy's rescue of its vulnerable citizens, some of the *navi bianche* contained a few non-Italian repatriates to Europe. The second mission in November 1942, for example, included sixty-six German citizens, five Hungarians, and one Romanian.[56] The *navi bianche* also brought succor to the remaining European populations in AOI, as when the *Saturnia* arrived in Africa on 30 June 1943 laden with goods sent by the CRI of Rome for needy civilians in Mogadishu (via the apostolic delegate there), as well as packages sent to individuals living in the city. These supplies included critically needed medicines.[57] In addition, the outbound voyages from Italy included a number of (former) Italian colonial subjects repatriating to Africa. Although the British complained about Italian refusal to recognize Ethiopians as anything other than Italian subjects even after Emperor Haile

Selassie had returned to Addis Ababa in May 1941, they ultimately succeeded in securing the release of Ras Imru, the emperor's cousin whom the fascist regime had imprisoned on the island of Ponza. Another nineteen Ethiopians or Eritreans (various documents refer to them differently) sailed from Trieste on the *Vulcania* in May 1943.[58] After the war, such two-way traffic in repatriations would continue, as East Africans, Libyans, Albanians, and others returned home from service or imprisonment in Italy, and Italian citizens made their way to the peninsula. As in the case of the *navi bianche*, however, the flows of former colonial subjects from Italy remained small in comparison to Italians leaving the former possessions. At the same time, the postwar period would witness a new phenomenon whereby Italians who had left the former possessions for the (imagined) safety of the peninsula now sought to return.

In contrast to postwar movements, the *navi bianche* traveled in treacherous waters where mines and other hidden dangers lurked. Forbidden by the British to travel through the Suez Canal, the ships made much longer passages (lasting about a month in duration) from the Red Sea, around the Cape of Good Hope, up the western coast of Africa, and into the Mediterranean. The British monitors left the ships at Gibraltar, after which they traversed the Mediterranean to various ports of disembarkation in Italy (Naples, Genoa, Trieste). The length of the trip provided the Italian officials on board plenty of time to conduct what Ertola has deemed a policy of "rehabilitation" and political reeducation, with the aim of inculcating fascist discipline and patriotism. The means of such reeducation included standard fascist propaganda, such as newspapers and films.[59] Children received particular attention, and a report of the second mission claimed that on arrival in Italy, those "children, who forty days earlier embarked in a state of moral abandonment presented themselves as ordered, disciplined and full of patriotic enthusiasm, singing hymns to the Patria in an exemplary manner, that were well received by all."[60] Children enlisted in volunteer work on board received a certificate attesting to service as part of the youth organizations of the regime.[61]

On the one hand, these ships served as microcosms (perhaps even heterotopias) of Mussolini's Italy,[62] with fascism's particular calculus of consent and coercion on prominent display. Repatriates filled out bureaucratic forms on the promise of an "extraordinary subsidy" (*sussidio straordinario*) available through the Ministry of Africa's Assistance Office (Ufficio Assistenza) in Rome; the regime also made available loans or advances (*anticipazioni*) to families whose breadwinner remained against his will in the former AOI.[63] While employing other classic instruments for forging consensus like film and ritual, the personnel on board simultaneously undertook tried-and-true practices of surveillance on repatriates and encouraged informers.[64] Members of the PAI, for example, mined repatriates' letters for any signs of potential subversive (antifascist) sentiments. A 1943 report claimed that such letters caught the civilians with their guard down: "The censorship of letters, on the return trip [to Italy], gave us the possibility to get to know the minds of the repatriates who had the maximum liberty to write, given that few believed in the possibility of a censorship service on board."[65] Those on board certainly would have been aware, however, of the monitoring of their everyday behavior, as when PAI officials were entrusted with the nightly screenings of films. The PAI collected information (whether spontaneously volunteered or actively solicited is not clear) about particular repatriates suspected of antifascism or collusion with the enemy. Several repatriates were noted as members of Italia Libera, an antifascist group with a branch in AOI, and suspected of serving as English spies.[66]

On the other hand, concerns about the repatriates' promiscuity and indolence after life in internment camps embodied common and pervasive fears about refugees, worries that would become more prominent after the conflict's end with the arrival in the metropole of significant numbers of displaced Italians and foreigners. Indeed, UNRRA would go so far as to make its motto "Helping people to help themselves," stressing the rehabilitative aspect of assistance to DPs and others, in contrast to charity-based models that positioned recipients as passive dependents. As had occurred on the *navi bianche*, after the war international agencies like UNRRA and its successor the IRO devoted particular attention to children and the dangers to home societies posed by those abandoned to their own devices during the conflict. In 1945, Martha Branscombe, who temporarily headed UNRRA's Child Welfare Section, wrote of the organization's enormous task in assisting war-torn children subjected to "shock and emotional disturbances"; these children, she warned, "have been schooled in deception and sabotage."[67] A year later, educator and writer Alice Bailey similarly sounded the alarm about "those peculiar and wild children of Europe and of China to whom the name 'wolf children' has been given. They have known no parental authority; they run in packs like wolves; they lack all moral sense and have no civilized values and know no sexual restrictions; they know no laws save the law of self-preservation."[68] If, during the war, Italian fascist officials worried that children from the colonies lacked adequate discipline as *figli di lupo* ("children of the wolf," one of the fascist youth group designations), after 1945 the specter of unruly and asocial "wolf children" symbolized the threat to the family posed by the war just past.

The role of the *navi bianche* as schools of fascist (re)education and refugee rehabilitation came to an abrupt halt midway during the final mission in July 1943, when news of Mussolini's ousting from the Grand Fascist Council and subsequent arrest on the orders of King Victor Emmanuel III became known. Marshal Pietro Badoglio—the Italian commander who had presided over the 1936 conquest of Addis Ababa and then served as Italian Ethiopia's first governor-general—became Italy's new prime minister. Badoglio ordered fascist insignia removed from the four *navi bianche* then making their way to the peninsula. Italy's division into two hostile governments after the Badoglio government's armistice with the Allies on 8 September 1943 meant that any further such organized naval evacuations from AOI were postponed until after the war. Just twenty days after the capitulation of the Italian military, Colonel Mirehouse in the British War Office noted that a fourth mission from AOI must be "shelved for the time being." Mirehouse reported that three thousand Italians in Ethiopia awaited repatriation, although many had changed their minds after the events of 8 September, and another fifteen hundred or so civilians and "decrepit prisoners of war" remained in Somalia.[69]

One British observer in Somalia in July 1943 claimed a muted response on the part of Italians still there. The most immediate concerns expressed were for those repatriates still en route to Italy:

> In assessing local reactions [in Somalia] to the Sicilian campaign and to the fall of Fascism, certain local factors must be taken into consideration. These events happened at a time when the dominant concern of the local Italians was the repatriation of over 2,000 women and children. Almost every person in Mogadishu had a relative amongst the repatriates on the high seas, and the immediate interest was their safe arrival in Italy. These personal sentiments almost completely overrode interest in the campaign, and most comments were confined to regret that the repatriation from Somalia, several times delayed, had arrived so late that their families would arrive in Sicily to come under British rule once more. . . . The current belief had been that if fascism fell, it would do so in a bath of blood. Consequently, the event was greeted with relief that their home-returning families would not be subjected to the dangers of internal troubles.[70]

Just as the British tried to discern the political sentiments of those Italians still in AOI and those repatriating home on the third mission, so too did Italian consular officials. In July 1943, incidents occurred in places like the city of Lorenco Marques (today's Maputo) in Portuguese Mozambique, one of the provisioning stops for the repatriation ships. After sending hostile letters to the Italian consul Campini, Italians there took down Mussolini's image and replaced it what that of the king, shouting, "Viva il Re!" (Long live the king!). Campini ordered the arrest of the ringleaders. British observers appeared more bemused than anything, noting that Campini's lack of "scruples" meant that he would soon become an antifascist once he understood the ramifications of the Duce's fall.[71]

The rapid mutation of the situation on the Italian peninsula meant that the remaining civilian population of Italians in former AOI, as well as Libya, would largely stay in place there until war's end. There were some exceptions, such as ten-year-old Mario Schifano (born in Homs, where his father directed the archaeological excavations at Leptis Magna), who in 1944 left Libya with his mother and siblings by plane for Rome. Schifano—whose image "When I Remember Giacomo Balla" graces this book's cover—would later become a leading proponent of the Italian Pop Art movement.[72] Those individuals who did come to the peninsula from Africa during the latter stages of the war experienced distinct and uneven conditions of assistance, depending on whether repatriates found themselves in the territory under the control of the Repubblica Sociale Italiana (RSI) at Salò or the areas liberated by the Allies.[73] Schifano and his family, for instance, received accommodation in the refugee camp at Cinecittà on the outskirts of Rome.

In East Africa and Libya, the British found it useful to retain some of the Italian civilians still resident there working in areas such as agriculture.[74] Italian farmers who remained on the land concessions of the INFPS and ECL in Libya (administered by the BMA between 1943 and 1951), for instance, no longer labored to provide foodstuffs in service to the dream of Italian empire, fascist economic autarchy, or (ultimately) small farmer self-sufficiency but rather to feed Allied troops. For the farmers, the demand created by the BMA brought about relative prosperity, although this changed by 1947 with the constriction of demand as troops went home and then prolonged drought set in.[75] Despite a few good years, many farmers became further indebted, and the overall quality of land development suffered, as settlers planted crops that offered immediate profits at the expense of planting trees and undertaking other long-term improvements.

The BMA found that the absence of Italians to work the land in places like Cyrenaica, where almost all Italian farms had been abandoned by 1943, created its own set of problems. As a result, in 1943 the Agricultural Department of the BMA instituted a "Hill Farms Scheme" in Cyrenaica in which Libyan farmers worked the land under the supervision of a BMA officer. On the rich Barce plain, the "Administration undertook direct responsibility for the cultivation of the Domain areas [ex-ECL], as well as for some private estates." Italian and German prisoners of war harvested wheat.[76]

Critical food shortages in East Africa similarly prompted the British military administrations there to encourage the resumption of agricultural activities by natives and, where possible, remaining Italians. Lord Rennell claims that by the end of 1943 agricultural output in Eritrea exceeded that of the Italian period and that Somalia became self-supporting in terms of food production.[77] The British took particular pride in this achievement, given that under Italy neither Eritrea nor Somalia had boasted significant numbers of Italian agricultural settler families, in contrast to Libya and Ethiopia. In Somalia, for example, the Villaggio Duca degli Abruzzi (with sixteen thousand cultivable acres) remained throughout the Italian period a concession run by employees of the Society for Italian-Somalian Agriculture and worked by largely native labor. Even those areas with Italian settlers like the Genale-Vittoria farm remained reliant on local labor. With the establishment of the BMA over Somalia, a British political officer assumed control at Villaggio Duca degli Abruzzi. The BMA encouraged those Italian settlers who had worked the land in places like Juba to return, with the result that "by the end of 1943 most of the reasonably fertile Italian farms were in cultivation under food crops, mainly maize, either by Italians or Somalis."[78] The administration in Somalia also organized an industrial exhibition in December 1943 with the aim of stimulating the initiative of Italians and native Somalis alike. In addition, a number of Italian colonists with skills in transport—such as truck drivers and mechanics—worked for the British in the Reserved Areas of Ethiopia.[79]

Although Italians from both Libya and AOI (as well as within different Italian ministries) differed sharply in their assessment of their treatment by their British overlords,[80] there is little doubt that between 8 September 1943 and war's end Italian civilians who remained in Italy's African territories on the whole faced less danger than did Italy's civilian populations in its Balkan territories: Albania, the Dodecanese Islands, Venezia Giulia, and parts of the Kvarner (Rijeka / Fiume, the islands of Cres / Cherso and Lošinj / Lussino), and Dalmatia (Zadar / Zara, Palagruža / Pelagosa). In these areas, the precipitous collapse of the Italian military and the Badoglio government's armistice with the Allies exposed Italian populations (military and civilian) to reprisals by either German or local forces, as well as other privations of war (notably hunger). As the result of occupation by the Yugoslav partisan forces and executions, followed by German occupation and intensive Allied bombing that destroyed much of the city, for instance, Zadar /

Zara's Italian population had almost completely abandoned the city by 1944. Many would relocate to Istria, only to face displacement once again after the war.

In recent years, episodes of violence that followed the collapse of Italian military control—notably the killings carried out by Yugoslav partisans in the karstic pits around Trieste and Istria known as the *foibe* and the massacres of Italian troops in places like Kos (part of the Italian Isole Egeo) and Cephalonia at the hands of their former German allies—have received considerable attention.[81] Long a focus of political contestation (and capital) at the local level in Trieste, by the late 1990s the *foibe* killings had entered broader public discourse in Italy. A memorial complex centered on these executions has now become bound up with the Giorno del Ricordo or Memory Day created in 2004 to commemorate the exodus from Istria-Dalmatia-Venezia Giulia.[82] Material on the massacres of Italians by German troops at Kos/Cos, Leros/Lero, and Kefalonia/Cefalonia instead came to light with the discovery in 1994 of the so-called "armoire of shame" (*armadio della vergogna*) in Rome, which contained details of various war crimes committed in Italy. During World War II and even today, the issue of violence remains key to which types of migrants potentially earn the designation of refugee and the moral capital attached to attendant claims for recognition and restitution.

Deportations, Detentions, and Assistance: The Italian Aegean Islands and Albania from 8 September 1943 to Liberation

In both the Italian Aegean and the Italian protectorate of Albania, the events of 8 September left Italian soldiers and civilians alike confused and uncertain about how to react. Ultimately, it would create conditions for repatriation very different from those in Africa, with the result that large-scale repatriation of Italian civilians would occur only after the conflict's end. Nevertheless, the picture of immobility (in contrast to the wartime evacuations out of AOI on the *navi bianche*) should not be overdrawn. In February 1943, for example, 322 women and children were repatriated from the Aegean Islands to Venice and then taken by train to various destinations on the peninsula.[83] Likewise, documents from the ICRC assert that Greek, Italian, Muslim, and Jewish refugees made their way to nearby Turkey from the islands once German occupation began. Then, as now, these clandestine flights in small boats carried the risk of shipwreck and drowning. As the ICRC delegate Raymond Courvoisier put it, "A very high number of these unfortunates disappeared in the waves as a result of the terrible storms raging in those regions, or were carried by the current and crushed on the reefs." The British established a reception center on the island of Simi, for those who survived the crossing.[84]

In these territories, as in the metropole, many Italian soldiers initially believed the 1943 armistice meant the end of the war and the possibility to go home. In the Dodecanese Islands the failure of British troops—employing an inadequate "shoestring strategy"—to wrest control of the Aegean from the German military after battles at Kos/Coo, Leros/Lero, and Ródos/Rodi meant that those Italian soldiers who escaped massacre at the hands of the Germans subsequently found themselves disarmed, rounded up, and deported to the Reich.[85] Some of these POWs never arrived at their destination; the British navy sunk the SS *Gaetano Donizetti*, and all 1,800 aboard died, for instance, while the *Orion* shipwrecked, and only 21 of some 4,115 Italian prisoners aboard survived.[86] The islands' highest-ranking Italian officials—Admirals Inigo Campioni and Luigi Mascherpa—instead found themselves sent to lager 64/Z in the concentration camp of Schokken, a camp section reserved for "traitors" who refused to adhere to the Repubblica Sociale Italiana headed by Mussolini until his death at the hands of partisans on 25 April 1945. After several months, the Germans sent Campioni and Mascherpa to face trial and execution in northern Italy.[87] The failure of the Allied campaign to take the islands also sealed the fate of Rhodes's Jewish population, deported en masse on 23 July 1944, first by boat to Piraeus and then by train to Auschwitz.

A minority of Italian soldiers and functionaries accepted collaboration with the Germans and carried on the task of administering the islands. The local fascist party group was reconstituted under the *centurione* Valenti Dante, commander of the Port Militia (Milizia Portuaria), and war correspondent Renato Burrini. Some 450 Italian civilians, mostly workers, still adhered to the *fascio*.[88] With Mussolini's rescue by German paratroopers and the establishment of the RSI by 23 September 1943, a military formation in the islands pledging loyalty to the RSI and under the command of Captain Ferdinando Cerulli came into being. Scholars have debated how to evaluate the actions and complicity of other Italians—required to swear loyalty to Mussolini's puppet state at Salò—who led the Italian community in the Dodecanese during the German period. In particular, opinion has diverged over how to judge the actions of Iginio Faralli, who became civilian governor of the islands upon the arrest of Admiral Campioni, and mayor of Rhodes Antonio Macchi. Whereas many authors have tended to accept the self-justifications offered by these men that they accepted a deal with the devil in order to protect Italian soldiers and civilians alike (by giving Italian soldiers positions within local government and thus helping them evade deportation, for instance), scholars Marco Clementi and Eirini Toliou have instead emphasized their complicity with the destruction of the islands' Jewish population. Clementi and Toliou note that Faralli apparently had valuables from a deported Jewish family in his home (as revealed by documents concerning those goods' theft by two servants and a maid). They likewise emphasize Macchi's silence after the war over the commune's role in drawing up the deportation list of Jews.[89]

For our story here regarding the experience of Italian civilians, Macchi played a decisive role, given his efforts (much lauded after the war) to assist at least some of the islands' civilian populations. In the final winter of the war, the islands faced severe food shortages. Whereas food insecurity in these islands was not new—indeed, the problem had prompted several waves of outmigration in the 1930s[90]—the situation became critical by late 1944. This reflected repeated Allied bombardments of the islands (particularly Rhodes), German requisitions of livestock and grain, and naval blockade. Things had become so bad that in January 1945 the German occupiers authorized the movement of civilians out of the islands, with a number of Italian citizens going to Syria, and Turkish subjects and other Muslims migrating from the islands to Turkey.[91] Italians frequently made their way first to Marmaris in Turkey and then on to Syria, as well as Simi and Cyprus. As with clandestine migrations out of the islands, there occurred shipwrecks, as in the case of two ships that sank in the waters off Marmaris in January 1945. In this instance, however, the Turkish authorities had been expecting the migrants and rescued and housed them.[92]

Outmigration ameliorated but did not resolve the fundamental problem of inadequate provisioning. In his capacity as mayor of Rhodes, Macchi appealed to the International Red Cross for food relief in the face of famine. Macchi's action was not unilateral, however. Heads of religious communities in Rhodes (the Catholic archbishop, the Orthodox metropolitan, and the Islamic mufti) similarly called on the ICRC to provide humanitarian assistance. Ester Fintz Menascé cites testimony that in early February 1945 these religious leaders also made clandestine contacts with the British on Simi to provide humanitarian assistance to the Dodecanese's civilians, aid that Macchi facilitated at risk to himself.[93]

Shortly thereafter, a Red Cross team, headed by Raymond Courvoisier and Luigi Jaquinet, organized three shipments of food and critical supplies for the islands in February and March 1945. In recounting the results of this work, Courvoisier—who spent two months in Rhodes—highlighted the tragic situation of the civilian population and the high mortality rate due to famine.[94] One report claims that at the time of Courvoisier's arrival in Rhodes in February 1945 an average of six or seven deaths a day occurred due to hunger.[95] As late as April 1945, a memo from the Italian consul general in İzmir/Smirne highlighted the problem of food on Rhodes as "an exasperating nightmare not only for the population but also for the troops of the [Italian] garrison who, with the stocks upon which they relied almost depleted, receive as a daily ration a piece of bread and a bit of vegetable soup."[96]

From their base on Simi, British forces liberated Rhodes on 9 May 1945. The British then established military administration over the Dodecanese, which operated until the islands' union with Greece on 31 March 1947. The BMA continued to employ ICRC assistance to supplement the work of the BMA Central Relief Committee, created in May 1945. In addition to two representatives from the BMA, six representatives from the Greek community and one representative each from the Turkish and Italian communities made up this body.[97] Macchi, no longer mayor, now became head of the Commissione per la tutela degli interessi Italiani nel Dodecaneso (CTIID), an assistance committee for local Italians created in June 1945 and recognized (if never officially authorized) by both the Italian government and the BMA.[98] As a summary report put it, the work of the committee was financed initially by individual contributions from well-off local Italians, donations in kind (such as fresh vegetables, grain, and wool) from local branches of Italian companies, free medicines from the Italian-owned pharmacy Rialdi, and donations of services by Italian doctors in order to alleviate the poverty and suffering of their co-nationals. With the help of Father Pier Grisologo Fabi, deacon of Rhodes, the assistance section (*sezione assistenza*) of this committee first conducted an informal census of needs. Subsidies to the needy were channeled through the diocese of Santa Maria della Vittoria, indicating the important role played by the Catholic Church in aiding Italians on the islands.

As its name suggests, the Commissione per la tutela degli interessi Italiani nel Dodecaneso focused exclusively on aiding Italians, drawing not only on private donations but also funds provided by the Italian Red Cross and those from the BMA's Central Relief Committee earmarked for Italians. The committee helped house and feed 987 Italian "refugees" (*profughi*) from the island of Kasos/Casos. Of these, 378 were considered (ex-)military and lodged in the POW camp at Peveragno to await repatriation. This number included children and wives of these former military personnel, underscoring the blurriness here of categories such as military and civilian. Other Italians displaced from the outer islands lived temporarily in Rhodes Town, receiving assistance from the CTIID.[99] The committee also helped in the maintenance of Italian schools and hospitals, published an Italian-language newspaper, ran camps for Italians, and facilitated repatriation.[100] As noted earlier, the bulk of repatriation from Italy's Aegean Islands would occur in this post-conflict period and with the cooperation of a variety of actors, notably the Italian government, the BMA, the CTIID, and UNRRA. Although UNRRA initially argued that Italians, as ex-enemy nationals, did not fall under its remit, it would ultimately reverse its decision and provide aid to both the Italian peninsula and to some "intruded ex-enemy nationals," including Italians in the Dodecanese and Albania.[101] This help reflected the changed political landscape within which Italian nationals would negotiate their migrations after the war's end, the topic of the next chapter.

As in the Dodecanese, the armistice of 8 September 1943 had put Italian military personnel in Albania into a precarious position. The Germans who had just yesterday been allies promised repatriation to those Italian military men who turned over their weapons and surrendered themselves. Like the suspicious Italian civilians in AOI who had worried whether the British would honor their promises of repatriation on the *navi bianche*, many Italian soldiers did not take the Germans at their word. In contrast to Africa, however, the fears of Italians in Albania were not misplaced. Most of the military men who agreed to the Germans' terms found themselves deported to the Reich to serve as forced laborers. Others hid in the countryside, aided by Albanian peasants.[102] Whereas some of these soldiers literally walked home to Italy, making their way through Yugoslavia to the peninsula, others joined groups of Albanian partisans or the Lëvizja Antifashiste Nacional Çlirimtare, directed largely by the Albanian Communist Party. In several celebrated instances, entire divisions—including the Perugia and Firenze infantry divisions of the Ninth Army—went over to the partisan side. Just twelve days after the armistice, these troops had been reconstituted as *Comando italiano truppe alla montagna* (Italian mountain command troops) within the Albanian National Liberation Front. Members of various former Italian regiments also came together in the Gramsci Battalion, the only Italian military formation directly incorporated into the Albanian partisan forces.[103]

Against this backdrop of confusion and shifting alliances, Italian civilians in Albania faced increasing hostility on the part of the German occupiers and their Albanian allies in the anticommunist, monarchist Balli Kombëtar (National Front) movement. The Provisional Executive Committee that administered Albania in this period required Italian citizens to obtain residence permits. Many Italian state and parastatal employees lost their jobs. As a result, some Italians sought to return to Italy across the Adriatic in clandestine fashion, paralleling the makeshift voyages from the Aegean Islands to Turkey. On the night of 25 October 1943, for instance, a group of twenty-six individuals that included thirteen soldiers, two policemen, a painter, a driver, and an employee of the Banco di Napoli made the crossing on a small fishing boat.[104]

In the hopes of exerting greater control over the movements and activities of Italian civilians, the German command permitted the operation of an assistance committee run and financed by local Italians, the Comitato d'assistenza tra gli italiani (alternatively, Comitato d'assistenza fra italiani). This committee walked a tenuous line, seeking to help Italians within the strictures of German occupation. The committee organized approximately a dozen repatriation convoys of Italians that made their way to Italy through Axis-controlled territories: first to Yugoslavia and then to either Hungary or Austria. Members of this group soon ran afoul of the Germans, with its president and two other members arrested by the SS on the charge of sabotage. A former soldier claims the committee furnished as many as four thousand military personnel with identity cards that enabled them to pass as civilians and thus escape deportation to Germany.[105] In Tirana, the cultural organization Società Dante Alighieri likewise helped Italian soldiers elude the Germans. Despite these varied efforts, the British Military Mission estimated in February 1944 that at least twenty thousand Italian soldiers remained in Albania.[106]

In November of that year, Tirana was liberated, and the nascent communist regime of Enver Hoxha moved from Berat to Tirana. Members of the Gramsci Battalion featured in the military parades celebrating the country's liberation, symbolizing an Italo-Albanian antifascist brotherhood given considerable emphasis by the Albanian partisans. At this point, however, the Italian government under Badoglio in the south had no formal diplomatic relations with Albania, complicating questions of assistance to Italian civilians and soldiers alike.[107] In negotiating the repatriation of Italians still in Albania, the Italian government appointed General Gino Piccini, former commanding officer of the Firenze Division who had gone over to the partisans as part of the Gramsci. In spite of Piccini's antifascist credentials and the sad condition of many Italian soldiers, the Albanian authorities created numerous obstacles to a mass repatriation of soldiers and civilians. As the war drew to a close, the regime confiscated much of the property of Italian firms and arrested and executed a number of Italians on the charge of sabotage.[108]

Just one month before VE Day, the Italian undersecretary of war and member of the Italian Communist Party Mario Palermo traveled to Albania. This visit resulted in the Hoxha-Palermo Accord, five of whose twelve clauses addressed repatriation. Insisting that Italy and Albania had never officially been at war, the Italians sought—to no avail—to keep their requests for repatriation separate from Albanian demands for restitution of properties seized during the Italian occupation. This accord reveals the difficulties in practice of isolating repatriation as an exclusively "humanitarian" question, distinct from larger political contentions between Italy and its former protectorate. Ultimately, the agreement guaranteed the urgent need to repatriate all Italians who desired it, regardless of their status as military personnel or civilians. Italy assumed sole responsibility for effecting repatriation, which created many practical difficulties. Although the Albanian government reserved the right to retain Italian specialists needed for critical reconstruction projects, the accord stipulated that these specialists be replaced over time by personnel voluntarily sent from Italy on specific work contracts.[109] Such an agreement was not without precedent in the recent history of former Italian territories. In 1941, for example, the Ethiopian government of Haile Selassie had requested that the British authorities in Ethiopia there retain as many as four thousand Italian workers with critical industrial expertise.[110]

In July 1945, the Italian government followed up its efforts to facilitate repatriation by sending the consul Ugo Turcato to Tirana. Sent without an official notification of appointment (*lettera d'accreditamento*), Turcato found himself stonewalled by the Albanian authorities until he returned to Rome to obtain the necessary credentials. Turcato's mission unfolded within a rapidly mutating political climate in Albania, as the regime drew closer to both the Soviet Union and a Yugoslavia eager to incorporate Albania within a Yugoslav-led Balkan Federation. As the United States and Britain dragged their feet on the question of recognizing Albania, the regime had shut down the Banco di Napoli and the Banca Nazionale del Lavoro (the only foreign banks operating in the country at that time), expropriated the goods of several Italian firms, and initiated an anti-Italian campaign in the press that took many of its cues from Yugoslav propaganda. In this climate of growing tension, the Albanian authorities ordered Turcato to quit Albania; he did so on 21 January 1946.[111] Before leaving, Turcato entrusted responsibility for documenting Italian repatriates to two of his secretaries, who worked alongside UNRRA staff.[112] UNRRA had taken over a building previously occupied by the Italian mission and in which some Italian civilians stored personal property. A few weeks after Turcato's forced departure, Albanian military police carried out a raid on the UNRRA premises in which, according to an UNRRA report, "No reason was given for this apparently unjustified invasion of the private property of UNRRA and no apologies were offered."[113]

In the interstices of these negotiations between states and intergovernmental organizations like UNRRA there also operated local committees that furnished assistance to Italians in Albania. In order to fill the vacuum on the ground and aid impoverished Italians, for instance, a Comitato Antifascista Italiano had come into existence in 1944, apparently taking over with the approval of the new Albanian communist authorities from the older Comitato d'assistenza fra italiani. At different points this antifascist committee was referred to as the Gruppo Democratico-Popolare Italiano or, alternatively, the Circolo Democratico Popolare. An internal document from the latter states that the Comitato Italiano Antifascista later dissolved, in the face of the fusion of the Gruppo Democratico Popolare Italiano with the "Circolo Garibaldi."[114] Branches of the Circolo Garibaldi existed in Tirana, Shkodër/Scutari, Durrës/Durazzo, Vlorë/Valona, Berat/Berati, and Korçë/Koritza. Members of the Circolo communicated with UNRRA, the ICRC, and the Italian and Albanian governments, suggesting this organization played an important but sometimes slippery role, not only as an advocate of the Italians in Albania but also mediator between very different actors and interests. In the autumn of 1945 and into 1946, for example, the Circolo Garibaldi actively petitioned UNRRA to expedite the repatriation of Italian women and children, as well as needy soldiers, camped out at Durrës/Durazzo, and to supplement the rapidly dwindling food rations handled by the Circolo.[115]

Analysis of documentation contained at the Central State Archive in Albania indicates that although the Circolo may have been born out of the need to provide immediate aid to Italians in Albania (particularly those seeking repatriation), it quickly expanded its scope. Critical gaps in humanitarian assistance thus made for a generative space in which the Circolo could extend its influence and create new kinds of connections between Italians (civilians and ex-military) in Albania. The Circolo contained diverse sectors assigned political, economic, cultural, and humanitarian tasks and framed in terms that proved common to socialist institutions: discipline and control; critique and self-critique; treasury/finances; theater and music; sport; work/labor; press and propaganda; and assistance.[116] Though its statute stated that it remained an apolitical association, the organization not surprisingly stressed an antifascist line and solidarity with Albanians in the partisan fight. Nonetheless, the Circolo declared that it would provide assistance to any and all Italians, including those who had not fought with the partisans.[117] This assistance included food and housing for needy soldiers and civilians, including some Italian women married to Albanian men.[118] Soldiers without shoes also received particular attention in 1944 and 1945.[119] In 1945, the Circolo began to distribute treats to needy children on Epiphany, taking on the role of the traditional witch or *befana* said to fill children's stockings.[120]

The Circolo also served as a social center for those Italians still in Albania. Doctor Vittorio Bruschi, who had worked with the partisans after the dissolution of the Parma Division, found himself employed in a Tirana hospital as a result of being deemed a "necessary" worker according to the language of the Hoxha-Palermo accord. The Circolo Garibaldi in that city provided him with a place to socialize and eat with fellow Italians, as well as listen to the radio—a "lifeline" connecting Italians to the mother country.[121] Among other things, the Circolo hosted dances, which served as fund-raisers. Indeed, the Circolo had semi-autonomy in the financial realm, as many documents mention donations by Italian companies in Albania and private citizens.[122] The Italian government also provided monies, although this created its own difficulties. The Turcato mission, for instance, had provided subsidies to members of the Circolo under the table. After the expulsion of the mission and the (illegal) opening of a diplomatic pouch containing receipts of the sums distributed, the Albanian government confiscated these monies.[123]

Whereas mass repatriation of soldiers—including members of the Gramsci Brigade—began almost immediately at war's end in May 1945, the majority of nonmilitary Italians did not return home until 1946 at the earliest. Some, detained as useful workers, would never return to Italy or would repatriate only in the 1990s after the collapse of state socialism in Albania. In these instances, links between family members in Italy and Albania remained attenuated at best and were frequently severed altogether. This situation echoed that between the armistice and war's end, when most Italians in Albania neither received news from nor successfully communicated with their families abroad. The Central State Archives in Tirana contain a collection of letters sent to Italians in Albania that never reached their intended recipients. Although the majority of the letters were sent by family members to soldiers in Albania, a number were directed to Italian civilians. One letter sent in June 1945 complains, "Why didn't they repatriate civilians instead of military personnel? At least these [soldiers] are given food to eat by the government and their families receive a subsidy. And you other poor creatures, how do you make it without work or means?"[124] This plaintive cry highlighted the challenges faced by those Italian citizens in Albania and their families whose experience of decolonization was not one of forced migration but forced immobility.

Civilians in the Italian Empire at the Conclusion of World War II

Some Italian settlers who wished to repatriate found themselves unable to or only did so after many years or, as in the case of some Italians in Albania, *decades*. As will be explored in the next chapter, however, others tried to return to or remain in the former possessions and build new lives in changed circumstances. In some instances, these individuals subsequently re-migrated to Italy or abroad only after trying to reestablish themselves in the former Italian possession. When the global conflict ended in 1945, then, what remained of Italy's overseas territories? As detailed in this chapter, military control over Italian East Africa had been definitively lost as early as 1941. At war's end, the British administered most of the former AOI under the BMA. Although Emperor Haile Selassie had returned to power in Ethiopia in 1941, four years later the British Military Mission in Ethiopia continued to operate in limited areas. In Libya, the British administered Cyrenaica and Tripolitania, whereas the Fezzan fell under French control. In Italy's former Balkan territories, the BMA oversaw the Aegean Islands. Together with US forces, the British also administered an Allied Military Government over Zone A of the contested region of the Julian March, whose ultimate fate would only be settled de facto by the 1954 Memorandum of Understanding and de jure by the belated 1975 Treaty of Osimo. Although the Dalmatian city of Zadar/Zara became part of Yugoslavia with the Peace Treaty of 1947, Italy had lost effective control over it after September 1943, and Yugoslav authorities governed it in practice from 1944 onward. Finally, in Albania the 1943 armistice meant the end of Italian rule, and a little over one year later the socialist regime of Enver Hoxha had assumed power.

It was within this highly varied landscape that Italian civilians who had inhabited Italia Oltremare, as well as those parts of the Julian March contested and ultimately annexed by Yugoslavia, made decisions—or had decisions made for them—about whether to remain in those territories or migrate. Although Italy's inability to guarantee the rights of its citizens in these territories seems obvious in hindsight, it did not necessarily appear to be a foregone conclusion in 1945. Even after the 1947 Peace Treaty with Italy renounced Italy's right to its colonies and ceded the Dodecanese Islands and large areas of Zone B in Venezia Giulia, Italian politicians on both the right and the left continued to argue for a truncated version of greater Italy, whether it consisted in permitting Italy to retain its pre-1922 colonies (Eritrea and Somalia) or proposals for Italian-administered UN trusteeships over parts of Libya (unsuccessful) or Somalia (achieved). Many Italians who had made their lives in these territories nurtured hope that conditions would permit them to remain where they had built homes, established farms and businesses, buried their dead, and raised their children. Yet others desperately sought to migrate to Italy but found themselves blocked by the authorities of the new states in which they found themselves (as in the case of socialist Albania and, in some instances, socialist Yugoslavia) or, even, by the Italian government itself.

In the complicated and protracted negotiations over final disposition of (former) Italian territories, the Italian government advanced a number of arguments for retaining some of those possessions. These claims ranged from those of historic right and highly debatable assertions of a majority ethnic Italian population in the case of the Julian territories, to the positive benefits of Italy's "civilizing mission" and the desirability of paternal(istic) guidance on the road to self-rule for colonized populations (an argument made about most of Italy's African territories), to Italy's perennial problems of overpopulation and the necessity of suitable outlets for emigration. While these arguments reflected continuities in Italian colonial thinking that extended from the liberal era through fascism to the First Republic, they also resonated with the belief of many postwar planners that problems of surplus population had contributed to the economic and social problems culminating in the two world wars. As various largely unrealized schemes to relieve population pressure by resettling post–World War II European refugees in parts of Africa and South America reveal, many experts in refugee management viewed the question through the lens of European overpopulation.[125] The Italian government also used this argument, to great effect, to resist any large-scale permanent resettlement of foreign refugees on its territory.

This fear of the danger of surplus population coexisted with a persistent belief that heterogeneity in Central and Eastern Europe—particularly the existence of large ethnic German and Jewish minority populations—had facilitated Nazi territorial aggrandizement. As recent scholarship has demonstrated, at Yalta the Allies sanctioned the expulsions of *Volksdeutsche* (historic communities of ethnic Germans living outside the Reich). Together with the Nazi policy of Jewish extermination, this postwar "ethnic cleansing" violently unmixed much of the Eastern European borderlands.[126] In this line of thinking, the presence of minorities (especially those with neighboring kin states, like Germany) opened the door to the risk of irredentist instrumentalization; European and global peace would best be served by homogenization, on the one hand, and a broader system of rights protections directed at the individual, rather than collective categories like minorities, on the other. Italians who remained in former territories failed to become a recognized and protected minority with one critical exception—in the socialist republic of Yugoslavia. This reflected socialist Yugoslavia's delicate balancing of ethno-linguistic diversity together with the politics of bilateral reciprocity, with Yugoslavia's official stance on Italians in its state conditioned by its desire to protect autochthonous Slovenes within Italy.[127]

From the point of view of the British administrators who at war's end controlled most of the former Italian overseas possessions in Africa and the Aegean, permitting significant numbers of Italians to remain in those territories—or, worse, amplifying those numbers through return migrations by those Italians evacuated to the peninsula during the war—could potentially create a troublesome minority within the eventual new states. Such a policy would also strengthen Italian demographic claims in the still open debates over the territories' fate, run the risk of antagonizing the majority (indigenous) populations of the possessions, and challenge British ambitions to assert dominance in the Mediterranean. In light of this, the British favored a policy of one-way repatriation out of the former possessions, even as they teased proposals for international trusteeships over Italy's African territories.[128] The most well known was the unsuccessful 1949 Bevin-Sforza Plan, which called for a partition of Libya into various trusteeships (with the British administering Cyrenaica, the Italians Tripolitania, and the French the Fezzan); the partition of Eritrea between Ethiopia and Sudan; and the creation of an Italian trusteeship over Somalia. Various British Military Administrations nonetheless had to balance their policy objectives with the desire of the Italian state to regulate carefully the flows of Italian repatriates and refugees into the metropole. Furthermore, the British occupiers had to at least pay lip service to wider humanitarian concerns, notably requests by spouses and children to repatriate back to the former possessions in the name of family reunification.

Just as frequently, however, non-state actors like the ICRC used humanitarian considerations to pressure the Italian government to facilitate return migrations to the peninsula by these civilians. According to one ICRC report, for example, in May 1946 there remained in Eritrea 37,787 Italians. That population included 1,685 unaccompanied women, another 13,557 women and children, and 18,058 single men. Many of these individuals lived in what the report deemed "evacuation camps" (*campo di sfollamento*). Located at Toselli, Godofolassi / Godofellasie, Ghinda, and Addi Cajee / Adi Caieh, these camps were presumably similar to the one at Dire Daua inhabited by those who, between 1941 and 1943, had awaited their departure on the *navi bianche*. Postwar migrants sought homeward passage on some of those very same ships. The author of the report concluded that, in light of the uncertainty of how long British assistance to these individuals would continue, "it would be extremely desirable that the Italian government proceed with the repatriation of these persons."[129] This recommendation points to the frequent foot-dragging by the Italian government on repatriation, which reflected both concerns about the future fate of the possessions and worries about further destabilizing a peninsula devastated by warfare. Although civilians seeking repatriation included men, women, and children, those advocating for them frequently resorted to gendered and emotive appeals that highlighted the particular vulnerability of women and minors.

Complex debates over and processes of repatriation in practice unfolded in the context of a dramatically altered geopolitical scene, one in which Italy occupied a peculiar position. As the only one of the three major Axis powers to have achieved the status of Allied co-belligerent with the creation of the Badoglio government in the south after September 1943, Italy could make a claim to sharing in the victorious war effort even as it simultaneously suffered treatment as a defeated power. Italian nationals within the former possessions would negotiate their conditions of mobility within the constraints set by Italy's categorical ambiguity, themselves coming to embody the liminal space between refugee and repatriate, refugee and citizen.

CHAPTER 3

Italy's Long Decolonization in the Era of Intergovernmentalism

> The interdependence of European states was, however, by no means purely economic. . . . Some national policies aiming at national reassertion had to be internationalized in order to make them viable . . . [and] the reinvigorated nation-state had to choose the surrender of a degree of national sovereignty to sustain its reassertion.
>
> Alan Milward, *The Rescue of the Nation-State* (1992)

When viewed through the prism of displaced persons, the history of relief and reconstruction in post-1945 Italy is at once a story of national redefinition and a transnational story that moves across borders and opens up onto the formation of regimes of international law and assistance. It is also an international history in its more restricted meaning, that is, an analysis "focused on diplomatic relations among nations,"[1] as evidenced by the Great Power negotiations that resulted in the 1947 Peace Treaty with Italy and the subsequent series of bilateral accords that finally determined the disposition of Italy's contested possessions. Finally, it is a story of multiple, overlapping *internationalisms*, a topic of growing interest among historians. In this chapter, I situate the story of relief to both national and foreign refugees in Italy in the immediate postwar years within these entangled internationalisms and Italian struggles to reassert and reframe sovereignty in the aftermath of defeat.

Historians have produced numerous and detailed studies of the international organizations, structures, and norms (like human rights) that gave expression to "liberal internationalism." The early postwar agencies of UNRRA and the IRO have received particular scrutiny. These organizations were aided in their work by a host of voluntary agencies or NGOs. The work of entities like the ICRC, technically neither an international nor an intergovernmental organization but rather possessed of a "legal international personality," paralleled these efforts.[2] Though less studied, religious internationalism of the sort promoted by the Catholic Church in its relief initiatives proved no less significant. At times, the Vatican's forms of assistance worked in tandem with those of the UN agencies and of national governments (such as the United States).[3] At other moments, the church gave particular attention to those—like the Italian children from Libya separated from their parents—who fell outside the remit of these international organizations.

Although the *bimbi libici* were (in theory, at least) the responsibility of the Italian state, their status and care became a source of contention between the BMA in Libya and the Italian government and thus resulted in Vatican advocacy on behalf of the children and their parents. This reflected not only the political and diplomatic wrangling over the fate of the territory but also the diminished sovereign capacities of the Italian state at war's end. This proved a critical vulnerability for Italy, operating as it did in a postwar system of entangled internationalisms that took the state as its cornerstone. Unable as it was to compel diplomatic agreements that would have permitted it to retain some of its overseas possessions, caring for and sorting out individuals displaced by those losses (together with non-Italian refugees) created both a practical dilemma and a rich opportunity for the Italian state to assert its authority at the domestic and international levels. In a very real sense, then, this case offers an early example of what Alan Milward, writing about postwar efforts to integrate Europe, deemed the postwar "rescue of the nation-state."[4]

The work of a new generation of historians has evidenced the key role played by the refugee and the refugee question in processes whereby national identities and sovereignties were rearticulated after the war and with the end of empire. Not only did the presence of foreign displaced persons in many European countries serve as a foil against which the national community was defined and protected through mechanisms like citizenship, but aid workers and governments alike affirmed the centrality of the national in their efforts to put refugees "in place," as amply documented by scholars such as G. Daniel Cohen, Matthew Frank, Peter Gatrell, Anna Holian, Jessica Reinisch, Silvia Salvatici, and Tara Zahra. This issue acquired particular urgency in the case of orphan or "kidnapped" children whose national affiliations appeared ambiguous.[5] *Renationalization* after the war was premised upon, enabled by, and rearticulated through transnational processes, among them the efforts of international organizations, US programs and policies like the Marshall Plan, and media such as film with potentially transnational audiences.[6]

Though Reinisch was writing of UNRRA specifically, her assessment nonetheless holds for the broader apparatus of postwar institutions and actors dedicated to care and maintenance of the displaced. As she puts it, "I argue that the organization cannot be understood properly unless we also see it as a forum for debates on, and a nexus of activities surrounding, not only questions of *internationalism*, but also of nationalism and the future of the nation-state—particularly concerning national reconstruction, nations' collaboration in international bodies, sovereignty, patriotism, and citizens' relationships to their state."[7]

Reinisch's comment typifies the approach of many recent studies of Europe's post-1945 displaced persons, which focus on the intersections of national and international interests, actors, and institutions.[8] In writing against a body of literature focused almost exclusively on the "internationalizing" aspects of UNRRA's work, for example, Reinisch rightly underscores how the UNRRA itself always "was presented as strictly in the national interest of participating member states. . . . National governments were UNRRA's clients and it worked through and for them, and only at their request."[9] Indeed, UNRRA publications reassured readers that the organization operated as a "service agency of 44 nations, and does not possess sovereign powers. While it is asked to operate on behalf of the United Nations, UNRRA is not a super-state. It is a creature of the governments which created it."[10] In light of this, Reinisch concludes, "UNRRA's overall project seems to have been shaped less by a concern for the universal rights of individuals, which the recent historiography has emphasized, than by ideas concerning the rights of sovereign nations, particularly in matters of repatriation and reconstruction."[11]

In her pioneering research, creation of scholarly networks, and establishment of a Centre for the Study of Internationalisms at Birkbeck College, Reinisch has helped set the scholarly agenda for the historiography of twentieth-century relief, refugees, and internationalisms. Nonetheless, Reinisch and many others have, rather surprisingly, failed to stress the obvious but often overlooked role played by intergovernmentalism in the early postwar world.[12] Although the *concept* of intergovernmentalism—defined as a process of "regional integration through which states accept the principle of cooperation depending on which common interests are at stake"—only originated in the 1960s in the context of nascent European integration,[13] in *practice* it proved a key aspect of interwar and early postwar politics. Indeed, the retrenchment after 1945 of the nation-state in the international state system gained its most obvious expression in the creation of a series of intergovernmental institutions, including the United Nations and its subsidiary agencies (such as UNRRA, the IRO, and finally the UNHCR). In the realm of refugees, these agencies quite literally mediated between the realms of the state and the international; the UNHCR's statute gave expression to this interstitial role with its requirement that aid provided by states to the displaced be distributed (for the most part) through NGOs.[14] In addition, decolonization—which took as its goal national independence and sovereignty—reaffirmed the centrality of the statist principle undergirding the UN.

The UN inherited this quality as "a regime of international oversight, not international government"[15] from its predecessor, the League of Nations. In particular, the UN trusteeship system—of which former Italian Somalia became a prominent example in its decade-long administration under Italy (1950–1960)—built upon the League's previous mandate system, even as the interwar world of a "League of Empires" gave way to the era of decolonization.[16] In some instances, intergovernmental bodies with origins in the interwar, notably the International Labor Organization (ILO), were incorporated wholesale into the new UN. In addition, many personnel from the League migrated to UN agencies like UNRRA.[17] Fittingly, perhaps, UNRRA required its staff to swear the same loyalty oath (placing the needs of the organization above those of the employees' home countries, one arena in which the international trumped the national) that the League of Nations had employed after 1930.[18]

Like the League of Nations, the UN and other intergovernmental entities exist only through the agreement of their constituent states, even as they may pursue common goods that are transnational in nature. And the intergovernmental arena is one in which many different strands of internationalism—liberal and otherwise—may come into contact, friction, and even entanglement. Bruce Cronin has identified the tension between intergovernmentalism and transnationalism as a defining one not only for the UN but for the wider international system more generally. "The fact that the UN assumes both intergovernmental and transnational tasks is not in and of itself a problem," acknowledges Cronin. Indeed, in many ways, intergovernmentalism might be seen to mediate the tensions between the national and international. Nonetheless, "Conflict arises when the organization fails to distinguish between its role as an intergovernmental organization coordinating the activities of its membership and its role as a transnational network promoting some type of common good."[19]

Promotion of the common good of transnational human rights enshrined in the UDHR and other UN covenants has proven an arena of particular tension within the UN's intergovernmental structure, one intensified by the expansion of human rights and humanitarian NGOs since the 1970s. For the period under examination in this study, however, and for the specific realm of refugee assistance, intergovernmentalism appears to have shaped and often contained the possibilities for transnational action within the UN system. Though the UN's institutional infrastructure encouraged transnationalism, "the institutional set-up of the relevant UN bodies [e.g., UNHCR] also reproduced intergovernmentalism and left limited room for transnationalism."[20] Whereas scholars like Cronin view intergovernmentalism and transnationalism as ultimately "incompatible,"[21] the early postwar world of refugee assistance rested on these precarious partnerships and shifting sets of claims. These different actors and claims found common ground in their affirmation of the national principle. Indeed, "With each successive refugee crisis the nation-state became more 'national' at the same time as the range and scope of international obligations became more extensive."[22] As we shall see, such a characterization certainly holds true for Italy as it emerged from the shadow of the war and tackled the challenges of both foreign and national refugees.

In light of this, it would be easy for historians to conclude that the methodological lesson is to focus on state actors. Frank and Reinisch, for example, say as much: "States also have to be the most important organizing principle through which historians can attempt to impose conceptual order on the refugee chaos."[23] Much of the recent scholarship on postwar relief and reconstruction employs such a top-down perspective, however, to the detriment of understanding the perspectives of refugees themselves, as well as the role played by lower-level officials.[24] In this chapter, I move between top-down and bottom-up perspectives, pursuing what has been deemed a "history-in-between," one that merges "international politics into national contexts and individual, local experiences" with the aim of understanding "how governments and state organisations engaged with the polices and actions of international agencies as well as how individual experiences fed back into international policies."[25] Likewise, I move between the scales of the national, regional, and global. Finally, this chapter and this entire book move back and forth between the worlds of policy and juridical classifications (themselves the products of messy and complex "histories-in-between") and their enactments and consequences for those subjected to them.

Aid to Italy and Its Displaced, 1944–1947: A Laboratory for Multiple Actors

In May 1945, Italy remained a state-in-between, with limited sovereignty at best and much of its territory occupied by Allied forces. In the war's immediate aftermath, Allied and local authorities alike struggled to gain a monopoly over force as political and other vendettas played out with exactions of summary justice and "insurrectional tribunals" to punish fascists and collaborators.[26] The form the new state would take—a republic divested of its monarchy—would only be determined by referendum in 1946. An immoral economy of prostitution, begging, and black marketing mirrored the physical devastation of much of the landscape. The sardonic comments made in 1944 by a British intelligence officer on the Neapolitans the Allies "liberated" hold for Italians more generally: "A year ago we liberated them from the Fascist Monster, and they still sit doing their best to smile politely at us, as hungry as ever, more disease-ridden than ever before, in the ruins of their beautiful city where law and order have ceased to exist. And what is the prize that is to be won? The rebirth of democracy."[27]

Those Italians awaiting the rebirth of democracy (whether eagerly or with trepidation) thus found themselves awaiting critical relief aid. While one could live without democracy (as, indeed, Italians under the dictatorship had done for two decades), one could not live without bread, potable water, medicines, or shelter. In spite of this, UNRRA initially refused to grant aid to Italy, given that its mandate prohibited assistance to ex-enemy states; it did, though, provide for assistance to nationals of Allied states located in the states of belligerents. Thus the task of control and relief, including assistance to displaced persons, first fell to the Allied command.

Beginning with the successful invasion of Sicily in July 1943, the Allies established military government over those parts of Italy they had liberated and occupied.[28] As noted previously, the BMA separately administered former Italian territories in Africa (with the exception of Haile Selassie's Ethiopia) and the Aegean.[29] Lord Rennell, who had served in the East African BMA, became the chief civil affairs officer of the Allied Military Government of Occupied Territories (AMGOT) established in Italy. The 1943 armistice that had created such confusion and precarity for Italian military and civilians alike in the overseas territories and Venezia Giulia and Dalmatia, described in chapter 2, also split the Italian peninsula and population. German forces occupied northern and central Italy and installed Mussolini's puppet regime in the northern town of Salò. In the regions held by the Nazis and their fascist allies, a bloody civil war that pitted fascist supporters against partisans would play out. Caught between the proverbial rock and a hard place, the vast majority of Italians in the north merely sought to survive the internecine conflict.

A multiparty Italian cabinet headed by Badoglio and King Victor Emmanuel III instead ruled over those areas already liberated by the Allies, although in practice the Allied command governed much of Italian life, from security to the economy.[30] As had occurred in former AOI with the BMA, Rennell preferred a form of indirect rule but found this impractical in many arenas. "It was always AMG policy to govern through the Sindaco [mayor]," commented one Allied assessment. In reality, however, "In Sicily and Southern Italy, the CAO [civilian affairs officer] was often forced by circumstances to be almost a Governor."[31]

By 1944, the different organizations of Allied government on the peninsula had been consolidated into the Allied Control Commission (ACC) based in Rome. Allied Force Headquarters (AFHQ) exercised ultimate authority over the ACC and the AMG in Italy. As Ben Shephard puts it, Italy's military governors quickly "became involved in politics, economic management and social policy, often with disastrous results, bringing inflation, starvation, prostitution and the restoration of the Mafia to the country"[32]—a characterization that echoes that made by Norman Lewis at the time. While Shephard acknowledges that Italy served as a valuable "training ground" for critical initiatives designed to contain and prevent diseases, he ultimately concludes, "Experience in Italy also brought out the limitations of the military's approach."[33] Critics at the time noted a lack of adequate planning and training for AMG officers, singling out Naples as a worst-case scenario of AMG mismanagement.[34] Civil affairs officers nonetheless organized food supplies and sought to fix prices, struggling against critical shortages in the transport network.

While largely a civilian-run affair under the chief of the Civil Affairs Division, the Displaced Persons and Repatriation Subcommission coordinated with the armies to facilitate repatriation of prisoners of war *within* the Italian peninsula. The ACC's Italian Refugee Branch also assisted Italians within the country displaced by the events of the conflict, overseeing refugee camps (some seven of them labeled "transit camps" by May 1944) in conjunction with Italian Red Cross personnel. In addition, the ACC coped with those non-Italians displaced into Italy. The division of labor proved flexible in practice, as the DP subcommission intended to help foreign DPs also assisted a number of Italian and Dalmatian Jews in camps established at Ferramonti, Bari, Palermo, Naples, and Lecce.[35] By September 1944, the ACC DP subcommission focused on foreign displacees in Italy, and the Italian Refugees Subcommission for Italian nationals established the previous year had fused into the Displaced Persons and Repatriation Subcommission.

As a military publication reveals, strategic concerns—"the evacuation and holding camps allowed AMG to keep roads and areas clear of refugees during advances"[36]—often took priority over those of humanitarianism. The AMG sought to direct refugee flows. By May 1944, for instance, refugees were being routed westward along the "Vairano-Capua-Aversa" axis, rather than eastward through Campobasso, Foggia, and Bari. At refugee and evacuation camps in "forward areas" of the front, AMG also sought to carry out "a quick check" of those persons coming from what remained enemy territory.[37] At times the Allies even organized temporary displacements, evacuating civilians in order "to relieve the congested conditions of troops and inhabitants and for security measures." The AMG Fifth Army, however, found stiff local resistance to this, as when trucks for evacuation arrived at Castiglione dei Popoli in October 1944 only to discover that "all the residents and refugees, in spite of cold rain and mud, had fled to the hills and nearby hamlets."[38]

As Silvia Salvatici notes, the differentiation between foreign and Italian refugees in both their status and treatment emerged during this early period of Allied control. The Italian state sought to aid its own through the Alto Commissariato Profughi, or High Commission on Refugees, established in 1944, though initially Italian refugees from the colonies were excluded from its remit.[39] After just a month of existence, the Alto Commissariato Profughi had assumed either direct or indirect responsibility for thirty-eight camps of various sorts (housing detainees, evacuees, and refugees). The Ministero dell'Assistenza Post-Bellica (Ministry of Postwar Assistance), created in June 1945, subsequently took over these responsibilities for care and maintenance.[40] At this time, however, the scale of destruction and need in Italy proved too great for the fragile Italian state to address adequately. The Italian state thus assumed the task of filling gaps in the ACC's approach. Despite employing both military and civilian personnel and solutions to refugee questions, the ACC continued to prioritize military needs.

The United Nations Relief and Rehabilitation Administration, created with an eye to the future peace, by contrast, took up the challenges of humanitarianism and placed them firmly in civilian hands. Reflecting back on her role as a relief worker in Europe for UNRRA, Francesca Wilson recalled both her hopes for and trepidations about the fledging organization when she first landed on the continent. Wilson encountered a mixture of idealism and incompetence, joy and misery. Arriving at the UNRRA Mobilization and Training Center in Normandy in April 1945, on the eve of the war's conclusion in Europe, Wilson met a Luxemburger who had previously served in the Foreign Legion. "Unrra he said, was like a Foreign Legion for peace instead of war. . . . In Unrra, where there were forty-four different nations, we must develop the same solidarity." Wilson replied, "'God knows you are right . . . and you must show us how—for it is harder in peace than in war.'"[41] For Wilson and others, then, UNRRA would have to wage war on the devastation and misery wrought by war itself. Not surprisingly, UNRRA was frequently promoted in militaristic terms, like those employed in a 1945 pamphlet: "To whip the Nazis and Japs, the United Nations mobilized armies and navies. To whip hunger and destitution and disease, the United Nations have created a special 'task force'—UNRRA."[42] Notably, this UNRRA publication did not mention the Italian fascist regime along with its fellow Axis belligerents, underscoring Italy's fundamentally ambiguous status.

Although UNRRA had been conceived and established in November 1943 as part of the general "planning-mindedness" that characterized the Allied war effort, its real work began with the end of the military conflict.[43] UNRRA possessed an ambitious and alliterative program of rescue, recovery, rehabilitation, reconstruction, and repatriation that extended beyond Europe, notably to Ethiopia and China. UNRRA combated hunger (particularly the European famine of 1946) in the short term through feeding programs and in the long term through agricultural recovery programs. It made vital interventions into public health, providing urgently needed drugs such as penicillin and typhus serum, medical equipment, and personnel in the short term and helping rebuild pharmaceutical production in the long term. UNRRA also aided industrial recovery through the importation of machines and transport, as well as raw supplies. Imports of cotton and raw wool, for example, made a critical difference in stimulating clothing production in Italy.[44] UNRRA also created fellowships in these different fields to train much-needed experts, deemed "the yeast for the future."[45] Despite these variegated activities, the work of UNRRA's Displaced Persons Operation remains the best remembered. UNRRA's efforts in this field consisted primarily in repatriation, as well as temporary care and maintenance for those awaiting repatriation. UNRRA did not engage in resettlement of those displaced persons who could not or would not go home, ceding that task to the Intergovernmental Committee on Refugees.[46]

As a great "experiment" in international relief,[47] UNRRA embodied the tensions of the new international order coalescing at war's end, and within whose interstices displaced persons would find their rights and possibilities debated. As an intergovernmental organization of the United Nations (a term that in 1943 applied only to Allied partners), UNRRA also coexisted—at times uneasily, at other moments with great complementarity—with Allied military commands establishing control and distributing assistance. This was certainly true in Italy, where UNRRA entered the scene only after overturning its initial decision not to provide aid to ex-enemy nations.[48] Initially, UNRRA gave priority to "assisting especially those gallant countries which bore the undiminished force of the enemy's attack"; in contrast, it possessed neither the will nor the authority "to operate in enemy or former enemy territories, except where requested by the military authorities to assist in the repatriation of displaced persons and in control of epidemics."[49] UNRRA's hostile stance toward Italy began to soften by 1944. That year, UNRRA staff member Loda Mae Davis traveled to Italy in order to learn from the ACC about how to deal with issues relevant to UNRRA's Balkans operation. Davis reported on the difficult conditions faced by both the Italian civilian population and foreign DPs in ACC-administered camps. Of the refugees in camps in Bari, she wrote, "Their condition was poor, with many children showing unmistakable signs of malnutrition, their clothing was in rags, and their filth pronounced." These problems and others prompted Davis to write her superiors, "I would suggest that consideration be given to the possibility of sending a small UNRRA mission to Italy, provided the military authorities are agreeable, to work with ACC officials and prepare for the day when UNRRA may be asked to operate there."[50] Davis added that she had encountered a number of Allied military personnel on the ground in Italy who shared her opinion.

An official UNRRA observer mission headed by Spurgeon Milton Keeny arrived in Italy two months later. At that time, however, provisional UNRRA budgeting for displaced Italians within Italy was nonexistent. As a memo written by E. R. Fryer put it, "Undoubtedly, by the time UNRRA takes over in Italy, permission will have been granted by the military for the return of those [Italians] who have been evacuated to their home areas and reconstruction of destroyed homes will be well under way." As a result, "I have made, therefore, no provision in this budget specifically to care for displaced Italians in Italy."[51] The report filed in December 1944 by Antonio Sorieri (future deputy chief of UNRRA's Italy Mission) quickly put paid to Freyer's unrealistic predictions about the rapid and easy repatriation of displaced Italians, many of whom no longer had houses to which they could return.

In his dispatch, Sorieri summarized the difficult conditions of displaced persons in the peninsula. Sorieri estimated that in liberated Italy alone were to be found 645,500 Italians who had been displaced and another 60,000 known to have already returned home. Whereas Davis had highlighted problems with ACC camps, Sorieri commented on the "deplorable" conditions in those camps instead run by the Italian government. "The lack of equipment, blankets, clothing, medical supplies and facilities results in standards of camp care which are generally indefensible." Sorieri added, "The needs of non-Italian displaced persons . . . are serious, but in general considerably less than those of Italian refugees. This is due to the fact that in general non-Italian refugees outside of camps were better off financially and because the program of assistance to them has been far more adequate than for Italian refugees."[52]

Such reports helped prepare the way for a significant shift. In the face of British opposition, the United States pushed through a program at UNRRA's Second Council Session in Montreal authorizing limited relief (totaling $50 million) to Italy for displaced persons, children, and expecting and nursing mothers.[53] Among the important provisions for DPs in Italy were those permitting UNRRA to assist repatriation of ex-enemy Italians "intruded" into other territories, notably Albania and the Dodecanese Islands. Several UNRRA delegates insisted on the exceptional nature of these efforts, however, noting that neither Italy nor Italians (including those outside the peninsula) possessed the *right* to assistance exercised by member states. As the French representative at Montreal put it, UNRRA "will not recognize to an ex-enemy . . . the right to assistance enjoyed by the United Nations but . . . only the benefit of benevolent charity."[54] Reduced to grateful recipient about whom decisions were made through a form of still discretional assistance, Italy in these negotiations remained semi-sovereign, at best. Fittingly, Italian schoolchildren would later pen UNRRA's second director general, Fiorello La Guardia, letters of effusive thanks that reflected Italy's position of servility within the emerging intergovernmental world of relief.[55]

The US Department of State had recommended from almost the beginning that UNRRA assume the ACC's responsibilities for welfare in Italy, thereby completing the shift from military to civilian control. The changes in responsibility made in 1944 instead required UNRRA operations to proceed with the agreement of either the military command or the "appropriate authority" (meaning either the ACC or, should it cease, the Italian government).[56] Over time, work with UNRRA offered a realm for Italian authorities to play a greater role in intergovernmental decisions about assistance to their people and their territory. In January 1945, the Italian government appointed Lodovico Montini as the liaison officer to UNRRA's Italy Mission. He would play a key role in negotiating the eventual agreement between the government and UNRRA and would head the Italian delegation that administered UNRRA relief.

Montini's brother Giovanni Battista, the future Pope Paul VI, likewise assumed a prominent role in the parallel relief efforts of the Pontificia Commissione di Assistenza ai Profughi (PCAP) created on 18 April 1944. In a very real sense, these Catholic initiatives filled the gaps created by Italy's initial ineligibility for UNRRA relief. Some authors have also seen in the early collaboration of Allied forces and the Vatican a symbol of the weakness of the Italian state and Allied recognition that only the Holy See possessed the organizational capacity required to distribute aid on a wide scale.[57] Others instead stress the political role played by the Vatican in serving as a key mediator between the Italian state and international organizations.[58] This assistance arm of the Vatican began its work with refugees and wartime needy, quickly becoming known as the Pontificia Commissione di Assistenza (PCA) after the merger with the Pontificia Commissione Assistenza Reduci in 1945; it was transformed into the Pontificia Opera di Assistenza (POA) in 1953. Within just a few weeks of the Allied occupation of Rome, the PCA had assisted 52,230 displaced Italians to return home. The PCA had several immediate precedents: the Opera Nazionale di Assistenza Religiosa e Morale degli Operai (ONARMO) founded in 1926 and in which Monsignor Ferdinando Baldelli, one of the PCA's founders, played a key role; the *refettori del papa* (pope's dining halls) created in Rome in 1943 to combat hunger; and aid to bombed-out Italians in 1943–1944.[59] While the PCA was never strictly limited to assisting refugees—as the just-noted work suggests—aiding the displaced (both foreign and national refugees, with a particular focus on women and children) formed one of its central activities until 1948. At that time, the PCA expanded its work to *braccianti* (day laborers) and other *lavoratori* as part of what one author has deemed a new activist vision of Christian charity.[60]

Most accounts of the PCA/POA stress its intensive collaboration with and financial support from American Catholic institutions, particularly the Catholic Relief Services (CRS). This organization came into being in January 1943 as part of President Roosevelt's War Relief Control Board. Like the PCA, Catholic Relief Services had deeper roots, in this case in the National Catholic War Council (NCWC) formed upon US entry into World War I. Important groundwork for the CRS was also laid by the discussions over postwar planning that took place at the 1942 meeting of the Catholic Association for International Peace meeting in Washington, DC.[61] In June 1944, the same month the Allies took Rome, the CRS undertook a nationwide clothing drive for needy Italians. With travel and entry permits facilitated by Roosevelt's representative to the Holy See Myron Taylor and Cardinal Spellman of New York, a CRS team made its way to Italy in October 1944 to distribute relief. Rev. Andrew Paul Landi of New York and the PCA's Monsignor Baldelli formed a partnership, harnessing the resources of the CRS to the energies and infrastructure of the PCA. A month earlier, Prime Minister Ivanoe Bonomi had announced the establishment of the Ente Nazionale per la Distribuzione dei Soccorsi (ENDSI), or the National Agency for Distribution of Relief Supplies in Italy. This organization funneled monies from the American Relief for Italy; representatives of the Italian state, the Vatican, and the Italian Red Cross composed its governing body.[62] Although Catholic publications and films made much of these collaborations between American Catholics and the Vatican, Carlo Falconi claims that the Italian state, not the CRS, was always the largest benefactor of the PCA/POA.[63] By the 1950s, though, Baldelli would explicitly reject Lodovico Montini's call for consolidation of "voluntary organization" assistance and the "statization" of assistance ("statalizzazione dell'assistenza").[64]

In the summer of 1945, however, a still weak Italian state negotiated with UNRRA, which clarified its responsibilities toward Italian displacees. It was authorized to help those who met the criteria of Category C, "Enemy or Ex-Enemy Nationals (Not Falling under Category B)." The three subcategories pertained almost exclusively to Italians:

1. displaced Italian nationals in Italy, all operations in this respect to be agreed upon between the military command or the appropriate authority in Italy on the one hand, and the Administration on the other . . . ;
2. found to be intruded in a liberated area, and whose removal is requested by the government or recognized national authority of the liberated area . . . ;
3. displaced Italian nationals in enemy or ex-enemy areas outside Italy (Central Committee Resolution of 28 May 1945).[65]

Full-scale UNRRA aid to Italy to the tune of $450 million began in 1946. As part of its responsibilities, the Italian government contributed to the so-called Lire Fund. This would eventually seed a housing scheme known as UNRRA-CASAS (Comitato Amministrativo Soccorso ai Senzatetto, or Administrative Committee for Assistance to the Homeless) that outlived UNRRA itself, falling under the competency of the Amministrazione per gli Aiuti Internazionali, or AAI.[66] National refugees from Italy's lost territories—most notably the ceded areas of Venezia Giulia—would number among those recipients of homes built by UNRRA-CASAS. In seeking both to repair damaged homes and build new ones, UNRRA-CASAS explicitly promoted the rehabilitation of the family through the literal reconstitution of the hearth.[67]

In its negotiations with UNRRA, the Italian state not only often appeared an unequal partner but also understood the division of labor and responsibilities in a distinctly different way. This proved true, for instance, for both the Lire Fund and UNRRA-CASAS. In a detailed internal memo dating from July 1946, UNRRA legal adviser Mitchell Franklin outlined his disagreement with the Italian state representatives, which centered on the Italians' erroneous assumption (in Franklin's opinion) that "'CASAS is *not* a direct UNRRA project, but a project operated by a committee of the Italian Government.'" Franklin countered that while "the Lire Fund belongs to the patrimony of the Italian state,"[68] the expenditure of such monies required agreement between the Italian government and UNRRA. A fundamental bone of contention lay in the distinction between rehabilitation and reconstruction, with Franklin arguing that long-term reconstruction, including the building of private homes, did not fall under UNRRA's remit of rehabilitation.

Not surprisingly, the area of greatest confusion and disagreement between Italian representatives and UNRRA centered on displaced persons. First, sorting displacees into UNRRA's own particular categories of eligibility and ineligibility proved anything but clear-cut in practice, a point to which I will return. Second, there existed frequent disagreement over responsibility for some of those determined to be "non-Italian displaced persons." The minutes of the first meeting of the Displaced Persons Committee of the UNRRA Italy Mission established in 1946 illustrate these challenges. Nevertheless, the discussion did reveal considerable consolidation of categories since 1944 and 1945. Those DPs in Italy eligible for UNRRA assistance included

> a) United Nations nationals, who have evidence of their nationality, displaced as a result of the war and in financial need.
> b) Persons of neutral, ex-enemy or indeterminate nationality, displaced as a result of the war from their normal place of residence because of religion, racial or political persecution.[69]

For the most part, only those who had come to Italy or who had been displaced within Italy (including Italian civilians) prior to the cessation of hostilities were considered eligible for UNRRA aid, a problem that would subsequently help prompt the creation of the International Refugee Organization. By 1946, approximately 60 percent of foreign DPs in Italy had arrived on the peninsula after the war's end; Yugoslavs, Bulgarians, and Albanians fleeing the newly emergent socialist regimes in those countries numbered among the principal categories of post-conflict displacees at that time.[70] Whereas UNRRA appeared to possess clarity on paper as to which displacees in Italy fell under its remit, in practice determining eligibility required time-intensive interviewing and data collection from military authorities in order to identify and screen out collaborationists, among other issues.[71]

By June 15, 1946, UNRRA had repatriated from Italy approximately 84,100 individuals identified as non-Italians. Sorieri, the deputy chief of UNRRA's Italy Mission, estimated that there remained 26,000 non-Italians on the peninsula eligible for UNRRA help, 7,000 Jewish refugees in camps run by the American Joint Distribution Committee, 17,000 foreign refugees in camps still under Allied control, and 9,000 DPs not residing in camps.[72] A few months prior, Allied command had asked UNRRA to assume care over those displaced persons in Italy who met UNRRA eligibility criteria. There nonetheless remained the thorny problem of who would care for those foreign DPs in ACC camps considered ineligible by UNRRA. UNRRA officials had already suggested "that for many of them it would be necessary to work out arrangements with the Italian Government for care."[73] By June 1946, UNRRA's Italy Mission was offering as a sop the possibility for Italian officials to use imported UNRRA supplies in assisting UNRRA ineligible non-Italian DPs.[74] Such proposals tacitly gave greater authority to Italian leaders over the foreigners in their midst but also created potentially greater burdens on a still weak state, obligations that Italian authorities did not wish to assume. At this same moment, the Italian state was consolidating assistance to national refugees created by changes in its eastern borders through the Ufficio Venezia Giulia, soon to become the Ufficio per le Zone di Confine.

In the negotiations between UNRRA and Italy over displacees, there existed plenty of room not only for disagreement but also outright misunderstanding. A 1946 letter from Spurgeon Keeny, chief of the UNRRA mission, to the Italian prime minister Alcide De Gasperi notes the confusion created by mistranslations from English into Italian of the word "ultimate" in a critical document. This had led to the false impression on the part of the Italian authorities that UNRRA held them "responsible for the assistance, maintenance and repatriation of refugees," whereas the original English version had read that UNRRA recognized the ultimate "authority and responsibility" of the Italian government. Keeny added further clarification when he stated, "non-Italian displaced persons ineligible for UNRRA assistance, are not the responsibility of UNRRA and remain the responsibility of the Allied armed forces. The maintenance and repatriation of such persons will remain the responsibility of the Allied or eventually of the Italian Government, in accordance with whatever relations may exist between the Allied armed forces and the Italian Government."[75] In this, Keeny defused a sensitive topic and kicked the can down the road, leaving unresolved the question of "ultimate" responsibility for certain displacees in Italy. This reflected, in part, broader tensions of intergovernmental humanitarianism created by blurred lines of authority between an intergovernmental agency (in this case, UNRRA), an occupying power (the AMG/ACC), and nation-states (here, Italy as host state for foreign refugees).

In certain contexts, the Italian government sought to turn its weakness into a strength, arguing that its nonmembership in the United Nations and its associated relief bodies should exempt Italy from the hardships of caring for UNRRA ineligibles.[76] In other contexts, Italian authorities instead highlighted how the state's hamstrung sovereignty rendered Italy victim of the ongoing problems created by foreign refugees. A 1946 "Nota Verbale" from the Ministry of Foreign Affairs, for example, implied that Allied laxity had created much of the initial conditions for these refugee flows. "When [after the cessation of hostilities], the borders were not yet controlled by Italian authorities, there poured into Italy undesirables expelled from Switzerland and in part from France and later Yugoslavs, Albanians, Greeks and other Balkan types originating from Central and Eastern Europe," asserted this memo. The author added that many of these individuals carried out political activities within Italy hostile to their home states, creating diplomatic difficulties for Italy. And despite their lack of stay permits, these "undesirables" competed with unemployed Italians for jobs. The memo continued on, repeating well-rehearsed tropes about the delinquency such refugees represented: "A considerable number of these refugees present, in short, a constant and notable danger for security and public order. These individuals don't exercise productive activities and instead carry on the most various and illicit clandestine traffic from weapons, ammunition, currency, valuables, foodstuffs to prostitution, arriving at the most serious forms of delinquency."[77]

While the memo blamed the refugees for a host of ills, it laid the real responsibility at the feet of the Allies. "The supervision of police has so far encountered obstacles because of the privileges that such foreigners enjoy in Italian territory as a result of the Allies and the few means of constraint to this point permitted to the Italian Government." The author went on to compare the camps administered by the ACC/AMG to "'hotels' where foreigners have full liberty to enter and to leave," denouncing how "the expenses for the maintenance of these camps weigh directly and indirectly on Italy." The conclusion drawn by this memo was the "absolute impossibility" of Italy absorbing these foreigners, particularly in light of the expected exodus of Italians out of Istria and ongoing migrations from Italian Africa.[78]

This *nota verbale* implied that Italy's requirement to help its own refugees leaving the contested territories in the Balkans and Africa (territories whose fate in 1946 had not yet been determined) rendered it unable to help foreign refugees in the peninsula. Yet Italian representatives had no difficulty in asking UNRRA for help with repatriating its nationals from those contested territories. By 1946 Sorieri, the deputy chief of UNRRA's Italy Mission, stated that while UNRRA "did not have a direct operating responsibility" for Italian civilians in the former colonies, it did have a role to play in assisting Italian repatriation: "(a) To serve as an intermediary between the Italian Government, and the Military Authorities here [Italy] and elsewhere in order to facilitate communications or arrangements for movements, (b) to arrange for the actual reception of these persons into Italy, or their movement therefrom."[79]

Despite such seeming clarification, throughout UNRRA's existence the question of whether UNRRA should or could provide (additional) assistance to Italians in the colonies and other overseas territories kept returning to the agenda. The fact that UNRRA had specific missions in several of the (soon to be former) Italian territories—notably Albania, the Dodecanese Islands, Ethiopia, and Yugoslavia—contributed to the confusion, particularly for Italian civilians who often sent specific requests for aid to UNRRA. Given this state of affairs, it should not prove surprising that repatriation to the metropole was not an obvious choice for some Italians in the overseas territories. Nor should it prove surprising that the fragile Italian state worried about its capacity to accommodate such arrivals.

Exceptions to the Rule: UNRRA and Italians in the Oltremare

As noted earlier, even before the extension of UNRRA relief to mainland Italy, a decision at UNRRA's Second Council session in 1944 permitted the organization to assist in the exceptional return of so-called intruded enemy nationals, that is, individuals from the enemy nations who had intruded into foreign territory and remained there after hostilities ended. One of the primary groups repatriated under this provision consisted of Italians from Albania, highlighting how despite its avowals of humanitarian neutrality, UNRRA took for granted Italy's de facto loss of sovereignty over such territories (rather than treating Albania as still part of Italian territory until the 1947 Peace Treaty).[80] In Albania, UNRRA staff had to improvise many of its policies for repatriating displaced persons, including but not limited to Italians. Displaced Greeks and Chamerians (ethnic Albanians from Epirus) also received UNRRA assistance. Thorny questions of which DPs proved eligible for UNRRA assistance complicated the task.

In January 1946, both the Circolo Garibaldi and individual Italians in Albania contacted UNRRA for help in returning Italians to the peninsula. According to UNRRA, most of these Italians lacked passes authorized either by the Italian government or the Allied High Command that would allow them to enter Italy. The mission chief D. R. Oakley-Hill noted, "Many Italians may have to wait for weeks and perhaps months at Durrës till the issue of entry permits to Italy is resumed. These persons fall outside the category of persons displaced by reason of war, as laid down in the UNRRA charter, and until they have received exit and entry permits and are actually awaiting shipment they are of no concern of this Mission." Having seemingly washed his hands of responsibility, Oakley-Hill nonetheless acknowledged, "But, though UNRRA has not special responsibility for these Italians, it is obviously necessary for this Mission to assure itself that they—like all other persons in Albania—receive enough food to keep them alive while they remain in Albania."[81] Brigadier Hodgson, head of the British Military Mission in Albania, had similarly disavowed responsibility for Italian repatriation. The minutes of a January 1946 meeting between the British Military Mission and two UNRRA workers in Albania, a Mr. Floud and a Miss Keir, noted of Hodgson, "The Brigadier had made it plain that he was not interested in displaced persons and that he had not the staff to deal with any extra work."[82] The meeting had apparently been called upon the insistence of the UNRRA workers, distressed by worsening food shortages. An internal UNRRA cable a week later stressed how the weakness of the Italian state, combined with Hodgson's hands-off policy, rendered particularly vulnerable Italy's citizens stuck in the former possessions: "BMM [British Military Mission] states matter is considered one between Albanian and Italian governments, but we emphasize there is no-one in Albania to look after Italian interests."[83]

Just a few weeks later, the situation had deteriorated. On 15 February 1946, an urgent cable went out from the UNRRA office in Tirana to UNRRA headquarters in London warning that in Albania "large numbers Italians [were] now being prepared for expulsion. . . . Under present exceptional circumstances all Italians here fall within Category DPs."[84] Ruby Oakley-Hill, a displaced persons officer for the UNRRA Albania Mission, recalls the effect of these threatened expulsions in 1946. "Enver Hoxha decided to be rid of all the Italians. Suddenly they were encamped all over the beach at Durazzo with trunks and children, dogs, and all with no food and no means of transport except the UNRRA supply ships!"[85] The regime, of course, made exceptions for those Italians considered "useful" and necessary for national reconstruction, even detaining specialists against their will.

One week after he sent his urgent cable, the mission chief D. R. Oakley-Hill complained in a letter to UNRRA's director of finance about the Albanian authorities stopping their trucks at a roadblock because of the presence of Italian nationals in the UN lorries. "London advises us that we may only assist the repatriation of those Italians who entered Albania after the Italian occupation, i.e. April 7th, 1939." Requesting clarification on the shifting policy regarding eligibility for UNRRA assistance for Italians in Albania, Oakley-Hill acknowledged, "As it stands it places us in an absurd position, having to distinguish between one Italian and another in this arbitrary fashion." As a result, he concluded, "The best plan therefore will be to refuse to carry any Italians at all."[86]

With the withdrawal of the British mission from Albania in the spring of 1946, however, UNRRA took over its role as liaison to the Italian government for obtaining exit permits for Italian repatriates.[87] By April 1946, UNRRA was facilitating the return of Italians who had moved to Albania before the 1939 occupation of the country, provided that either the Italian state or the individual repatriate paid the shipping costs. Eventually, UNRRA did carry out large-scale repatriations of Italian soldiers and civilians, employing a range of ships such as the *Marvia*, the *Thimble Eye*, and even some Yugoslav transports.[88] The last such UNRRA-assisted returns to Italy occurred in June 1947.[89]

In addition to providing shipping, UNRRA helped screen Italian repatriates, using lists drawn up by the Circolo Garibaldi. In attempting to block any potential Albanians masquerading as Italians and "to assure only bonafide Italians allowed entry," the Italian government insisted on screening the repatriates upon their arrival in Bari, Brindisi, and Taranto. As an UNRRA cable stated, "Italian Government expresses view that no rpt no Albanian be permitted entry Italy."[90] Despite (or perhaps because of) its weakness, Italy asserted its sovereignty as best as it could in controlling entry of foreigners—just as it also sought to regulate the flow of Italians back to the peninsula.

Like regime officials who had worried about the behavior of Italians repatriating from AOI on the wartime *navi bianche*, Italian officials after the war continued to fret over the possible deficiencies of such national refugees. Italian officials complained about some of the repatriates coming from Albania, for example. A cryptic message from Ugo Turcato warned that the "unworthy" actions of Italian families who had been offered accommodation in the officers' cabins of the UNRRA ship *Zena* had led to a temporary suspension of UNRRA repatriation of Italians. Echoing those who had seen the *navi bianche* as sites of political reeducation, Turcato urged the need for an "educative" role in communicating appropriate behavior to would-be repatriates.[91]

Like UNRRA's other relief work in Albania, these repatriations of Italians took place in the absence of meaningful Albanian cooperation, highlighting the complex juridical and political landscapes within which Italian repatriation from former territories typically transpired. From the start, UNRRA officials in Albania confronted suspicious and obstructionist attitudes. Delivery of much-needed supplies was held up, for instance, as Hoxha delayed signing the initial contract with UNRRA and insisted that Albanians alone could handle the logistical delivery of relief and reconstruction supplies. Once operations finally began in August 1945, and shipments of food, leather, and medicines began arriving, Hoxha made increasingly extravagant demands, particularly for trucks and vehicles. In light of this, it is not surprising that UNRRA's official historian concluded, "The UNRRA program for Albania proved one of the most difficult to carry out."[92] In his memoir, mission chief and former Special Operations Executive officer Oakley-Hill likewise remarked on what he saw as the regime's lack of gratitude: "The ordinary person might think that 25 million dollars' worth of supplies of almost any kind would be worth having and would be met at least by a mild thankyou. . . . This government not only made a fuss about allowing us to enter the country, but when we did they began to expect to get everything they wanted as of right, and to criticise a good many things we did bring."[93]

In this instance, Hoxha's regime understood intergovernmentalism through a particularly narrow lens. Jealously guarding its newly won national sovereignty, the Albanian state saw UNRRA as useful only in so far as it doled out resources. Albania did not appear to conceive of itself as a partner in the organization, despite numbering among the antifascist United Nations. We see here, then, a clash of different visions of internationalism, with socialist states understanding the role of intergovernmental organizations like UNRRA very differently from the British or the Americans.

The lack of gratitude shown by emerging communist regimes for aid from UNRRA (funded overwhelmingly by the United States) and the fulsome thanks given instead to the Soviet Union figures as a common trope in assessments by UNRRA personnel and sympathetic observers.[94] As had occurred in Albania, for example, Yugoslav officials greeted UNRRA with suspicion. While happily receiving supplies necessary to kick-start agricultural production and rebuild transportation infrastructure, Yugoslav leaders sought to delimit other activities by UNRRA staff within the country. They particularly mistrusted the process of supply distribution. Indeed, from the very beginning of negotiations between UNRRA and Yugoslavia in 1944, the Yugoslavs had worried about infringements on their sovereignty.[95]

Such concerns became particularly acute in the case of the disputed Venezia Giulia territory, with Zone A under AMG control and Zone B administered by Yugoslav military authorities. In stressing UNRRA's impartiality and purely humanitarian mission, the organization's director Herbert Lehman had urged, "UNRRA would, as provided in resolutions, act in agreement with JUGOSLAV authorities and Allied military authorities in their respective Zones of Occupation. In same way UNRRA would act in agreement with ITALIAN authorities concerning areas which they administer." In a subsequent cable Lehman added, "This agreement and the provision of supplies by UNRRA for distribution there [Zone B] by the YUGOSLAV Government area [are] entirely without political significance and are without prejudice to the ultimate decision by the appropriate authorities of the claims of YUGOSLAVIA and ITALY to the area, a question not within the functions of UNRRA."[96] This did not stop actors on the ground, like the antifascist leader of the autonomist party in Rijeka / Fiume Riccardo Zanella, from making politically sensitive requests, in this instance, that a city under Yugoslav control be furnished with UNRRA supplies through Italy.

As a letter to Paolo Contini, legal adviser to UNRRA's Italy Mission, put it, Zanella asks for assistance from UNRRA to the "'Free State of Fiume' . . . The 'Free State of Fiume' does not exist since 1922. The city was Italian since 1922. <u>It is occupied by Yougoslavia now</u>. Its future status is uncertain. But I do not for one moment anticipate that it will be Italian again. Therefore it is a mistake on Zanella's part to appeal to <u>UNRRA, ROME</u> rather than to <u>UNRRA, BELGRADE</u>. I would like Fiume to get food, no matter wherefrom. And I think it will stand a better chance if food comes from <u>UNRRA, BELGRADE</u>."[97]

The author of this memo, who deemed Zanella's request "most pathetic," implied that pragmatic humanitarian needs must override political consideration. Yet the writer failed to note that Zanella's requests went beyond those of direct assistance to the city. Zanella had another reason for appealing to UNRRA Rome rather than Belgrade. He asked "that the refugees of Fiume who reside in Rome or in Northern Italy be given the same help that is usually extended to those who, for war causes, have been compelled to abandon their country of origin."[98] Zanella thus highlighted one of the limitations of UNRRA's DP work, which focused on repatriation and excluded post-hostility displacees. Individuals from Rijeka / Fiume who had made their way to the Italian peninsula after the city fell under Yugoslav administration occupied the gray zone inhabited by many Italian nationals from the contested territories, whose juridical status remained as ambiguous as that of the lands from which they had migrated. Writing of his city, whose legal status remained undecided at war's end, Zanella concluded, "Fiume cannot be considered as an ex-enemy or enemy City by the United Nations, but rather as a helpless and most unfortunate victim both of national-fascism (now finally wiped out) and by the same systems of violence and oppression, now being applied to its detriment by those at present occupying the city."[99]

In its broader relief work, UNRRA sought to avoid becoming embroiled in the political dispute between Italy and Yugoslavia.[100] Following Lehman's proposed division of labor, UNRRA relief to Zone A went through Trieste, while supplies to Zone B moved through the Zagreb office of the Balkan mission. By 1946, though, UNRRA was moving relief supplies for the Yugoslavia Mission through Trieste with the permission of the AMG, reflecting the fact that Italy did not possess sovereignty over the city; Trieste also handled supplies for UNRRA's Austria Mission. "Pilfering" and theft in the port quickly became a pressing problem, necessitating UNRRA's request for the "receiving governments to furnish armed guards—and by that I mean armed guards. We don't want observers."[101] Such a comment points to the limited capacity of an intergovernmental organization like UNRRA to carry out effective enforcement. As in all its fields of operation, UNRRA remained dependent on the goodwill or at least the acquiescence of the host government or local authorities, in this case the AMG and Yugoslavia.

Worries about violating or overstepping sovereignty troubled UNRRA's relationships with a range of states, not just new socialist regimes. UNRRA workers in the Ethiopian mission found leaders distrustful of any type of foreign intervention or benevolent "assistance," not surprising after the fascist war of aggression and subsequent half decade of colonial occupation waged in the name of an Italian civilizational mission. Ethiopians worried that UNRRA would renege on its promises and fail to deliver the promised quantity of supplies.[102] At the same time, the Ethiopian delegate to UNRRA noted the disparity between relief to his country—"the first country to be invaded by one of the Axis powers and the first to be liberated"[103]—and that to Italy. For Ethiopians, there was no ambiguity about Italy's status as a former enemy nation and Ethiopia's pride of place among the United Nations that had defeated the Axis powers.

In protecting their reclaimed sovereignty, Ethiopians also reacted angrily to proposals forwarded by UNRRA's Italy Mission for resettlement of European displaced persons in their country. In 1947, the chief of the Ethiopia Mission Willard Park wrote to Keeny, the head of UNRRA's Italy Mission:

> With reference to your memorandum of 13th March . . . enquiring about the possibility of displaced Persons settling in Ethiopia, I have to state that the Ethiopian Government is not now considering any plan by which 12 to 15,000 displaced persons will be accepted in Ethiopia for re-settlement.
>
> Officials of the Government have expressed to me very considerable surprise that such a plan should ever have been considered by the Government and they are completely at a loss to account for the rumours you mention.
>
> It should be noted that in the experience of this mission entry permits into Ethiopia are extremely difficult to secure at the present time.

> I doubt very much that the Ethiopian Government would issue permits for entry if the object were re-settlement. *Further, if the displaced persons were of Italian origin, it would be practically impossible to arrange for their entry into Ethiopia* [my emphasis].[104]

In Ethiopia, then, UNRRA's primary repatriation responsibilities centered on helping Ethiopians displaced outside the country as a result of war return home, not on assisting Italians. This did not stop Italians and Italian authorities, however, from forwarding requests to UNRRA from Italians seeking to reenter Ethiopia. Frequently, these consisted of entreaties to join a spouse who remained there.[105]

In contrast to these often fraught interactions between UNRRA and officials of newly independent or liberated states, UNRRA eventually established an "effective working partnership" with the BMA in the Aegean Islands.[106] Although a Greek liaison mission to UNRRA had been posted in the Dodecanese since August 1945, UNRRA's primary interlocutor here remained the BMA. The BMA operations subdivided the archipelago (with roughly twenty islands) into six administrative groups, with the principal headquarters on the largest island, Rhodes. UNRRA provided critical food rations and medical supplies to the islands and also ran small camps for islanders bombed out of their homes. UNRRA assumed responsibility for local displacees, foreigners who had been displaced to the islands, and Dodecanesians seeking to return home, whereas the local authority (in this case, the BMA) assumed primary responsibility for repatriating Italians.[107] Given the considerable role played by UNRRA, the BMA, and the ICRC in assisting the residents of the Dodecanese Islands (including but not limited to Italians) up until the territory's transfer to Greece in 1947, the Dodecanese case offers an interesting counterpoint to that of Italian civilians in Albania. In both cases we find sometimes competing, sometimes complementary authorities involved in the repatriation of Italians. In contrast to the Albanian situation, however, the BMA stood in for a sovereign state and thus maintained a different position as placeholder power. This likely facilitated UNRRA and BMA collaboration, although even here the BMA did guard its temporary sovereign prerogatives.

The Dodecanese Islands: Entangled Authority, Overlapping Responsibilities

In extending aid to the Dodecanese Islands, UNRRA ultimately treated those islands—as it did Ethiopia and Albania—as territories that had been liberated from Italian rule, rather than as integral parts of the ex-enemy state of Italy. In reality, however, the final disposition of the islands and their annexation by Greece would only be determined by the 1947 Peace Treaty with Italy. UNRRA's decision to help followed out of entreaties both by the Vatican and the ICRC, which reported dire conditions in those islands at war's end.[108] In recognition of ICRC efforts to ameliorate starvation conditions in the islands in the winter of 1945, the BMA—established over the island group in May 1945—had invited the ICRC to participate in the BMA's Central Relief Committee from its inception; Jean Munier, the ICRC delegate to the Dodecanese, served as the committee's vice chairman. Sales of Red Cross supplies helped fund the committee's work. In July 1945, the ICRC delegate to the islands proposed that the Red Cross not only carry on its traditional role as a "neutral, impartial and independent element" but also serve as "eventual liaison between [local] population on one side and civil and military authorities on the other."[109] Brigadier Acland of the BMA graciously accepted the ICRC offer—after clarifying that the delegate presumably intended to serve as liaison *only* in the area of relief.[110]

In addition to working with the BMA through the Central Relief Committee, the ICRC toured the islands in November 1945, documenting conditions and the organization's accomplishments there.[111] Certainly, the ICRC possessed a moral authority in the islands distinct from that of the British military command. Islanders commemorated with an Orthodox Te Deum and a Catholic Mass the one-year anniversary of the first ICRC relief that had helped them through the starvation winter of 1945.[112] That anniversary, in February 1946, coincided with the withdrawal of the ICRC delegation from the islands. The previous summer, the mayor of the town of Kremasti on the island of Rhodes had announced the naming of a principal street after the Red Cross in recognition of the organization's heroic efforts.[113]

Whereas the BMA likely feared challenges to its authority (a provisional or discretional sovereignty) should the ICRC overstep its bounds in administering assistance, the ICRC—somewhere between a nongovernmental and an intergovernmental organization—faced its own jurisdictional dilemmas. As early as September 1945, a Miss Saddler from the BMA had approached the ICRC about establishing a specifically Dodecanese Red Cross distinct from that of either Italy or Greece, an initiative deemed juridically untenable by the home organization in Geneva. In the same month, Munier met with local Dodecanese interested in extending the work of the Greek Red Cross to the islands. Those promoting this initiative included the wife of the mayor of Rhodes and two nurses from the Greek Red Cross. While Munier welcomed the goodwill and intentions of these humanitarians, he recognized the difficulties created by the insistence that the Dodecanese Islands be included within the national Greek Red Cross organization, given that the disposition of the islands had yet to be determined.[114] Likewise, internal ICRC documentation suggests that at least some of the delegation in the Dodecanese initially perceived UNRRA as an unwelcome competitor in the humanitarian landscape. As the ICRC wrapped up its activities in the winter of 1946, however, a final report concluded, "Contrary to what we had believed, we did not lose ground since UNRRA was installed in the Dodecanese. We might even venture that we have gained ground."[115]

Just as the BMA had first sought to delimit and contain the ICRC's capacities and authority in the islands, UNRRA aid to the Isole Egeo had been delayed by similar concerns. Keeny in the Italian mission reported that despite discussions in October 1944 about sending relief through UNRRA's Greek mission, the Allied command had told UNRRA in no uncertain terms that relief to the civilians of the Dodecanese fell under British military control.[116] As Keeny had been informed three days earlier, "Civil Affairs Committee [of the BMA] have complete responsibility and authority and neither want nor will they permit relief and rehabilitation activities by UNRRA in the islands."[117] Lord Rennell likewise confirms that the commander in charge of the Dodecanese did not initially favor the plan to bring UNRRA in as a partner. "His views were, in substance, that the Dodecanese Islands were a British commitment and that B.M.A. must remain fully responsible for their administration." Added Rennell, "Such responsibility, until regular trade channels were re-opened, included the procurement of essential supplies for purchase by the local population: there would be no advantage and some disadvantages in inviting U.N.R.R.A. to participate in this business."[118] An UNRRA letter in June 1945 noted that UNRRA supplies to the Dodecanese had been discontinued, owing to the "full responsibility" of the British military for the islands. A handwritten note on the margins that the British had "not invited" UNRRA assistance drove the point home.[119]

The commander began to come around over the summer, though, and by August 1945 an official agreement between the BMA and UNRRA was in place. At this point, UNRRA deemed the problem of displaced persons "acute," offering a figure of at least six thousand externally displaced Dodecanesians in the Nusereit camp in Palestine in addition to those Italians awaiting repatriation from the islands.[120] In November 1945 an UNRRA representative, a Mr. Wankowicz [here spelled Wancowica], finally joined the Central Relief Committee.[121] When UNRRA concluded its mission in the islands in December 1946, Wankowicz became chairman of the Dodecanese Welfare Association, to which remaining UNRRA funds rolled over.[122]

As occupying power and supposedly neutral intermediary, the BMA sought to ensure order while avoiding overt antagonisms with either local Greeks or the Greek government to whom it was assumed the islands would pass. Although the British government had issued private assurances to the Greek government about the inevitability of Greek rule over the islands, the rapidly changing political context in Europe and the delicate question of Greek claims on territories respectively held by Albania, Bulgaria, and Yugoslavia complicated public expressions of British support for eventual Greek sovereignty over the Dodecanese. In practical terms on the ground in Rhodes, this meant that the BMA referred all requests to enter the islands from Greece to the Greek authorities in Athens and sought to achieve a rough demographic balance between those entering the islands from Greece and those traveling to Greece out of the archipelago. Nonetheless, BMA authorities risked irritating Greece when they combated irregular or unauthorized entries from that state, a problem exacerbated by the tendency of Greek authorities to issue permits for permanent residence in the islands without informing the BMA.[123]

In maintaining order within the islands, the BMA also facilitated the practical work of UNRRA through crowd control. A February 1946 memo from the BMA civil affairs officer on Karpathos hints at the kinds of problems that could erupt. The letter refers to aiming to prevent "a repetition of the disorderly conduct which took place in several villages when the Red Cross representative visited CARPATHOS." With this in mind, the BMA police "will ensure that people of the village who wish to present their cases to U.N.R.R.A. officials do so in an orderly manner i.e. there will be no disorderly mobs, screaming and shouting." Anyone contravening these orders would be arrested and relief delayed to the village involved in such an incident.[124]

UNRRA documents testify to the generally "cordial relationships" that prevailed between UNRRA and BMA personnel, while admitting "a lack of co-operation" on the part of some BMA officers, particularly on the islands of Kalymnos and Kos. In addition, UNRRA efforts to reorganize child health services and training of nurses encountered "passive but effective resistance" from the BMA matron in charge of the hospitals.[125] UNRRA established welfare officers throughout the islands to coordinate distribution of supplies (including food, clothing, and monies for public works projects). Overall, UNRRA's work with refugees in the Dodecanese complemented BMA efforts. UNRRA provided primary relief to internal refugees, that is, those displaced between the islands, and Dodecanese returning from the war and exile abroad. The BMA, with assistance from UNRRA, focused on three principal groups and tasks involved in repatriation: (1) returning Dodecanesian

Greeks to the islands who had fled during the war, (2) repatriating Jewish survivors to Rhodes, and (3) repatriating Italians back to the peninsula. Over the course of 1945, a total of 17,765 Dodecanese refugees returned to the islands (most of them coming from camps in the Middle East and Cyprus or from Turkey and Greece), 595 Italian officials and their families migrated to Italy, and 55 of an estimated 303 Jewish survivors had repatriated to Rhodes.[126]

The BMA, the ICRC, and UNRRA worked with Elia Soriano, president of the Jewish community, to address the particular needs of returning Jews. A representative Jacobson of the Joint Jewish Distribution Committee also visited the islands.[127] Confronted by both rumors and actual requests for repatriation by Jewish survivors from Rhodes, many of whom had made their way to Rome upon liberation, UNRRA and the BMA struggled to work out how many of these Jews actually wanted to return permanently to Rhodes. Despite estimates in November 1945 that as many as 204 Jews (including 180 young women) sought to return, the majority actually appeared inclined to remain in Italy or relocate to live with kin in Rhodesia and the Belgian Congo.[128]

In coordination with the UNRRA office in Athens, UNRRA's Dodecanese Mission worked to facilitate further repatriations to the islands by ethnic Greeks, Turks, and Jews the following year. As in Albania, however, it proved almost impossible to determine whether the 864 applicants UNRRA had planned to return in early January 1946 actually qualified for UNRRA care as "genuine displaced persons." A British report summarized the difficulties: "Much correspondence and discussion followed and the help of the British Embassy, Athens, was enlisted. Screening reduced the total of 864 to 632. Just how many of these have actually returned to the islands it is impossible to say."[129] The uncertainty about both the identities and whereabouts of these applicants for repatriation underscores the very real challenges to controlling mobility on and in the islands. These challenges did not stop officials from scrutinizing cases as carefully as possible.

The request of a Professor Cotzias sent to UNRRA in 1946 proved typical of the types of cases that came before UNRRA officials. Cotzias testified that he, his wife, and their three children had migrated from the Dodecanese after the Italian fascist authorities had fired him from his job as a high school teacher. Moving to Greece, Cotzias spent the war years working as a teacher on Crete, and had returned to Rhodes in March 1946 in the employ of the Allied forces. He asked UNRRA for assistance to his family, still waiting in Athens for a permit to repatriate to the Dodecanese and without money or means.[130] UNRRA staff interrogated closely such claims to fascist persecution. UNRRA permitted one man, Vassilios Spirou—born in Karen [Keren] to a Rhodian father and Ethiopian mother—to travel to Rhodes to obtain documents necessary to prove that he had suffered fascist persecution while studying in Brindisi. UNRRA personnel nonetheless insisted that his claimed right to return to East Africa had to be established, and they closely monitored his case.[131]

The BMA/UNRRA housed Dodecanesian refugees at the Miramare Transit Camp and the former Italian military hospital, among other sites, until they could be returned to their home islands. Italians also could be found in these camps. If these displaced persons refused to go to the outer islands or to smaller villages on the island of Rhodes, they forfeited additional UNRRA aid.[132] Prior to the arrival of UNRRA, the ICRC had also debated relocating those refugees in Rhodes who came from outer islands or had lived on the principal island for less than a decade. The ICRC representatives worried that overcrowding of displacees on Rhodes had created an explosive situation of moral laxity. Upon his visit to a school housing DPs, for instance, one Red Cross delegate discovered "the refugees were destroying the fittings, and the director of the orphanage had no peace and no control over their movements. He found considerable overcrowding and the place was filthy; People were still in bed at 11 o'clock."[133] Despite varied efforts to remove individuals from Rhodes, many islanders who had made their way to the capital claimed to have always been resident there, assertions BMA officials and their colleagues in the ICRC and UNRRA found difficult to either verify or disprove. By the end of 1945, the influx of such out-islanders to Rhodes had resulted in a surplus population of approximately one thousand persons lacking employment and housing.[134] Given this, the BMA sought to regulate *all* movement between islands, evaluating requests by non-displaced Dodecanesians for temporary visit permits and any permanent moves between islands. Between August and November 1946, the BMA on Karpathos handled 301 such requests to visit Rhodes. Whereas most applicants sought to visit the hospital there, other motivations for these journeys included "trade" and "privet affairs" [*sic*]. Those requesting to move to Rhodes Town, the administrative capital of the island chain, typically justified such moves on the grounds of family reunification or employment.[135]

As noted previously, the BMA assumed primary responsibility for repatriating Italians out of the islands, although UNRRA provided considerable material support. That all Italians would necessarily wish to leave the islands was not a foregone conclusion, nor did the Italian government encourage such movement, particularly before the islands' fate had been determined. Just a month after VE Day, Brigadier Arundell in the British War Office worried, "The anti-Italian feeling in the Dodecanese Islands is so strong that there is a serious risk of outbreaks of violence unless certain classes of them are removed at an early date." In light of the sensitivity of the issue with Italy, however, Arundell conceded that the BMA needed to limit its requests for removal at that point in time. Arundell thus recommended the repatriation of those who posed a "danger to the peace of the Islands" (some fifty men, thirty-eight women, and fifty-eight associated children found on Rhodes); eighty-two discharged officials ("Metropolitan Italians"), plus six women and seven children; those Italians anxiously awaiting repatriation to the peninsula (fifteen hundred to two thousand individuals then living in refugee camps); and "the whole Metropolitan Italian population of the island of Cos against whom the local Greek feeling is dangerously hostile" (comprising 165 men, 140 women, and 119 children). In addition, the BMA recommended a series of cases of medical repatriations for Italians suffering from both chronic and acute health conditions.[136]

This policy appears to have helped defuse local tensions. In his history of British Military Administration, Rennell contends that despite strong anti-Italian sentiment at the end of the war, local Italians and Greeks got along fairly well after the deportation/evacuation of the most noted fascists. The internment of Italian carabinieri (with the exception of those born in the Dodecanese) further calmed the waters. "The Italians, in their turn, lost their fear while remaining unsettled over the problem of their future."[137] Having said this, both British and Italian observers at the time did report threats and antagonism toward specific Italians; during the peace treaty negotiations, for instance, slogans such as "Italians Leave Now! Union or Death" (Partono subito gli Italiani! Unione o Morte) and calls for the expulsion of remaining Italians appeared on buildings like the Franciscan orphanage.[138]

The extent of intimidation and its role in prompting repatriation, however, proves hard to gauge. As Nicholas Doumanis has documented through his oral historical work with Dodecanese residents, a Greek nationalist historiographical tradition positing implacable hatred between Greeks and Italian occupiers obscures the more positive memories many islanders held of the colonizers. Local Dodecanesians often attributed bad behavior to a small group of "fascists" who they set apart from the general mass of "Italians." Many of these islanders also drew a temporal distinction between the more benevolent or paternalistic governorship of Mario Lago and the harder-line one of Cesare Maria De Vecchi, with the latter's rule commonly used to denote "when fascism came."[139] In the end, fears about Greek violence and nationalism toward Italians proved exaggerated.

The potential *threat* of nationalist violence by Greeks did enter into British calculations, however, and may have proved useful to the BMA in arguing for the necessity of large-scale Italian repatriation out of the islands. Into the summer of 1945, the Allied command debated whether the BMA should hold off on any subsequent large-scale repatriation, particularly in light of the Italian government's foot-dragging on the issue and the "unsettled future" of the territory. In July, for example, the Italian government said it would permit the return of some ex-officials from the islands but did not wish to make this a general policy. In the handwritten notes scribbled alongside the telegram referring to this decision, a member of the British Foreign Office registered his dissent with the Allied Commission's recommendation that Italians in the islands remain in place until the islands' status had been determined. According to this observer, Italy would lose the islands "sooner rather than later," and to delay the departure of Italians "will only cause difficulties for BMA in the islands and lead to bitterness of feeling."[140] By September 1945 even members of the Allied Commission shared such worries that "it would be non-repatriation, rather than repatriation which might be harmful, owing to the trouble which may arise with the Greek population in the Dodecanese on account of the presence of the Italians there." British representatives in Rome thus urged the Allied Commission to resubmit the question of repatriation to the Italian government.[141] The War Office seconded this: "Delay [in repatriation] is embarrassing."[142] By November, according to the report of an Italian officer recently repatriated through the islands, the BMA had invited all Italian family heads into their offices and asked them to declare whether they intended to remain or repatriate. In the Dodecanese, then, the British sought to balance a wide range of ambitions: preserving local order, providing assistance, retaining good relations with the governments of both Italy and Greece, and, of course, protecting British prestige. Not surprisingly, officials closer to the realities on the ground in the islands often disagreed with the distant directives of the Allied Commission and the Foreign Office, where strategic considerations outweighed those of either humanitarianism or daily interethnic relations. And, not surprisingly, Italian officials suspected the British of harboring their own "imperial" ambitions in the islands,[143] a belief shared even by some of Britain's staunchest allies.[144]

In the midst of competing national interests and overlapping political and humanitarian agendas, the Commissione per la Tutela degli Interessi italiani nel Dodecaneso, headed by Antonio Macchi, served as the principal advocate for the Italians in the islands. The commission established its own section for assistance under Dr. Aldo Levi, offering aid to Italians. In the last part of 1945, the CTIID concentrated its refugee relief on those approximately 987 Italians displaced from the island of Kasos, 378 of them POWs awaiting repatriation in the transit camp at Peveragno. Other Italian refugees found accommodations in the Knights Hospitaller at Acandia or the camp at Monte Profeta. In its work of distributing aid, the commission drew on funds and supplies obtained through the Italian Red Cross, the Central Committee, and from within the Italian community itself in a manner similar to that of the Circolo Garibaldi in Albania.[145]

Large-scale repatriations of Italians overseen by the BMA and UNRRA began on 29 December 1945, when 502 Italians departed Rhodes on the SS *Marigot*. Another 495 Italian citizens left on 13 January 1946. The Italian government then agreed to approve the repatriation of all those wishing it who could demonstrate a guarantee of housing with family or friends, subsequently seeking to screen arrivals for possible collaboration with the Nazis during the German occupation of the archipelago.[146] With the cancellation of a planned transport in March 1946, however, a number of would-be repatriates who had already liquidated their assets found themselves stranded until the SS *Kathleen* delivered 579 individuals to Italy. The SS *Miraglia* carried out the final voyage overseen by the BMA, taking another 1,257. From that point on, the CTIID organized roughly fifty convoys of repatriates and movable property, as both UNRRA and the BMA argued that they did not bear responsibility for the personal effects of repatriates.[147]

In his capacity as CTIID head, Macchi applied considerable pressure on the Italian government to accept repatriates, even traveling to Italy in September 1946 at the request of the BMA. Indeed, a letter sent by an Italian of Rhodes to the Italian Ministry of Foreign Affairs two months earlier had highlighted the many difficulties faced by repatriates, "principal among them those created by the Italian Government."[148] This same letter writer singled out for criticism the Comitato di Gestione Amministrativa delle Isole Italiane dell'Egeo, created by ministerial decree on 18 February 1946 to settle Italy's administrative and financial matters. Admittedly, the Comitato di Gestione did establish an Ufficio Rodi, or Rhodes office, that eventually helped remaining citizens to repatriate. Nonetheless, in his complaint letter, our unknown author asserted that the Rhodes office became home to "many former Italian functionaries in Rhodes noted for their incompetence and lack of propriety [who are] poorly viewed by the local population."[149] By the beginning of 1947, a month before the union of the Dodecanese Islands with Greece, the BMA estimated that as a result of these various repatriation convoys, only eleven hundred Italians remained in the Isole Egeo. Of these, most "were born in the islands or at Smyrna, many never having visited Italy."[150]

The BMA did not invent these distinctions between "metropolitan" and "local" Italians but rather drew on categories and hierarchies of identity elaborated within the Italian empire. These categories reflected complex histories of migration, belonging, and citizenship. A few of these "local" or so-called "domiciled" Italians had been born in the Dodecanese to families who came during the liberal era (1912–1922). Most, however, were individuals with some claim to Italian identity who had moved from various parts of the (former) Ottoman Empire to the islands. Others were Italians who had married Greek subjects. One case that came before the BMA involved a fifty-year-old man, P. Crocchianti, who had migrated to the islands from Tivoli (outside of Rome) in 1918. Two years later, he married a Greek woman with property on Karpathos. Employed by the BMA as a mechanic and driver on Karpathos, by July 1946 Crocchianti had already requested twice to emigrate abroad (not to Italy). A BMA civil affairs officer reported that "he is extremely unpopular with the locals, and fears violence when the GREEKS take over." Crocchianti had previously served as mayor of the town of Menetes and "has scores of enemies, many of whom threaten to cut his throat when the GREEKS arrive." The BMA officer, who praised Crocchianti's service as a driver, recommended his relocation to Rhodes, owing to the impossibility at that point in time of organizing emigration out of the islands.[151]

As will be detailed in chapter 4, the citizenship option clause in the 1947 Peace Treaty would render the juridical and cultural status of such individuals an open—and pressing—question. This, in turn, would complicate decisions about whether such individuals qualified for assistance as either Italian national refugees or foreign refugees, an issue that came before the International Refugee Organization (in operation between 1948 and 1952) that picked up the work of refugee relief where UNRRA and the IGCR had left off.

UNRRA and the IRO inhabited and inherited an intergovernmental structure that viewed the world—and its residents—largely in terms of ethnonational categories. In determining who counted as a displaced person, these organizations hoped for an easy mapping of individuals onto national territories. In practice, however, a number of Italians who sought repatriation from the Dodecanese did not necessarily view Italy as home. UNRRA and the BMA received requests to emigrate to join family in places like Jerusalem, Alexandria, and Cairo, reflecting the existence of a large "Italian" diaspora across the lands of the former Ottoman Empire. This also pointed to the islands' imbrication in a wide range of economic, cultural, religious, and kinship networks spanning the Mediterranean—both a potential asset and liability that Italy's colonial governors had monitored closely.[152] Macchi claimed that a number of Italian subjects had fled to the islands from Turkey with the establishment of Ataturk's regime. In July 1946, he wrote the Italian ambassador in Ankara to inquire whether it might be possible for those Italians to return permanently to Turkey.[153]

In some instances, Italians in Rhodes even appealed to UNRRA to move them to *refugee camps* abroad where relatives resided. One man, G. De Marchi, an Italian resident of a Rhodes BMA/UNRRA transit camp, requested assistance to join his two young daughters, son, and their mother (a Greek woman from whom he was separated) in the El Arish camp in Egypt. In Rhodes, UNRRA officer Wankowicz endorsed this application, but several months later, T. T. Waddington, the chief of UNRRA's Middle East Office, roundly rejected it, sputtering, "It would be folly to introduce this fresh complication. Family friction, with resulting ill-effects on the children, would be inevitable." In its stead, Waddington recommended De Marchi's repatriation to Italy, where he could (re)establish himself and provide for his children upon their eventual "return" to Italy. Born in Istanbul in 1891, De Marchi had two older children living in Italy, though it is not clear whether they were by the same Greek mother with whom De Marchi was engaged in a custody dispute.[154] What does come through is that Waddington envisioned the De Marchi family's rightful place in Italy and saw the patriarch as its main provider, highlighting the ways in which staff of the intergovernmental agencies UNRRA, and later the IRO, helped reinscribe both the national and gendered orders in the early postwar period. In addition to those appeals to join kin in places other than Italy, the requests to UNRRA made by Italians from a number of the (former) possessions for assistance in repatriating *back* to places like Libya and Rhodes further confounded any neat understandings of what repatriation and returning home—and, by extension, *displacement*—meant, as well as the role to be played by organizations like UNRRA or powers like the BMA in effecting such migrations.

Complicating the Meaning of Repatriation

At the conclusion of the war, many of those Italian civilians who had been evacuated or otherwise displaced from territories in Africa and the Balkans (as described in chapter 2) sought to return to them and phrased their demands—to the Italian state, the BMA, and intergovernmental agencies like UNRRA—as ones of repatriation. In its common usages, repatriation refers to return to one's native land and/or to one's place of citizenship. For those born in the Italian possessions or who had set down roots in them (sometimes migrating from other imperial lands, like those of French Tunisia or British Egypt), repatriation to their "native land" did indeed mean traveling back to Africa or the Dodecanese. And before the 1947 Peace Treaty had renounced Italian claims on those territories, such individuals might argue on legalistic grounds that repatriation to their land of citizenship included those possessions. At war's end, British authorities had sought to sidestep the issue of what (and where) home meant by stating that Italian prisoners of war must be repatriated to Italy regardless of where they had been "domiciled." In this, the British implied that the Italian peninsula was the true homeland of those decommissioned soldiers who requested to be sent "home" to places like Eritrea or Tripolitania.[155]

Certainly, as we have seen, the Italian state did not favor mass repatriations to the peninsula as long as there existed some hope of Italy retaining a portion of its empire or acquiring a trusteeship over one of its former territories. Where hope was already lost, as in the independent Ethiopia of Haile Selassie, Italy sometimes found its hand forced, as when Ethiopia expelled eighty Italian industrialists and confiscated their property in August 1946.[156] Yet even here, the willingness of Italy at this point to accept repatriation of its citizens from Ethiopia should not be overstated. Numerous appeals in 1947 to the Italian government made by family members for husbands or brothers or sons to be permitted to repatriate (either permanently or temporarily) from Ethiopia to Italy reveal a continued policy of limiting and regulating repatriation.[157] In light of this, British authorities administering those territories whose fates remained unresolved—Eritrea, Somalia, Libya, and the Dodecanese—worried that any significant returns of Italians to those areas might antagonize local populations and unduly influence the peace negotiations. In pursuing their own individual and familial agendas, Italian civilians (including ex-POWs)—many of whom conceived of themselves as refugees, even if relevant authorities did not—nonetheless ignored such regulations and doggedly applied to the relevant authorities to reenter the territories.

In the Dodecanese, for instance, UNRRA received numerous requests by Italians for assistance to repatriate to the islands. On this question, UNRRA ultimately deferred to the BMA's authority. In December 1945, Major Miles-Bailey of the BMA informed UNRRA (after receiving a query from Deputy Chief Wankowicz), "The general present policy is that it is not considered wise to allow entry of Italians into the islands during the present phase of repatriation to Italy of ex-Italian and Italian families." The major added, "When this is completed the above question will be reviewed when you will be informed of any alterations in policy."[158] This policy had not changed by April 1946, its "wisdom" likely reflecting the state of negotiations for the peace treaty with Italy. Although a number of Italians residing in refugee camps in the Middle East (primarily Egypt) had made applications to UNRRA requesting repatriation to the Dodecanese, Major Miles-Bailey reaffirmed at that time, "It is regretted, but permission of entry into the Dodecanese CANNOT be granted by this Administration for permanent residence (or visit) of these Italian families."[159]

In July 1946, the policy began to soften. At this point, the BMA command informed both UNRRA and Macchi's Italian committee that entry for Italians would be granted only "on the strongest humanitarian grounds." Such circumstances included the return of children if the breadwinner resided in the islands—that is, "the return to the breadwinner of dependent children if the breadwinner here is able to support them and life on a reasonable standard is not possible for them in ITALY or wherever they may be."[160] This policy proved identical to one put into practice by the BMA in Tripolitania regarding requests to repatriate to the territory. In Libya, in contrast to the Aegean Islands, the return of children would become a fraught issue.

By the end of 1946, the BMA and UNRRA had begun to allow some Italian civilians to return to the islands. Although these numbers were never large (particularly in comparison to those of Greek and Turkish Dodecanesians seeking repatriation to the island chain), they do underscore the multidirectional nature of repatriation by Italian nationals to the former possessions and complicate the narrative of a quick Italian withdrawal. Add to this the fact that some former Italian residents of the islands were petitioning to be permitted to return as late as 1951.[161] In December of 1946, for example, UNRRA's Dodecanese Mission weighed in on a request sent by the Italian mission to assist a group of thirty-eight individuals in the UNRRA transit camp at Bari desiring to make their way back to the Aegean. UNRRA classified eleven of these thirty-eight as being of Italian nationality. Nine of these Italians were children (fourteen years old or younger).[162] In the autumn of that same year, UNRRA had approved several requests for Italian children to repatriate back to join (breadwinner) parents in the islands; following Allied/BMA strictures, however, those children had to possess Italian passports (rather than mere *lasciapassare* or travel permissions).[163]

Other Italians requesting repatriation to the Isole Egeo in this same period included two widows and a woman who had moved to Italy with her husband in June 1945 and, upon divorcing him eight months later, had made her way to UNRRA's care in Bari. Whereas these latter cases reflected the fragmentation of families that necessitated humanitarian repatriation, other Italians adopted the breadwinner language to argue that they could best maintain their family financially by returning to their businesses and homes in Rhodes. This was the case made by one Giovanni Paradiso, whose wife and children had been evacuated to Italy in 1942. Though the documents fail to mention how Paradiso himself either remained in Rhodes or made his way back there, he claimed that he possessed steady employment and could support his family. On these grounds and those of family reunification, he requested that his wife, two children, and niece—whom he labeled "refugees" (although it is unclear what this status signified juridically in such a situation)—be permitted to migrate back to Rhodes. Paradiso also noted that he could pay the family's travel expenses for such repatriation.[164]

That individuals like Paradiso made applications to UNRRA, even though the BMA and the Allied authorities in Italy possessed the final say over such matters, likely points to continued confusion over who possessed both responsibility and authority for the repatriations of Italians to and from the former possessions. At the same time, however, it also suggests how individuals sought to exploit such ambiguity in the pursuit of their interests. In light of the BMA's relatively hard stance against Italian returns to the islands, for example, perhaps Paradiso hoped that UNRRA might intercede in his case or that somehow he could slip through the cracks between interim governance (the BMA) and intergovernmental operations (UNRRA). Certainly, some displaced Italians were willing to try whoever and whatever might permit them to return "home." In Tripolitania, this meant clandestine immigration when all other means failed.

As discussed in chapters 1 and 2, the mass evacuation of Italian settler children and some women from Libya in 1940, as well as conscription of adult men and internment of POWs, led to long and painful separations for families that had called Italy's "fourth shore" home. Italian propaganda had encouraged such settlers to see their absence from Africa as temporary, and the dream of return had sustained many during long years of war and even imprisonment. Despite Italian claims (and illusions) that most Libyans would welcome the return of Italian rule, the BMA knew otherwise. In October 1944, a group of Libyans submitted a petition opposing a possible return of Italian administration in the country and carried out a protest in Tripoli. The Libyan Nationalist Party (al hizh- al-watani), initially an underground group at its formation in 1944 and then officially recognized by the BMA in April 1946, pledged itself to working with the BMA to maintain order and to halt Italian immigration into Libya.[165]

The BMA's political considerations soon clashed with humanitarian ones, particularly demands for family reunification. As early as September 1945, some of the children evacuated to the peninsula had begun to rejoin their families in Libya, with five groups totaling 1,491 individuals departing Italy for Libya. The return of these children owed much to the efforts of Tripoli's bishop, Monsignor Facchinetti. Well known for his fascist sympathies, Facchinetti had traveled to Rome in July 1944 one month after its liberation to intercede with both Pope Pius and the Allied authorities to permit the children of Italians still in Libya to rejoin their parents.[166]

Italian documents refer to an accord reached on the question of Italian children between the Pontificia Commissione di Assistenza and the Allied authorities during the summer of 1945. Acting as intermediary at the request of the Ministry of Italian Africa, the PCA facilitated the return of children to the colony on ships staffed by CRI personnel.[167] The ACC and the BMA sought to regulate such movements through what was called the "breadwinner's scheme." Similar to regulations set out for the Dodecanese, the breadwinner's scheme stated, "in whatever country the breadwinner is found, his family will be authorized to join him in that country"; thus, "if the head of the family is in Italy and his family is in Tripoli, the family can be authorized to join him in Italy," and, vice versa, "if the breadwinner resides, for example, in Tripoli and his family is in Italy, the family can be authorized to join him in Tripoli."[168] In later negotiations with representatives of the Ministry of Italian Africa who visited Tripoli on an official mission in October 1946, the BMA further specified that breadwinners needed to be "usefully employed" and included among permissible dependents the elderly (persons sixty-five or older).[169]

Under the breadwinner principle, the Italian government had approved the arrival of a ship from Tripoli in August 1945 carrying fifty-eight women and children whose breadwinners resided in Italy. But just as the BMA worried about too many Italians seeking (re)entry in Libya, the still fragile Italian government sought to control repatriation from the territory and accused the BMA of allowing unauthorized repatriations to the peninsula. In November 1945, for instance, the Ministry of Foreign Affairs sent a memo to the Allied Commission complaining about the arrival in Naples in September of a ship carrying 118 repatriates. The BMA had given the Italian authorities no notice of this sailing, nor could the repatriates—almost all of them male workers or artisans—be considered dependents joining breadwinners in Italy. The following month another ship, carrying 380 repatriates from Tripoli, had arrived in Taranto without Italian authorization. By contrast, only in rare cases did those Italians seeking to repatriate to Tripolitania and with legitimate claims to join breadwinners in Libya find themselves permitted entry by the British authorities. In practice, then, the British generally promoted one-way repatriation to Italy and rejected claims about home and kin (that is, claims of belonging) in Libya. After underlining the failure of the BMA to follow its own principles on repatriation, the Italian Foreign Ministry requested that the ACC (re)consider this problem from a humanitarian, as well as social and economic, point of view.[170]

The BMA, however, later yoked its humanitarian breadwinners policy of family reunification to a head-to-head scheme designed to ensure that at least as many Italians repatriated from Libya as repatriated back to it.[171] Similar attempts to balance flows between those repatriating *to* and those repatriating *from* the African territories (or at least to ensure that those repatriating back to Africa did not exceed those repatriating to Italy) also appear to have operated in Somalia and Eritrea.[172] Italian settlers stranded in the peninsula and frustrated by the BMA's selective policies of return in practice began to take advantage of Libya's porous sea border and proximity to Italy to make their way across the Mediterranean as clandestine immigrants. The Sicilian city of Syracuse became a well-known departure point from which small-boat operators smuggled Italians—particularly children and young adults—back to Tripolitania. During the war years, Sicily had become home to a number of Italians displaced from Libya; large concentrations of Italians from Libya were to be found in the towns of Catania, Caltanisetta, Messina, Ragusa, Termini Imerese, and Trapani, many of these receiving assistance from Italian authorities in the form of housing and food rations.[173]

Lord Rennell highlighted such movements from Sicily to Libya as having "caused the Administration much trouble." Although these unauthorized reentries had occurred from 1943 on, he noted,

> But early in 1946 the movement assumed the form of an organised traffic: this could hardly have been carried on without the knowledge of the Italian Authorities, since nearly all the boats came from Syracuse, leaving that port in daylight, with up to 250 persons aboard each craft. The boats reached the Tripolitanian coast under cover of darkness, unloaded their passengers, and endeavoured to be away again and out of sight of land before daybreak. No two landings were made at the same place. The arrivals had all formerly lived in Tripolitania, and most were women and children seeking to rejoin their family breadwinners.[174]

In response to these flows, after 26 February 1946 the BMA temporarily suspended reentry not just of children but of all Italians, including those who claimed to be "refugees" from Libya. UNRRA documents state that by 1946, Italians seeking return to Libya or any of the former colonies had to "apply through the UNRRA Repatriation Office. They then communicate with a relative in the area to which they wish to return, asking them to apply to the local Military Authority for permission to enter this area." At the same meeting at which this procedure was laid out, however, it was admitted that there existed confusion in practice as to the extent of UNRRA's responsibilities and its appropriate ministerial interlocutor and partner within the Italian government.[175] In the midst of this ambiguous situation, the BMA began to deport intercepted migrants and continued to do so into 1947, when clandestine flows again began to tick upward. The BMA sent 140 illegal immigrants back to Italy on the *Endeavour* and another 30 on the *Toscana* in April 1947.[176] At that time, the British authorities claimed they had shown "extreme leniency in dealing with this problem." The BMA contended that "out of a total of 2,600 Italians who have entered the territory illegally only 190 have been deported to Italy, in spite of the considerable hostility which had been aroused among the native Arab population by their illegal arrival." The British embassy warned that from this point on, their representatives would take a harder line toward both the migrants and the boat operators trafficking them.[177] Such deportees may have been more fortunate, however, than clandestine migrants who ran across Libyans. Rumors circulated that, upon landing, some illegal migrants had been robbed and beaten up by locals.[178]

These restrictive BMA policies prompted petitions and appeals of various sorts. Individual Italians continued to send appeals to UNRRA for assistance in returning to Libya and other colonies. In July 1946, the Italian mission estimated it received approximately twenty-five such requests each week. In the spring of that year, a local representative of Italians in Tripoli had also sent a memo to Brigadier General Blackley of the BMA requesting that Italian citizens with land, property, or businesses in Libya be granted entry "regardless of sex or age," but these requests fell on deaf ears.[179] Monsignor Facchinetti likewise appealed to UNRRA, and Monsignor Baldelli of the Pontificia Commissione di Assistenza urged the Italian prime minister to press the BMA to permit "repatriation" to Libya as a humanitarian gesture to reunite families.[180] According to Baldelli, as late as August 1946 over eight thousand Italian children still remained separated from their parents in Libya.

Memoirs and testimonies of former colonists often focus on the anxiety of waiting for news about and the safe return of family members to Libya. As noted in chapter 2, for example, the diary of settler Giacomo Cason was filled with anguish regarding his separation from his daughters. In June 1947, the three girls finally returned to Libya after seven years on the Italian peninsula.[181] In other instances, the age limits placed by the BMA on who counted as "children" (sixteen years for boys, twenty for girls) prevented or delayed such family reunifications. One repatriation request filed in 1947 revolved around a worker in Tripoli who wished for his wife and seven children to join him in Libya. His oldest son, Massimo, was three months too old for the age cutoff and had been denied permission to return to the ex-colony. Massimo's parents pleaded that he be allowed entry on compassionate grounds, as he had suffered a hand injury during a bombardment while in one of the mainland camps for *bimbi libici*; although those children had been evacuated in the name of their safety, in reality they often faced neglect and after 1943 greater dangers of actual warfare than those children who had managed to remain in Tripoli. On his own in Italy and unable to work owing to his injury, Massimo would be left alone with few prospects. The BMA demanded a medical certificate of his disability. In responding to such requests, the colonists themselves asserted whatever agency they possessed, tailoring narratives to the humanitarian requirements of the BMA.[182] INPS officials who temporarily resumed control over its agricultural settlements in Libya with the cessation of the BMA in 1951 similarly scrutinized health claims made by settlers seeking repatriation and complained about the circulation of fraudulent medical certificates.[183]

Individuals thus employed a number of strategies to overcome the restrictions placed on repatriation, particularly repatriation back to Africa: appeals based on compassionate grounds to the BMA and to UNRRA and, in the final instance, illegal migration. Settlers employed other stratagems, as well, as in the case of Fabio Chiodi, who returned as a young man to Libya in 1947 on a boat from Naples by lying to BMA officials that his parents remained in Tripoli. In reality, his parents in Florence had sent him to his grandparents, who in Libya enjoyed plentiful food in comparison to his impoverished family members in the metropole.[184] Although Chiodi's parents no doubt saw their choice as one to best ensure their child's future, the Italian government looked skeptically upon similar cases. An Italian mission to Tripoli in 1946 (the first such delegation permitted by the BMA) reported that "many of these clandestine immigrants were pushed to adventure more by the discomfort in which they lived in Italy and the hopes of finding a good setup in Tripolitania."[185] Like UNRRA, the IRO, and subsequently the UNHCR, the Italian government drew a sharp distinction between so-called economic migrants and those compelled to move by force or fate.

By the end of 1946, the Italian authorities appear to have established a better working relationship with the BMA in Tripolitania as a result of two official delegations to the territory in October and November of that year. The Italian government had obtained the BMA's reassurances that it would not allow Italians to repatriate to Italy without the approval of Italian authorities, suggesting that many in Italy remained unwilling to host flows of impoverished colonial settlers. In accepting the principle of equal exchanges of repatriates to and from Libya, according to the terms of the head-to-head plan, the Italian authorities even admitted to the disparities in organization of such movements. Reporting on the arrival of repatriates in Tripoli, members of the second Italian mission there recounted that the BMA's organization on the receiving end was "really perfect."[186] Members of the mission had traveled with the children and family members returning to Tripoli on the *Miraglia*, the same ship previously employed in repatriating Italians from the Dodecanese Islands. Monsignor Facchinetti, accompanied by a nun and two friars, also traveled with the group in his role as protector and advocate of the *bimbi libici*. After arriving in Tripoli, the disembarked families "were already home in their houses by early afternoon while the same evening almost all the children of the colony were taken by truck to the villages where their parents lived."[187]

According to the Italian representatives, Italian arrangements for those leaving the former colony lacked the precision of the British. Until the last moment, there was confusion over the candidates on the repatriation rolls and multiple changes. Repatriates also routinely ignored the limits on personal baggage, arriving in port with excess trunks and cases. Even more troublesome was the discovery of fifteen stowaways among the returning POWs and approved repatriates on the return voyage to Italy. Snuck aboard with the complicity of the crew and the officials, these clandestine migrants to Italy claimed to have feared applying for repatriation through the BMA since they lacked the necessary documents.[188] As this incident suggests, the traffic in illegal repatriation / migration went both ways across the Mediterranean.

The demand for Italian repatriation *to* Africa, including illegal immigration, thus assumed its greatest dimensions in Tripolitania. As late as March 1948, the BMA reported on six hundred individuals who had been evacuated from Libya as children and wished to return to Tripolitania.[189] At the same time, BMA officials worried that the attempt to correct the previous imbalance between repatriations from Libya versus those to Libya threatened to create a precarious underclass of impoverished Italians in the former colony. "In the period between October 1948 to January 1949 some 1197 persons have been allowed to return from Italy to resettle in Tripolitania, while only 101 persons have returned to Italy from Tripoli," noted one memo. "While in this way the over-all balance between movements in either direction has been adjusted, the British Military Administration cannot overlook the fact that during that period there have been no less than 1400 destitute Italians in Tripoli depending for their existence on relief organisations." Echoing the concerns of earlier fascist colonial authorities, the BMA worried about the "unfavourable impression in local native circles" created by such impoverished Italians and demanded that Italy repatriate these pauperized citizens. If Italy did not, the BMA would "be regrettably obliged to suspend the issue of entry permits to persons in Italy desiring to resettle in Tripoli."[190]

In contrast to Tripolitania, the majority of Italians still in the former AOI sought repatriation back to Italy, although even here some Italians requested repatriation *to* East Africa and others demanded the right to move freely between their two homelands of Italy and Africa.[191] Some of the same ships—including the *Vulcania*—that had served as *navi bianche* evacuating civilians from Ethiopia, Eritrea, and Somalia in 1942 and 1943 once again plied the waters of the Red Sea and the Mediterranean carrying Italian nationals to the peninsula after the war. In October 1946, the *Toscana* brought the first Italian diplomatic mission to Somalia since the 1943 evacuations. A local Comitato Italiano della Somalia, similar to the civilian committees sanctioned by the BMA in Libya, Eritrea, and the Dodecanese Islands, presented the mission with a memo in which members lamented the plan for one-way repatriations. In the months preceding the delegation's arrival, a few Italians had succeeded in traveling to Italy, only to learn they could not return to Somalia. Those Italians now being promised passage to Italy on the *Toscana*, continued the memo, feared that this, too, would be "a voyage without return," and the committee stressed the urgency of finding a "remedy to this state of things," which the author considered "contrary to the most elementary rights." After praising the loyalty and attachment of these Italians in Somalia to the motherland, the memo nonetheless urged, "These Italians thus need to be able to travel to and from Italy with a certain liberty and to travel on their own and to also see free travel of their kin, their dependents or their representatives."[192] In addition, given that Italians traveling out of Somalia often crossed through other states, the memo writer requested diplomatic assistance to facilitate the procuring of relevant travel documents and permissions. After years of isolation, then, many Italians asserted their right to move freely between Somalia and Italy, rather than a desire for a definitive and one-way departure from East Africa.

The Italian governmental representatives who received this appeal from the Italian community of Somalia appear to have taken it to heart. When Enrico Olivieri arrived in Mogadishu on the *Vulcania*'s first postwar voyage to ex-AOI as part of an Italian mission there in February 1947, he presented to BMA officials a list of 505 individuals seeking repatriation back to Somalia in order to join the family breadwinner. He also discussed the need for Italians to receive temporary transit visas to Italy. Olivieri reported that the BMA proved cooperative.[193] The 1946 and 1947 voyages of the former *navi bianche* thus repatriated some civilians back to East Africa, although the numbers repatriating to Italy were always much larger. Whereas the BMA operated a head-to-head scheme in Libya and the Dodecanese, a 1947 note from the British Embassy in Rome to the Italian Ministry of Foreign Affairs suggests that the BMA in Eritrea instead held to a 1-to-5 ratio (one repatriation to Eritrea for every five from the former colony) as a minimum.[194]

The *Vulcania*'s voyage in February 1947, for example, brought 77 Italians "home" to Somalia and then carried back to Italy 2,400 civilian repatriates and former POWs from Mombasa, Mogadishu, and Massaua.[195] A month later, 325 Italians (including 10 friars and 9 monks) returned to Somalia. Encouraged by this, the head of the Italian mission Bruno Santangelo recommended the repatriation to the African territory of "a contingent of Italians, greater in numbers and quality, than those who must be accepted for repatriation [to Italy]." Santangelo further recommended initiatives to stimulate the local economy in order to prevent a mass exodus by Italians out of East Africa.[196]

The report filed by the governmental representative Mario Franco Rossi, part of the Italian mission to Eritrea, indicated such a danger had become all too real there. In November 1946 Rossi wrote, despairingly, "The desire to repatriate [to Italy] among our co-nationals in Eritrea has assumed a morbid form of collective psychosis." As a result, the mass of Italians there "want to repatriate and repatriate immediately, without delay," a comment that pointed to the Italian government's continuing desire to control and regulate repatriation out of the former colonies.[197] A few months earlier, the British government had pressed the Italian government to accept greater numbers of Italian repatriates from Eritrea, claiming that twenty thousand Italian civilians "are most anxious to return to Italy," together with another ten thousand internees in British East Africa.[198] In response, there had arisen a lively trade in illicit voyages between Massaua and Italy; for the cost of £50 sterling, one could illegally migrate to the peninsula. Rather than demonstrating compassion for the desperation that drove such trips, Rossi further pathologized these Italians languishing in the former colony. "A mass that has reached such a degree of selfishness and indifference to any ideal is more likely to injure than benefit us [Italy]." In rhetoric reminiscent of fascist concerns over settler behavior that could damage white prestige, Rossi lamented that some of these Italians lived off thefts and petty cons and, what was most damning in the eyes of natives, even allowed local prostitutes to support them. This antipathy to the Italians of Eritrea appeared to be reciprocated, as Rossi recounted violent threats made against him by Italian nationals in the camp at Ghinda.[199]

Where possible, then, the Italian government hoped to keep its nationals in place in the overseas possessions. This policy reflected the desire to maintain a viable presence and claim upon these territories until their disposition had been settled, as well as the fear that influxes of impoverished repatriates—who had become increasingly vocal in pressing claims upon the Italian state as national refugees—could overwhelm an already fragile political and economic situation in the Italian peninsula. Attempting to control and regulate the return of Italian nationals also offered the Italian state a form of agency, although the decisions of other actors (like the British in Africa and the Dodecanese) often forced the hand of the Italian government. The 1947 Peace Treaty with Italy altered this situation and the calculus of both Italian settlers and the Italian state alike about the prospects for permanent residence in the overseas territories.

The Shock of 1947: Delimiting the New Italy, Shrinking and Expanding Sovereignty

> At this hour, night will fall on one of the saddest days in our history. . . . My brothers, you who have been unfairly forced out of your homeland, may you have in your hearts the certainty—and nurture that certainty every day—that Italy will not abandon you, because there are no borders that can break ties of blood and civilization, the ties that unite you to the populous and ever growing Italian family.
>
> May this voice of mine, sad but resolute, be of consolation also to those in the refugee camps in Africa and among the Italians left in the old colonies which, through the hard work and the adaptable intelligence of our colonists, were economically renewed and raised to a civilized way of life.
>
> Alcide De Gasperi on the Peace Treaty of 1947

The 1947 Peace Treaty with Italy delineated a new cartography for the Italian state, as well as specifying agreements on issues such as disarmament, debts, and reparations. While many observers in Italy then (and now) claimed the treaty proved less the result of a negotiation than a diktat imposed by the Allied powers[200]—the inevitable outcome and symbol of Italy's limited sovereignty—the treaty actually restored formal Italian sovereignty. One legal scholar has underlined how "the day the Treaty became effective Italy returned as an equal member of the community of nations."[201] For many, however, this sovereignty remained limited in the sense that Italy now ruled over much less territory than it had before 1943. Unsurprisingly, not only did the treaty's ratification in the Italian Constituent Assembly occasion bitter debate (with the treaty approved in August 1947 and entering into force 15 September 1947) but also immediate demands for its revision.[202]

The moment of the treaty's signing in Paris on 10 February 1947 prompted mourning, protest, and angry resignation: flags were lowered to half mast, a siren was followed by a moment of silence, veterans massed in front of national monuments, and the Constituent Assembly suspended its session for a half hour.[203] In Pula / Pola, the principal city of the Istrian peninsula and part of the territory ceded to Yugoslavia by the treaty, Italian patriot Maria Pasquinelli assassinated British brigadier Robert de Winton. In a letter found on her person at the crime scene, Pasquinelli railed against de Winton as a representative of what critics of the Peace Conference called "peace by force,"[204] that is, as "the man who is unfortunate enough to represent the Four Great Powers that, at the conference in Paris, in violation of justice, against humanity, and against political wisdom, have decided to tear out once again from the maternal womb the lands most sacred to Italy, condemning them either to the experiments of a new Danzig or, with a chilling sensibility and complicity, to the Yugoslav yoke."[205] Pasquinelli's dramatic act, as well as the widespread outcry over the treaty, puts paid to the myth that Italian decolonization occasioned no "traumatic" aftershocks.

Despite the perceived harshness and definitive nature of the treaty, some Italians in places like Libya, Somalia, and the areas of Venezia Giulia that became the redrawn Zone B of Istria (including the towns of Koper / Capodistria, Izola / Isola, Piran / Pirano, and Buje / Buie) actually held out hope that they might still remain under Italian rule. The Italian government nurtured such hopes; just nine months after the treaty's signing and two months after it entered into force, Italy made a formal request to the UN that it be awarded trusteeships over Eritrea, Somalia, and Tripolitania.[206] This act was emblematic of Italian priorities, for, as Giampaolo Calchi Novati has noted, "On the agenda of Italian foreign policy in the aftermath of World War II, the colonial issue was second in importance only to the dispute with Yugoslavia over Trieste."[207]

The negotiations at Paris that resulted in the treaty had mobilized considerable support within Italy for the maintenance of (at least) some of Italy's overseas possessions. Groups defining themselves as *profughi* from the African possessions—as well as individuals still in Africa who considered themselves refugees, like those Italians evacuated from Cyrenaica to Tripolitania in advance of Allied forces in 1942 and 1943—offered testimonies to the negotiators at Paris. One document prepared for Paris, for example, made familiar arguments about Italy's right to the African colonies on the basis of the considerable money and energy invested in their betterment, as well as the sacrifices of settlers who had built Italian Libya and AOI and now faced unemployment and hardship in the peninsula. According to this line of argument, the repatriations of Italians from places like the Balkans and Tunisia only worsened the situation of these Italians who had come to the peninsula from Italian Africa and who longed to return "home" to reap the fruits of their labor.[208] Aiming to reach a broad audience, refugee groups presented memoranda in English and French; others sent letters to James Byrnes, US secretary of state, and Harold Macmillan, among others, demanding, "Give Italy a Just Peace, not a rancorous one!"[209] If De Gaulle and his supporters later sought to reframe defeat and decolonization in Algeria as the inevitable and positive outcome of both a linear civilizing process and the "tide of history," as Todd Shepard has argued, in Italy forcible decolonization instead prompted a sense of being struck by a disastrous tidal wave of history that threatened to obliterate the labors of generations of Italian emigrants to the possessions.[210]

As efforts by groups of "refugee" settlers from these possessions to make their voices and wishes heard demonstrate, the 1946 Peace Conference (at which peace treaties were determined not only with Italy but also Bulgaria, Finland, Hungary, and Romania) became a site for intense campaigning by lobby groups. Though these actors remain much less remembered or studied than the various groups and minorities inspired by the "Wilsonian moment" who sought self-determination at the 1919 Paris Peace Conference, they often cited similar principles.[211] In particular, delegates at Paris, like a pro-Italian one from the contested Julian lands, invoked articles 2 and 3 of the 1941 Atlantic Charter. As the Julian delegate argued, these articles rejected "territorial changes that do not accord with the freely expressed wishes of the peoples concerned" and respected the "right of all peoples to choose the form of Government under which they will live; and they wish to see sovereign rights and self-government restored to those who have been forcibly deprived of them."[212] Such sentiments echoed those of more prominent delegates, such as the former Italian prime minister Ivanoe Bonomi, who likewise invoked the Atlantic Charter as compatible with Italian trusteeships over its African territories.[213] With the war's conclusion, some in the Italian Ministry of Foreign Affairs had encouraged the refugee associations in their efforts, seeing in them (particularly those from Africa) "the best instrument, given their essentially humanitarian character, with which to keep alive in Italian public opinion the Italian colonial question, and which therefore should be encouraged."[214]

The voices of colonial displacees also sought to counter those of the former colonized and occupied calling for the prosecution of Italian war crimes. The Ethiopian delegate to the Peace Conference at Paris, for example, helped press for the recognition that for Ethiopia, World War II would be considered to have begun with the Italian invasion in 1935 (articulated in article 38 of the treaty), thereby making it possible for the UN War Crimes Commission to prosecute war crimes and crimes against humanity committed during the East Africa campaign. The Ethiopian delegation did succeed in submitting the names of ten Italians to that commission, but diplomatic wrangling, logistical and political problems, and the weakness of Ethiopia vis-à-vis the West ultimately derailed these efforts.[215]

Even more than in the case of the African colonies with which it was entangled, the Julian dispute led to a furious propaganda war, with many pro-Yugoslav and pro-Italian pamphlets published in English and French with the aim of influencing negotiators at Paris.[216] Both sides massed bodies and space in this contest, as the city of Trieste's central square, Piazza Unità d'Italia, became the site of frequent demonstrations for either the Italian or the Yugoslav side. The Istrian peninsula's landscape was marked by pro-Tito writings and graffiti, some of them the product of a top-down campaign orchestrated by local authorities, others the expressions of spontaneous support.[217] The immediate audience for these demonstrations of loyalty was the Council of Foreign Ministers' Commission of Experts made up of delegates from Great Britain, France, the United States, and the USSR and sent to visit the territory between 9 March and 5 April 1946 with the aim of providing "objective" information to the Great Powers at Paris determining Italy's eastern borders. In April of that same year a similar commission visited the contested Briga and Tenda area ultimately given to France. Each delegation to the Julian region recommended at Paris a different demarcation of the border. Ultimately, this commission failed "to provide the peace talks with a scientific border, or strategy for the Venezia Giulia and Istria regions that might have distinguished an objective ethnic line or a predominant local preference, or transcended the political differences amongst its experts," contends Glenda Sluga.[218]

As Sluga's assessment highlights, the 1947 treaty left many issues surrounding Italy's former territories unresolved. James Byrnes, US secretary of state and a key protagonist at Paris, included the Italian agreement among the "unfinished treaties" that resulted from the 1946 Paris conference.[219] Tracey Watts, the legal secretary of the BMA in Cyrenaica, maintained that the treaty actually rendered Italy's legal position in its former colonies "one of considerable uncertainty."[220] In a speech in Paris the month before the treaty's signing, Prime Minister De Gasperi went so far as to call it a "provisional peace" (*una pace provvisoria*). He gave expression to the Italian belief that the treaty took inadequate account of Italy's efforts to liberate itself from fascism and Nazi occupation through military cooperation with Allied forces as a co-belligerent, as well as of the sacrifices made by the partisans. De Gasperi asked pointedly of those negotiating with Italy, "Italy would have suffered the sanctions for its fascist past, but, putting that past in its grave, everyone should find themselves equal in the spirit of a new international collaboration. But can we believe it is such? Evidently, this is your intention, but the text of the treaty speaks another language."[221]

So what did this other "language" actually lay out? Articles 1–14 (part 1) of the treaty demarcated Italy's frontiers and borders. Article 23 (part 2, section 4) referred to territorial possessions in Africa (Libya, Eritrea, Italian Somaliland), over which Italy renounced all claim. Articles 33–38 (section 7) dealt with Ethiopia, whose sovereignty Italy recognized. Articles 27 to 32 (section 6) acknowledged Albanian sovereignty. The disposition of the Aegean Islands and the areas awarded to France was similarly clear and unambiguous; article 14 ceded the Dodecanese Islands to Greece, and article 2 redrew the French-Italian border. Likewise, article 3 awarded a large area of the disputed region of Venezia Giulia to Yugoslavia, including the city of Pula / Pola. The remainder of the contested territory became part of a Free Territory of Trieste (FTT) encompassing the area roughly from Duino / Devin in the west to the Istrian town of Novigrad / Cittanova in the southeast and whose autonomy was to be guaranteed by the UN Security Council (articles 21 and 22).

The growing tensions of what would become the Cold War meant that the Free Territory never was realized in practice as a functioning entity. The FTT's Permanent Statute called for a governor appointed by the UN Security Council and a Council of Government derived from an elected Popular Assembly. Cold War rivalries, however, prevented any agreement among members of the Security Council upon a candidate for governor. Given the inability of the Security Council to provide for governance over the FTT, the area was divided into a Zone A administered by an Anglo-American Allied Military Government and a Zone B administered by Yugoslav military authorities.[222] This situation replicated in miniature the stalemate that had existed prior to the 1947 Peace Treaty, even as it finalized Italy's loss of large swaths of territory in Istria, as well as the Kvarner (the islands of Cres / Cherso and Lošinj / Lussino) and Dalmatia (Zadar / Zara, Palagruža / Pelagosa). The FTT, then, demonstrated the weakness of a certain form of intergovernmentalism—"free cities" guaranteed protection by an international body like the United Nations or, before it, the League of Nations. The provisions for the Free Territory of Trieste looked back to recent historical precedents (blasted by zealous patriots like Maria Pasquinelli) such as the Free City of Danzig created by the 1919 Versailles Treaty and under the protection of the League of Nations, and the Free State of Fiume (Stato Libero di Fiume) delimited by the Treaty of Rapallo and in existence between 1920 and 1924.[223] The Stato Libero di Fiume became a member of the League of Nations in 1921. Neither arrangement succeeded for long, revealing the weakness of autonomist solutions promoted and "guaranteed" by intergovernmental organizations in the aftermaths of both the World Wars.

The 1954 Memorandum of Understanding would clarify the ambiguous status of the Julian area, awarding Zone A to Italy and Zone B to Yugoslavia. Although this decision was seen as signaling the return of Italian sovereignty over Trieste and its environs and "rejoining" or redeeming an irredentist territory to the *madrepatria* yet again, as had happened in 1919, this occurred as a result of pressure by Great Britain and the United States. Weary of long and thankless years maintaining Allied Military Government over Zone A, after 1948 the British and Americans proved more favorably disposed to a socialist Yugoslavia that had definitively broken with the Soviet Union and the Cominform. As a result, they pushed forward the negotiations that broke the political and diplomatic impasse over the territory. While this solved the situation on the ground, it was only the 1975 Treaty of Osimo between Italy and Yugoslavia that finalized and formalized what amounted to a territorial partition of the Free Territory of Trieste and the wider territory. Not surprisingly, ratification of the 1975 treaty gave rise to considerable protest within Trieste. While Osimo ostensibly resolved at long last the Trieste question, Yugoslavia's dissolution in 1991 led some Italian nationalists to press unsuccessfully for a reopening of the territorial controversy. The protracted and messy nature of the dispute over Trieste and the wider Venezia Giulia area puts into question the claims by some international studies scholars that Trieste represents an exemplary case study in successful dispute resolution.[224]

Whereas the 1947 Peace Treaty's provisions regarding the FTT made for a long period of uncertainty over that particular territory's status, the treaty instead renounced Italy's claims to its African colonies. Yet even here, "final disposal" of those territories was "to be determined jointly by the Governments of the Soviet Union, of the United Kingdom, of the United States of America, and of France within one year from coming into force of the present Treaty." Annex 11 stipulated that the Four Powers would send out commissions to the former colonies in Africa in order "to ascertain the views of the local population." If they were unable to make a decision, the issue would be referred to the United Nations for a recommendation, entrusting the final disposition of the Italian colonies to an emergent form of intergovernmentalism.

This is precisely what occurred in the case of Libya, Eritrea, and Somalia. In keeping with the stipulations of annex 11, in 1948 a Four Power Commission composed of French, British, American, and Soviet representatives visited Libya to gauge the desires of the local population. Two organizations represented the Italian community: the Comitato rappresentativo (neofascist in its outlook) and the much smaller Associazione per il progresso della

Libia (left oriented and in favor of Libyan independence).[225] The commission also made a three-day stopover in Rome to hear out associations of Italian refugees from Africa. When the commission failed to reach agreement, the assistant secretary-general of the UN Adrian Pelt assumed the role of UN commissioner in Libya. Beginning his work in 1949, Pelt oversaw the creation of a constitution and the establishment of an independent Libyan state in 1951. There nonetheless remained many unsolved questions between Italy and Libya, and the negotiations that ultimately resulted in the 1956 Italo-Libyan Accords stalled for years over the issue of war reparations and the distinction between Italian public and private property.[226]

A similar scenario unfolded in Eritrea, where the Four Power Commission of Inquiry visited that same year. Traveling to fifteen centers across the territory, the commission received 173 written statements. Though representing a wide range of opinions, the declarations captured the sense of polarization between the emerging Eritrean Unionist and Muslim League parties.[227] When the commission failed to reach agreement, the issue went to the UN. A UN commission visited Eritrea in 1950, arriving in a moment of increased political tension between competing political parties around the issue of possible union with Ethiopia. The visit also "coincided with a wave of attacks on the Italian population in Eritrea," including the killing of nine Italians, according to reports at the Italian Ministry of Foreign Affairs. The months following the commission's visit witnessed assaults on a train station, the murder of an Italian police officer, and the fatal attack on Vittorio Longhi, a member of the Associazione Italo-Eritrea, a pro-independence group composed of mixed-race Italo-Eritreans.[228] A secret memo from the Italian Ministry of Foreign Affairs that year transmitted police reports from Naples on the arrival of the ship *Caserta* carrying seventy-eight "Italian refugees" from Eritrea who had pretended to be Holy Year pilgrims to Italy in order to receive BMA permission to depart.[229] The BMA in Eritrea would continue until 1952, at which time Eritrea was joined to Ethiopia in an unequal and ultimately disastrous federation.

The original Four Power commission also made a fact-finding trip to Italian Somalia. The arrival of the commission members on January 6 and 7, 1948, prompted demonstrations by pro-Italian Somalis (including *ascari* or former colonial soldiers) and pan-Somali political groups (most notably the League of Young Somalis, or SYL). In general, scholars have tended to discount the so-called Pro Italia parties, seeing them either as merely opportunistic responses to promises of Italian backing or "as a clan-based reaction to the SYL and more specifically a reflection of traditional cleavages between agro-pastoral and pastoral communities."[230] Annalisa Urbano has instead

FIGURE 8. Eritreans welcome the UN commission, 1950. Reproduced with permission of the United Nations Photo Archive. NICA ID=111611; Massawa, 01/02/1950. Copyright: UN Photo (Eritrea).

argued that questions of land played a critical role in debates over Somalia's future. In particular, the dynamic of Italian-British imperial rivalry and the cultivation of alliances with groups within Somalia "not only exacerbated tensions among different groups but also reduced the range of discussions about future dispositions."[231]

As the commission delegates in Mogadishu prepared to officially begin work on January 11 eliciting the views of these various groups, bombs were detonated at a printing press run by the Catholic mission and at a café popular with Italians. Clashes with demonstrators and an attack on the SYL headquarters sparked a riot, variously described as a massacre or a pogrom. Members of the Young Somali movement, some of whom had joined the local gendarmerie, began to attack Italians and loot their homes and businesses. The incident resulted in fifty-two Italian dead and forty-eight wounded, with fourteen Somalis killed and forty-three wounded. The BMA quickly appointed a commission of inquiry, though Italian and British observers disagreed over the interpretation of events and the assignation of blame.[232]

The riots prompted a wave of migration out of Somalia by frightened Italians. Almost immediately after the attacks, 142 Italians left Somalia (and another 62 Eritrea) as refugees on the ship *Sparta*, on which many survivors of the violence gave testimony about the events. Many of the individuals aboard accused British officials in the police force of connivance with anti-Italian demonstrators or even of outright participation in the violence, although these charges were never officially substantiated. This episode also led to protests in Italy, making highly visible the fate of the Italian community in Somalia and provoking anti-British comments in the Italian press.[233] The impact of this event at the time—particularly on the critical 1948 elections for the first Italian General Parliament—should not be overlooked. The events at Mogadishu "aroused a unanimous and spontaneous wave of indignation across the peninsula, foregrounding the African question. All the press were in agreement in deploring this as an offense to the dignity of Italy and as indicative of British opposition to Italy's return to Africa."[234] At the same time, the left-wing press also used this as an occasion to denounce the Western powers backing Italy's center-right against the Italian Communist Party in the elections. Less clear is the impact these events had upon the visiting commissioners.

Among other stakeholder groups, the commission representatives met on 22 January 1948 with the Comitato Rappresentativo Italiano headed by Barone Pietro Beritelli. This committee had already presented the commissioners with a memorandum urging that an Italian fiduciary trusteeship be established over former Italian Somalia. After quizzing the members of the *comitato* present on their views regarding issues such as the projected length and cost of a trusteeship, provisions for local education, and abolition of the fascist racial laws, the head of the US delegation asked about the argument made in the memorandum for the need to expand the Italian population in Somalia. Beritelli responded, "We were referring not to Somalia but to Italy in general, which has a proletariat that can provide manpower and intelligent work to all the colonies,"[235] thereby repeating long-standing claims about the need for outlets for Italy's surplus population. When the US delegate pressed the question, asking whether the committee believed Somalia *in particular* could sustain (Italian) immigration, Beritelli responded in the affirmative and countered that such migrants could find work in agriculture, fishing, and saltworks. In Beritelli's estimation, such emigration would contribute to Somalia's development, thereby honoring the terms of a potential fiduciary trusteeship. Italian rhetoric justifying maintenance of its colonies thus appears to have changed little with the demise of fascism, even if it now adapted itself to the new realities of the postwar world and the possibilities that Italy might hang on to limited sovereignty in the form of a trusteeship. Serious discussions occurred within the Ministry of Italian Africa in 1948 about the potential not only for Italian trusteeships in Africa, for example, but also the extension of Marshall Plan aid (granted to Italy in June of 1948) to such "colonial territories" (*territori coloniali*).[236] Likewise, some refugee organizations such as FeNPIA (Federazione dei Profughi Italiani d'Africa) continued to invoke the fascist regime's famous poster vowing "We will return," challenging the view that Italian Africa was lost forever.[237]

As with the Free Territory of Trieste, proposals for Italian trusteeships in Libya and Eritrea foundered on divisions between the Great Powers, divisions that (de)limited the power of the UN's brand of intergovernmentalism. These included not just East-West tensions but also differences among the Western Allies. In the case of Somalia, for example, the British floated the proposal for joining British and Italian Somaliland into a British trusteeship of Greater Somaliland; not only did the Soviet Union reject this idea as an imperial gesture, but the French and Americans did as well.[238] Ultimately, UN Resolution 289 (21 November 1949) awarded Italy the administration of fiduciary UN trusteeship over Somalia (Amministrazione Fiduciaria Italiana della Somalia or AFIS) between 1950 and 1960. AFIS thus entrusted to Italy, a state so recently renewed to its own full sovereignty, the task of preparing Somalia economically and politically for eventual independence. Italy's first act as administrator was to send sixty-five hundred troops and carabinieri to the former colony to replace the forces of the BMA. This also encouraged some of its citizens still resident and firms still operating in Ethiopia to migrate to trusteeship Somalia.[239]

This represented the only case in UN history of a trusteeship created with a fixed duration / end point and with oversight awarded to the former colonizer. Despite the modest or even questionable achievements of AFIS, in the estimation of historian Gian Paolo Calchi Novati it represented "the sole episode in which at the end of its presence in its African colonies Italy succeeded in creating the minimal conditions for a process of emancipation in which the two parties, the colonizers and the colonized, recognized and knew one another."[240] As I have suggested, however, into the 1950s and 1960s Italian entanglements continued even in those territories over which Italy no longer had any legal or formal control.

As the complex histories of the Four Power and subsequent UN commissions reveal, the 1947 Peace Treaty did not resolve the legal and political question of the disposition of Italy's Oltremare possessions and the fate of Italian citizens residing in them. Into 1951, in fact, the Italian government authorized considerable "secret political expenses" for pro-Italian propaganda among local Italophile elements in the former African territories.[241] While even after 1947 the Italian state sought to modulate repatriation out of its former African possessions, however, events like the pogrom in Mogadishu revealed that for many Italian citizens still in those territories, an irrevocable shift had occurred that made remaining much less desirable or even possible.

In Italy's former Balkan territories, the situation was different. As we have seen, in Albania the majority of Italians had been repatriated by 1947–1948. In 1949, most of the (ex-military) medical personnel detained in Albania by Hoxha finally received permission to return to Italy.[242] In 1951, further repatriations occurred, after which the Italian Ministry of Foreign Affairs claimed "there remain practically no Italians who are not imprisoned who desire to return to the Patria; very few co-nationals have asked and obtained permission to remain in Albania for personal reasons."[243] Nonetheless, another document from the same year acknowledges that Italians living "freely" in Albania were, in reality, "subject to strict surveillance and subjected to continual harassment. In fact, none of these tries to approach our Legation and if they meet someone from our Legation on the street they pretend not to know him."[244] Such an assessment demonstrates the Italian government's awareness that some Italian citizens remained in communist Albania, even if the Italian government treated the story of Italian presence there as a closed chapter. Many of these individuals and their descendants would remain in Albania until socialism's collapse there in 1991–1992.

In the areas of Venezia Giulia ceded to Yugoslavia by the 1947 Peace Treaty, by contrast, the fate of Italians would become highly publicized and instrumentalized. The most dramatic episode of mass migration out of that territory occurred in the period stretching from the conclusion of the treaty negotiations to its signing, as the city of Pula/Pola largely emptied in the space of several months. Admittedly, this exodus had already been under way, but the treaty intensified and accelerated the process. Smaller movements out of the city had already begun during its occupation by Yugoslav forces in May 1945. During the interregnum constituted by Pula/Pola's inclusion as an enclave in the Anglo-American AMG-administered Zone A, acts of violence like the deliberate explosion in August 1946 on the beach of Vergarola/Vergarolla of twelve pieces of ordnance that had been cleared from the sea disseminated fear. As with the Mogadishu Incident, the responsibility for this act (which killed some seventy individuals) remains hotly disputed by historians. Nonetheless, as also occurred at Mogadishu, the effect (whether intended or not) was to convince many residents who identified as Italian that there could be no future for them in a Yugoslav-controlled Pula/Pola.[245]

As events at the Paris negotiations wound up and made clear that Pula/Pola would be awarded to Yugoslavia, pro-Italian groups like the irredentist Lega Nazionale began to urge the AMG there to prepare for a large-scale migration out of the city. In response, Major J. A. Kellett, the AMG's chief public welfare officer in the city, prepared a special report on eventual evacuations. While Kellett expressed skepticism that the city's entire population would leave, he did note that assisting such a migration would become the responsibility of the Italian government, not the AMG, a division of labor already well established even before the war's conclusion.

This mass migration from Pola commenced in late December 1946. For both protagonists of the events and many Italian historians, this has often been viewed as a "preventive exodus" (*esodo preventativo*) that gave spontaneous expression to the Italianità of the city's population. In making this argument and reconstructing the psychological effect upon inhabitants as they saw businesses shuttered and their neighbors departing, historian Enrico Miletto draws on the extensive newspaper and newsreel coverage from the time.[246] The intense coverage of Pula / Pola's evacuation, however, could also be (and has been) interpreted as part of a more orchestrated form of political theater intended to send a message to the Great Powers and their publics about the fate of those Julian lands still in dispute. Whether in an act of humanitarianism or political strategy or a combination of both, the Comitato di Liberazione Nazionale dell'Istria (CLNI) helped direct the transfers by sea, which began on Christmas Eve 1946 in a well-timed display of Christian fear of persecution by Yugoslav communists.

By the beginning of February 1947, the Italian government began to provide direct assistance in the form of ship transports. Among the ships carrying Italian families and their personal effects out of Pula / Pola to the port cities of Venice, Ancona, and Bari was the *Toscana*, one of the ships that had repatriated Italians to and from AOI and Libya during and after the war.[247] Again, although the role of the Italian government in directing and orchestrating, as opposed to merely *responding* to, such migration remains debated, the authorities certainly sought to accelerate processes once they began.[248] An AMG briefing note contended, for example, "As the Italian Government plan for evacuation was working reasonably well there was a tendency for a number of people to attempt to delay their departure until the last possible minute. The announcement however by the Italian Authorities that the evacuation ship 'Toscana' would not be available after the first week of March had the desired effect and nearly all intended to leave left before the middle of March."[249] The government also issued certificates for those who were part of the "official" exodus that began on 24 December 1946. Initially, those who left prior to this date and thus lacked these certificates (which allowed family heads a daily assistance subsidy of 300 lire) were ineligible for aid. The Presidenza del Consiglio dei Ministro finally overturned this decision, ordering that in cases of exceptional need those without such certificates be provided an extraordinary subsidy.[250] Interestingly, as early as 7 December 1946, the CLN of Pola was informing frustrated supplicants that "the exodus from Pola has not yet 'officially' begun," revealing a clear-eyed understanding of the politics of recognition and the role of the Italian government in naming and legitimating (if not directing) such a migration.[251]

The special care and attention for the migrants from Pola also prompted demands by migrants from other former territories for similar assistance. Repatriates from the Dodecanese Islands, for instance, appealed to the Ministry of the Interior for subsidies like those provided "refugees" from Pula/Pola. The ministry replied that the Pola funds had an exceptional character and depended on the particular funds of the Ufficio per le Zone di Confine,[252] despite the fact that the 1947 treaty had decided the territorial disposition of both the Aegean Islands and the areas of Istria annexed by Yugoslavia. Other migrants from lost Julian territories, like the Dalmatian city of Zadar/Zara, used the Pola precedent to inquire whether they might also receive Italian state assistance with their movable property.[253] During this same period, complaints were registered in places like Bolzano, where Istrian migrants from Pola appeared to be receiving favored status over other Istrians.[254] Such debates point to what in 1947 was an emergent hierarchy of refugeedom—what we might even deem a "nesting refugeeism"—within Italy, as the Italian state addressed the needs of its own displacees over those of foreign refugees and also sought to distinguish deserving national refugees from other Italian migrants.

The creation of this hierarchy reflected the expansion of Italian sovereignty in the period under crisis. As I have demonstrated, the 1947 Peace Treaty remade Italy's boundaries and formally restored Italy's sovereignty, one that had been both challenged and forged through Italy's peculiar cobelligerency from 1943 to 1945, its prolonged occupation after the war by the Allied Military Government, the politics of aid and assistance of UN intergovernmentalism (particularly UNRRA), and the decolonization by Great Power fiat that occurred at the Paris Peace negotiations. In the aftermath of the 1947 treaty, determining, policing, and regulating the borders of citizenship would become a key site of sovereignty-making for the neophyte Italian Republic. As we shall see in the next chapter, the citizenship option set out in the 1947 treaty's articles 19 and 20 mapped imperfectly onto the identities of many residents of the ceded territories. "Indeterminate" individuals caught in the gaps between national refugee and international refugee, citizen and stranger, would prompt extended debates within the IRO over their eligibility for assistance. The challenges of classification extended far beyond those created by the treaty citizenship options, however, and provided a critical arena for rethinking the boundaries of belonging for a decolonizing, postfascist Italian state.

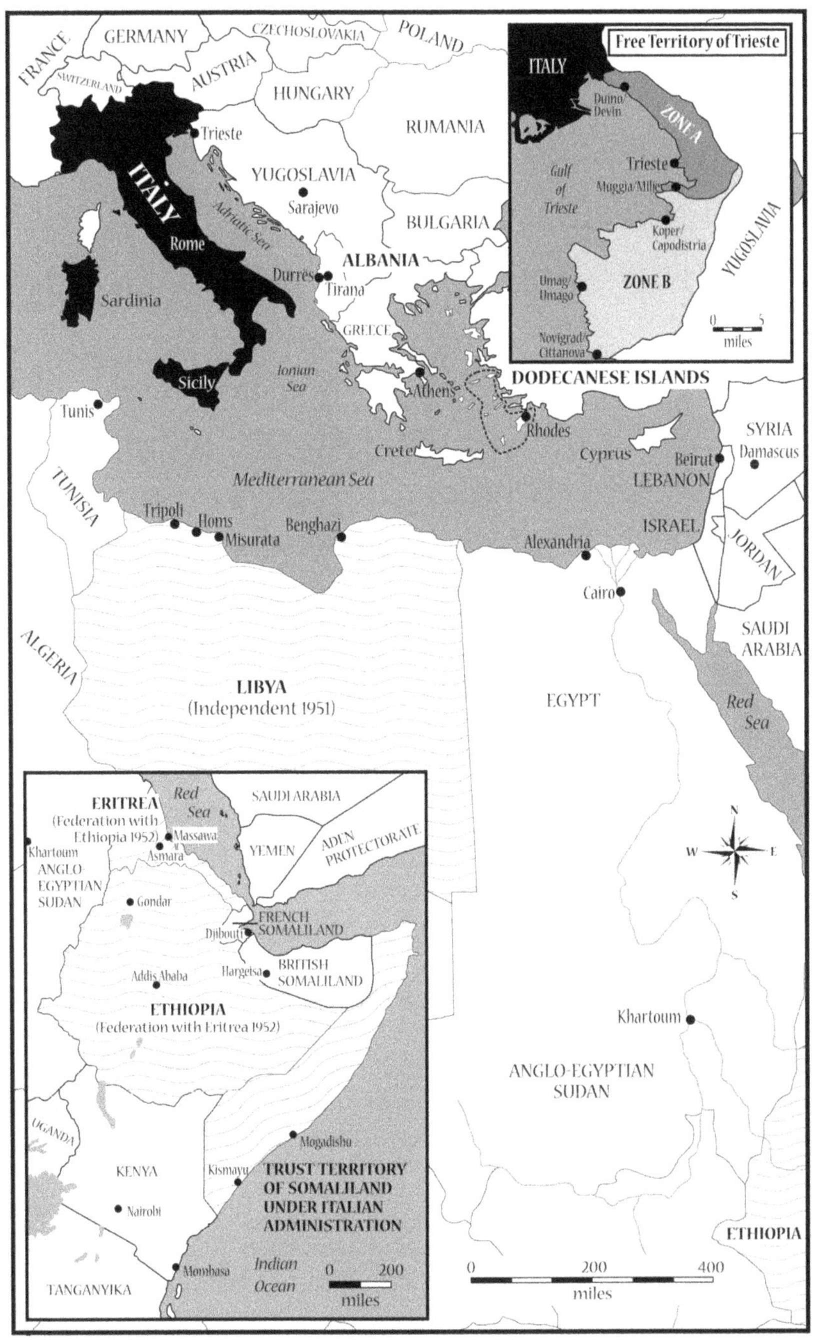

FIGURE 9. The road to decolonization: Italia Oltremare in 1952. Map designed by Mike Bechthold.

CHAPTER 4

Displaced Persons and the Borders of Citizenship

> The passport that you hold in your hand as you approach the immigration officer has a purpose and a coherence that is governed by its own rules. The passport chooses to tell its story about you. Is that story one of your own making? Can it ever be?
>
> Amitava Kumar, *Passport Photos* (2000)

> Crowds were walking towards the station where uniformed policemen stopped and searched them. Jama had never needed identification before, he had no paper saying who he was and where he belonged but from this point on, it would become a priority for him. In this society you were nobody unless you had been anointed with an identity by a bureaucrat.
>
> Nadifa Mohamed, *Black Mamba Boy* (2010)

In *Black Mamba Boy*, the fictionalized account of her father's difficult childhood, Nadifa Mohamed's young Somali protagonist Jama makes his way across the African continent in search of his father. He travels from Yemen to Italian East Africa to mandate Palestine and finally to Egypt, where in 1947 he is given work on a ship going from Port Said to Britain. On his journey, Jama is questioned at each turn for his papers. At a certain moment, Jama finds himself threatened with deportation from Egypt, his fate shared by many of his kinsmen. "The whole carriage was full of Somalis who had also entered Egypt illegally, all roamers who had only known porous insubstantial borders and were now confronted with countries caged behind barriers."[1] While Mohamed likely overstates the openness of colonial borders, she does capture a critical moment in time—the birth of the postwar international order—as states, borders, and citizenship regimes were redefined and solidified as a result of the Second World War, the global refugee crisis, the beginnings of decolonization, and the emergence of what would become the Cold War.

Historian Silvia Salvatici has characterized the postwar management of migratory flows of Italians from the former territories and of non-Italian displaced persons as producing a "binary regime for refugee care—[setting off] 'nationals' versus 'internationals,'"[2] a regime that reflected the broader "rescue of the nation-state" enshrined in postwar intergovernmentalism. Similarly, Italy's loss of empire and debates over classifying displacees produced a binary citizenship regime whose primary differentiation lay between citizens and aliens. At first glance, this appears a rather commonplace and uninteresting observation. After all, isn't the goal of citizenship to sort people into the categories of citizen and alien? In reality, however, the process of (re)making citizenship in Italy after 1945 flattened and simplified the complex hierarchical structure of citizenship that had existed during Italy's colonial era.

In theory, the distinctions that emerged after 1945 in Italy between citizen and foreigner—like those between national refugee and international refugee—were clear. These binary distinctions implied a division of labor and entitlements. The Italian state was responsible for its own citizens and national refugees, while foreigners remained under the protection of their country of citizenship. Those foreigners with no recourse to their home governments, who were stateless or who qualified as international refugees, instead became the responsibility of the UN agencies (first UNRRA, then the IRO, and subsequently the UNHCR) or organizations like the IGCR and ICEM (later the International Organization for Migration, or IOM).[3] As evidenced in chapter 3, however, in practice there existed a good deal of ambiguity and debate as to who should or would help Italy's "own" refugees. These debates over assistance reflected deeper dilemmas over determining just who among the displaced counted as an Italian.

In teasing out these ambiguities and entanglements, then, Salvatici's language of binary regimes proves most useful when we draw on the multiple meanings of the Italian term *binari*. *Binari* may refer not only to binaries and binarisms but also to *tracks* in both the figurative and literal sense. Like train tracks, which can run parallel, converge, or intersect at switching points, at key moments in the early postwar period the regimes of juridical classification and assistance established to manage the displaced in Italy intersected and overlapped. While in theory, for example, the Italian state ran camps for its nationals displaced from the lost possessions in Africa and the Balkans, and the intergovernmental UN agencies maintained eligible foreign refugees in IRO/UNHCR camps, in practice Italians often lived alongside foreigners in camps like that at Risiera di San Sabba in Trieste or Aversa, near Naples, or Cinecittà in Rome. Likewise, there existed a whole series of individuals and groups whose ambiguity reflected categorical confusion and crossings and switchings across the tracks. Indeed, this book has highlighted the extensive ideological and practical labor involved not just in the bureaucratic "anointing" of identity (to return to the *Black Mamba Boy*'s protagonist's assessment of the new era dawning in 1947) but also in the consolidation of truly *categorical categories*, that is, unambiguous and clear-cut distinctions. Though the citizen/alien distinction seems commonsensical and unremarkable today, it was rearticulated in postwar Italy through the process of reckoning with the dual displacements of decolonization and war. This chapter examines these post-1945 transformations, first offering a brief discussion of the development of Italian citizenship codes during the era of imperial expansion before turning to detailed analysis of those displaced persons whose statuses challenged and tested the limits of Italian republican citizenship, as well as the incipient category of international refugee.

Italian Mobilities and Citizenship before 1945

Most scholarly genealogies of citizenship in Italy stress how citizenship codes and related documentary instruments such as passports, entry and exit visas, and identity cards—constituting what Horng-luen Wang has deemed the "regime of mobility"[4]—developed largely in response to the challenges of people leaving the Italian peninsula, rather than migrating to it. In his influential work on the creation of what he calls the "passport regime," for example, John Torpey has argued that the 1901 Italian Passport Law that required transatlantic travelers to hold a valid passport before purchasing passage "arose not from an urge to choke off exit," as many critics at the time claimed, "but rather a desire to ensure that Italian emigrants would not be denied *entry* into American ports."[5] Indeed, from the beginning of Italian statehood, Italian lawmakers repeatedly endorsed a notion of citizenship grounded in a belief that nationality (*nazionalità*) constituted a tenacious bond that could endure emigration and be passed down to descendants in the diaspora. As a result, after a series of parliamentary debates the new Italian state embraced a category of citizenship largely rooted in *jus sanguinis*, or the right of blood.

Sabina Donati has argued that, in contrast to the much better known example of Germany's descent-based citizenship regime, the rules put in place in 1865 in Italy "endorsed a relatively inclusive definition of national citizenship that, together with the *jus sanguinis* rule, took into account the presumption that birth combined with long years of settlement in the country as well as with civil and military service rendered to the state were sufficient factors to transform aliens into Italians."[6] Naturalization nonetheless came in two forms—small or *piccola naturalizzazione* (with only local rights) and large or *grande naturalizzazione* (full political rights). In the period between 1861 and 1912, full naturalization remained rare (with fewer than twenty cases).[7] In those exceptional cases where colonial subjects requested naturalization during this period, the overriding criteria determining approval appear to have been "good conduct and the role played in serving the colonial State."[8] As such comments imply, the issue of foreigners in Italy was hardly a novelty by the twentieth century, even if foreigners turned naturalized citizens were. Rather, "foreign residents in Italy have long been a key element in national self-definition."[9]

Between 1861 and 1943, Italian policies toward immigrants became increasingly exclusive. Although groups of Hungarian and Russian refugees in Italy had provoked some concerns during the liberal era, for example, it was only during World War I that the Italian state began to require and scrutinize the passports of foreigners seeking to enter the country. As Torpey notes, "The papers necessary for moving around within Italy as a foreigner"—which included not only passports but consular visas from the point of departure, as well as registration documents made within twenty-four hours upon arrival in Italy—"began to multiply."[10] Despite the fact that the number of aliens present in the country at the time of Italy's entry into the Great War remained small, "spy fever and Germanophobia spread throughout the country," with German wives the particular object of fear, and antisemitism also figuring in nationalist propaganda. Over the course of the conflict, the Italian government issued over thirty decrees pertaining to "enemy aliens" and interned many of them (particularly those from Austria-Hungary) in Sardinia.[11]

These strictures on aliens were accompanied by increasing control over the movements, internal and external, of Italian nationals, largely in the attempt to prevent flight by conscription-age males. It was only in 1926, however, that centralized supervision of immigrants—which increasingly became bound up with other issues of public order, such as the monitoring of politically "subversive" elements—received extended attention from state authorities. In the same year, the fascist regime also passed laws that permitted the stripping of citizenship from Italians based on their "political character" or if they behaved abroad in a manner that diminished the "prestige" of the Italian race, evidence of the state's willingness to use citizenship explicitly as cudgel. Three years later, the regime created the Central Registration Bureau for Aliens; Russians, Albanians, Spaniards, and foreign Jews constituted the primary groups of immigrants and refugees monitored by authorities.[12] In contrast, then, to those like Torpey who see the particular dimensions of Italian citizenship as largely the product of a protective gesture prompted by Italian emigration abroad, I argue here that focusing on the dialectical articulation of inclusion-exclusion both at home and abroad (including but not limited to the metropole-colony) proves more instructive.

Italian citizens who went abroad to work had successfully lobbied for changes to the Civil Code of 1865, which ultimately resulted in the new citizenship law of 1912. This law reinforced the conception of Italian citizenship as based primarily on ancestry and stipulated that (with some exceptions) Italian nationality passed on to descendants could be lost only through choice or voluntary action. If the "spontaneous" acquisition of foreign nationality had resulted in the loss of Italian citizenship, the latter could be attained by repatriating to Italy and "'after two years of residence in the Kingdom' (art. 9, para. 3, Law 555/1912)."[13] At the same time, the 1912 law also made naturalization for "aliens of non-Italian nationality" more difficult, highlighting the ways in which inclusionary and exclusionary policies remained entangled. The 1992 citizenship law repeated this pattern, facilitating acquisition of citizenship by members of the diaspora and tightening the path to naturalization. By contrast, individuals who could make some claim to Italianness and who hailed from lands viewed as "historically" Italian—such as the Veneto (under Habsburg control until 1866), Malta, Corsica, and the Republic of San Marino—had an easier time of acquiring either denizenship (residency rights) or full citizenship. The 1912 law also abolished the distinction between small and large naturalization for *metropolitan* citizenship, even as the acquisition of colonies from the 1880s onward made for a new hierarchy of citizenship statuses in Italia Oltremare.[14] Valerie McGuire has noted the noncoincidental timing of the 1912 citizenship law and the acquisition of Libya and the Aegean Islands, with the law entrenching the link between notions of blood and citizenship.[15]

Until Italy began its course of colonial expansion in Africa in the 1880s, the terms denoting Italian citizens had included *cittadini* (citizens), *sudditi* (subjects), and *regnicoli* (subjects of the realm). These were often used interchangeably and with relatively little precision. With the acquisition of territory in the 1880s and 1890s in what today forms parts of Eritrea and Somalia, however, the term *suddito* or subject became reserved for native peoples in the colonies and *cittadino* or citizen for the Italian in the metropole or colony.

In Etritrea, for example, the Royal Decree of 2 July 1908 (Regio Decreto 2 luglio 1908, Ordinamento giudiziario per l'Eritrea) codified these distinctions and became a foundational juridical text for questions of colonial citizenship.[16] As Donati puts it in her pioneering study of Italian citizenship, "The notion of citizenship thereby gained its full significance and was to be used to distinguish the higher and thicker status of the Italians from the lower one held by the native subjects."[17]

On the one hand, then, colonialism introduced the binary logic of metropole/colony, settler/native, and citizen/subject. On the other, it led to complex differentiations between and within the populations of Italy's overseas possessions as Italy expanded.[18] As we know, Italy's victory in the 1911–1912 Italo-Turkish War brought Italy two additional territories: Libya and the Dodecanese Islands. In contrast to its East African possessions, in Libya the Italian liberal regime created an intermediate form of citizenship—*cittadinanza italiana in Tripolitania e Cirenaica*—as a reward for loyalty and service to Italy; this contrasted with the general subject status accorded the "indigenes" of Libya. Alessia Maria Di Stefano has gone so far as to deem Libya under liberal Italy a "juridical laboratory" characterized by a multinormativity that acknowledged and recognized existing legal codes, including Ottoman regulations, Sharia, and rabbinical law. Statutes passed in 1919 promised Libyans near equal rights to Italians, as well as representation in elected assemblies.[19] Such equality never materialized in practice, however, and under fascism, this special Italian citizenship in Libya would be reformulated as *cittadinanza italiana libica*, often referred to (imprecisely) as *piccola cittadinanza* or "little citizenship." Small citizenship carried neither political rights, such as the right to vote, nor the obligation of military service. In 1939, a new wrinkle would be added with the possibility of *cittadinanza italiana speciale* for select Libyans from Cyrenaica and Tripolitania as a form of individual naturalization. Although a proposal for a similar special citizenship for Eritreans and Somalis who loyally served empire failed to come to fruition, it revealed how even within AOI the regime viewed (and sought to reward) certain populations as more loyal than others.[20]

In the Dodecanese Islands, by contrast, Italy initially kept in place Ottoman codes of belonging, given that Italy occupied this archipelago from 1912 on but only formally acquired the islands in 1923. Beginning in the fifteenth century with the Republic of Genoa, the Sublime Porte had made a series of bilateral trading agreements with various Christian powers that provided those powers' merchants and other agents with extraterritorial rights. This "capitulatory regime" gave rise to various groups of protégés living in

Ottoman territories but claiming the protection of foreign powers, such as France, Britain, and Italy. In the Isole Egeo, these protégés included so-called *Levantini* or Levantines who often made distant claims to Italian ancestry in the maritime Republics of Venice and Genoa. Many, but not all, of these Levantines in the Islands were Jews, and just as the Levant label gestured toward "an amorphous geographic entity" redolent of Orientalist connotations, the Levantine appellation proved at once capacious and indeterminate.[21] The Levantines of the Dodecanese likely included "Italian" protégés expelled during the Italo-Turkish War by Ottoman authorities from Aleppo, Beirut, and Jerusalem.[22] These *Levantini* were among those who acquired the *cittadinanza italiana egea*, or Italian Aegean citizenship, introduced in 1925. Like Italian Libyan citizenship, Italian Aegean citizenship offered a reduced or limited form of Italian citizenship that rewarded loyalty to Italy. Nonetheless, it did accord some citizenship rights, in contrast to the colonial subjecthood codified in the 1936 establishment of AOI, which joined together Eritrea and Somalia with the Ethiopian territory acquired through the brutal Abyssinian war.

Italy's last major territorial acquisition (leaving aside the military occupation of territories during World War II) occurred in 1939, when Albania and Italy were joined in "brotherly union" and Victor Emmanuel III became "King of Italy and Albania." In reality a protectorate, Albania retained the civil code that had governed King Zog's monarchy. As Donati notes, while not actually acquiring full-fledged (metropolitan) citizenship, Albanians nonetheless enjoyed "the most substantial civic position, held *de jure*, by a nonmetropolitan people within Mussolini's imperial community" in light of "the unprecedented introduction of equality of certain rights between them and the Italian metropolitans."[23] As we have seen elsewhere, however, there often remains a large gap between theory and practice, and the actual rights enjoyed by Albanians proved remarkably less robust than those on paper.[24] Throughout the period of Italian colonialism, most of the citizenship benefits provided to non-Italians in the Oltremare operated less as rights and more as privileges accorded at the will (and whim) of the colonial power, giving rise to what Nicola Camilleri has deemed a form of "discretional citizenship" (*cittadinanza discrezionale*).[25] Not surprisingly, some officials in the Ministero degli Affari Esteri (MAE) explicitly described the naturalization process in possessions like the Dodecanese as a means of "patronage," one that operated largely on a case-by-case basis.[26] The Aegean Islands offer a useful case study of the complexities of Italian imperial citizenship and its discretional nature in practice.

Categorical Confusion, I: The Dodecanese Islands and *cittadinanza italiana egea*

In her study of the Ottoman Empire's Jewish populations, Sarah Stein highlights how "the emergence of a passport regime" transformed many "Ottoman-born extraterritorial subjects [into] . . . legally liminal subjects with ill-defined rights and responsibilities."[27] The efforts of successor states to compel these former Ottoman protégés to adopt national citizenships often failed, as in the case of Greece and the Jews of Salonica. Whether through conscious resistance of new citizenship practices or lack of understanding of their import or of the procedures by which they could be obtained, many residents and former residents of the Isole Egeo remained in such a state of legal and documentary liminality during the period of Italian control. Residents of the Ottoman Dodecanese—who included Muslims, Christians, and Jews, as well as individuals who self-identified as "ethnic" Turks, Greeks, and Italians—had proved as peripatetic as peninsular Italians, emigrating frequently in search of work and tapping into transnational kin and trade networks that spanned the Mediterranean and beyond. According to Stein, "Italian protégés from Rhodes" were almost all Jewish. Stein estimates a community as large as forty-five hundred Jews on Rhodes at the time the islands came under Italian control. With the advent of World War I, these Jews (as well as Rhodesli Jews living outside the islands) "had been 'protégé Italians' for but a few short years. Indeed, those who lived in émigré settings (including South Africa, Rhodesia, the Belgian Congo, Tunisia, and Egypt) received Italian protection through local consuls and representatives despite having never set foot on the island in its [Italian] incarnation."[28]

By the 1930s, however, the Italian state did not necessarily recognize as its own all those who claimed status as former protégés, even if some other states like France did view those subjects as "Italian." For those Dodecanesians living outside the islands, the Second Treaty of Lausanne of 1923 established the procedure for obtaining or retaining Italian protection. Article 34 of the treaty declared,

> Turkish nationals of over eighteen years of age who are natives of a territory detached from Turkey under the present Treaty, and who on its coming into force are habitually resident abroad, may opt for the nationality of the territory of which they are natives, if they belong by race to the majority of the population of that territory, and subject to the consent of the Government exercising authority therein. This right of option must be exercised within two years from the coming into force of the present Treaty.[29]

Given the extensive network of Dodecanesians, Italian officials not surprisingly found themselves deluged by requests by individuals who had been living outside the islands at the time they came under Italian sovereignty and who had not exercised their right of option within the time limit. The resulting situation of categorical confusion foreshadowed the messiness of the citizenship "option" for residents of both the Dodecanese Islands and the Istrian-Julian-Dalmatian lands laid out in article 19 of the 1947 Peace Treaty, discussed later in this chapter. It also complicates the claims by Italian officials themselves that they had largely sorted out the citizenship question in the islands by 1926.[30] In an actual situation of continued ambiguity, administrators in the Dodecanese treated requests for entry and residence, connected to claims of belonging, in a discretional manner.

The global Depression that began in the early 1930s heightened the desire of some former inhabitants to return to the islands, while it prompted others to leave. In 1932, for example, officials in the islands noted the movement of workers to Morocco.[31] In that same year, the government of the Belgian Congo began pressuring Italian officials in the Dodecanese to repatriate indigent and unemployed "Italians" from Elizabethville (today Lubumbashi) and Léopoldville (present-day Kinshasa). Referring to those who claimed Italian belonging but had not opted by the terms of Lausanne for citizenship, the islands' governor Mario Lago underlined, "The crisis of work is felt in the Possession no less than elsewhere. Rather than favor the repatriation of these islanders, it would be better for us to keep them far from the islands, where we have no interest in increasing the population."[32] Four months later, the secretary-general of the Italian administration in the Dodecanese noted that for reasons of subjecthood (*sudditanza*) and, above all, for political implications, such requests for repatriation should "be considered with extremely restrictive criteria." In fact, the secretary continued, "many Dodecanesians resident in Belgian Congo pass for Italian subjects [*passano per sudditi italiani*], without being such."[33] Such comments perhaps encoded suspicions about the ethnic provenance of the largely Jewish populations requesting return from the Congo, although into the early 1930s both Mussolini and Lago had looked favorably upon the settlement and naturalization of Jews (in contrast to Muslims) in the islands.[34]

In contrast, requests to emigrate to the Isole Egeo made in the same year by "Italians" in places like Turkey found a more sympathetic reception among officials in the islands. Citing high unemployment among members of the "colonie Italiane" in places like Istanbul, one observer recommended to the MAE that while such emigration must be undertaken with care, "the presence in some centers of the islands of nuclei of our co-nationals could be considered useful to the aims of Italianization of those lands, a process that the Government of Rhodes follows with tact and prudence."[35] While the precise citizenship status and religious background of these (Levantine?) "Italians" in Turkey remains unclear from the documentation, they apparently could make greater claims on the Italian state than either the Italians in Congo or other former residents of the Ottoman Dodecanese. Governor Lago contended that his administration had adopted more generous criteria for "connazionali levantini" seeking to emigrate to the islands than for "expatriate Dodecanese," the latter term apparently referring to all non-Italian islanders abroad.[36] Indeed, documents from the same time period reveal close scrutiny of ethnic "Greek" Dodecanesians and Levantines applying to return to the islands. One such case involved a Greek subject and mariner, Sotirio Sicofilo, who had previously lived in Alexandria and then in Italian Benghazi and Tripoli. Sicofilo requested a one-year visa to Kalymnos. Sicofilo had apparently entered the islands in a clandestine fashion in 1928, but this "crime" was subsequently pardoned by a general 1930 amnesty. Nonetheless, his request to stay on Kalymnos was rejected.[37]

Of such potential migrants to the islands, Lago cautioned, "It will be necessary to ascertain by the most rigorous means the morality of these new [Levantine] arrivals who, neither being allowed to return to Turkey *nor to be expelled* [my emphasis], would remain in the islands like a deadweight and discredit to the Regime." Lago added, "Unfortunately, that little bit of the underworld that exists here is formed in large part by bad Levantine Italian elements who have infiltrated."[38] In a number of instances, requests made by "Italians" from places like İzmir/Smirne with close relatives living on Rhodes were rejected solely on the grounds that the prospects for employment of these *Levantini* remained dim, the implication being that idle "Levantine Italians" could create disorder.[39] Italians born in the metropole and possessed of good fascist credentials instead found few obstacles to their emigration to the Isole Egeo. Consider the case of Pietro Scala and his wife, born in Torre del Greco (near Naples) and in 1932 resident in İzmir/Smirne. Owing to his membership in Smyrna's local fascio, Scala's request to embark in the Egeo was viewed as "favorable in all aspects."[40]

By contrast, Lago proposed employing a landing permit (*permesso di sbarco*) to surveil and regulate the arrival of less desirable Italians. The case of an Italian, Umberto Mancuso, who arrived on a three-month visa to Rhodes in 1932 and then expressed his intention to remain even if he did not secure employment, prompted discussions within the Aegean administration about strictly controlling permits. In this instance, it was urged that obtaining consular approval for a passport should not be sufficient for entry into the islands. This highlights the ways in which the Italian state sought to employ other types of travel documents to mitigate claims made on it by "citizens" or semi-citizens.[41] Whereas Torpey reminds us, "Formal citizenship is not necessarily the foundation of a claim to a passport for travel,"[42] it is important to keep in mind that in this case neither a passport nor a claim to or possession of a demi-citizenship necessarily provided sufficient grounds for reentry and residence.

Nevertheless, those *sudditi* who possessed an Italian passport as a result of having opted for one by 1925 and who returned from places like the United States could be granted a visa to the islands without needing the government's preventive authorization (*preventiva autorizzazione*)—as long as these subjects were of good moral and political conduct. This example demonstrates both the flexibility and the limits of *cittadinanza italiana egea* in practice, since officials continued to refer to those who possessed it as subjects and made determinations as to their moral fitness to return.[43]

Within two years, the Italian administration had begun to liberalize its naturalization process, in part to meet the needs of Italian military conscription for an expanding imperial war machine. Despite the criticisms expressed by Governor Lago, the MAE pushed for the expansion of *cittadinanza italiana egea* even to ethnic Greeks from the islands resident in Egypt and facilitated the transformation of *grande naturalizzazione* to full metropolitan citizenship through military service.[44] The increasingly explicit racial dimensions of citizenship and the turn toward harder Italianization policies in the islands under the governorship of Cesare Maria De Vecchi (1936–1940), however, soon prompted a bitter debate over the discretional nature of *cittadinanza italiana egea*. Valerie McGuire has detailed how Governor De Vecchi zealously enforced the antisemitic legislation of 1938, which included the denaturalization of those Jews who had acquired citizenship after 1919.[45] He did so in the face of opposition from Count Ciano, the minister of foreign affairs, who agreed with the appeals made by Dodecanesian Jews as to the non-revocability of their "small citizenship" status. De Vecchi counterargued not only that *cittadinanza italiana egea* occupied a place below that of *piccola naturalizzazione* but that its discretional nature permitted such rapid reinterpretations and shifts in policies. As McGuire concludes, "The deployment of the anti-Semitic Racial Laws finally laid bare the lack of clarity that had always existed about the juridical construction of Dodecanese inhabitants as either colonial subjects or protected persons of the Italian nation."[46] Italian officials continued to debate how to operationalize citizenship as questions arose over Jews with Turkish citizenship in the islands (who could not be expelled on the same grounds as Italian Dodecanesian Jews), as well as mixed marriages.

The ambiguities of citizenship in this Italian possession gave rise to a new set of definitional debates after the war, prompting the creation of the label of "undetermined Dodecanese." The option clause for the Dodecanese laid out in the 1947 Peace Treaty with Italy that created problems for UNRRA and IRO personnel avoided the language of race that had figured so prominently in the debates of the 1930s. Praising the "innovation" represented by what he called an "ethnical option," legal scholar Josef Kunz underscored how "the Treaty of 1947 has dropped the criterium of 'race' and has decided the problem of 'language'—mother tongue or customary language."[47] This contrasted with the vocabulary of race found, for instance, in the 1923 Lausanne Treaty's option. Nonetheless, the 1947 treaty's embrace of ethnic identity—which in Italy had long rested juridically on a notion of blood (*jus sanguinis*)—did not do away with race as completely or handily as Kunz might have wished. Although the fascist regime explicitly racialized citizenship in both the metropole and the Oltremare in the 1930s and 1940s with tragic consequences, the structures of Italy's citizenship codes had carried racial connotations from at least the beginning of its colonial expansion. The logics of this "vincolo di sangue" (blood tie) would continue to unfold even after empire's formal end.

Race, Citizenship, and Belonging in Italian Empire

The differing possibilities for legal belonging in Italia Oltremare reflected the differential statuses of the territories, which in turn mapped onto the racial hierarchies of Italian rule over its possessions. After 1934, for example, Cyrenaica and Tripolitania were joined together with the Fezzan as the colony of Libya and in 1939 made a direct department of Italy. The Aegean Islands possessed a similar status as province/department rather than colony, in contrast to AOI. This territorial hierarchy both reflected and refracted racial hierarchies, in particular the perceived putative racial proximity of subject peoples to Italians. As colonizers, for example, Italians often stressed their shared European heritage with the majority Greek subjects of the Dodecanese Islands, even as they pointed to the effects of centuries of Ottoman Oriental backwardness as justifying or necessitating Italy's "benevolent" and modernizing rule in the archipelago. The recollections of many locals of that period simultaneously highlight their cultural and racial affinity with the Italians, as expressed in the popular saying, "una faccia, una razza," or "mía fátsa, mía rátsa" ("one face, one race"), along with the occupiers' technological superiority.[48]

Italy's appeal to Greek (Orthodox) Dodecanesians as fellow "Europeans" nonetheless did not hamper the pursuit of policies of religious and linguistic assimilation, though the governorship of Mario Lago undertook these with greater caution and much less coercion than did his successor, Cesare De Vecchi.[49] Nor did this vision of a shared "razza" necessarily embrace other residents of the islands, including Muslims (some of them Turkish citizens) and Jews, as discussed in the previous section. Indeed, De Vecchi's insistence after 1938 on revoking citizenship and expelling those Jews previously protected by *cittadinanza italiana egea* reflected the racial logics expressed in the pages of *Difesa della Razza*, where Umberto Angeli (and others) warned of the need to distinguish "true Italians" from "false Italians," that is, "Italians in fact" from "Italians by right" (*veri italiani / falsi italiani*; *Italiani di fatto / Italiani di diritto*).[50] Interestingly, at the 1938 Reale Accademia d'Italia conference on Africa, De Vecchi (like fellow colonial governor Italo Balbo) had assumed a dissident position on the racial laws that criticized the overly zealous application of German-style norms. When the Ministry of Italian Africa protested De Vecchi's statements, De Vecchi hastily deleted them and stressed his agreement with the need to rigorously enforce antisemitic legislation.[51] In the Aegean Islands he proved true to his word in a case of tragic overcompensation. This example underscores the continual push and pull between the administrative centers of power in Rome and in the possessions, as well as the specificities of each of the territories. Where De Vecchi was busily revoking Jewish citizenship and "encouraging" Muslims to emigrate from the Isole Egeo in 1938 and 1939, for example, Muslim Libyans who had served in the Ethiopian campaign instead became eligible in 1939 for a new *cittadinanza italiana speciale* that recognized their service to empire.[52]

Overall, the sharpening of racial stratifications in the second half of the 1930s found expression in antimiscegenation laws in the African colonies, the Racial Laws of 1938 that restricted the civil and political rights of Jews, and reversals on the possibilities of citizenship for mixed-race children (*meticci*) in AOI,[53] all of which would continue to create definitional dilemmas around citizenship long after the regime that had enacted those policies had disappeared. Whereas in the past mixed-race children from AOI (as well as Italo-Libyans) who had been recognized by their Italian fathers could obtain full metropolitan citizenship, this became impossible after 1940. Beginning in 1936, colonial legislation had begun to erode the already limited rights of mixed-race children and their possibilities for citizenship.

No similar prohibition under fascism existed regarding offspring of mixed unions (Orthodox-Catholic or Muslim / Orthodox-Catholic, respectively) in the Aegean islands or Albania, underscoring how these Balkan possessions—and at least some, if not all, of their inhabitants—figured as racially similar to the metropole, despite religious and linguistic difference.[54] When the issue arose after 1945 regarding the citizenship of the spouses (usually wives) of Italian citizens repatriated from these Balkan former territories, however, the similar but not quite the same quality of these subject peoples (as well as the legal status of religiously mixed weddings) opened up a space for ambiguity and even exclusion.[55]

In highlighting these racialized hierarchies of citizenship, it should be noted that the origins, meanings, and salience of racial classifications in Italy (particularly during the fascist era) have provoked considerable, if belated, debate among scholars. For several decades after fascism's defeat, scholars often contrasted relative Italian indifference to racialist understandings with the enthusiastic promulgation of such appeals by their Nazi allies, a thesis promoted most forcefully by Renzo De Felice. Eliding antisemitism with racialism more generally, De Felice argued that not only did the majority of Italians disagree with the Racial Laws but also that the embrace of antisemitism occurred only during the period of Salò and the German occupation.[56] Scholars like Menachem Shelah, Jonathan Steinberg, and Susan Zuccotti emphasized Italian efforts during the war to rescue both their own Jews and those who came under their control and protection in zones of occupation in France and Dalmatia, lending further support to the widespread view that Italian antisemitism possessed shallow roots.[57]

The careful research of scholars like Michele Sarfatti, however, has challenged the popular thesis of antisemitism as merely an "alien" imposition wrought by the alliance with Nazi Germany. Indeed, the very image of Italians (particularly soldiers and officers) as humane rescuers of Jews during World War II has come into question.[58] Furthermore, a burgeoning body of work has examined the roots of home-grown Italian racial and eugenicist ideas, including but not limited to antisemitism, from the nineteenth century on in a wide range of contexts stretching from the peninsula to the irredentist lands to the colonies and other possessions.[59] Admittedly, a discernible shift occurred with the official promotion from 1938 on of the line that Italians belonged to an Aryan, rather than Mediterranean, race, leading to furious and ever more tortured debates among racial thinkers within Italy.[60] Olindo De Napoli has documented in extensive detail the legal contradictions and circularities created by the introduction of more extreme imperial racial logics into a law system whose foundations rested on Roman principles. Nonetheless, the emerging scholarly consensus not only highlights the deep roots of racialized ideas and practices in the Italian peninsula well beyond the legal realm but also the complex intertwining of notions of race in both the metropole and overseas possessions, a point seconded by de Napoli.[61]

While possessing distinct histories, then, Italian stereotypes about southerners or *meridionali*, depictions of the eastern Adriatic's Slavic peoples as rural savages deficient in *civiltà*, antisemitic tropes, Orientalist notions of backward Levantines and rootless Libyan pastoralists, and racist images of African "primitives" shared common grammars of domination and exclusion and, in the context of imperial expansion, nesting logics of social and legal alienness.[62] As a result, some scholars have gone as far as to view southerners and so-called allogenes or *allogeni* (Italian citizens of non-Italian ethnicity, such as Slovenes in Venezia Giulia and Germans in Alto Adige) as subject to mechanisms of internal Orientalism and colonialism not so different from that experienced by colonized Libyans or Ethiopians.[63] Certainly, the regime itself conceived of the projects of "reclaiming" and purifying domestic and overseas spaces and peoples in quite similar terms. In Venezia Giulia, for example, the Ministry of the Interior launched a project of "bonifica nazionale" or national reclamation in 1931 that possessed many analogues to the reclamation efforts elsewhere in the peninsula and the Oltremare. In this instance, the plan called for eventual expropriation of land held by *allogeni* (ethnic Slovenes), with redistribution to fascist veterans and agriculturalists.[64]

Despite the discrimination experienced by internal Others like Italian Slovenes, it must be remembered that as citizens they could make claims on the Italian state that colonial *sudditi* or subjects could not. Nonetheless, the *allogeni* remained vulnerable to the threat of denationalization in ways that citizens of the old provinces of the *Regno* did not. As Roberta Pergher notes, for these nonethnic Italians, "citizenship became a weapon for assimilation."[65] Indeed, in practice, the *allogeni* became subject to intense assimilation processes, through often forcible Italianization. As Triestine journalist Ragusin-Righi put it in 1920, the *allogeni* consisted in "new Italian citizens who still need to be cultivated/cultured [but] . . . with time . . . could become truly Italian, even in sentiment."[66] And, as occurred in 1936 when a contingent of nine families (with 180 individuals total) of woodcutters from the Alto Adige were sent to the Dodecanese, *allogeni* could on occasion even be considered appropriate colonizers in the name of Italian empire.[67] In this instance, the colonization process was likely simultaneously intended as one of Italianization and fascistization of the colonizers themselves, as was also true with ethnically Italian settlers throughout Libya and AOI.

One consequence of the extended and often fierce debates about the entangled genealogies of racialism in Italy has been to temper the myth of the "good Italian." As occurred earlier in the context of Holocaust studies, scholars have critiqued tired notions that Italian colonialism proved more humane than that of other European powers by detailing the extreme (even genocidal) violence perpetrated in subjugating territories like Libya and Ethiopia, on the one hand, and by examining moral panics and prohibitions provoked by interracial mixing, on the other.[68] Under fascism, the long-standing practice (indeed, norm) of Italian men in the colonists cohabiting with African women (a form of concubinage glossed in Italian as *madamismo*) became the object of ever more stringent prohibitions. These were formalized in antimiscegenation laws that preceded the metropolitan Racial Laws focused on Jews. Law 880 of 19 April 1937, for example, made relations of a "conjugal" nature in AOI a crime punishable by between one and five years of prison. In liberal Italy, by contrast, an Italian man could marry a native African but at the cost of a position in colonial administration; in practice, however, this depended very much on the Italian man's position within the colonial elite. After 1914, mixed-race offspring were prohibited from serving as colonial functionaries.[69] Within two years of the 1937 law, the regime had also begun to apply this prohibition to mixed Italo-Libyan couples.[70] The criminalization of *madamato*, argues Luciano Martone, was "intended to resolve once and for all the problem of miscegenation, negating absolutely any possibility of integration and citizenship for mixed-race offspring."[71] Interestingly, too, the 1937 law punished the Italian citizen engaging in this practice, rather than the native, thereby reversing the laxity previously shown toward Italian men who engaged in sexual unions with African natives. The idea of a female Italian citizen pairing with an African male, by contrast, had always aroused horror.[72]

Prior to this, children born of an Italian father and African mother automatically acquired Italian citizenship in those instances (always the exception) where the father legally recognized the child. Although even this rule did not prove straightforward in either theory or practice, the juridical status of "meticci" remained largely unchanged from 1916 until the 1930s. For most of this time, patrilineal descent trumped race in determining whether such children belonged (formally at least) to the Italian national community. In the case of the Tigrinya people of Eritrea, for instance, Giulia Barrera has identified a "'patrilinear convergence' between colonizers and colonized: for both groups, paternal descent defined individual identity."[73] Some of these children attended Catholic mission schools in the colonies in recognition that such children should be raised as Italians. Indeed, even when Italian fathers abandoned their children, their African mothers often encouraged their offspring to identify as Italians and to practice Catholicism (as opposed to the Orthodox Christianity of the Eritrean Tigrinya), in keeping with Tigrinya conceptions of descent. By the end of the 1920s, Catholic campaigns had also begun to advocate for and draw attention to the growing problem of abandoned and impoverished meticci.[74] As late as 1933, legislation came into effect that permitted children of mixed race in Eritrea and Somalia whose paternity remained unknown or unacknowledged to acquire Italian citizenship, under certain circumstances. The colonial authorities exercised discretional authority in such cases.[75] However, Law 822 of 13 May 1940, detailing "Norms Concerning Children of Mixed Race," reversed these earlier policies by prohibiting the recognition of such children by their fathers and rendering all meticci colonial subjects or *sudditi*.

Parallel policies of racial exclusion converged in the increasing marginalization experienced by Jews resident in Italia Oltremare—where there lived as many or more Jews under Italian control than in the metropole—and the (slightly delayed) application of the Racial Laws there. By 1942, Italian authorities had interned approximately three thousand Cyrenaican Jews at the Tripolitanian camp of Giado (Jado, Jadu); some 560 individuals perished from malnutrition, disease, and forced labor. Others, including Jews with foreign passports, were deported to Italy and onward to Bergen-Belsen.[76] Between 1947 and 1951 some twenty-five thousand Libyan Jews who survived the war would depart in the face of pogroms in 1945 and 1948.[77] The majority of Rhodes's Jews would perish at Auschwitz. Only the Falasha or Ethiopian Jews (*i falascia* or *falascià* in Italian) would escape this tragic fate as a result of AOI's occupation by the British in 1941. Although the provisional or discretional nature of many of the Oltremare Jews' legal statuses facilitated the nullification of protection, it must be remembered that the protection offered by the full citizenship held by metropolitan Jews ultimately proved just as precarious.

For our purposes here, then, let us sum up what the complex and multistranded histories of racialized categories in liberal and fascist Italy meant for citizenship in theory and practice by the time the war ended in 1945. According to Donati, the creation of a fascist empire (including the occupation of Balkan territories in World War II) had brought some thirteen million Europeans and ten million Africans into an increasingly complex citizenship system grounded in the metropolitan citizen / colonial subject binary but also characterized by many ambiguous, in-between statuses. The fragility of such statuses was revealed in the face of ever greater racialization, as well as the prerogatives exercised by local administrators like De Vecchi in the Dodecanese.

After 1945, a form of republican citizenship would emerge that reflected the new territorial configuration or truncation of the nation and that mapped citizens to national territory more tightly, albeit still imperfectly.[78] With the loss of Italy's overseas territories came a concomitant loss of its confusing colonial hierarchy of juridical subjecthood. There nonetheless remained problematic categories—including mixed-race children in AOI, foreign spouses, and persons of so called "undetermined" nationality from the Dodecanese Islands and Venezia Giulia—that required both ideological and actual labor to separate the tracks of citizenship (and by extension, the related ones of refugee assistance) into a binary one (citizen/alien), the topic to which I now turn. In this flattened version of republican citizenship, the principle of *jus sanguinis* would remain central, as it had from almost the beginning of Italian statehood.

Categorical Confusion, II: The Peace Treaty with Italy and the Citizenship Option

The 1947 Peace Treaty stipulated that individuals in former Italian territories in the Aegean, Adriatic, and the areas that Italy ceded to France could opt to retain Italian citizenship. According to article 19, all "Italians" resident in the ceded territories on or before 10 June 1940 had the legal right (though by no means the obligation) to choose Italian citizenship. Those who acquired or retained Italian citizenship were, for the most part, required to leave the former Italian territory and take up residence in a territorially reconfigured Italy. The treaty stipulated that this depended on the discretion of the state that annexed the former Italian territory. Those who did not opt for Italy instead automatically became citizens of the states that had acquired sovereignty over those territories—Greece, Yugoslavia, and France, respectively.

The principal requirements of Italianness in the case of the option were Italian as the *lingua d'uso* (language of customary use) and *domicilio* (domicile) in Italian territory on the determined date, the former standing in imperfectly for Italian identity. In the context of the Isole Egeo, domicile was more often interpreted along the lines of the Italian civil code as the place where the concerned party held the principal seat of his affairs or interest, whereas for those parts of Venezia Giulia ceded to Yugoslavia, domicile was more typically interpreted as primary residence. Evidence exists, however, for slippage between the two meanings in both contexts. In the territories ceded to France, the French government instead interpreted domicile as "effective and habitual residence."[79] The notes for a meeting of the Consiglio dello

Stato concerning such diverse legal interpretations of the term "domicile" voiced the pervasive resentment that the Great Powers had decided Italy's fate at the Paris Peace Conference. The minutes of the meeting complained about the brokering of the treaty terms by "foreign politicians and diplomats belonging, for the most part, to diverse nationalities" who failed to appreciate the legal traditions and specificities of Italy; this presumably included its traditions of citizenship. It should be noted, though, that this problem was not unique to the 1947 treaty; the drafters of the 1951 Geneva Convention on Refugees also struggled with defining "country of [former] habitual residence."[80]

Enshrining the principle of reciprocity, article 20 of the 1947 Peace Treaty provided for Italian citizens domiciled in Italy and whose customary language (*lingua d'uso* or *lingua usuale*) was one of the Yugoslav languages to opt for Yugoslav citizenship. The treaty did not contain similar provisions for either Greek- or French-speaking Italian citizens in the Italian peninsula.[81] Writing at the time of events, Josef Kunz declared this option process "theoretically correct and apt to avoid difficulties."[82] He could not have been more wrong. Determining Italianness on the ground proved no easy feat, either in the borderlands of the eastern Adriatic or the former Ottoman Aegean territories, albeit for somewhat different reasons. Nor was the decision as to who possessed the right to opt for Italian citizenship a unilateral one made solely by the Italian government.

In the case of Venezia Giulia, both Italian and Yugoslav governments made decisions on individual option cases, with the Yugoslav government actually rejecting or blocking a number of applications to opt for Italian citizenship. In his analysis of the option process, Kunz highlighted the discretionary power of the Yugoslav government. In those cases where Italian citizens exercised their option for Yugoslav citizenship, such optants "acquire Yugoslav nationality only if the Yugoslav authorities accept their request, which is entirely discretionary with them."[83] Similarly, from the Italian side, language of customary use remained a "question of fact and proof."[84] A memo from the Ministry of the Interior, for example, clarified that in practice "lingua d'uso" really should mean "lingua materna" or "the 'native language,' the 'language of the patria,' that is, the language of the nation to which one belongs."[85] For Italian authorities, then, speaking Italian in daily use constituted necessary but not sufficient proof of one's genuine Italianness; in practice, "lingua d'uso" was often taken to imply "lingua di sentimento" or "lingua di cuore" (the language of sentiment, the language of the heart), which in turn was said to indicate the "lingua di Patria." These glosses on "language of customary use" underscore how, in the context of sorting out citizenship claims by residents of the former Italian lands along the eastern Adriatic, language stood in as the exterior marker of a deep and interiorized ("di cuore") ethno-national identity. Concurrent debates in the Constituent Assembly over how to define "Italian nationality" for the case of "italiani non appartenenti alla Repubblica" (Italians outside the Republic) further reveal a (continuing) appeal to "'origins, to 'blood,' to 'tradition' as connotative elements of 'Italian nationality.'"[86] During the drafting of article 3 of the Constitution, which guaranteed equal rights to all Italian citizens regardless of religion, sex, or race, heated demands to eliminate the vocabulary of *razza* or race altogether failed to produce results.[87]

Given the difficulties in actually determining this "lingua di cuore"—indeed, what bureaucracy has ever been able to know truly the heart of its subjects?—Italian authorities fretted that ethnic Slavs who were former Italian citizens and possessed the requisite Italian fluency were using the option process to infiltrate the border area around Gorizia and Trieste. Documents from the Comitato di Liberazione Nazionale of Gorizia to the Presidenza del Consiglio claimed that as many as fifty thousand "white Slavs"—that is, opponents of Tito—were trying to reacquire citizenship, sometimes through fraudulent means such as false statements as to their *lingua d'uso*. Despite their opposition to Tito, these Slavs supposedly nurtured a "profound hatred of Italy." In the border city of Gorizia, in particular, this situation appeared to pro-Italian groups to represent a "grave" danger in its potential to destabilize the relationship of the Italian majority to the autochthonous Slovene minority.[88] Given the legal impossibility of refusing all such requests to opt and the practical difficulties of establishing *lingua d'uso*, the Italian authorities sought to transfer these Slavic Italians to other regions in Italy, far from the eastern border.[89] These attempts by the Italian and Yugoslav authorities to control and regulate which optants they would recognize as citizens represented assertions of sovereignty by two young regimes still consolidating their legitimacy.

The sensitivity of the border dispute and the imprecision of the citizenship option in practice also complicated the task of the intergovernmental organizations charged with assisting refugees. UNRRA and, after 1947, the International Refugee Organization struggled to interpret whether (and if so, how) their own definitions of eligible international refugees applied to individuals coming from the formerly Italian parts of Istria and Venezia Giulia. Clearly, those individuals who presented themselves at IRO offices seeking assistance such as placement in an IRO-run camp and help to emigrate overseas considered themselves refugees and hoped that the IRO would, too. Some of these migrants had opted for and received Italian citizenship, others had found their applications blocked, and yet others had not sought Italian citizenship and thus had become de facto Yugoslav citizens but had still made their way to Italy.[90] Who, if any, among these individuals counted as international refugees according to the emerging criteria of international law?

Confronted with the growing phenomenon of "post-hostility" refugees, the IRO had embraced a definition of displaced persons different from that used by UNRRA. Essentially, the IRO narrowed UNRRA's definition in a process that increasingly excluded those groups we might label internally displaced persons and national refugees. A June 1947 memo laid out the basic terms of eligibility:

> To qualify as a person of concern to the IRO, a refugee or displaced person, as defined, must satisfy one of two conditions set up in Section C, paragraph 1 [annex 1 of the IRO constitution]. He must be either (1) a person who can be repatriated and requires the help of the Organization, or (2) a person who, in complete freedom and after receiving full knowledge of the facts, expresses "valid objections" to returning to his country of nationality. The list of objections was intended to be exclusive. However, broad discretion rests with the IRO to determine what is a "political objection."[91]

The IRO also exercised discretion to determine what constituted the "country of nationality" and whether an individual was displaced outside of it. Initially, IRO officials deemed individuals who had opted for Italian citizenship ineligible for aid. The IRO considered these optants as Italians who "remained" in Italy, despite the fact that Italy's border had moved, and hence retaining Italian citizenship generally required moving with and to Italy. As stated in a March 1949 "Memorandum on the question of Refugees from Venezia-Giulia,"

> Since it was felt by the Eligibility staff of the Italian mission that these persons who are for the most part of Italian ethnic origin, whose language is Italian and who have been Italian citizens since 1918 could have no sound grounds for declining to reacquire Italian citizenship they were declared to be outside the mandate of the organization on the grounds that they are to all intents and purposes in their country of origin and cannot be considered to be bona fide Refugees according to the terms of the IRO Constitution.[92]

The IRO's acting director-general P. Jacobsen explicitly endorsed the assumption built into article 19 of the 1947 Peace Treaty that language proved an accurate measure of "origins"—that is, ethno-national identity. While acknowledging that Venezia Giulia proved home to many different groups, including persons of "Austrian" and "Hungarian" background, Jacobsen nonetheless contended that most of these groups would not be of Italian customary language. As a result, in his mind the Italian government bore responsibility for all Italian speakers displaced from the ceded territories. "It is our view that the problem of Italian speaking persons in Italy who have been Italian citizens only recently," Jacobsen argued, "is at least as much a part of the Problem of the Italian population generally as the problem of the 'Volksdeutsche' is part of the problem of German populations."[93]

In advancing this position, Jacobsen ignored the earlier assessment by Italy's IRO head, G. F. Mentz, who maintained in a letter to W. Hallam Tuck, director-general of the IRO, that comparison of the Venezia Giulia refugees to the *Volksdeutsche* was unwarranted. As Mentz put it, the latter category "is a very particular and negative exclusion based on racial terms, [thus] to extend it to groups other than German would be very clear violation both of the letter and of the spirit of the IRO Constitution."[94] Like those Italian representatives drafting the Italian Constitution in the same moment and struggling over terms such as "race," Mentz and others in the IRO were painfully aware of the history of such racialized conceptions but nonetheless remained caught in the ethno-national logics of identity that still dominated the intergovernmental system of states after 1945.

Initially, then, IRO staff presumed or, at least, accepted the dictum that the citizenship option and its language criterion adequately mapped onto ethno-national identity. An eligibility officer in the early preparatory stages of the IRO's work in Italy pronounced that persons of customary Yugoslav language "are to be considered as Yugoslav and cannot opt for Italian citizenship,"[95] ignoring the ways in which individuals' self-understandings might not match those of state authorities evaluating option requests, or applicants with Slavic customary languages might nonetheless successfully attain Italian citizenship. The Preparatory Commission for the IRO Eligibility Office in Rome, in fact, made a key distinction between "Persons of customary Yugoslav language (Slovene, Croat, or Serb)" and "Persons of customary Italian language," with the former eligible for IRO assistance and the latter excluded. IRO interviewers in Trieste and Gorizia received instructions that optants who "i) are of Slav ethnic origin, and ii) genuine political refugees because of persecution for political opinion (or religion) be given special consideration and declared (as a group) prima facie within the mandate of IRO." The area intake supervisor Michael Sedmak questioned whether such displaced persons even met the criteria for opting for Italian citizenship, adding, "Many of them are not only of Slav ethnic origin but of Slav customary language (or bilingual) and thus it is doubtful whether they had the right to opt or not."[96]

While the commission did recognize that some applicants were bilingual, it still sought to identify a primary customary language. In cases of multilingualism, the criteria employed to determine "customary language" included "house language, parents' language, family name, parish church, cultural and political associations, etc." In practice, however, such bilingual applicants proved difficult to classify, and by May 1949, IRO personnel reported receiving 165 applications from persons whose customary language was said to be "Istrian dialect" or who were bilingual. One month later, the IRO was reconsidering the applications of some five hundred individuals—previously excluded from the IRO's mandate—deemed bilingual or of Italian customary language.[97]

The reconsideration of these applications points to the difficulties that the IRO soon ran into with its exclusion from eligibility of "Italian" refugees from Venezia Giulia, as well as with its general adherence to the linguistic criterion of identity that had been built into the treaty's understanding of citizenship. Displaced persons from the ceded territories in Istria and Dalmatia requesting help from international agencies included individuals who had not opted for Italian citizenship (or whose options the Yugoslav government had rejected) and therefore were considered de facto Yugoslav citizens but whose "customary language" appeared to IRO staff to be Italian. Initially, the IRO's policy had been to exclude any "Italian speakers," even if they had *not* opted, as they were seen to be the responsibility of the Italian government. IRO personnel soon recognized the problems with this policy. In a "Report on Operations of the Eligibility Division in Italy Covering the 3 months period September—October—November 1948," I. H. D. Whigham, chief of the Eligibility Division, commented on the fact that many of these so-called Italians ruled ineligible were Italian *only* in terms of their language of daily use:

> One of the most pressing problems encountered by the Eligibility Division is that of refugees from Italian territory ceded to Yugoslavia as a result of the Peace Treaty, whose customary language is Italian but who have not opted from Italian citizen(ship) within the time prescribed by the terms of the Treaty—i.e., before September 15, 1948. Many of these refugees are not racially Italian or of Italian ethnic origin but are more familiar with the Italian language than with other tongues owing

to the extreme nationalist policy adopted in the now ceded territories by the Italian Government in the years between the wars (this policy included the enforced teaching of Italian in schools, etc.).[98]

Having contended that many of these DPs were not of Italian "ethnic origin," Whigham added that many likewise did not consider themselves Italian.

Some of these refugees have strong cultural affiliations with the Italian race, others have not. Many do not feel themselves in anyway Italian, and some have a strong hatred of Italy as a result of past persecution on racial grounds. Until September 15th some of them had been harbored in Italian Post War Assistance camps but have since been, or are about to be, ejected. Many of them, together with their families, are quite destitute, have no possibility of obtaining work and are regarded as undesirable foreigners by the Italian authorities. Some have already found their way into Italian Internment Camps for foreigners. Their disposal has been a matter of discussion between this Mission and the Italian Government and their eligibility status is at present under consideration at Geneva.[99]

Mentz seconded this view, underlining the ways in which individuals with some markers of Italian cultural identity (e.g., language) could possess a specific, local identity that did not extend to or map onto a broader sense of "Italian nationality."

An Italian speaking Istrian who left his country of origin because of the establishment of Tito's regime in the State of Yugoslavia to which Istria was transferred, but who did not opt for Italian citizenship because the only strong tie he formerly had with Italy was represented by the Istrian town where he was born, is a clear case of a refugee who is unable or unwilling to avail himself of the protection both of the Yugoslav and the Italian government, and so he is the concern of the Organization.[100]

As a result of these discussions over eligibility, the IRO changed its policies in early 1950 and began offering assistance to this type of Venezia Giulian refugee—that is, an individual who had not opted for Italian citizenship (and thus legally became a Yugoslav citizen), regardless of customary language.[101] Also included in this decision were individuals who had opted but whose option the Yugoslav government had not accepted. In some instances, the Yugoslav authorities rejected option applications on the supposed grounds that Italian was not the language used at home, in spite of what prospective optants had declared. In Istria, authorities required an attestation before the local Comitato Popolare or People's Committee that the language spoken by the optant was Italian.[102] Not surprisingly, this situation made for possible intimidation and abuse. Some of these migrants who had not received the option nonetheless held provisional passports issued in Zagreb that had permitted them to cross into Italy. These provisional passports would prove to be a source of enduring controversy within the IRO. The IRO required these individuals to have "valid objections against returning to Yugoslavia." In addition, to be considered eligible for IRO help, these DPs could not be "firmly established in Italy," a situation that would negate the need for assistance with emigration.

In revising its eligibility policies, then, the IRO came to technically privilege the legal criterion of citizenship over that of ethnicity (as linguistic identity)—what they had initially considered to be largely coterminous. The eligibility evaluation of individual cases of Venezia Giulia from the 1950s on also reveals greater attention to the aspects of local identity highlighted by Mentz and others. IRO staff often used these as indicators of rootedness in deciding whether migrants merely sought to exploit IRO aid or if they possessed legitimate reasons for not opting for Italy. Ultimately, for those refugees who belied easy classification as either "Italian" or "Slavic," IRO officials adopted the label "Undetermined Venezia Giulian." The IRO, and UNRRA before it, had used the notion of "undetermined nationality" to denote a number of ambiguous situations, so the concept did not prove unique to the Italian case. A 1946 UNRRA memo, for instance, had stated that the classification "undetermined" was part of "a broader category designated as 'others and unclassified.'"[103] Even here, however, the Venezia Giulian case stood out for its complexity. In an interview in 1952 as the IRO was winding up its operations, the chief eligibility officer R. L. Gesner was asked, "What was the most interesting group that you had to deal with?" He responded, "As a whole the Venezia Giulians, because of the constant change of policy, commencing in 1948 right through."[104]

For statistical reporting on ambiguous refugees in camps or IRO intake centers, for example, Alva Simpson, chief of the Department of Health, Care and Maintenance, ordered that the nationality of such refugees should be registered as "Undetermined Venezia Giulia."[105] Whereas the Italian government frequently flattened ambiguity and read claims to Italian belonging by "Slavs" as akin to deception and subterfuge, then, IRO personnel instead came to recognize officially the national indeterminacy of many such refugees from Istria and the larger region of the Julian March. In addition, IRO staff changed their policies to allow a number of these "undetermined" individuals to emigrate abroad with IRO help, thereby relieving the Italian government of some potential citizens whose "Italianness" proved questionable.

The IRO, however, would or could only go so far. The organization, for instance, refused the demand of the refugee Association for Venezia Giulia and Zara either to award the classification of "indefinite citizenship" to those whose options had not been approved or to drop any pressure "for a declaration of Yugoslav citizenship as a condition for emigration to other countries."[106] In 1951 and 1952, as well, the IRO revisited its eligibility decisions yet again. First, the mission excluded a number of Venezia Giulia refugees with provisional passports previously included within the mandate. Although some officials deeply regretted this shift, others adopted a much tougher line. V. A. Temnomeroff, a member of the IRO's review board, insisted,

> persons who duly opted [for Italy] in Yugoslavia are to be considered as Italian citizens as soon as their options are approved by the Yugoslav authorities—in other words, before they are issued with Italian passports by the Italian Consul in Zagreb. Therefore, the motives of the Italian consul in issuing these provisional passports are not relevant. . . . The motives of the Yugoslav authorities in approving the option are also irrelevant. It is not up to the Organization to attempt to correct the determination of the customary language made by the Yugoslav authorities, or to examine their motives in approving the options. . . . It would not be consistent to adopt other than a formal attitude towards the problem in question.[107]

These reversals prompted numerous letters of protest by Julian refugees. With the reclassification as ineligible of certain refugees previously deemed to fall within the IRO's mandate, a group of Julian refugees in the IRO camp at Carinaro d'Aversa sent a letter to the organization's director-general. Many of these individuals had liquidated their savings in preparation for emigration overseas under IRO auspices. As the result, these individuals found themselves "at present in a critical material and moral position, for the prolonged stay in the camp has exhausted all their material and financial resources, because of the inadequate assistance."[108] Sadly, such displaced persons ultimately found their indeterminacy extended not only to their ethnicity/nationality but also to their status as international refugees.

While different from that of Venezia Giulia, the situation in the Dodecanese raised similar questions of indeterminacy. As we have seen, the primary actors involved here in repatriation of those opting to retain Italian citizenship by the terms of article 19 were officials of the British Military

Administration and the Italian government, though UNRRA/IRO and the Greek government also played significant roles. Even before VE Day, the language of indeterminacy appears to have gained salience on the ground, if the complaint of a BMA major is to be believed. In a letter dated May 1945, he wrote, "There seems to be a tendency among islanders to claim that they are no longer Italian Aegean subjects, or in some cases Italian nationals, and to call themselves Greeks or of indeterminate nationality when neither is true. This should not be countenanced in this connection."[109]

In contrast to the BMA, both UNRRA and the IRO took seriously such claims of indeterminacy, given that citizenship and nationality determined, in part, which persons came under the mandate of the intergovernmental bodies. In the case of UNRRA, of course, the organization focused on returning individuals to their national homes (for details, see chapter 3), while the IRO's efforts focused on facilitating emigration for those displaced persons who could not safely be repatriated home. By October 1949, some three thousand "Dodecanese refugees" in Italy had filed applications for IRO assistance, rather than making claims on the Italian state; some documents referred instead to two thousand such individuals.[110] Marquis Chiavari, special adviser on Italian affairs to the IRO, inquired whether the organization would honor these requests. In response, a 1949 cable from the IRO's headquarters in Rome to Geneva clarified that there existed three primary categories of Dodecanese in postwar Italy:

> FIRST NATIVES OF DODECANESE BECAME ITALIAN CITIZENS AFTER ITALO–TURKISH WAR BY LAUSANNE TREATY 1913 [*sic*] SECOND NATIVES OF TURKEY MOVED TO DODECANESE AND RHODES AFTER WORLD WAR II THIRD EMIGRATED FROM ITALY AFTER 1913 ON JUNE 1940 WERE RESIDENTS ON ISLANDS CEDED TO GREECE OPTED FOR ITALIAN CITIZENSHIP UNDER PARA 19 PEACE TREATY LIKE VENEZIA GIULIANS OPTION NOT REGULARLY APPROVED BY GREEK GOVERNMENT THEY WERE EVACUATED TO ITALY AFTER WORLD WAR II BY ALLIES OR ITALIAN NAVY FEARING PERSECUTION AND HOSTILITY OF GOVERNMENT AND LOCAL GREEK POPULATION APPLICANTS NOT FIRMLY ESTABLISHED IN ITALY STILL LIVING IN ITALIAN CAMPS HAVE NO RELATIVES IN ITALY REESTABLISHMENT HERE EXTREMELY DIFFICULT.[111]

A small number of Jews from the islands who had survived Nazi concentration camps and made their way to Italy upon their liberation numbered among these "Dodecanesian refugees."

This memo—sent to the IRO's major players, including the acting general director Jacobsen, Myer Cohen in Health and Maintenance, and L. M. Hacking of the Historical Section—apparently raised as many questions as it sought to answer. On this document, someone scribbled at the bottom: "this doesn't help much," "customary language," "valid objection to returning to Greece—pol[itical] grounds? persn or pol grounds? pol opinion not in conflict with U.N.?," and "approved option?"[112] In the Dodecanese case, then, the IRO was clearly experiencing dilemmas similar to that of Venezia Giulia in translating the citizenship terms laid out in the 1947 Peace Treaty into its own procedures of eligibility. Not surprisingly, in the internal IRO debates opened up by Chiavari's request, Hacking commented, "The problem was in many respects similar to the problems raised by Venezia Giuliansrefugees [*sic*] and particularly by that group of Venezia Giulians who opted to retain Italian citizenship while they were still in Yugoslavia." Hacking also indicated the considerable degree of work the IRO undertook to interpret the treaty's article 19 in relation to these displaced persons from the Isole Egeo.

> We thought that in the first place it was necessary to have texts of the Greek legislation and administrative directives implementing Article 19 of the Peace Treaty which you will remember is the Article governing the citizenship of persons living in areas transferred by Italy to other countries under the Peace Treaty. It appeared that Mr. Asscher had a good text of the Greek law on the subject and that Mr. Asscher is checking this text with the original Greek one which exists in the library at the Palais des Nations. We felt, however, that it would be well to cable to Athens to ask for the Royal Decree mentioned in the law, to be sent to Geneva for examination.[113]

Beyond the formal issue of citizenship remained the question of possible political persecution should such individuals be repatriated back to the islands. "In addition to citizenship issues," commented Hacking, "there is of course the most important question of the validity of any objections to repatriation that may be expressed by the Aegean refugees in question." Nonetheless, such possible objections appeared to hold little weight. Hacking admitted, "So far the Organisation has made a firm rule that it will not accept as valid objections to repatriation to Greece."[114]

This initial decision did not dissuade representatives of the Italian government, however, from insisting that the IRO recognize some of these migrants from the Dodecanese in Italy as bona fide international refugees, as had occurred in the Venezia Giulian case. Just a few months after the IRO's judgment as to the noneligibility of these refugees, Prince del Drago in the Ministry of Foreign Affairs pressed the case. Del Drago argued the invalidity of the Greek Law No. 517 (3 January 1949) laying out the process by which optants could make their applications to Greek consular officials, including those in Italy.[115] According to IRO documents, most of the nineteen hundred non-Jewish individuals from the Dodecanese in Italy had exercised the citizenship option before such consular officials on the Italian peninsula. By contrast, most of the one hundred or so Jews from the islands had not.[116] Arguing on a technicality, Del Drago contended, "The law promulgated by the Greek Government . . . does not appear sufficient to settle the question of the nationality of the refugees from the Dodecanese who have opted in favour of Italian nationality and are at present living in Italy, inasmuch as it is a one-sided act of the Greek Government." Del Drago added, "In the present circumstances, and since the ratification [in Italy of the Greek law] has not yet been carried out, the above refugees should be considered, from the legal point of view, in a position of undetermined nationality like the refugees from Venezia Giulia."[117]

In Italian eyes, at least, approval of option requests by Greek authorities did not constitute a recognition of the optant's genuine Italian identity in terms of language or sentiment. Del Drago also claimed that the majority of these individuals had been persecuted "on account of their religion and political ideas," implying affiliations with the former Italian regime that seemingly contradicted his statement as to their indeterminacy (unless he referred only to the small number of Jewish survivors). In language familiar from Italian authorities' evaluations of requests to repatriate to Italy from former possessions, Del Drago also underlined the "strain on the very limited Italian assistance budget [created by these Dodecanesians], inasmuch as they have neither financial resources nor relations in Italy."[118]

In a certain sense, we might read the enthusiastic endorsement by Del Drago (and, by extension, the Italian government) of the "undetermined nationality" label in the Aegean case as strategic and pragmatic, an attempt merely to reduce the burden of caring for national refugees. Indeed, Del Drago made this burden explicit when he maintained, "Even if these refugees constitute a serious problem for the Italian Government, which has already to assist many of its own refugees, they would not be a heavy burden for IRO either because of their limited number (approximately 2,000) or because of their professional ability which will permit ready acceptance by the immigration countries." In the same letter, however, Del Drago refers to the ambiguous citizenship statuses in the Dodecanese that had prevailed under fascism. "On the other hand . . . several of these refugees are in possession of the 'little Italian citizenship' and, even if their status is definitely established, they would be able to maintain such little citizenship but with limited rights, unless special provisions are established in their favour." In another sense, then, Del Drago pointed to the problematic legacies of indeterminate citizenship as embodied by the limited rights of the *piccola cittadinanza* and *cittadinanza egea*.

Although IRO staff took seriously such requests from Italian representatives, they ultimately did not accept Del Drago's line of reasoning. In urging careful consideration of eligibility of individual cases (rather than blanket group designations), Myer Cohen stressed that for persons from the Dodecanese, "the most important criteria are their citizenship (apart from one inapplicable exception, refugees cannot be within the mandate under the IRO Constitution unless they are outside their country of citizenship) and their objection to return to the Dodecanese." In regard to the argument that the Greek government had established a unilateral procedure for option, Cohen urged, "The Peace Treaty does not demand any agreement between the Greek or Italian Governments regularizing options, nor any acceptance by either Greek or Italian Government of such options. It demands merely the promulgation of appropriate legislation by the Greek Government or the Government to which territory has been ceded." Acknowledging the IRO's delicate position as an intergovernmental body operating in a world structured through and around the logics of state sovereignty, Cohen noted, "The Italian Government has a sovereign right to report as Italian citizens whomsoever it chooses. We submit, however, that this right is subject to provisions of international instruments, in particular, the Peace Treaty, which is binding on the Italian Government, and that IRO is not competent to agree to a position clearly contrary to its terms." Cohen thus concluded, "The IRO should therefore consider as Italian citizens, all persons who have duly opted within the terms of the Peace Treaty and the appropriate implementary legislation to retain Italian citizenship. Persons who have not so opted should be considered as Greek citizens."[119]

In contrast to the Venezia Giulian case, then, the IRO did not reverse its initial ruling on the ineligibility of certain individuals from the Aegean who had opted for Italian citizenship. In both instances, however, the status of migrants from the former Italian territories troubled the seemingly straightforward divisions between national and international refugees that rested on understandings of citizenship, as well as persecution. Were migrants to the Italian peninsula from the ceded territories of Venezia Giulia or the Aegean to be considered to have remained within their home countries and thus under the protection of the Italian state? What about in those instances where the Italian government did not recognize the Italianness (in terms of customary sentiment and language) of those who had legally opted for Italian citizenship before either Yugoslav or Greek authorities? Just as Italy sought to assert and strengthen its sovereignty through the control of "alien refugees" in its midst, so too did it seek to reinterpret the citizenship clause of article 19—part of a larger peace treaty over which Italians had relatively little say—by urging the IRO to facilitate the emigration of a number of individuals who could make legal claims on Italy but whose Italianness appeared questionable. In other ambiguous questions of citizenship, Italian authorities would endorse an understanding of Italianness that included not only such criteria as language as ethnicity but also blood.

Categorical Confusion, III: Mixed Unions and Their Offspring

As we have seen, from unification onward, Italian citizenship codes made naturalization cumbersome and rare. Fascism's defeat and the establishment of the First Republic did not fundamentally alter this. In the aftermath of the Second World War and the empire's dissolution, there arose the question of the status of "foreign" partners (many, but not all, of them colonial subjects) of Italian citizens, as well as their offspring. The files of the Archivio Centrale dello Stato and the Ministero degli Affari Esteri, for instance, contain numerous requests by "foreign" wives of Italians in the Dodecanese both to repatriate and opt for Italy. In the case of inter-confessional marriages in the Aegean, one key issue involved the type of marriage rite performed (civil or religious, and if religious which faith) and its validity under Italian law. BMA officers on Karpathos, for instance, told Greek wives seeking repatriation to Italy that neither the Vatican nor Italian civil courts recognized marriages between Catholics and Orthodox without a dispensation and the presence of a Catholic priest at the ceremony.[120] These dilemmas extended to those Italian soldiers on the Greek mainland who had contracted marriages during the war. In December 1945, the Greek UNRRA mission headquartered in Athens received instructions: "It is imperative to forward the marriage certificate drawn up abroad, <u>duly translated and legalized by the Italian consular authority</u>." The delays in obtaining and forwarding such documents had already created "a situation greatly prejudical [*sic*] to the interests of the married couples recently repatriated from Greece, as, owing to the non-recognition of the legality of their marriage by the Italian authorities, their families do not enjoy the advantages provided by the law in favour of the wives and children of the ex-service men." Adding to the problems, "without these documents the Italian Judicial Authority is similarly unable to provide for the prosecution necessary <u>in certain cases of bigamy</u>."[121]

Bigamy and the related problem of abandonment posed very real threats to the postwar reconstruction of the family. As UNRRA and Italy negotiated the terms of repatriation in the early years after the war, "It was also agreed that Greek wives of Italian soldiers could be sent to Italy, but only if there was good assurance of the validity of the marriage and acceptance of the wives by their husbands."[122] As this last clause suggests, an important consideration appeared to be whether the Italian male wished his companion to be allowed into Italy—which would have given bigamists an easy escape clause. As a 1946 UNRRA memo noted, "The Italian government reserves its right to withhold permission of entry into Italy for these women [here, Greek wives of Italian POWs], pending definite proof that the Italian husband wishes to have his wife brought to Italy."[123] Dodecanesian women married to Italian POWs also made requests for help to the BMA and the Italian Committee in Rhodes run by Antonio Macchi. The BMA took a line similar to that of UNRRA, confirming that requests for the requisite marriage documents must "be initiated by the husband in each case."[124] One woman who appealed to the BMA for help with repatriation received the reply, "The initiation of the movement must in the first instance come from the husband, who has to state that he is able to house and feed, etc his family, before they are accepted in Italy."[125] In another case that did not prove at all uncommon, BMA officers on Karpathos had determined that a legal marriage between an Irene J. and Nicola G. took place in June 1944. The wife "has one small child, by her marriage, and has had no money from her husband since he went to Italy." Fearing that her husband had remarried in Italy (thus becoming a bigamist), Irene sought only financial support for their child.[126]

For those spouses of non-Italian citizenship from the Dodecanese Islands or the ceded areas of Venezia Giulia who succeeded in repatriating to Italy, the option process remained separate from that of their husbands. In contrast to many earlier options, the husband's citizenship did not extend to his wife, though it did for minor children under eighteen. Still, the treaty option clauses made no provisions for a whole range of persons, including illegitimate children, nonmarried orphaned minors, and adopted children.[127] In this, the citizenship clauses of the treaty *did* represent a break with earlier citizenship policies of liberal Italy that had automatically assigned married women their husbands' nationality; fascist changes to the 1912 Citizenship Law had exerted even greater control over the citizenship of married women. In his commentary on the treaty, legal scholar Kunz lauded the lack of extension of the husband's option to his wife as a significant "expression of the movement for the emancipation of women."[128] Undoubtedly, the mandating of separate options for husbands and wives helped rectify gender inequities built into previous Italian citizenship policies. This innovation provided women resident in the former possessions who could satisfy the criteria for Italianness greater freedom to decide whether or not to opt on their own for Italian citizenship. Nonetheless, in the case of foreign wives, it appears to have given some Italian husbands the opportunity to "emancipate" themselves from their domestic partners and attendant obligations.

It should be noted, however, that not all such hesitation about whether to naturalize foreign wives came from the Italian side of the process. The attitudes of the home states of potential optants also mattered. Italian authorities received many urgent requests for assistance concerning "Yugoslav" wives of Italian citizens whose options had been repeatedly turned down in Istria, for example. Likewise, in Albania both Albanian wives and *husbands* of Italian citizens found their requests to go to Italy blocked by the Hoxha regime.[129] Indeed, marriages between Italian women and Albanian men—which resulted in the wives' automatic loss of Italian citizenship and acquisition of Albanian citizenship—proved an exception to the prevalent pattern elsewhere in which only Italian men married or cohabited with imperial subjects.

One relatively rare request for naturalization by a man originally from the former possessions who had married an Italian citizen concerned the Albanian-born Abdul Luku. Luku had served in the Austrian military in World War I, after which he moved to Rijeka / Fiume. Soon afterward, he settled in Duino Aurisina, near Trieste, and married an Italian woman by whom he had a daughter. Luku remained Muslim, though his wife and daughter practiced Catholicism. In recommending that Luku's 1952 naturalization request be granted, the prefect of Trieste Gino Palutan asserted that Luku was "completely assimilated to our environment and while knowing numerous other languages, expresses himself correctly and prevalently in the Italian language. He does not manifest any national sentiment, however, he has never assumed an attitude contrary to Italy."[130] The Ministry of Foreign Affairs concurred with Palutan's assessment, characterizing Luku's request "particularly worthy."[131] This example evidences how language, political sentiment, and assimilability were key in deciding which foreigners might become citizens or immigrate to Italy in the early postwar period. In this case, at least, the otherness of Islam did not appear as significant as Luku's adaptability to an Italian way of life. Similarly, a number of Jews originally from Rhodes and resident in the Congo at the time of the 1947 option process chose Italian rather than Greek citizenship and were recognized for being "well disposed" toward Italy.[132]

In such cases, the Europeanness of the optants—and hence their potential for assimilation—was likely assumed, even if their Italianness remained in question. But what happened in the case of the mixed African-Italian populations in the newly independent colonies? The majority of those who lived in the colonies did not have the option to move to Europe, similar to other cases of decolonization. R. E. Ovalle-Bahamoń notes of the population of former Portuguese Angola, "For the majority of people in Angola, namely 'blacks,' the exit to Europe option was nonexistent."[133] And, as in the Portuguese case, where no explicit reference was made to race in defining citizenship, in the case of Italy's former colonies an implicit understanding about race nonetheless operated: as former colonial subjects, rather than Italian citizens, "black natives" acquired the citizenship of their respective countries. Such logics reflected a common colonial grammar. In the words of Ann Stoler, these policies of exclusion were "contingent on constructing categories, legal and social classifications designating who was 'white,' who was 'native,' who could become a citizen rather than a subject, which children were legitimate progeny and which were not. What mattered were not only one's physical properties but who counted as 'European' and by what measure." Silences proved critical to these exclusions, for "Skin shade was too ambiguous; bank accounts were mercurial; religious belief and education were crucial but never enough. Social and legal standing derived not only from color, but from the silences, acknowledgments, and denials of the social circumstances in which one's parents had sex."[134]

In the Italian case, the meticci or persons of mixed race from the former AOI complicated this colonial grammar's neat classificatory distinctions between citizen and (former) subject, shattering those silences and making visible the frequency of interracial relationships. Indeed, although much of the travel literature on the empire remained silent on the widespread practice of *madamismo*, these writings nonetheless expounded at length on the degenerational dangers represented by mixed-race children.[135] These politics of nonrecognition and denial, of course, contradicted a form of citizenship based on blood. Alberto Pollera—colonial official, ethnographer, and brother of a onetime governor of Italian Eritrea—pointed this out in his appeal to Mussolini in 1939. Pollera, himself the father of six (recognized) children by two African wives, pleaded, "Our meticci children are thus by the blood of the father, by their physical being, by education, by sentiment, perfectly Italian." In case the blood criterion seemed insufficient, then, Pollera threw in for good measure language and sentiment. In a parting shot, he asserted, "They [meticci] are officials, functionaries, professionals, traders, artisans, honest workers; and the women joined with Italian men are good mothers whose offspring for their intellectual, moral, and physical qualities are often superior to Italians of pure race [*razza pura*]."[136]

As noted earlier, the increasingly stringent legislation in the late 1930s prohibiting and punishing miscegenation, as well as the stripping of citizenship from those relatively few meticci who had been formally recognized by their Italian fathers, indicated the regime's increasing moral panic over the problem of mixed-race children. This official obsession in spite of the frequent denials of the phenomenon was evidenced by a 1938 census, which collected specific data for the AOI on "meticci per nazioni e razza della madre e il sesso per territorio"—meticci by nation and race of the mother and by sex. The statistics offered an extremely conservative figure of 2,518 meticci total for Eritrea, Ethiopia, and Somalia combined. Of these, only 1,291 had been recognized by their fathers.[137] Estimates by the UN and the BMA of the population of Italo-Eritreans alone in the early postwar instead give figures of around 15,000 individuals, of whom only a small fraction (some 2,750) had been recognized by their fathers.[138]

In the immediate aftermath of the war, the Italian government pushed for the abolition of the fascist-era legislation prohibiting miscegenation. At the beginning of their occupation of AOI, BMA authorities had agreed, proclaiming in May 1942 the suspension of the law until the end of British rule. By June, however, the British had reverted to the Italian legislation, arguing that as a neutral occupier it would serve merely as a placeholder, including in the juridical sense. This set the stage for a long-running dispute between the British and Italians over the racial law, which Valeria Deplano has situated within the broader wrangling over the future of the territories. In preventing the (re)acquisition of citizenship by those meticci recognized by their fathers, for instance, the British sought to block the increase in "Italians" within the ex-colonies[139]—just as they sought to do by regulating and stemming repatriation back to Italian Africa. Some Italian jurists still working in the former AOI adopted a line closer to that of the British than that of officials on the Italian peninsula. In particular, a 1949 decision by a *procuratore* Montefusco in Asmara rejecting an Eritrean mother's attempts to win her son Italian citizenship prompted frustration and anger within the Ministry of Foreign Affairs and the Ministry of Italian Africa. Whereas Montefusco interpreted the question of citizenship in the colonial terms of a discretional privilege accorded to subjects, Italian officials on the mainland stressed that citizenship was a right.[140]

In the midst of these broader geopolitical struggles over the former colonies and internal Italian debates over the meaning of citizenship, mixed-race children in AOI continued to pay the price in the form of stigma, as well as broken relationships with their parents. In a testimony given to historian Gabrielle D'Agostino, Giovanni Mazzola—born in Asmara just a few weeks after the 1940 law went into effect—remembered how his Italian father had succeeded in registering his son and thus recognizing him (presumably after the war, although this is unclear). Mazzola recalled that the year 1949, when any hopes of an Italian trusteeship over Eritrea faded, witnessed an "exodus" of Italians back to the peninsula. His father numbered among those Italians leaving. Neither Giovanni nor his five brothers ever saw their father again, although Giovanni arrived in Italy in 1963 in search of him, only to learn he had died a week earlier. Like so many before him, the father of the Mazzola brothers had a fiancée in Italy, with whom he established a second family upon his return. Not only was Giovanni's mother abandoned by her European partner, but she also suffered discrimination from her fellow Eritreans. "The [Eritrean] woman of that time, according to the local mentality, in the moment in which she got together with an Italian lost all her rights, she no longer had the right to own land, a house . . . she was ignored completely."[141]

Giovanni later married a *meticcia*, Maria Bertellini, who noted that other Eritrean children frequently taunted her as a "bastard." In contrast to Giovanni's father, Maria's father could not recognize his children because he was already legally married in Italy. Until 1975, the Italian Civil Code prohibited both inquiries into paternity and the legal recognition of children born out of wedlock. As Barrera concludes, many of these children of mixed descent "suffered not only due to the colonial relationship, but also because of the patriarchic imprint of the Italian legislation. . . . A distinctly *colonial* paternity was at work in both cases."[142] Maria's father, Salvatore Mauro, thus resorted to a stratagem employed by a number of Italians anxious to recognize their children: he asked another Italian (Bertellini) to give his name to his daughter and son. Salvatore Mauro remained in Asmara until the civil conflict of the 1970s, when he was assaulted and expelled to Italy. Like so many Italians who suffered from *mal d'Africa*, Mauro dreamed of returning. He told his daughter Maria, "'I'm ready, I keep my passport updated, I want to return.'"[143] Giovanni Mazzola's father similarly waxed nostalgic. Mazzola's relatives in Italy told his brothers that their father would occasionally go down to the seashore and murmur, "'One day, I will return to Africa.'"[144] Whereas the iconic fascist image featuring the pledge "We will return" had depicted a settler father (or grandfather) and son, the Italian men here instead longed for an African home in which the children they would return to were of mixed race.

Legally, the situation for meticci in Eritrea changed in 1952, when the BMA finally abolished the 1940 legislation. In that same year, Eritrea was joined in federation with Ethiopia.[145] UN Resolution 390(V) of 2 December

1950 had laid out the plan for federation. According to the Ethiopian state's laws on citizenship, all meticci automatically became Ethiopian citizens. Yet some meticci sought either to retain or newly acquire rights as Italian citizens—following the option for Italian citizenship laid out by the UN Resolution—by renouncing their Ethiopian citizenship. The year 1952 saw the opening of an Italian consulate in Addis Ababa, where most requests for recognition and/or citizenship arrived. Between 1952 and 1955, some 48 meticci had been recognized. A total of 1,950 meticci had opted for Italian citizenship by April 1953.[146]

In the context of lingering bad feeling between Italy and Ethiopia over Italy's crushed hopes for a trusteeship over Eritrea, the Italian government supported the right of these meticci to opt, and saw their choice of Italy as a validation of Italy's accomplishments and civilizing mission there. The Ethiopian government responded by creating bureaucratic obstacles, such as substituting a new form for opting just three days before the closing date of the request process. The Ethiopian government also used an implicit appeal to racial solidarity in its assertion that opting for Ethiopia, rather than Italy, appeared "more just and natural." Italian officials interpreted the Ethiopian government's actions as motivated by a need for prestige and the wish to demonstrate that Ethiopia was more attractive to the meticci than was Italy.[147] As Barrera has noted, however, this policy may have also reflected the cognatic conception of descent that prevailed among Ethiopia's Amharic peoples; this contrasted with the patrilineal understanding of identity subscribed to by the Tigrinya of highland Eritrea, the ethnic group of most of the Eritrean women who had children by Italian men.[148]

Italian diplomats went so far as to denounce as "discriminatory" the Ethiopian government's refusal to issue visas to Italian citizens—presumably former settlers and those few meticci living in Italy as citizens—wanting to visit Ethiopia.[149] Yet despite the Italian government's seeming openness toward the meticci, a 1953 document that exulted in the meticci's choice of Italy over Ethiopia nonetheless admitted, "If these meticci had conserved en masse federal citizenship [that of Ethiopia], it would not have been bad either for them or for us."[150] This reflected the fundamental ambivalence toward this Italo-African population and the widespread belief that such hybrid subjects could never become genuine Italian citizens in the fullest sense of social belonging. Silvana Patriarca has detected a similar ambivalence to the "brown babies," almost all of them Italian citizens, that resulted from unions between Italian women and black Allied servicemen.[151] As occurred in the former AOI, in the 1950s many of these biracial children in Italy suffered abandonment, frequently ending up in the care of Catholic institutions. Meticci children often lived in Catholic-run schools and orphanages and sometimes went to summer camps organized by humanitarian groups like the Italian Red Cross. This entrenched the pervasive discourse that such children constituted a "problem." The fact that the same child actor played the part of a "mulatto" and a colonial "meticcio" in the films *Il Mulatto* and *Angelo tra la folla*, respectively, symbolizes the easy slippage in the Italian imagination between these populations of mixed-race children whose histories are quite distinct.[152]

As the 1950s wore on, Italian officials continued to report on the numbers and conditions of both the meticci in Eritrea-Ethiopia and the "Italians" there. In some accounts, meticci and their mothers figured as problematic for their role in prompting the abandonment of "true" families in Italy. In a 1955 assessment of the "Italian collectivity in Ethiopia," for example, the Italian consul general to Ethiopia Francesco Smergani complained, "Every day I receive letters from the most remote regions of Italy where mothers, wives and legitimate children who are now adults beg for news of their loved ones. I know where and with whom they live, how many meticci children they have as their burden and I also know that I cannot humiliate them for fear of destroying those slight vibrations of patriotism in their hearts that comprehend the bitterness of the situation from which they can longer extricate themselves."[153] Smergani went on to invert the colonial tropes of Africans as childlike naifs in need of rescue and civilizing. In his mind, Italian men had become the virtual slaves of their African partners, who established "families" that mocked the decent values of those genuine families lost back in Italy: "The piety that every one of us feels for the abandoned families in Italy is profound and it is no less for these bereaved men who labor under the exploitation of women of color, relentless in their robbery. To latch onto an Italian man is considered a feat here, because it's known that this guarantees not only maintenance of the woman and her meticci children but also of the whole band of beggars from which she comes."[154] Just a few lines later, however, Smergani wrote of the meticci how "reasons of human piety recommend that we extend to these innocent derelicts [*derelitti*] our help/aid." Smergani noted that this had to be done with great delicacy through the Italian fathers, avoiding contact with the African mothers out of political sensitivity. Unlike in the Eritrean part of the federation, where a *festa della befana* or celebration of the witch that delivers treats to children on the eve of the Epiphany had been held for Italian children of "any color" (*qualsiasi colore*), tense relations with the Ethiopians meant that a *befana* event could only be held there for legitimate Italian children. Given that unrecognized children typically exhibited the greatest need, such an event would only provoke resentment. Smergani's admission of this extreme need, of course, contradicted his claims about the children's rapacious mothers. Smergani's account thus exhibits toward the meticci an admixture of racism, empathy, obligation, and political opportunism that proved pervasive among Italian officials.

Ultimately, despite political posturing designed to depict Italy in a favorable light, in the period under study here, the majority of mixed-race children in the former African colonies found themselves unable to make claims as citizens on the Italian state. This did not, however, resolve the issue, and in succeeding decades meticci from both Ethiopia/Eritrea and Somalia continued to press for recognition as Italian citizens. This became particularly urgent as individuals sought to flee the violent conflict between Ethiopia and Eritrea (1961–1991), the tumult of the Ethiopian Revolution with Selassie's overthrow in 1974 by the communist military regime of the Derg, the devastation of the Ethiopian famine (1983–1985), and the atrocities of the Siad Barre regime in Somalia. Within Italy, the 1990s witnessed a flurry of largely empty political discussions and promises over Italian obligations toward these African descendants of Italian citizens. The 1992 citizenship law permitted requests by second-generation descendants ("in linea retta di secondo grado"), prompting several hundred requests for citizenship by Italo-Eritreans alone. By 2014, only eighty of these requests had been successful, with another three hundred or so pending.[155]

The problem of citizenship for some Italo-Somalis also remains open, particularly as there occurred a boom in births after 1949 during the period of the Italian-administered UN trusteeship. The civil war in Somalia led to the destruction of many birth records, required to establish a possible claim to citizenship. Many of the Italo-Somali children born between 1949 and 1960, the year of Somalia's independence, were taken from their mothers and placed in special boarding schools or religious institutions in which they were educated in Italian. Those who succeeded in obtaining Italian citizenship and moved to Italy, sometimes after a period of formal statelessness, nonetheless feel set apart—what they deem "category C citizens." As the head of the Associazione Nazionale Comunità Italo-Somala, or National Association of the Italo-Somali Community (ANCIS), Gianni Mari, put it, "We are aliens with Italian passports."[156] In June 2008, the Italian government declared it would offer compensation to several hundred such Italo-Somali. Although groups such as ANCIS express satisfaction at the government's pledge to offer compensation, they also want a formal apology, and continue to press their cause and work to bring it to a wider Italian audience.[157] The decades-long struggle by such descendants to win recognition as essential members of the Italian national community further underscores how Italian decolonization unfolded over a much longer arc of time than usually imagined, as well as the enduring exclusions that resulted specifically from the narrowing of Italian citizenship norms with the end of empire.

As this chapter has demonstrated, as the colonial juridical hierarchy gave way over time to a flat one of national citizenship, there was little place in Italy for those seen as indeterminate or in between. It was for precisely this reason that the Italian government had pushed the IRO to accept as eligible for emigration abroad those individuals who came to bear the label "undetermined nationality"—even in some instances where the migrant had opted successfully for Italian citizenship. Despite efforts by Italian officials or migrants themselves to claim "indefinite citizenship" for some subjects from the Dodecanese and Venezia Giulia so that those individuals could be classified as international refugees, international agencies proved wary of embracing a notion of indeterminate citizenship. In the world of the emerging international refugee regime, one either had citizenship or did not (i.e., was stateless). The pressing question for UNRRA, the IRO, and later the UNHCR centered on whether those requesting recognition as refugees who did possess citizenship resided in their country of citizenship or outside it. If the latter, did their claims merit recognition as refugees on the familiar grounds of persecution in their home countries?

For Italian authorities, the process of sorting through individuals making claims to be refugees—whether national or foreign—sharpened and tested the limits of Republican understandings of citizenship. As evidenced by debates over who from the former territories could rightfully opt to retain Italian citizenship and thus legally move to the Italian peninsula, understandings of Italian identity and belonging in the early postwar period rested explicitly on linguistic affiliation qua ethnicity and implicitly on a racialized notion of Europeanness and whiteness. In the case of those "ethnic" Greeks and Slavs excluded from opting for Italian citizenship, being a white European was necessary but not sufficient for inclusion within the Italian national community. Language of use and "Italian ancestry" were additionally required for both legal citizenship and social belonging. In this sense, understandings of Italian identity displayed considerable continuity with older understandings, even as certain aspects of identity such as race became naturalized to the point of invisibility. A patrilineal and thus consanguineal understanding of identity continued to underwrite codes of Italian citizenship after World War II, even as the citizenship of married women became independent of that of their husbands. Likewise, previously explicit understandings of race central to colonialism became muted in a context where the "racial" identity of the "Italian" migrants was not questioned, even if their Italianness remained a question of "fact and proof." The small numbers of meticci eligible for Italian citizenship constitute the notable exception here; among the various categories of repatriates from the former possessions, this group has, not surprisingly, faced the most daunting challenges to acceptance as Italians.

The story of citizenship recounted here does not prove a mere historical anecdote but rather an enduring legacy that continues to shape the reception of migrants to Italy. With the advent of mass immigration to Italy from the 1970s on, new migrants to the peninsula have continued to run up against the restrictive policies for Italian naturalization created by a system anchored by *jus sanguinis*. A controversial and politicized vote over whether to reform Italian citizenship law and award citizenship to those children born in Italy to noncitizens has long been postponed. At the heart of the "jus soli" debate and movement in contemporary Italy are the terms of both legal and sociocultural belonging.[158] After World War II, the citizenship question was settled in a distinctly exclusive and restrictive manner. Over seventy years later, it remains to be seen whether the Italian state will expand the legal boundaries of citizenship.

Chapter 5

Reclaiming Fascism, Housing the Nation

> Today there are eucalyptus trees all over Italy, whole forests of them, or rows and windbreaks stretching far as the eye can see. But every eucalyptus in the land—even in the most desolate, lonely uplands in Sicily or Sardinia—is a permanent and tangible sign of what at the time was called the "Fascist Era." Some legacy, some *damnatio memoriae*. If you really wanted to root out all memory of that period, come 25 July 1943, you wouldn't just have gone round removing all the Fascist symbols and inscriptions from the walls and towers. If you wanted to make a thorough-going job of things, you'd also have had to go and pull every eucalyptus tree up by the roots, *ab radicibus*, as Cato put it, to rid our native soil of them.
>
> Antonio Pennacchi, *The Mussolini Canal* (2013)

> It is a society's aspirations for peacetime that determine whether a ruin is rebuilt, replaced, or preserved—or, rather, the ruler's interpretations of society's wishes.
>
> Christopher Woodward, *In Ruins* (2001)

During the period of Italy's long decolonization, the migrations of settlers from former Italian territories proved multidirectional, as we have seen in chapter 3. Some displaced colonists sought to return to their homes in places like Rhodes, Tripoli, and Mogadishu; others "repatriated" to Italy (sometimes arriving in their putative homeland for the first time); others joined kin in centers of Levantine Italian life like Alexandria or İzmir; and yet others emigrated to the New World or the Antipodes. Even as the Italian government struck agreements with UNRRA, then the IRO, and later the UNHCR and ICEM that essentially created a division of labor, there remained troublesome categories (mixed-race children, foreign spouses, and persons of undetermined ethnicity and citizenship from Venezia Giulia and the Aegean Islands), as detailed in chapter 4. Furthermore, the assistance provided by religious organizations such as the World Council of Churches, the Catholic Relief Services, the National Catholic

Welfare Council, and the PCA/POA to both foreign and national refugees in Italy at times blurred the categorical distinctions between these tracks of assistance. Ultimately, however, these exceptions proved the rule that Italy's "national refugees" were ineligible for aid as bona fide international refugees. Yet even after the long and complex process of consolidating these categories of national refugees and international refugees had been completed, there remained the pressing challenge of just what to do with these human remnants and reminders of empire, many of whom arrived on the Italian peninsula with few prospects of housing or stable employment. Rightly or wrongly, metropolitan Italians often saw these migrants as willing participants in the fascist project, interpreting their displacement as symbolic not only of Italy's humiliation but also the consequence of complicity with the former regime.[1]

The efforts by the Italian state at certain moments to slow processes of repatriation by requiring guarantees of work and housing proved merely stopgap measures. Despite worries about the potentially destabilizing effect of introducing impoverished Italian repatriates and refugees into an Italian peninsula devastated by the war, the Italian government worried equally about the corrosive consequences of lengthy residence in refugee camps on its inhabitants, as well as for neighboring communities. This prospect carried with it the risks of ruination not only of the generation of adults displaced by the war and the collapse of fascist empire but also of succeeding generations raised in the camps. Examining debates about how to reclaim the children of Italy's lost empire for the nation after 1945, this chapter explores such questions through the prism of resettlement policies and refugee housing. In particular, I ask whether we can read these efforts as instantiations of the famous fascist projects of land reclamation or *bonifiche integrali*—what Ruth Ben-Ghiat has identified as the unifying trope of fascism[2]—and thus as attempts to reclaim and render productive the ruins of the fascist project. In turning my gaze to imperial aftermaths in the metropole, I focus on what Stoler signals as "sites of decomposition that fall outside historical interest and preservation, of those places that are not honored as ruins of empire proper and go by other names."[3]

Housing the Nation

In both the popular and scholarly imaginations, 1945 figures as "year zero" in Western Europe, a label signaling both the ruins and devastation wrought by the war and the potential for a rupture with that past. In Italy, this understanding of "anno zero" remains indelibly associated with the school of neorealist filmmakers and their vision of a new cinema for a new Italy. In 1948 Roberto Rossellini released *Germania anno zero*, his dark Berlin rubble film depicting a family destroyed by the still-toxic influence of Nazism. As Noa Steimatsky has demonstrated, the film displaces the Italian "Fascist presence-of-the-past to German soil."[4] Working out of the literal ruins of the Cinecittà studio, Rossellini and his fellow neorealist filmmakers further displaced the legacies of what was both a fascist and imperial present-past when they made Italy's streets and working-class neighborhoods the subjects of gritty authenticity and hopeful renewal and ignored the refugee camp that had arisen in the former fascist studio. As Steimatsky puts it, "Neorealist culture could not tackle the ironic implications of a refugee camp being situated within the entity that was Cinecittà."[5] This camp—like that of Risiera di San Sabba in Trieste and others scattered throughout the Italian peninsula in which the national and international assistance tracks converged—housed both Italian citizens/former citizens from the lost territories and foreign displaced persons. Steimatsky makes a powerful case for Cinecittà as a very particular type of ruin of the fascist "state apparatus," a ruin that is at once both literal and figurative. Steimatsky contends that despite the neorealist disavowal of the refugees in their midst, "reality was being constructed, quite literally, out of the colossal sets and the ruinous remains *of* that apparatus, and in Cinecittà."[6] In this chapter, I examine how key aspects of Italy's reconstruction—notably the settling of citizens migrating from the *ex possedimenti*, many of whom lived in Cinecittà and similar camps on their arrival in the Italian peninsula—built on, rather than dismantled or erased, the literal and figurative ruins of fascist empire. In this process of reconstruction, national refugees/repatriates became critical agents.

Although the 1950s are often remembered as the takeoff years of the postwar "economic miracle," the benefits of that boom were unequally distributed. Italians who made applications to repatriate to Italy from former possessions often found themselves living in shabby refugee camps, as earlier arrivals in the 1940s had. Government officials fretted that potential repatriates nurtured unrealistic expectations "of finding an optimal placement and easier living in the Patria."[7] These fears reflected the problems of housing shortage and surplus population that persisted despite the development of a variety of housing schemes. A 1953 study offered a statistic that 2.8 million families (24.1 percent of the population) lived in overcrowded conditions, with 870,000 (7.5 percent) struggling with four or more persons per room and living in inadequate housing. The situation was most acute in the south, particularly Campania, Calabria, Puglia, and Basilicata.[8] The 1950 Fanfani Plan, which tasked the Istituto Nazionale Assicurazione (INA) with the provision of working-class housing through INA-CASA, and the 1955 Vanoni Plan (a larger program for the Mezzogiorno or the south that contained provisions for housing construction) numbered among the initiatives designed to address these housing problems. In addition, the Comitato Amministrativo Soccorso ai Senzatetto (CASAS), created under the aegis of UNRRA, continued its existence long after UNRRA itself ceased to exist in 1947. Combining unused UNRRA monies with those from the European Recovery Plan (i.e., Marshall Plan monies), the Fondo Lire partially financed the work of both UNRRA-CASAS and INA-CASA.[9]

The vast majority of housing built by these two entities did not go to *profughi nazionali*, and, indeed, available documentation suggests a perpetual battle to hold UNRRA-CASAS to its promises of refugee housing. By 1957, however, UNRRA-CASAS had built fourteen *villaggi* (villages or small housing settlements) specifically for Italian refugees from the lost Adriatic territories. The majority of these were sited in the border region or neighboring Veneto (Gorizia, Udine, Monfalcone, Ronchi, Grado, Gradisca, S. Giorgio Nogaro, Venezia Marghera), but some construction also took place further afield at Brescia, La Spezia, Taranto, Rovereto, Trento, and Fertilia.[10] These activities formed a small, if highly publicized, part of the broader recovery program of UNRRA-CASAS, which built some one thousand villages throughout Italy. The "ideal house type" (*casa-tipo*) promoted by UNRRA-CASAS consisted in small-scale units conceived of as the "antithesis to the large agglomerates of mortifying buildings devoid of any expression of personality." An UNRRA-CASAS building would ideally have no more than four apartments, each with separate entrances, and a small garden attached to the apartment to "develop a sense of property ownership."[11] Ironically, this was one of the same goals of those villages built for Italian settlers in Libya, suggesting how "problems" targeted by fascist ruralist and colonial policies persisted in the postwar era. Despite the claims to housing with individual personality, "the board of UNRRA-CASAS came to develop prototypes for standardized houses whose almost imperceptible elements of differentiation were represented by the slope of the roof and other minor details. . . . In this way, the UNRRA-CASAS programme propounded an architectural language inspired by a generic regional re-reading of the local vernacular tradition."[12]

These seemingly traditional views of the home, however, also refracted changing notions of the private sphere as both the refuge of the family from the state (a rejection of fascism's attempts to collapse the private and the public spheres) and the site of new forms of consumer citizenship enacted through performances of domesticity in kitchens and living rooms. Marshall Plan or ERP programs, in particular, stressed the necessity and right of each family to a home; these ambitious building plans were intended to both stimulate the construction industry and forge community.[13] These visions of home and community drew not only on ideas imported from the United States but also traditions like the prewar European municipal movement, in which Italian industrialists Adriano Olivetti (who became vice president of UNRRA-CASAS in 1958) and socialists like Alessandro Schiavi played an important role.[14] As Betts and Crowley have noted, after the war "the power of the emotion-laden home took on heightened significance amid the impoverished conditions in which many Europeans now found themselves." Not surprisingly, housing became "the centre of social policy in every European country after the war."[15]

Programs like UNRRA-CASAS and ERP-CASE thus addressed Italy's (and Europe's) much broader housing problems after 1945, the result (at least in part) of both Allied and Axis bombing. Many Italians residing on the peninsula had found themselves displaced by the conflict, as over a million homes were destroyed. In some instances, these *sinistrati* ("bomb-damaged" persons) and *sfollati* (displaced) found temporary refuge in camps and shelters before returning to their homes; in other cases they no longer had homes to which they could return.[16] As late as 1959, for example, populations displaced by fighting in Anzio and Cassino remained in precarious shantytowns at the edge of Rome in the areas that would be developed for the Summer Olympics held in the city the following year.[17] With their removal of unsightly reminders of the war (squatters), on the one hand, and the recovery of an imperial Roman past appropriated and abused by the fascist regime, on the other, the 1960 Rome Olympics symbolized a broader process of national reclamation that acquired particular intensity in the years between 1945 and 1960.

In Rome, the Olympic Committee repurposed, expanded, and redesignated spaces that Mussolini's regime had built for the staging of mass spectacles. Foro Mussolini became Stadio Olimpico, and the EUR zone, built in 1942 for the intended but never realized Esposizione Universale di Roma, became home to the Palazzo dello Sport and Velodrome. Rather than destroying these monuments of a ruined ideology and regime, then, planners "quite deliberately marshaled 2,713 years of the city's history,"[18] thereby epurating and reclaiming a built environment that bore the unmistakable imprint of fascist monumentalism and modernism. A similar process occurred at Cinecittà, restored as a film studio as the refugees were moved out. The construction of EUR, in particular, had never been completed, owing to the interruptions of the war. It was only after 1945 that EUR properly came into being as a usable built environment.

Like other urban peripheries in Italy, EUR became home to new apartment buildings that, together with the completion of grand ministry buildings, actually realized the fascist dream for a new Rome. The new housing at EUR features prominently in Michelangelo Antonioni's acclaimed 1962 film *L'eclisse.* Karen Pinkus has read the film as symbolic of the displacement of memories of colonialism onto Italy's postwar "conquest" of its urban peripheries with their transformation into residential neighborhoods.[19] In one sense, this reading is apt, as the realization of sites like EUR represented a ghostly continuation of imperial building projects halted by the war and fascism's defeat. Mia Fuller has detailed the dialogic relationship between the colonial city plan for Addis Ababa and that of EUR, contending that, although located in the metropole, the latter "most thoroughly fulfilled the agendas of Italian colonial city planning."[20] In another sense, however, Pinkus misses the fact that displaced Italians from the African colonies and other possessions lost after World War II were among those groups for whom the new neighborhoods featured in Antonioni's film were built. Individuals *literally* displaced with the collapse of empire arrived to inhabit what Pinkus characterizes solely as sites of *psychological* displacement for the memories of empire. An entire neighborhood of EUR, for example, became the Villaggio Giuliano Dalmata—still in existence today—for resettlement of refugees from Italy's lost eastern Adriatic territories. Some repatriates from Africa also came to live alongside their fellow national refugees from Istria and Dalmatia in the EUR quarter. This neighborhood was constructed under the auspices of the parastatal entity Opera per l'Assistenza ai Profughi Giuliani e Dalmati.[21]

Although refugees/repatriates from the lost possessions settled throughout Italy in a variety of locales and settings, I will focus in this chapter on those instances where resettlements arose on the remnants of fascist architectural showpieces such as the Sardinian "new town" (*città di fondazione*) of Fertilia, which became home to Istrian-Julian-Dalmatians, as well as some repatriates from Africa and the Aegean. Like EUR, these sites remained inextricably associated with the fascist political project. How are we to interpret these double displacements of the past, as problematic memories of fascism became literally mapped onto those populations who lost their homes as a result of fascism's defeat? On the one hand, the refugees' putative complicity with fascism assumed cartographic form with their resettlement in landscapes saturated with fascist imagery. On the other, the refugees' status as symbols of Italianness opened up the possibility (however incomplete or problematic) of reclaiming spaces contaminated by fascism for a notion of nation now severed from fascist imperialism.

The Politics of Reclamation

The fascist regime's policies of land reclamation profoundly transformed the Italian landscape. Although projects of integral reclamation—particularly those designed to drain malarial swamps—were not new in Italy, the scale of investment under fascism was. Rooted in fascist ideologies of ruralism, corporatism, and autarchy, many but not all of the reclamation projects took place under the aegis of the veterans' organization Opera Nazionale Combattenti (ONC). In addition to taming the lands and waters where popes and princes had failed to do so, these schemes were designed to put veterans to work as agriculturalists. With the conquest of nature followed the establishment of rural towns and settlements designed to fashion ideal fascist subjects. Pioneered first on the Italian peninsula in the Pontine region, Sicily, Sardinia, and Puglia, as well as in the Dodecanese Islands and Istria, this model of *bonifica integrale* was exported to Ethiopia, Eritrea, and Libya after 1936 and Albania after 1939.[22] Settlers (*coloni*) brought to work these lands included not only veterans but families of peasants and day laborers (*braccianti*) from overpopulated and impoverished regions, notably the Veneto and Emilia-Romagna.

The "new towns" (*città di fondazione*) and village settlements (*borghi*) built on reclaimed land in the Italian peninsula and its overseas possessions shared a common logic that rested on the myth of conquering virgin land. The conceptualization and execution of these projects revealed the ways in which, under fascism, processes of formal colonization and internal colonization became entangled.[23] As we have seen, the desire to redirect emigration abroad to Italian colonies provided a key ideological justification for fascist imperialism; likewise, the regime aimed to diminish rural-urban migration on the peninsula by sending colonists from impoverished and overpopulated regions to those in need of agricultural reclamation. From 1930 onward, a General Commissariat for Migration and Internal Colonization regulated these movements. In many ways, then, the new towns that remained within the confines of the reconfigured Italian state after 1947 may be understood as colonial traces. For a long time after the war's end, though, they merely appeared as ugly reminders of the fascist past. Italian philosopher Lucio Caracciolo captures the distaste many Italians felt for these settlements when he recalls his parents' responses to Latina, one of the Pontine towns: "On one point . . . my father and mother never budged. Latina disgusted them. They found it vapid."[24]

With the broader cultural turn in fascist studies that took off in the 1980s, scholars belatedly reclaimed these new towns as objects of academic study, situating them within fascism's cultural logics. Nonetheless, studies of these settlements have tended to remain restricted to more formalist architectural accounts of the built environment or analyses of the mediatic nature of these schemes.[25] Both approaches frequently focus on the utopian aspects of these projects, a perspective that tends to remove them from the realm of everyday life and into the space of fantasy and projection. In her analysis of the Pontine projects, for example, Suzanne Stewart-Steinberg emphasizes the links between these reclamations and fascist use of film (both cinema and newsreels), arguing that these towns were conceived of as grand stage sets.[26] While this may be true, such an analysis (like those focused on the formal aspects of the architecture) obscures the fact that these spaces were inhabited—and continued to be inhabited long after their "director" and "star" (the Duce) had disappeared from the scene. Pinkus's discussion of EUR as one of decolonization's "empty spaces" replicates such omissions. Only a few scholars, notably anthropologists Mia Fuller and Joshua Samuels, have taken up the question of what it actually meant—and means today—to live in these spaces stamped with the brand of fascism. Keeping in mind Stewart-Steinberg's comments, too, we might note that no one actually lives on a stage set, with the exception of the repatriates and refugees who lived in the camp at Cinecittà![27] Viewing these sites exclusively as dead ruins of fascist colonialism ignores their long afterlives and the ways in which many of these sites were completed or enlarged only *after* the fall of fascism. As Frank Biess has argued in his reframing of the notion of the "postwar," such an approach "does not see the war merely as the 'prehistory' to the postwar period but seeks to unearth and render visible the persistent hidden—and sometimes not-so-hidden—traces of the Second World War [and the fascist *ventennio*, I would add] within postwar societies."[28]

Even as these new towns hide in plain sight, their precise number and definitional criteria remain disputed. Antonio Pennacchi, born to a family that migrated from the Veneto to the new town of Littoria (rechristened Latina after the war) has counted at least 160 such new settlements scattered throughout Italy and the parts of Venezia Giulia annexed to Yugoslavia. Writing against a body of scholarly work that recognized only twelve such "new towns," Pennacchi has revealed just how extensive was the intervention made by such reclamation of the Italian landscape.[29] Indeed, many of the areas of swampy marshland reclaimed along Italy's shores became sites of the postwar boom in seaside tourism and development; this radically altered the relationship between land and sea in places like Calabria and Puglia, where for centuries malaria (as well as the threat of piracy) had hindered the development of large population centers on the coast. How are we to understand the lack of recognition of most of these fascist settlements? On the one hand, it would appear that certain towns—particularly those close to Rome, like Latina and Sabaudia—came to stand in for the broader project of fascist reclamation, the process of ruination being displaced onto these specific sites. On the other hand, it suggests that much of the broader space of reclamation has been so naturalized as to be detached from its fascist origins and reclaimed as part of the post-fascist nation. In this sense, we might think of these "ruins" as laying the foundations for the postwar nation in a manner akin to those eucalyptus trees planted all over Italy during the fascist era. Though often taken for granted, the trees (like the reclamations) are recognizable markers of a superseded era.

The process of reclaiming these spaces for the democratic nation, rather than fascist empire, required a new form of redemption, distinct from the rite of *redenzione della terra* or redemption of the land that had characterized the fascist projects. In referring to this broader process as postimperial reclamation, or *bonifica post-imperiale*, I distinguish it from the related notion of *bonifica nazionale*. The fascist regime had undertaken "national reclamation" in those newly "redeemed" territories that became integral parts of Italy after World War I. In Venezia Giulia, for example, national reclamation entailed projects of cultural Italianization (particularly in the realm of language policies) and expropriations from small-scale cultivators (for the most part, ethnic Slovenes and Croats) to provide land for migrants from the old provinces of Italy.[30] In his groundbreaking study of the politics of the resettlement of Istrian-Julian-Dalmatian refugees in the region around Trieste, Sandi Volk has evidenced the deliberate postwar continuation of these policies of *bonifica nazionale*. The territorial dispute between Italy and Yugoslavia occasioned a mass migration of individuals out of the territories that became part of Yugoslavia, as we have seen. Approximately one-third of those migrants settled in and around the border city of Trieste. With the support of the OAPGD, the parastatal entity created to assist refugees from Italy's eastern territories and whose remit later came to include repatriates from the colonies,[31] local communes expropriated land from ethnic Slovenes (citizens of Italy) in order to build housing complexes for "Italian" refugees from the Istrian peninsula.

The explicit justification for such actions was the need for a *bonifica nazionale* that would Italianize the corridor between the cities of Trieste and Monfalcone largely inhabited by Italy's autochthonous Slovene populations.

In addition, the creation of the *Villaggio del pescatore*—a settlement for refugee fishermen—at Duino Aurisina on land expropriated from Slovene fishermen aimed to stake an Italian claim to a coastline historically fished by ethnic Slovenes.[32] In this case, the continuation of fascist projects of ethnic reengineering was intended to nationalize a historically mixed border territory. Volk acknowledges the success of this policy, given that "in the arc of only 20–30 years from the end of the war, the 'Slovene coast' became, in fact, 'Italian.' And here this transformation was obtained almost exclusively thanks to the mass settlement of Istrian and Dalmatian refugees."[33]

I have not found evidence for a *bonifica nazionale* with a clear-cut ethnic design in other parts of postwar Italy where refugees from the former possessions settled. This likely reflects the peculiarity of the ethnic situation along Italy's eastern border. That there were explicit designs to settle national refugees in the zones of fascist *bonifica integrale* that awaited completion, however, is clear. Two socialist members of the Italian Constituent Assembly tasked with creating a constitution for the nascent Italian First Republic, Antonio De Berti and Angelo Corsi, proposed the resettlement of such refugees in areas where the work of reclamation remained incomplete.[34] In the contested region around Trieste, displaced Italian citizens from Istria and Dalmatia were the means by which local administrations sought to cleanse and purify the "contamination" represented by ethnic Slavs. These Slavs represented the human analogue, in nationalist rhetoric, of the murky swamps and their disease-bearing mosquitoes cleansed through the *bonifica*. Elsewhere, as at Fertilia, Italian refugees and repatriates instead became the means to reclaim spaces and practices associated with fascism, even as these human reminders of fascism's failure were removed to peripheral spaces within Italy. As a 1955 pamphlet describing the creation of the settlement of Gebelia near Anzio for Italian refugees from Libya put it, "This is an appeal to social reconstruction, to a *bonifica* that is not only rural but civil and human."[35]

Fertile Grounds

The town of Fertilia, today practically a suburb of the town of Alghero in northwest Sardinia, possesses multiple origin stories. Technically, it was founded on 8 March 1936, intended to serve as the urban heart of the reclamation zone on the marshy Nurra plain. In contrast to many other such *città di fondazione*, the settlement of Fertilia developed with the intention of settling not veterans of the ONC but colonists from Ferrara selected by the Ente ferrarese di colonizzazione (EFC). The EFC had obtained the concession on land from the Istituto Nazionale Fascista della Previdenza Sociale in

1933, and in 1934 took over the former penal colony of Cuguttu (rechristened L'azienda agricola Maria Pia).[36] An initial master plan by the architect Arturo Miraglia in 1935 was largely abandoned in 1937 in favor of the new design drawn up by the Roman architecture group 2PST.[37] Despite high hopes and the fanfare of the ceremony in which the first stones for the church and the youth organization were laid, many of the EFC's plans never materialized.

Still, the EFC did undertake a number of interventions onto the terrain, including the creation of a water system (aqueduct, wells, canals, cisterns) and sixty-five homes for settlers (*case coloniche*), as well as the planting of pines along the dunes of Maria Pia. Nonetheless, malaria continued to make regular appearances during the summer months. By 1942, Fertilia itself consisted of a cinema, post office, buildings for police and customs personnel, the fascist youth headquarters (Opera Nazionale Balilla), a hotel, and town hall. Construction had begun but not been completed on the church and Casa Doria, the latter which would become a dormitory for refugees after the war. A 1943 Allied bombing raid left the military airport of Fertilia in ruins, and the use of various buildings to house troops and later interned civilians from Yugoslavia further degraded what remained.[38] The city of Alghero also sustained considerable damage.

FIGURE 10. Former refugee dormitory at Casa Doria, Fertilia, Sardinia. Photo by author, June 2012.

After the war, the incomplete and half-ruined Fertilia became the site for another origin story. A newspaper article in *La Nuova Sardegna* described the visit by a governmental-sponsored commission to assess Fertilia's suitability for resettling Istrian-Julian-Dalmatian refugees in terms that replicated the fascist regime's rhetoric of virgin territory, even if the abandonment of this site owed more to the pernicious acts of man, rather than nature: "In the zone there was no human presence. Not even shepherds, who instead lived in the zone opposite the Nurra. And it was precisely that loneliness, that sense of abandonment, that convinced the commission that this would be the new city of the Julian refugees. No one would have looked at them badly, because there was no one to look at them."[39]

In this telling, refugees from Italy's lost lands became positioned as colonial pioneers, taking the places left by the Ferrarese settlers who had preceded them. This omitted the reality, of course, that approximately one hundred colonists from Ferrara continued to live around Fertilia. The plans to realize Fertilia as a kind of refugee "new town" coalesced with the negotiations for the 1947 Peace Treaty with Italy, which awarded a large swath of territory to Yugoslavia and laid out the terms by which Italians resident in those territories could opt to retain their citizenship, an act that required moving to the now territorially reduced Italy (discussed at length in chapters 3 and 4). As Italians began to opt and leave the Istrian towns of Pula / Pola, Rovinj / Rovigno, and Vrsar / Orsera en masse, the prime minister at the time, Alcide De Gasperi, invited Monsignor Raffaele Radossi, the bishop of Porec / Parenzo and Pula / Pola, to help convene the commission of experts that would visit Fertilia in February 1947. Radossi sent Don Francesco Dapiran, the exiled parish priest of Vrsar / Orsera, to represent the church. Only thirty-two when he first visited Fertilia, Dapiran would remain there as its parish priest from 1948 to 1992.[40]

In a testimony given toward the end of his life, Dapiran recalled his first encounter with Fertilia: "The condition in which we found the town was frightening: there weren't any roads, just a stony track where now lies Via Cherso. . . . Despite these conditions, our report was not negative. The place had potential, as long as streets, sewers, and houses would be built, as well as the purchase of nets for the fishermen from Istria."[41]

Dapiran returned to Fertilia for good soon after this initial visit, arriving in the nearly deserted town on the cold and dark evening of 18 February 1947. Refugees from Italy's lost lands on the eastern Adriatic had already begun to make their way to Sardinia by this point, some on the mistaken information from the Comitato di Liberazione Nazionale dell'Istria that at Fertilia they would find ready-made accommodations. Some fifty-three or fifty-four of these refugees were subsequently sent on to either Alghero or Sassari. Others found accommodation in the barracks at Fertilia's airport. To some degree, the movement of these refugees toward Fertilia and Alghero propelled the state to formalize a resettlement plan, even if the skills of many of these initial arrivals did not match up with the recommendations that fishing families be brought.[42]

Fertilia's gradual transformation over the next decade into a habitable town for Italian refugees involved many actors: the Italian state, local and regional authorities in Sardinia, the church, UNRRA, the Rockefeller Foundation, the Ente di Trasformazione Fondiaria della Sardegna (EFTAS), the Ufficio per le Zone di Confine (a state organization under the prime minister's oversight), entities created specifically for Fertilia like the Ente Giuliano Autonomo di Sardegna or EGAS, and the refugees themselves.[43] At the most fundamental level, the development of the region required the eradication of malaria. Between 1946 and 1948, a DDT campaign sponsored by UNRRA and the Rockefeller Foundation and channeled through the Ente Regionale per la Lotta Anti Anofelica in Sardegna (ERLAAS) achieved what fascism had not. UNRRA and Rockefeller made similar interventions on the Italian peninsula, notably in the Pontine marsh area where retreating German troops had destroyed the waterworks that had permitted fascism to claim its premature victory over mosquitoes.[44] Despite this reclamation of the land, the initial plans to develop Fertilia as a new home for Italian refugees rested on a vision of Fertilia as a fishing village, in part because of the sea's proximity. The report of the commission sent to Sardinia concluded, "Given the distance of the agricultural land [from Fertilia] and the immediate proximity of the sea, the settlement should welcome only families of fishermen, some artisans and some office workers."[45]

In a much-publicized event, the crews of thirteen Istrian fishing boats that had escaped sequestration in Yugoslavia took the vessels from Chioggia (near Venice) through the Adriatic, around the boot of Italy and up the Tyrrhenian Sea to Sardinia. The Luce Institute dedicated one short film and a newsreel to this voyage. The 1949 short, *Fertilia dei Giuliani* (alternatively titled *Giuliani in Sardegna*), captured the boats on their journey with Dapiran at their head. Describing the fishermen as "modern Ulysses," the film depicted the "small incomplete city" (*piccola città incompiuta*) that awaited the refugees. The gaze of the film lingers on the ruins of the city—at once spectral and deserted but possessed of "good foundations" (*buone fondamenti*). Portraying the arduous work of reclaiming Fertilia in order to render it habitable, the film then cuts to the joyous arrival of a truck with the men's wives and children. Although the short film shows refugees engaged in a variety of economic activities—including farming, cultivation of vegetable hemp, and shopkeeping—the focus remains on fishing. "To say Istrian is like saying man of the sea" quips the voiceover, closing with a shot of Istrians fishing a new sea in their sturdy wooden boats.[46]

The initial plans to recast Fertilia as a fishing center, rather than an agricultural one, ultimately failed. Some of the earliest refugees who had preceded the fishermen, including miners from the Istrian new town of Raša/Arsia, migrated once again.[47] Some of the original refugees at Fertilia later migrated to the United States through the IRO, included among those exceptions discussed in the previous chapter. By the 1950s, a "second exodus" out of Fertilia to the cities of the mainland, particularly the industrial center of Turin, began.[48] The story of Lidia M. is a fairly typical one. Born in Vodnjan/Dignano (Istria), Lidia and her family migrated to Italy when she was just six months old. Her family passed through several refugee camps (including that at Cinecittà) before ending up at the IRO camps in Bagnoli and then Pagano. When her father was rejected for emigration abroad because of his health, the family moved to Fertilia in 1953. In 1960, however, Lidia migrated to Turin, where she lived for thirty-eight years before returning to Sardinia.

One explanation for Fertilia's initial failure as a fishing hub and the subsequent re-migration of refugees there pointed to the undeveloped nature of the fishing market and distribution networks in Sardinia at the time. Piero Massarotto, who led a group of four boats to Fertilia in 1948, later remembered, "We used our own fishing methods [in Sardinia], those which in Rovigno allowed us to provide the factory for tinned fish with a continuous supply. Our 'sacca a leva' net closed and brought aboard an incredible quantity of fish. . . . The catch was great but nobody wanted our fish. We had to go around the villages trying to sell it, and after a few days, without refrigeration it would start to rot."[49] Whereas Massarotto eventually abandoned fishing and turned to construction work, some of his fellow fishermen left Fertilia and joined those who had headed to the mainland.

Without a doubt, the Istrians found underdeveloped markets for their fish in Sardinia, and their technology likely outmatched that of local fishers. Istrians had migrated to an island with relatively underdeveloped maritime traditions, owing to centuries of malaria and piracy that encouraged pastoralism and small-scale agriculture away from the coasts. Yet Istrians also appear to have endorsed, consciously or not, a long-standing rhetoric that depicted southern Italy in general and Sardinia in particular as backward. Such a rhetoric would be invoked, as we shall see, to justify further refugee settlement on the island, with displaced persons cast as agents of modernity and civilization.

In reality, then, the obstacles to establishing Fertilia as a fishing village proved political and organizational in ways that extended far beyond the limited capacities of local markets. The Unione Pescatori Giuliani, an entity founded in Venice in 1947 to assist Istrian-Julian-Dalmatian refugees, had—with the Italian state's generous contribution of 20 million lire—helped to equip and organize the fishing boats immortalized in the Luce Institute film. Contrary to the heroic rhetoric of the film (a mythic narrative that I often heard repeated by informants in Fertilia), refugees at the time accused the Unione Pescatori of corruption. A 1952 document from the then–undersecretary of state Giulio Andreotti summarizes the gist of these charges, the most egregious being that the founding journey of the fishing boats to Fertilia "ended with the general sale [of those boats] to the profit of the participants who had received the outfitted boats on concession in Venice. The poorest refugees were then abandoned to themselves in Fertilia until the Presidency [PCM] assumed the management of the colony; the directors of the Unione . . . returned to Venice with no interest in the fate of their needy companions."[50] Andreotti went on to lay out several other charges, including the Unione's request for a merchant marine ship said to be for the refugees' use but actually intended to enrich the Unione's administrators.

Other entities that took up the question of fishing at Fertilia—most notably the Ente Giuliano Autonomo di Sardegna (EGAS), formed in 1949 with the remit of overseeing the development of Fertilia—likewise encountered problems. Only dissolved in 1979, EGAS has proven a source of continuing controversy. Some scholars and residents of Fertilia view it as having served as a positive agent for the improvement of the refugees' lives; others instead see it as a source of division and even exploitation of the refugees. A 1948 note from the exile organization Associazione Nazionale Venezia Giulia e Dalmazia (ANVGD) to the Ufficio per le Zone di Confine urged the necessity of establishing EGAS: "One must use all means to prevent the locality [i.e., Fertilia], built with such noble intentions, from itself becoming a refugee camp."[51] Ten years later, however, the ANVGD's Sassari branch called for the incorporation of EGAS into the OAPGD. In the letter, the ANVGD's president and executive committee noted that while the government had created EGAS with an initial six-month mandate, it had continued to prolong that mandate. Administration of EGAS had passed to non-refugees who did not represent the interests of Fertilia's inhabitants.[52] Even *esuli* who had played significant roles in EGAS, like Dario Manni, criticized the fact that Istrians and Dalmatians almost never held the key positions.[53] My informants also differed in their assessments of the role played by the priest Don Francesco

Dapiran, some claiming he had been scapegoated for Fertilia's problems, others complaining that he acted like a "boss."

Under the direction of EGAS and with assistance from UNRRA-CASAS and the OAPGD, among others, Fertilia developed a mixed economy based on agriculture, cultivation and processing of vegetable hemp, fishing (organized through the Nazario Sauro Cooperative), artisanal trades, tourism, and employment at the nearby airport. A handful of Italian refugees from Africa (Libya, Eritrea), Rhodes, and Romania arrived to live alongside the Istrian-Julian-Dalmatians in Fertilia. In 1957, UNRRA-CASAS built forty-seven houses—referred to colloquially as "Case Canada" (Canadian homes) for refugees in Fertilia. The OAPGD built another four.[54]

The development of Fertilia's agricultural potential followed out of the agrarian reforms of the mid-1950s, as some refugees moved out of the center of Fertilia to tame the nearby rocky, *macchia*-covered area known as Lazzaretto. Over time, these labors transformed the area, today known as Maristella and made up of tidy homes and vineyards. By 1961, forty Istrian and sixteen Sardinian families had obtained thirty-year mortgage contracts for these lands.[55] When I visited Lidia M. and Marisa B. in their homes in Maristella in 2012, they showed me photos of the formerly barren landscape that their parents encountered there. "It was a desert. . . . My parents went on foot from Fertilia to the countryside. . . . At that time, it was all ugly—there weren't any trees. . . . My parents had to take out all the rocks from the soil." These women also repeated a story I heard repeatedly about how in the 1940s and 1950s the backward local Sardinians were shocked by the emancipated nature of the Istrian women, who ventured out on their own on bicycles and to the beach.[56] This account thus offered a gendered take on the civilizational rhetoric that characterizes the tale of Istrians' reclamation of the "wild" zone of Fertilia.

As such comments suggest, the story of Fertilia consists in a multilayered narrative of ruination and redemption/reclamation. Although Fertilia's literal reclamation (physical and moral) lay in the hands of the refugees and their representatives—and received considerable financial inputs from intergovernmental and nongovernmental organizations such as UNRRA and the Rockefeller Foundation—ultimately it was the Italian state that provided much of the land and the means for such a reclamation. This underscores the state's increasing assertion of control over questions of assistance to national refugees, with the limited capacities of the Italian government in the period 1945–1947 a distant memory by this point. Whether or not the "statization" of assistance advocated by AAI head Lodovico Montini (see chapter 3) had been achieved is debatable. What appeared incontestable, though, is that by the 1950s the Italian state had affirmed its national "right" to regulate flows of displaced persons into its territory and provide assistance to those who met the criteria of citizenship and refugeedom it established. This had occurred in the wider context of an Italian rearticulation of assistance and welfare, one in which the very constitution "treats relief as a duty of the State and therefore something to which the citizen is entitled," contended Montini in his role as vice president for the Parliamentary Inquiry into Destitution in Italy.[57] Italy's success, however mixed, in resettling national refugees and exiles in places like Fertilia nonetheless opened it up to questions of whether *foreign* refugees might also become agents of reconstruction and reclamation.

Did these foreign DPs have some rights to relief from the host state in which they found themselves, or were such rights reserved exclusively for those who had lost their homes in Italy's Oltremare and their fellow metropolitan citizens? This was precisely the question that John Alexander-Sinclair, head of the UNHCR's Rome office and later a staff member of the International Rescue Committee (IRC), asked in 1953 when he began to promote a plan to permanently settle refugees in Sardinia. Inspired in part by the success of Fertilia, Alexander-Sinclair included Sardinia as a potential site in UNHCR's then emerging "permanent solutions" program.[58]

"Everybody Here Is for Sardinia"

As we have seen, Italian leaders had successfully argued again and again that Italy's economic weakness—as well as its pressing obligations to its own refugees—made it unsuitable for large-scale resettlement by foreign refugees. In 1948, Lodovico Montini had recommended to the Chamber of Deputies that Italy should join the International Refugee Organization in order to "defend" Italian interests, which in his mind included seeking the extension of IRO help to Italian refugees. He noted, in particular, the "sad contrast in the treatment, on the same Italian territory, given to United Nations refugees versus Italian refugees."[59] Sympathetic observers agreed regarding the burden presented by Italy's own refugees, as well as the victim status of such repatriates. Looking back on her experiences in postwar Italy, Eileen Egan of Catholic Relief Services recalled,

> Into a country unable to feed itself, came 510,000 Italians from the ceded territories outside the peninsula. They streamed back from Venezia Giulia, from Dalmatia ceded to Yugoslavia, from the Dodecanese Islands restored to Greece, and from Africa. . . . From Libya,

> Somaliland, and Ethiopia came poor and hardworking colonists who were themselves victims, like the sons of the poor Irish in the lower ranks of British colonial forces, of colonial incursions in whose planning they had no part.[60]

Egan described the sad encampments in which Italian "returnees" lived and then repeated a line of argumentation that had already become common sense by the 1950s: "The 'overseas Italians' who were dumped on the ravaged peninsula, besides needing shelter, exacerbated an unemployment situation of almost unimaginable proportions."[61] As evidenced by the use of the passive voice ("were dumped") that denied any agency to these overseas Italians, Egan left unquestioned the possibility that refugees (whether national or foreign) could be anything other than a burden on the fragile postwar Italian economy. Such a view accorded with the opinion of those like Montini who cited population pressure owing to lack of emigration possibilities as a fundamental problem in large cities like Naples.[62] Nonetheless, some Italian authorities had instead begun to reposition national refugees as agents of positive changes in places where the work of fascist *bonifica* remained incomplete. Like Fertilia, many though not all these sites were also in those areas considered culturally as belonging to the south, and hence part of the "Southern Question."

Fascism had marked a rupture or, perhaps, a temporary hiatus in understandings of *meridionalismo* within Italy. As Mariella Pandolfi has argued, "This 'auto-orientalist' construction of a double Italian identity was overcome only for the briefest moment when the Fascist regime proclaimed its agenda of transforming Italy into a late colonial empire."[63] In keeping with this, fascist patterns of land reclamation did not single out the south as a privileged space of intervention but instead addressed pressing issues from Istria to the Veneto to Puglia to Sardinia, as well as the overseas territories. Within the fascist colonial imaginary, the south thus occupied the simultaneous position of colonizing and colonized subject, as notions of southernness were projected onto overseas lands to be settled by both Italian southerners and northerners alike. The reemergence of discourses pathologizing "the Southern Problem" after 1945 thanks in part to the 1951 sociological study of the "cave dwellers" of Matera and the Parliamentary Inquiry into Destitution, together with a host of proffered political and economic solutions, transformed the once capacious and diffused notion of *bonifica* under fascism into a distinctly southern concern. Edmondo Cancellieri's 1953 documentary *L'ora del Sud* mocked this development with its "claim" that in southern Italy belief in the "legend" of *bonifica* had supplanted belief in fairies.[64]

Other documentary films took *bonifica* more seriously, however. As Paola Bonifazio has pointed out,

> In democratic Italy, to inform viewers about the success of the bonifica projects meant to spread knowledge about the success of Italian workers and also to enlighten them with the technical knowledge of modern times. The older opposition between an idle southern soul and a working northern soul was replaced by two newer oppositions: one between those who worked towards and participated in the solution of the Southern Question and those who remained idle, and another between those who could see the results and the implementation of the reconstruction and were, therefore, knowledgeable about modern technology against those who still reasoned according to common sense.[65]

Within this reconfiguration of the Southern Question, Sardinia figured as a prime object for intervention. In a 1953 publication that drew heavily on the Parliamentary Inquiry into Destitution, Giovanni Spagnolli of UNRRA-CASAS lamented that "in Sardinia, misery and destitution is reflected in the inert, atavistic ignorance of the population that perpetuates this situation in a truly worrisome manner. The condition of the accommodations of people on the edges of the cities and of fishermen presents startling characteristics."[66] Such comments drew on pervasive stereotypes of Sardinia as an untamed landscape marked by banditry and savage pastoralists, what Tracey Heatherington has called a "dark frontier."[67] As Dario Gaggio notes, "Sardinia was at times perceived as utterly different and remote, and at others as intimately familiar and as the possible stage for dreams of redemption."[68] A 1955 American Universities Field Staff report titled *Everybody Here Is for Sardinia* emphasized the island's "quasi-colonial" character within Italy but nonetheless saw great opportunity as the result of the successful antimalarial campaign and the infrastructural investments in the region made by the Cassa per il Mezzogiorno.[69] In contrast to Sicily (the Mediterranean's largest island), which possessed a high population density, Sardinia (the Mediterranean's second-largest island) remained underpopulated, and refugees were imagined as useful agents of development, rather than drains on the economy or competitors for jobs. With the flurry of interest in and proposals for resettlement of refugees in Sardinia in the 1950s, then, we find a convergence of multiple interests: those of Italian authorities keen on developing and disciplining the "backward" island of Sardinia; individuals and groups seeking homes for national refugees; and non-Italians in international agencies hoping that foreign refugees might also find durable resettlement solutions in Italy.

As early as the mid-1950s, officials within UNHCR like Alexander-Sinclair had begun urging Italy to accept some foreign refugees for resettlement given the poor prospects for emigration for many of the hard-core refugees, on the one hand, and the opportunities presented by the country's postwar economic boom, on the other. Alexander-Sinclair also dared to question the usual assumptions about the problem of surplus population in Italy. Drawing on demographic and statistical projections, Alexander-Sinclair argued that by 1980 Italy would actually suffer from negative population growth.[70] He also diagnosed contemporary Italy's problems as ones of maldistribution of capital and "under-capitalisation" rather than overpopulation per se. Maintaining that "Europes [*sic*] empty spaces must be filled, before additional burdens are assumed in overseas countries," Alexander-Sinclair wrote to a US State Department official in 1953 that the initial idea for placing refugees in Sardinia developed out of a discussion with Bartolomeo Migone in the Ministry of Foreign Affairs.[71] Minister Migone "then suggested that use should be made of the principal Mediterranean islands which happen to be the possessions of different European countries and which, being near enough to the Iron Curtain [which was generating migrant flows], might provide useful centres for selection for emigration, for local integration etc. He mentioned Corsica, Sardinia (Sicily is too close to the mainland) Crete and Cyprus."[72]

Migone no doubt had in mind the efforts already undertaken by the Italian state to settle its national refugees on the island. The initial seed for Fertilia's reconstruction as a refugee town had been laid not just by the pioneer priest Dapiran and enterprising exiles who made their way to the town, as discussed in the previous section, but also by two socialist members of the Italian Constituent Assembly, Antonio De Berti and Angelo Corsi, who proposed that Italian refugees be placed in areas where the work of *bonifica* or land reclamation awaited completion. Corsi, himself a Sard, took particular interest in developing his home island through refugee resettlement. As president of the INPS from 1946 to 1966, he confronted head-on the challenges of repatriating Italian settlers from the villages the INPS had administered in Tripolitania. In the mind of Corsi and many others, Fertilia was not a unique or singular experiment in refugee placement. In fact, the 1947 commission of governmental experts that visited Fertilia had also traveled to Castiadas (a former penal colony in southwest Sardinia) to evaluate its potential.[73] In the mid-1950s, Castiadas would become home to many Italians leaving Tunisia. Foreign entities had also eyed Sardinia for refugee resettlement, with Aide Suisse purchasing land to create a model farm at Siniscola. In 1952, Aide Suisse had also floated a plan to work with the AAI and UNRRA-CASAS to settle foreign refugees at Nurra, just north of Fertilia.[74]

Drawing on these precedents, in May 1957 an initial "Sardinia plan" developed by Migone, Alexander-Sinclair, and others was presented formally at the International Conference on Refugee Problems Today and Tomorrow.[75] The project envisioned the resettlement of twenty thousand families and called for the provision of homes and necessary infrastructure. Entities expressing interest in sponsoring the scheme included the World Bank, the Council of Europe, the Food and Agriculture Organization (FAO), the National Catholic Welfare Council (NCWC), and Aide Suisse. In order to gain the support of the Italian state, the plan provided for resettling both "alien" or foreign refugees and national refugees,[76] as well as some impoverished Sardinians. Another iteration of the plan called for fifty thousand individuals, including ten thousand Sards, fifteen thousand continental Italians, and twenty-five thousand alien refugees; "continental Italians" presumably referred here to displaced Italians (*sinistrati*) or national refugees, since this particular proposal for the Sardinia plan acknowledged, "To this day no Italian will willingly leave the continent—as they call the mainland of Italy—and live in Sardinia."[77] Earlier discussions of the plan had highlighted that the only real obstacles to Sardinia as a site of resettlement existed in the minds of continental Italians "and not in the minds of Italian refugees from the Balkans, or from the ex-Italian colonies, nor indeed in the minds of alien refugees in Italy or other countries of Western Europe." One projection claimed Sardinia could support double its population.[78]

The proposed project called for refugees to engage in a range of industrial, agricultural, and fishing activities (particularly lobsters for export).[79] Italian prime minister Antonio Segni, himself a Sard, was said to have expressed interest in the plan, though Segni's resignation in 1957 rendered this support less significant.[80] Whereas some of the project's international backers saw this as a potential model to deal with a "new emergency of the Hungarian Revolution type,"[81] others—like one skeptic in the International Rescue Committee (IRC)—wondered aloud, "If this idea is sound, why don't Italians do it for their own surplus population?"[82] Such a question hinted at the ambivalence of Italian authorities to the plan. As Alexander-Sinclair's personal papers reveal, the project ultimately foundered on Italian indifference.

Whereas Lodovico Montini (at that time a member of both the Italian Chamber of Deputies and the Parliamentary Assembly of the Council of Europe, as well as head of the AAI) first asked for a delay in discussing the plan,[83] he then failed to turn up at scheduled meetings held in July and September 1958 with the Council of Europe. This provoked frustration and irritation among council members.[84] Alexander-Sinclair claimed that the reluctance came from above, thereby excusing Montini, who he claimed was "most embarrassed and as charming as usual, but he was simply powerless."[85] A note to Montini in July 1958 indicates that a discussion on the plan "was cancelled at the request of the Italian authorities, who are not open to examining such plan." Montini then replied confidentially that "the project of Mr. Alexander Sinclair is seen with some diffidence. In particular, this project was seen in absolutely negative terms by the Sardinian representatives at the Council of Europe: by our colleague Azzara, above all."[86] In addition, strong opposition to the plan existed within the Italian Ministry of Foreign Affairs. In a June 1958 internal MAE memo, an official named Pescatori within the "Emigration" section complained, "These vague proposals [for Sardinia] have for years been presented, in the most disparate circumstances, by Mr. John Alexander-Sinclair (who is well known and not in a positive way, by this Ministry)." Pescatori fretted that successful implementation of the plan threatened to "confirm the legend of the inexhaustible and virgin possibilities for insertion—even of foreign refugees—in Sardinia." Furthermore, claimed this official, the plan could imperil Italian efforts to obtain financial assistance from the United States in settling Italian emigrants in "ethnographic settlements" abroad (in Brazil, Chile, and Costa Rica).[87]

Giovanni Vassallo in the "Profughi Stranieri" section of the MAE went even further in his criticism. Seconding Pescatori about the "disfavor" (*sfavore*) with which Alexander-Sinclair was seen within the MAE, Vassallo added in a letter to Montini, "The impression that I took away [in various meetings with Alexander-Sinclair] was that this project concealed some hidden interests, political more than financial, of groups that are not identified but are probably British." Just in case such suspicions weren't sufficient to damn the project, Vassallo concluded, "The project is extremely absurd and utopian."[88] Regardless of whether members of the Council of Europe proved aware of such controversies behind the scenes, they quickly turned their attention to other potential underdeveloped sites for similar resettlement, including the Landes in southwest France. Alexander-Sinclair's efforts thus failed to produce concrete results in resettling foreign refugees in Sardinia.[89]

During the same time period, the Homeless European Land Program (HELP) established in Simaxis (a hamlet on the edge of Oristano) offered an important exception to the rule that Italy would serve only as a transit country for alien refugees. Alexander-Sinclair proved well aware of HELP's work; discussions of the Sardinia plan even referred to it as a positive model.[90] Pescatori, the critic in the Ministry of Foreign Affairs, instead dismissed it as "a simple private entity [*azienda*], a source perhaps of publicity but irrelevant on the international scene."[91] Though HELP's genesis paralleled that of the Sardinia plan in time, it was a more organic, bottom-up scheme formulated by two young Americans, Belden Paulson and film actor Don Murray. Paulson and Murray had become friends as social workers at the Casa Mia project in Naples in the early 1950s. Distressed by the enduring problem of hard-core refugees languishing in camps in Italy, Murray and Paulson hatched a plan to resettle some of these longtime foreign refugees in Italy. After an initial but fruitless scouting visit to Calabria in early 1957, Paulson met with the head of the Cassa per il Mezzogiorno (Fund for the South). Paulson wrote home in a letter to his family, "We were almost lifted out of our chairs when the director, Engineer Orcel, told us that if we wanted favorable conditions . . . the place to go was Sardinia. . . . La Cassa would be prepared to help financially and would provide experts."[92] Belden and Murray thus conceived of a small resettlement project of about twenty-five families in the "historically depressed area" of Sardinia. With the support of the Cassa, UNHCR, the AAI, and EFTAS, as well as Murray's own money from his movie salaries and funds raised through a direct appeal on US television (with Murray surprising Paulson with a *This Is Your Life* episode), Paulson and Murray obtained a piece of land for the project in 1957 and began to tour camps on the mainland, recruiting refugees.

As had occurred with Alexander-Sinclair's project, however, the Italian government sent mixed messages, at best. "Only later did we learn why our dealings with AAI, the Italian Government refugee authority, were so difficult," confessed Paulson. "The government was convinced our project would fail 'because these refugees will never make it.' Further, if we did succeed, it would be too expensive, since it would lead to other, similar efforts. Even more basic, the Ministry of Interior really didn't want these refugees integrated into the Italian economy. On the surface, however, AAI had to cooperate in order to receive international support."[93] The comments made by the UNHCR representative Ernest Schlatter who attended the inauguration of the first house on the project in July 1958 must have confirmed the worst fears of these Italian critics. Schlatter—the same UNHCR official urging Italy to accept foreign refugees for permanent settlement whom we encountered in the introduction—lauded HELP as "a pilot project, an important experiment." Underlining the project's uniqueness in the Italian context, Schlatter continued,

> May I confirm that the UNHCR, with the means at its disposal, will do everything possible to help assure the success of this project. In a country like Italy, traditionally one of migration, for a refugee to achieve *integration* and work here is nearly impossible. It is therefore all the more interesting that precisely in Italy, in Sardinia, a project is

being created which can serve as an example for the world. Of necessity, this experiment will be duplicated elsewhere, and we hope also in other parts of Europe.[94]

Despite such hopes, the project appears to have been an outlier in the Italian landscape. The gains of HELP were modest, settling at most fifteen refugees. All the refugees were men, and they included a Spaniard who had been a refugee since the Spanish Civil War, a Czech who had collaborated with the Nazis, a Slovene, and a Serb. The inclusion of Yugoslavs into the project was significant, since on the Sardinian project proposed by Alexander-Sinclair, Minister Migone had sought to "swap out" or replace Yugoslav refugees with displacees from other parts of Eastern Europe. As Alexander-Sinclair noted in one of his memos on the failed project, "The only condition he [Migone] put was that Yugoslav refugees should be housed in islands other than Sardinia so that Italy could avoid complications with her eastern neighbour."[95] While Migone phrased this demand in the name of good relations with Yugoslavia, there also existed considerable hostility toward and suspicion of Yugoslav refugees within Italy, even when those refugees opposed Tito and communism (see chapter 4). Ironically, HELP organizers instead worried about anti-Tito Yugoslav refugees resettling near a town—Oristano—at that point in time dominated by the Italian Communist Party.[96]

In December 1958 Paulson and Murray established the Don Murray Agricultural Cooperative (Cooperativa Agricola e Responsibilità Limitata Don Murray), which gave the project a firm legal footing. By the late 1950s, the refugees-turned-farmers were even hiring local laborers. They worked alongside volunteers (mostly young Americans and Europeans) from the Brethren Christian Service. The project was economically viable and made a small but positive contribution to the local economy, seen in the existence of a hen and egg farm still in operation today.

From the start, Paulson and Murray had conceived of the HELP project as one of rehabilitation for the refugees and reconstruction and development for Sardinia. In regard to the latter, the refugees were to constitute a valuable labor force, and, in reality, the families of HELP completed work of land reclamation, clearing agricultural land and producing crops such as tomatoes, melon, and eggplants. In presentations to the local audiences, one refugee who had no previous agricultural experience proudly recounted "how he had become a peasant."[97] The descendant of one refugee noted that the painstaking work of reclamation had been mostly done by hand. "Bonifica! Bonifica!" she exclaimed, pointing to the capaciousness of the *bonifica* notion to include, at least in this singular instance, foreigners as both agents of Italian modernization and actors worthy of reclamation themselves.[98] In this project, then, we find on the terrain of underdeveloped Sardinia the literal intersection of the Italian metaphor of *bonifica* with the UN agencies' remit to facilitate rehabilitation, that is, to "help refugees help themselves."

Paulson had explicitly aimed to combat the apathy and distrust created by long years in refugee camps. He argued that Italy's "rigid social structure" and the typical closure of the islanders toward outsiders (their literal insularity) reinforced a *necessary* sense of refugee community. In a report on "refugee attitudes," Paulson asserted, "The values being nurtured on the project are beginning to create more mutual trust among themselves than with anyone outside. They now see the desirability of inviting over more refugees—and if possible some of the best elements in the camp—to make the growing community more substantial."[99] At the same time, he acknowledged that a number of the more educated refugees viewed themselves as superior to the local Sards, an attitude that provoked resentment. As occurred at Fertilia with the "emancipated" Julians and Istrians, the HELP refugees became "extremely critical of local customs centered in the Church, social conformity, rigid ideas about women, and lack of outside contact. . . . [Refugee] 'worldliness' is often distant from views found in Sardinian villages. Moreover the refugees are franker than local people steeped in 'face' and at times they are insensitive to local feelings."[100]

In the end, though, such differences appear to have been overcome, as at least six of the original refugees married local women and established families. In 2015, I interviewed a group of the widows (none of the refugees is living today) and their children. Though bearing names like Vlada, the descendants possess a stronger identity as Italians and Sards than as Italo-Slovenes or *figli di profughi* (children of refugees). The traces of the HELP project remain, then, in both infrastructure like homes and the hen operation, as well as kin. Contrary to the fears of Italian officials that such refugees would "never make it," the foreigners settled by HELP contributed to the reclamation of Sardinia and the postwar Italian nation. Although rather tellingly none of the refugees themselves ever obtained Italian citizenship, their children have been "claimed" for the postwar Italian nation, suggesting that Italy could have potentially played a larger role as a place for foreign refugee resettlement after World War II had there existed the political will to do so.

The history of schemes to settle refugees (foreign and Italian) in Sardinia underscores, yet again, the entangled nature *in practice* of assistance to these two populations—that is, the intertwined threads of international (intergovernmental and nongovernmental) and national relief. Placing refugees in either Fertilia or Simaxis would not have been possible without the initial

Figure 11. Wives of HELP refugees, Simaxis, Sardinia, 30 June 2015. Photo by author.

joint efforts of the Rockefeller Foundation and EFTAS to rid the island of malaria, for instance. Likewise, the AAI worked (if at times grudgingly) with UNRRA-CASAS and the UNHCR, among others, to find such durable solutions for the displaced. In one version of the Sardinia project, there was even stipulated a head-to-head plan, suggesting that the earlier lessons of BMA efforts to control migratory movements had not been lost on those national and international actors dealing with refugees. In a missive written on the letterhead of the "Special Committee on Long Term Integration Projects" and sent by Alexander-Sinclair to Migone, it was noted, "On the Italian side it might be stipulated . . . that alien refugees in Italy should have absolute priority for resettlement and that any alien refugees moved to Italy from other European countries for resettlement should be exchange[d] on a 'one-for-one' basis against refugees in Italy as far as this may be humanly possible and practicable."[101]

Beyond Sardinia, refugee policy experts engaged in transnational conversations designed to solve pressing problems of both national and international refugees in mainland Italy and, more broadly, Europe. In a 1958 letter to Alexander-Sinclair (at that point an employee of the IRC), for instance, C. Balmelli of the NGO Aide Suisse suggested that the Sardinian plan might be put on the back burner. Instead, he saw a more effective model in Gebelia, a rural settlement near Anzio-Nettuno created in 1955 for repatriates from Italian Cyrenaica. Although largely an Italian project that drew on significant state help, Gebelia and its associated agricultural cooperative—the Società Cooperativa Agricola fra i Colonizzatori Italiani d'Africa, or SACIDA—also received loans from Aide Suisse, highlighting the ways in which the tracks of domestic and international relief frequently crossed and intersected. Ironically, Balmelli discounted the prospects for Sardinian projects because "the island actually permits only actions of a pioneering character [*carattere pionieristico*]."[102] It was precisely, in fact, this *pioneering* quality of reclamation that provided the moral and political impetus for projects like those at Fertilia and Simaxis, as well as that of Gebelia on the mainland. These projects reinscribed and reclaimed reclamation from a failed fascist state project, rendering refugees (including former colonial settlers) the new pioneers of postwar and postimperial *bonifica*.

New Pioneers, New Foundations?

In contrast to Fertilia, the village of Gebelia arose not on the incomplete foundations of a fascist new town but rather on land yet to be reclaimed. In this instance, we find a project whose guiding spirit replicated many of the principles of fascist colonialism, even as it transformed them in the new conditions of postimperial life in the metropole of a now democratic country. The very name of the project established an explicit genealogical link to fascism's colonization projects in Libya's Gebel plain. A pamphlet published on the inauguration of the settlement opens with a foundational scene: four men begin the backbreaking task of clearing forest and building a barrack and stables in order to house the eighty-two family heads who would complete this work as part of a cooperative (SACIDA). "Those who happened to see in those days, those 82 men of SACIDA . . . won't easily forget the spectacle, one that seems to renew the deeds and enterprise of pioneers in far-off lands," asserted the publication. "However, this was at the gates of Rome; these were Italian colonists, whom the war had driven out of Africa and now came to plow and transform another desert."[103]

Distancing the settlers from a common image of the repatriates as nostalgic and unrepentant fascists, the text continued, "Gebelia: a memory with a touch of bitterness but no nostalgia for the Cyrenaican hills to the east of Benghazi. . . . There, on the Gebel, thousands of Italian colonists, in the course of a few years, sowed wheat. Even the English called that a miracle."[104] The origin story laid out in this publication attributes the initiative for the project to a refugee from Africa, lawyer Enrico Barra, who founded SACIDA in 1946. The text claims that the refugees placed their faith in the Italian state but instead found only hardship. "Only refugee camps [awaited them]: it seemed that agrarian reforms, reformed institutions, new social structures in agriculture weren't intended for them."[105] This narrative depicts SACIDA as the product of these refugees' agency, the passive inhabitants of the camps now transformed into pioneers of the land. Doing this distances these "new" settlers from their past lives as fascist colonial settlers, who went as agents of the state-backed colonial entities and found everything provided (homes, tools, seeds, etc.). Whereas in Libya these colonists took their directions from the fascist state and its agents, at Gebelia they controlled their own fate through a cooperative.[106] Balmelli of Aide Suisse later highlighted the agency of the former refugees for having obtained, "after courageous and gigantic works of *bonifica* and division of land [*appoderamento*], a stable insertion into agriculture."[107] Such language fused long-standing images of colonial settlers as pioneers with a rehabilitative idiom that sought to transform refugees into masters of their own destiny.[108]

In actuality, as the inaugural text for the project later acknowledges, the creation of SACIDA—like the reconstruction of Fertilia—required substantial state assistance from a number of entities, as well as private help and support from the Catholic Church. Crucially, too, the Marquise Donna Elena Dusmet Borghese donated the original plot of land. The INPS, which had administered one of two colonial entities in Libya, contributed monies to the project and claimed SACIDA as one of the most successful of its attempts to settle its former colonists in the metropole.[109] As an internal document noted, "The work of S.A.C.I.D.A. is of notable interest to the Institute given that the former facilitates the definitive settling of the repatriating colonists, thereby preventing these refugees from turning to the Institute for subsidies and requests for accommodation."[110] Refugees settled at SACIDA came from camps located throughout the Italian peninsula, including those at Aversa, Bari, Brescia, Centocelle (Rome), Cibali, Civitavecchia, Laterina, Marina di Carrara, Nesima Superiore, and Termini Imerese.[111]

Despite the celebration of Gebelia/SACIDA as entailing a successful reclamation of both land and individuals previously abandoned to the "promiscuity" and disorder of the refugee camps, protagonists and their descendants whom I interviewed in May 2011 told a somewhat different story. Most of those I spoke with had come through the refugee camp at the former military barracks at Aversa (province of Caserta in Campania), where they lived alongside Istrian-Julian-Dalmatian refugees. "We all knew each other from the camp," quipped one man, who then mentioned the "multicultural" nature of Aversa, which housed Italians from various lost possessions. My interlocutors described the devastation to Anzio created by the war, in particular the protracted and bloody battle after the Allied landing at Anzio-Nettuno in January 1944, which displaced many inhabitants to the outskirts of Rome where the Olympic structures later arose. Into the 1950s, the towns of Anzio and Nettuno remained half abandoned, increasing the sense of isolation among the settlers at nearby Gebelia. The land given to them proved difficult to work, in contrast to the fertile soil of Cyrenaica.

Mauro (pseudonym), born in 1937 in the colonial village of Luigi di Savoia in Derna, described the "alarming" (*spaventoso*) condition of Gebelia when he arrived there at age fourteen with his family. After the Allied occupation(s) of Cyrenaica, his family had relocated first to Tripoli and then made their way to Aversa after the war before joining the community near Anzio. Conditions in Gebelia remained rudimentary through the 1950s, with limited electricity and one television, housed at the cooperative's office, for the entire community. In his hatred of agricultural work, Mauro typified many of the young people at Gebelia. A good number of them emigrated to the industrial cities of northern Italy (as also occurred at Fertilia), rejecting their parents' agricultural vocation.[112] The construction of a Colgate Palmolive factory on Anzio's outskirts in 1957, however, provided new opportunities for the young people who remained. In the opinion of Mauro, who worked there for forty years as a technical assistant, "Palmolive saved us." Enrico Barra, the lawyer who helped conceive of Gebelia, apparently agreed, as by 1958 he urged the need for further projects "of prevalently industrial character" to assist national refugees. Balmelli of Aide-Suisse had apparently read these proposals when he recommended Barra's work as a model superior to that of the Sardinia plan.[113] Today, the zone formerly known as Gebelia is a suburb of Anzio. The neighborhood now goes by the name of Sacida (not Gebelia), despite the cooperative having closed decades earlier. Apart from the refugees and their descendants, only a few individuals know the history of the area or what "Sacida" (transformed from an acronym into a toponym) signifies, suggesting how once distinct agricultural settlements have been gradually absorbed and naturalized in a manner not unlike that of the eucalyptus trees planted by the regime as part of its efforts to reclaim marshy land.

Rethinking Ruinology

When I learned that sites such as Fertilia and processes (*bonifica*) inextricably associated with fascism had been employed in the resettling of refugees and repatriates from the territories that Italy lost after World War II, my first inclination was to read them through the lens of contemporary ruinology and its focus on spaces devastated by warfare, postindustrial decay, and imperial decline. Indeed, much of the burgeoning literature on ruin draws a sharp distinction between the picturesque ruins favored by the Romantics—who treated them as sites of both pleasure and gloom, as well as allegories for the limits of man's control over nature—and those created by modern forms of violence.[114] The latter become metonyms for a view of history as catastrophe. As Julia Hell and Andreas Schönle put it, "When history piles wreckage upon wreckage, ruins evoke not only the buildings from which they hail but also a transhistorical iconography of decay and catastrophe, a vast visual archive of ruination."[115] Such an understanding accords with the notion of colonialism as entailing a corrosive and open-ended process of ruination,[116] one whose variable effects persist in both the metropole and former colonies. It also maps onto problematic but pervasive views of refugees and repatriates as "human relics."

While such a take on ruins possesses utility for my analysis here of the resettlement of Italian national refugees, viewing these sites *exclusively* through such a prism proves overly reductive. Indeed, the limits of such an understanding become evident in those accounts of fascist new towns that focus on their formalist, architectural elements—treating them as empty repositories of past ideological formations—rather than their continued existence as lived spaces. In turn, the neglect and even abandonment of parts of Fertilia and Sacida visible to a contemporary visitor could easily lead one to wrongly attribute that decay directly to the collapse of fascism's empire. In reality, these places expanded (or, like Gebelia, were created) after 1945 and the years of the postwar economic takeoff. Their relative decline in more recent decades is another story that I cannot detail here.[117] As I have argued, despite the literal collapse of the fascist regime and its ideology, some of its most visible material expressions—such as vast tracts of reclaimed land and the new towns built on that terrain—not only remained largely intact after 1945 but, in many instances, were only fully realized *after* the destruction of the fascist regime and with the support of the new republican government. In places like Fertilia and Gebelia, the agents of their realization were migrants from the regime's overseas colonies and Adriatic territories. In the Italian peninsula, these refugees and repatriates often completed the work of internal colonization spearheaded by the regime in the 1930s, albeit through different means. As occurred in the former colonies, then, in the metropole itself the process of decolonization proved protracted and profound, rather than abrupt and transitory. In this sense, sites like Fertilia and Gebelia serve as "foundational ruins,"[118] repurposed ruins that helped form the basis of the postwar, postimperial nation. This selective and strategic re(use) of literal and figurative ruins—even of something as discredited as fascism and colonialism—should not strike us as overly remarkable on the Italian peninsula, where the salvaging and bricolage of strata from previous historical formations has long been the norm.

In arguing this, however, I do not wish to foreclose the multiple meanings of ruins and ruination at work in places like Fertilia and Gebelia. Here, I heed Tim Edensor's caution about overinterpreting or offering *the* definitive reading of ruins: "There is an excess of meaning in the remains: a plenitude of fragmented stories, elisions, fantasies, inexplicable objects and possible events."[119] The memories of my interlocutors in Fertilia and Gebelia hint at the plenitude of stories and meanings attached to those former refugees who lived, worked, and built upon these productive ruins.

Conclusion
"We Will Return"

The preceding chapter concluded with a caution about foreclosing alternative analyses of ruins, reminding us of the broader dangers of assuming that displaced persons necessarily or merely stand in as the human analogue of such physical relics or ruins.[1] Throughout this study, I have aimed to consider the multiplicity of stories and meanings attached to the experiences of displacement and (re)emplacement to and from the Italian peninsula in the decade and a half following fascism's end. Where possible, I have recovered the understandings of those who deemed themselves "refugees" (whether or not others accorded them that status) and, in particular, the complex if asymmetric negotiations between displaced persons themselves, state actors, and intergovernmental and nongovernmental organizations that resulted in the codification of concepts such as international refugee and national refugee. In light of the complicated entanglements between the international and national regimes of refugee assistance, it is no coincidence that the Geneva Convention that laid out the definition of the international refugee came into being during the same period as major Italian legislation that consolidated the Italian state's responsibilities to its own displaced citizens.[2] Nor is it coincidence that as a signatory to the Geneva Convention on Refugees, Italy was among those few states that (initially, at least) adopted the geographic reservation exclusive to European refugees. John Alexander-Sinclair, who dreamed of the "Sardinia plan," was only one of many UNHCR officials who would unsuccessfully press Italy to change its policies and become permanent home to foreign refugees. As we have seen, despite Italy's spectacular postwar economic growth, Italian officials repeatedly invoked the twin specters of Italian surplus population and the pressing needs of its "own" refugees to argue for Italy's unsuitability as a country of permanent resettlement.

The arrival in the 1950s and 1960s of Italian refugees from the territories of other decolonizing powers—notably (formerly) British Egypt and French Tunisia and Algeria—merely reinforced the Italian government's stance that its priorities for assistance must lie with its own citizens. These new arrivals often followed the pathways established by the *profughi* from Italy's former possessions, sometimes even inhabiting the same camps previously occupied by Italians from Libya or Istria, as did foreign refugees. The "Rossi Longhi" camp in Latina (former Littoria) illustrates the long trajectories of such spaces. After housing Italian national refugees (primarily, but not exclusively, from the ceded eastern Adriatic territories), in 1957 the camp became Il Centro di Assistenza Profughi Stranieri. Until 1989, it served as a transit point for displaced foreigners awaiting emigration.[3]

Although the "durable solutions" advocated for by the UNHCR sometimes eluded displaced persons, the labels that attached to them have demonstrated durability. The processes that gave rise to displacement in the particular case explored here—wartime defeat and decolonization—likewise possess durable afterlives in Italy and beyond, challenging claims that Italian decolonization was brief or even noneventful. Ruth Ben-Ghiat has argued that Augusto Genina's 1942 film *Bengasi*, which portrayed the first Allied occupation of Cyrenaica and the region's subsequent reconquest by the Axis powers, signals the end of the genre of fascist imperial cinema. Nonetheless, as we have seen, empire itself and its affects actually had a long fade-out.

Ben-Ghiat points out that the film *Bengasi* saw reissue in 1955, evidence of both continued interest and perhaps yearning within Italy for its lost possessions but also a broader "sense of an Italian imperial history that had been suspended or interrupted, rather than concluded."[4] As Daniela Baratieri has detailed, while the film's re-editing as *Bengasi anno '41* downplayed the presence of fascist symbols, as well as Italian-British antagonism, it did display strong continuities in the representation of Italy's colonial ventures.[5] In 1955, of course, Italy and Libya were still engaged in the bilateral negotiations that would ultimately settle the status of the agricultural settlements in Tripolitania, and Italy had completed only half of its mandated decade as trusteeship administrator in Somalia. In a very literal sense, then, when viewers in Rome or Brindisi or Catania settled into their cinema seats in 1955 to watch the film *Bengasi anno '41*, they were viewing past (the triumphant Italian empire) and present (the still then ongoing diplomatic questions regarding Italian colonial settlements in Libya). For some repatriates, the film also evoked a still possible future, one signaled by the famous slogan "(Ri)torneremo" (We will return). Baratieri rightfully comments that the reissue of *Bengasi* in the 1950s reveals how "the past has not been acknowledged to be past and clings onto the present."[6]

Even with the close of Italy's formal decolonization in 1960, the classifications for migrants coming from the lost territories—repatriates and refugees—possessed continuing salience. Many of the individuals to whom they were applied embraced those identifications, ones that not only marked out their difference from metropolitan Italians but also left open the possibility of political and legal claims on the Italian state and the successor states in the former Italian Oltremare. Still today there exist a host of political and cultural associations for *rimpatriati* and Istriani-Giuliani-Dalmati and their descendants in many towns and cities across the Italian peninsula, as well as in the Italian diaspora. Although scholars of refugees and colonial repatriates often face challenges in locating their subjects along the archival grain, it nonetheless remains true that refugees remain a visible and marked category, in contrast to those who rejected such a label or failed to obtain any of the benefits accorded to refugees. Thus, this book has told a story of those who fought for recognition as refugees and who saw themselves as such, even when denied eligibility by intergovernmental organizations like the IRO (as occurred with many Venezia Giulians, discussed in chapter 4) or by the Italian state (like Italians from Cyrenaica in Tripolitania in the 1950s who insisted they were refugees *within* Libya). Given the scope of this task, I have not been able to recover the voices and stories of the many individual migrants who neither sought status as refugees nor joined a refugee association but rather merely drew on kin and friendship networks on their "return" to Italy. Having left relatively few archival traces, the stories of these displacees await their chronicler.

Likewise, for those relatively few Italians who stayed in the former territories there remains a still largely untold story of how these populations *failed* to become recognized minorities. Despite recent publications focused on the experience of "the Italian minority" in places like Libya,[7] Italians retained no privileged juridical status in independent Libya or anywhere else in Africa. The only former territory where Italians did constitute a recognized and "protected" minority—with rights, among other things, to bilingualism and minority language schools—was Yugoslavia and now the successor states

Slovenia and Croatia. It would be easy to conclude that this difference reflects the fact that this was the only former Italian land where those who felt culturally Italian possessed meaningful claims to autochthony, as well as the reality that the Julian territories had been integral parts of the Italian state. Furthermore, it is tempting to locate this practice in Central European traditions of thinking about minorities. Nonetheless, there exists tantalizing evidence from other parts of the former Italian empire regarding Italians who *almost* became (official) minorities.

In the period leading up to Libyan independence, for example, there occurred lively discussions as to whether to accord particular rights and protections to Italians as one of Libya's four largest minorities. An American Jewish Committee report in 1950 listed these minorities in order of their size: Italians (estimated at forty-five thousand) followed by Jews (thirteen thousand), Maltese (two thousand), and Greeks (four hundred).[8] During the period of Adrian Pelt's work as UN commissioner in Libya, a number of proposals—none of them successful—were advanced to provide these minorities with representation in the National Assembly and even to permit use of Italian in public offices. A representative for all the minorities did, however, sit on the Advisory Council to the UN commissioner. In his history of Libya's Jewish populations, Renzo De Felice contends that during this period of UN tutelage, the criteria for citizenship and the role and status of the territory's principal minorities proved among the most contentious questions.[9] Just one year after his rise to power, Muammar Gadhafi would resolve any lingering questions or ambiguity, brutally reinforcing the binary logics of citizen/alien by expropriating the property of and expelling the approximately twenty thousand Italians in Libya. The call in chapter 4 to examine the redefinition of citizenship in Italy after the war through the dialectical articulation of inclusion-exclusion at home and abroad reminds us of the critical role also played by emergent forms of citizenship from which many Italians were excluded in the newly independent states.

In contrast to Libya, where Italians, as well as Jews, who wished to stay ultimately faced expulsion, in Albania several thousand Italians instead found themselves unable to leave Hoxha's communist state after 1945. As discussed in chapters 2 and 3, these Italians remained immobilized in Albania either because they were deemed to possess skills essential for the reconstruction of Albania or because as Italian women married to Albanian men they had lost the protection afforded by their Italian citizenship. As the Italian and Albanian regimes wrangled over the fate of these Italians, the Circolo Garibaldi provided assistance on the ground. This Circolo soon expanded its scope beyond that of emergency provisioning and aid with repatriation, however, and began to concern itself with a variety of questions related to the moral and spiritual health of the Italian community. In 1945, for example, the Circolo established a Scholastic Commission for Italians in Albania, forwarding offers by nuns to teach elementary school classes. These efforts, together with the organization of a variety of cultural activities, hint at the possibility that the Circolo's leaders may have hoped it could provide the institutional basis for an Italian minority in Albania along the lines of those organized in Yugoslavia in the Istrian and Kvarner regions. A memo written in 1944, for instance, expressed the desire that "once the situation normalizes, the Circolo Garibaldi will be the Italian Association open for moral and physical assistance, for physical and intellectual culture and for a healthy democracy free of any sectarianism or violence."[10] Given the influence of Tito's Yugoslavia on Albania until Yugoslavia's 1948 expulsion from the Cominform, it would not be surprising if some in the Circolo took inspiration from the Unione degli Italiani dell'Istria e di Fiume founded in 1945, though this is a hunch that I have yet to prove.

As in Libya, however, Italians in Albania never acquired status as a recognized and protected group—another story of an *almost* minority. With the rapid mutations in the Albanian political scene and Tirana's shifting international alliances (from Yugoslavia to the USSR to China to isolationism), those Italians who remained in Albania found it best to hide their identities. It was only in 1992, after the collapse of state socialism in Albania, that the Italian Ministry of Foreign Affairs organized Operazione CORA (Comitato Operativo per i Rimpatriandi dall'Albania), by which the Italian military repatriated approximately eighty individuals and their families to Italy.[11] These repatriates and their descendants, many of whom belong to the Associazione Nazionale Cittadini Italiani e Familiari Rimpatriati dall'Albania (ANCIFRA) founded in 2001, continue to press claims on the Italian state to the present day. Nor are they alone among repatriates and refugees from the former possessions. Groups like the Italo-Somali ANCIS (discussed in chapter 4) still seek an apology from the Italian state; protests over the (now invalidated) 2008 Treaty on Friendship, Partnership, and Cooperation between Italy and Libya led to requests by Italians expelled from Libya for a meeting with Gadhafi during his 2009 visit to Rome;[12] and some mixed-race children from former AOI still battle to attain Italian citizenship. For these groups, the dislocations of decolonization are anything but past or uneventful, even if scholars have been relatively slow to recognize this.

Of all the populations of national refugees analyzed here, the Istrian-Julian-Dalmatians have been the most successful in finding new audiences for their story and claims—among scholars, in the press, and at the level of public commemoration. The *esuli* community has succeeded in the creation of monuments to the "martyrs" of the *foibe* (the pits in which Yugoslav partisans executed Italian soldiers and civilians) in various towns and cities scattered throughout Italy. In 2004, representatives of these communities even attained a national day of recognition. The Italian government proclaimed 10 February—the date of the signing of the 1947 Peace Treaty with Italy—a day of official remembrance of the "exodus" of Italians from the Adriatic territories ceded to Yugoslavia. The treaty, of course, also renounced Italy's rights to its African colonies, as well as the Dodecanese Islands and Albania. Nonetheless, the "Giorno del Ricordo," or National Memorial Day of the Exiles, exclusively commemorates the experience of Italian exiles from the Julian lands, and it has frequently reduced even that complex and varied experience to the "precipitating" violence of the *foibe*.

The exclusivity of this memory day underscores the hierarchy of national refugeedom that emerged in postwar Italy. In part because of the concentrated flows and resettlement of Italians from the Adriatic territories and in part because of the emotive resonance of losing territories "redeemed" through the sacrifice of World War I, the *profughi giuliani* sat at the apex of this hierarchy. Time and again, documents I read spoke of the risks that repatriates from Libya or AOI would not find accommodation in refugee camps, overflowing as they were with displacees from the eastern Adriatic.[13] The associations of Italians from Venezia Giulia worked hard over the succeeding decades to obtain additional recognition of their status, thereby differentiating them from other Italian refugees such as the African repatriates. Situating the experiences of national refugees in this hierarchy—as well as within the broader hierarchy of international and national refugees—reminds us that national refugees did share common experiences of classification and assistance in the Italian peninsula, even if their trajectories in and out of the lost possessions proved distinct. While this finding now seems obvious and uncontroversial to me, it was not when I began the research for this project nearly a decade ago, as I noted in the preface. Both my Istrian informants and many scholarly colleagues warned me that my project dealt with distinct and incommensurable experiences—that the situation of autochthonous Italians displaced from the Venezia Giulian lands directly incorporated into the Italian state had nothing or very little in common with those of "short term" Italian colonial settlers who had left Africa or Albania or the Aegean Islands.

I had begun to seriously doubt my methodological and theoretical assumptions until I interviewed a representative from an umbrella organization for associations representing various repatriated groups from Libya,

Eritrea, Ethiopia, and Somalia. With a hint of disdain, this individual contended, "The Istrians have sought greater protections because they want to be seen as special." This comment highlights that despite such efforts at differentiation, some colonial repatriates—moving as they did through a humanitarian infrastructure in which they rubbed elbows with and lived alongside Italians from other *ex possedimenti*, as well as foreign refugees—did perceive their commonalties with the Istrian-Julian-Dalmatian refugees. The desire of some representatives of the latter group to set their experiences apart reflects not only an effort to obtain more resources from the Italian state but also, I would venture, an attempt to divorce further the Istrian story from a problematic history of fascism that raises questions about complicity, as well as Italy's historical responsibilities toward the non-Italian victims of the fascist regime. Positioning Italian refugees from the Julian region exclusively as victims of ethnic cleansing focuses on the wrongs committed by the Yugoslavs and emphasizes the role of ethno-national ideology, rather than the struggle between fascism and socialism or the broader question of fascist imperialism and its legacies.

Since I began this project, the ground has shifted both at the level of scholarship and in political discourse. Already beginning in the mid-1990s, scholars of the Italo-Yugoslav border had begun to insert the history of the exodus into a broader story of forced population transfers and movements in Central and Eastern Europe during and after the Second World War. Only in the last few years, however, have historians begun to investigate the linkages between the various groups of national refugees and the place of these Italian refugees within larger histories of refugee relief.[14] New works on specific groups of national refugees, such as Italians from Libya, are appearing with great frequency. In light of all this, it is not surprising that a young researcher at a 2015 conference at the University of Cagliari excitedly told me, "We really need to start comparing the Istrian exiles and African repatriates!" I had to chuckle when I remembered the stubborn resistance such a suggestion had met only a few years earlier.

No doubt the "rediscovery" of this shared refugee history reflects the broader interest in refugee questions provoked by ongoing migration crises in the Mediterranean and Europe. I conducted much of my research in 2010–2011, as the events of the Arab Spring drove desperate asylum seekers across the sea, and wrote the book over long years as new refugees came to Europe from Syria, Afghanistan, the Democratic Republic of Congo, and beyond. These events often raised pointed questions about previous waves of refugees to Italy. At many turns in my research, I had encountered these refugee pasts—like empire's past—hiding in plain sight. Nonetheless, I was

FIGURE 12. "Ritorneremo": Political poster in the Monteverde neighborhood of Rome advertising a political rally for the "memory day" remembering the exodus of Italians from the Adriatic lands after World War II. Poster made by the group Noi Oltre, which reused the image of the boy and man (see figure 6) for this purpose. Photo by author, March 2011.

still startled when in March 2011 I ran across a poster in the Monteverde neighborhood of Rome that explicitly fused Italy's colonial past in Africa with its lost lands in the Adriatic. Employing the famous fascist image of the grandfather and the young boy dreaming of a return to Africa, the poster put its theme of return in service to the Giorno del Ricordo honoring the victims of the *foibe* and the Adriatic exodus. The placard bore one of two captions that had accompanied the original wartime image: "There where we were, there where our dead await us, there where we left powerful and indestructible traces of our civilization, there we will return." The poster thus explicitly joined the dreams of "return" long shared by Adriatic exiles and African repatriates, even as it privileged the former. Such traces of conflict and displacement possess what Rebecca Bryant deems a latent "'potentiality' . . . a temporal dynamism capable of exploding, twisting, or braiding the past."[15]

In February 2018, the Giorno del Ricordo events braided together past and present in particularly explosive ways. In the context of an electoral campaign that had put front and center questions of Italy's fascist past and its migration present, large antifascist protests turned out in some 150 Italian cities including Turin, Milan, Macerta, and Piacenza. These encounters with the police and with groups commemorating *foibe* victims turned violent in several instances. Antifascist supporters carried signs that linked historical fascism, neo or "crypto" fascism, and xenophobia against migrants in contemporary Italy. As I have evidenced here, such entanglements should not surprise us. Though frequently kept apart, the histories explored in this book were neither repressed nor entirely forgotten. The dream of return, then, does not signal a return—rather, it is a sign of an ongoing, if uneven and always contested, reckoning with Italy's long decolonization.

Notes

Acknowledgments

1. Henry Miller, *Big Sur and the Oranges of Hieronymus Bosch* (New York: New Directions, 1957), 25.

Introduction

1. Archivio Storico Diplomatico del Ministero degli Affari Esteri (ASDMAE), Rome, Direzione Generale Affari Politici (DGAP), Ufficio III 1948–1960, b. 281, fasc. 1023, Prefetto Gaia, "Problemi Profughi Cirenaica," 25 September 1958; Prefetto Celona, "Unione Coloni Italiani Africa," 25 September 1958.

2. Andrea Smith, "Europe's Invisible Migrants," in *Europe's Invisible Migrants*, ed. Andrea Smith (Amsterdam: Amsterdam University Press, 2003), 9–32. For an outstanding and comprehensive recent work that pierces this selective visibility see Elizabeth Buettner, *Europe after Empire: Decolonization, Society, and Culture* (Cambridge: Cambridge University Press, 2016).

3. Jacqueline Andall and Derek Duncan, "Memories and Legacies of Italian Colonialism," in *Italian Colonialism: Legacy and Memory*, ed. Jacqueline Andall and Derek Duncan (Oxford: Peter Lang, 2005), 21. See also Alessandro Triulzi, "Displacing the Colonial Event: Hybrid Memories of Postcolonial Italy," *Interventions* 8, no. 3 (2006): 430–443.

4. The figures for returns from Italian Africa (between 1940 and 1961) come from Colette Dubois and Jean-Louis Miège, introduction to *L'Europe retrouvée: Les migrations de la décolonisation*, ed. Jean-Louis Miège and Colette Dubois (Paris: L'Harmattan, 1994), 9–22. Drawing on the work of Hamid Etemad, Andrea Smith instead estimates between 320,000 and 480,000 Italian migrants from the colonies. Smith, "Europe's Invisible Migrants," 32. When terms like "colonies" are used in such statistics, it often proves unclear whether this refers only to the formal colonies or also to possessions like the Dodecanese or Albania. According to a publication commemorating the work of the Committee for Assistance to Refugees of Venezia Giulia, 1,089,516 "national refugees" from Venezia Giulia and the former colonies (and other powers' colonies, such as Egypt) received assistance in the fifty-year period between 1947 and 1997. Istituto Regionale per la Cultura Istriana, *Esodo e Opera Assistenza Profughi: Una storia parallela* (IRCI: Trieste-Roma, IRCI, 1997), 5. The numbers of national refugees from each of the lost possessions are, not surprisingly, the object of contestation and political manipulation, particularly in the Julian case. The standard statistical study endorsed by Istrian Italian exiles gives a figure of 350,000 ethnic Italians; see Amedeo Colella, *L'esodo dalle terre adriatiche. Rilevazioni*

statistiche (Rome: Stab. Tip. Julia, 1958). Other studies estimate between 188,000 and 200,000 migrants from the Adriatic territories Italy ceded to Yugoslavia.

5. Here I have given the most inclusive dates for the operation of UNRRA and the IRO. The UN archives actually list UNRRA's dates of operation from 1943 to 1946, although some operations continued after that, and the final employee ceased work only in 1949. Likewise, the UN General Assembly adopted the constitution of the International Refugee Organization in December 1946, but operations only really began in earnest in 1948. In 1951–1952, IRO work overlapped with that of the young UNHCR.

6. After 1954, the AAI became the Amministrazione per le Attività Assistenziali Italiane e Internazionali. On parallel systems for aid to foreign refugees in Italy see Matteo Sanfilippo, "I campi in Italia nel secondo dopoguerra," *Meridiana* 86 (2016): 41–56.

7. United Nations, *Convention and Protocol Relating to the Status of Refugees* (Geneva: UNHCR Media Relations and Public Information Service, 2007 [1951]), 16.

8. Ibid., 16–17.

9. On the geographic reservation and Italy refer to Luca Einaudi, Le politiche dell'immigrazione in Italia dall'Unità a oggi (Rome: Editori Laterza, 2007), 49. The text of the convention published by the UN in 1954 contains this statement by Italy's representative, Gastone Guidotti: "In signing this Convention, the Government of the Republic of Italy declares that the provisions of articles 6, 7 (2), 8, 17, 18, 19, 22 (2), 23, 25 and 34 are recognized by it as recommendations only. It also declares that for the purpose of the obligations assumed by the Republic of Italy under this Convention, the words 'events occurring before 1 January 1951' in article 1, section A (2), shall be understood as referring to events occurring in Europe before 1 January 1951." Refer to United Nations, "Convention relating to the Status of Refugees (with schedule)," in Treaty Series: Treaties and International Agreements Registered or Filed and Recorded with the Secretariat of the United Nations, vol. 189 (Geneva: United Nations, 1954), 192 fn. 1. In 1964, Italy withdrew its reservations to articles 6, 7, 8, 19, 22, 23, 25, and 34 of the convention.

10. Section (1) of article 40 stated, "Any State may, at the time of signature, ratification or accession, declare that this Convention shall extend to all or any of the territories for the international relations of which it is responsible. Such a declaration shall take effect when the Convention enters into force for the State concerned." UN Convention and Protocol Relating to the Status of Refugees, 34. Many thanks to Max Cherem for pointing this out.

11. Cited in Atle Grahl-Madsen, *The Status of Refugees in International Law*, vol. 1 (Leyden: A. W. Sijthoff, 1966), 265–266. Section E of Article 1 proves identical with Article 7(b) of the 1950 UNHCR statute. Article 1(D) of the convention contained another important exclusion for individuals already receiving assistance from UN agencies (such as the IRO and the United Nations Relief and Works Agency for Palestine Refugees in the Near East, or UNRWA). The term "national refugee" is sometimes used interchangeably with the term "con-national refugee," as in the work of Grahl-Madsen. Given the prevalence of the terminology of national refugee, in this book I employ that more straightforward vocabulary and leave the parsing of possible distinctions between national and con-national refugees to other scholars.

Though rarely used, the con-national term is often associated with those refugees excluded by the criteria of Article 1(D). I am grateful to Max Cherem for bringing to my attention the "con-national" language and for his insights on the complexities of, as well as confusions surrounding, the categorization.

12. Grahl-Madsen, *Status of Refugees*, 92–33; see also 265–270.

13. Robinson has argued that the "South Asian refugee regime emerged in dialogue with, and in deliberate opposition to, the refugee regime developing in Europe." Cabeiri debergh Robinson, "Too Much Nationality: Kashmiri Refugees, the South Asian Refugee Regime, and a Refugee State, 1947–1974," *Journal of Refugee Studies* 25, no. 3 (2012): 349.

14. For a sampling of studies on repatriation with the end of Japan's empire see Mark Caprio, "The Detritus of Empire: Images of 'Japanese-ness' in Liberated Southern Korea, 1945–1950," Occasional Paper 14 (Rikkyo University, Asia Research Center, 2009); Mariko Tamanoi, *Memory Maps: The State and Manchuria in Postwar Japan* (Honolulu: University of Hawai'i Press, 2009); and Lori Watt, *When Empire Comes Home: Repatriation and Reintegration in Postwar Japan* (Cambridge, MA: Harvard University Asia Center, 2009).

15. See, for example, Lucy Mayblin, "Colonialism, Decolonisation, and the Right to Be Human: Britain and the 1951 Convention on the Status of Refugees," *Journal of Historical Sociology* 27, no. 3 (2014): 423–441; Anna Holian and G. Daniel Cohen, introduction to *Journal of Refugee Studies* 25, no. 3 (2012): 315.

16. Guy S. Goodwin-Gill, "Different Types of Forced Migration Movements as an International and National Problem," in *The Uprooted: Forced Migration as an International Problem in the Post-War Era*, ed. Göran Rystad (Lund, Sweden: Lund University Press, 1990), 28. Grahl-Madsen remains one of the few scholars in the early postwar period to acknowledge the existence, let alone the significance, of national/con-national refugees, who he recognized were "found in great numbers in various countries such as Germany, India, Italy, Korea, Pakistan, Turkey, and Viet-Nam." Nonetheless, his discussion focuses almost exclusively on the German expellees. Grahl-Madsen, *Status of Refugees*, 3; see also 89–91.

17. Phil Orchard, "The Contested Origins of Internal Displacement," *International Journal of Refugee Law* 28, no. 2 (2016): 212.

18. Grahl-Madsen, *Status of Refugees*, 262. Orchard ultimately locates the exclusion of IDPs and (con-)nationals from the refugee definition as the product of "the deliberate effort by the US government to frame refugees as having two constitutive properties: they were both outside their own State and lacked its protection." Orchard, "Contested Origins of Internal Displacement," 233. Focusing on the issue of ethnic German expellees, Orchard makes a persuasive, if incomplete, case. The Italian example instead underscores the importance of the colonial context to the wider debate.

19. James Hathaway, *The Rights of Refugees under International Law* (Cambridge: Cambridge University Press, 2005), 74. As a historian, I adopt an approach different from that of Hathaway, who examines the specific debates among the convention's framers along with "evidence of contemporary factual challenges to the treaty's effectiveness, and synthesizes the interpretation so derived with analysis of the vast array of primary and secondary materials which elaborates the interpretation of cognate rights under general international human rights law." Ibid.

20. United Nations Archives, New York, UNRRA Papers, S-0527–0848 PAG-4/3–0-14–0-2:6, UNRRA Subject Files 1944–1949, Special Assistant to the Chief of Mission Special File on Displaced Persons, Letter from P. Contini, "Policy on 'Infiltrees,'" 9 January 1947. Also, UNRRA S-0527–0981 D.P. Operations (Italy), De Gasperi, "Censimento stranieri," 19 January 1947. In the closing months of the war, the Italian authorities in the south (under Allied control) had conducted censuses of both Italians and non-Italians. By contrast, the 1947 census focused on aliens and worked in tandem with policing. This placed UN workers who sought to aid arrested and detained foreigners in a delicate position. On this go to Archives Nationales, Paris, International Refugee Organization (IRO), AJ 43/1042 Italie, 44/8 Legal protection of persons in Italian collecting centers, closed camps, etc., Varrichione to Contini, "D.P.—Refugee Relations with Questura," 22 July 1947; Mentz to Tonglet, 16 December 1948.

21. On the IRO negotiations, Maria Eleonora Guasconi, "I rapporti dell'AAI con l'IRO e l'assistenza ai profughi in Italia (1947–1956)," in *L'Amministrazione per gli Aiuti Internazionali*, ed. Andrea Ciampani (Milan: FrancoAngeli, 2002), 159–160. On the Joint Eligibility Committee consult Arthur and Elizabeth Schlesinger Library on the History of Women in America, Radcliffe Institute, Cambridge, MA, Louise W. Holborn Papers, 1989–1975, MC 680, box 37, file #3, Italy 1961–1970, UN General Assembly, Executive Committee of the High Commissioner's Programme Twelfth Session, "Report Submitted by the Italian Delegation on Assistance to Alien Refugees in Italy, 8 October 1964," 6.

22. Law no. 763 of 26 December 1981 consolidated the various legislative acts recognizing and protecting such Italian *profughi*. On the particularities of Cyrenaican refugees, especially those remaining in Tripolitania after 1945, turn to Pamela Ballinger, "Caught in the Double Bind? Italian Settlers and Refugees from Cyrenaica, 1943–1960," *Archivio Storico dell'Emigrazione Italiana* 14 (2018): 68–82.

23. United Nations High Commissioner on Refugees Archive (UNHCR), Geneva, fond 11, series 1, Classified Subject Files 1950–1971 6/12/ITA Protection, Naturalization—Italy, "Granting of Italian nationality to refugees within the mandate of U.N.H.C.R.," 12 June 1958.

24. Ibid.

25. IC(E)M Library / IOM Historical Section, Geneva, Refugees General Statistics: European Ref. Ex Africa, etc., Tenth Session, Summary Record of the Eighty-Eighth Meeting, 6 May 1959, 19–20. The Italian government did, however, pledge some 500 million lire to the WRY and additional monies to be raised through a state lottery. Minutes of UNHCR/ICEM meeting held in the ICEM Conference Room, 18 July 1960, 2.

26. IC(E)M Library / IOM Historical Section, Refugees General Statistics: European Ref. Ex Africa, etc., Thirty-ninth Session, "World Refugee Year and the Refugee Program of ICEM (Submitted by the Director)," 7 November 1960, 1.

27. Cohen attributes the DP terminology to US planners during the war. Gerard Daniel Cohen, *In War's Wake: Europe's Displaced Persons in the Postwar Order* (Oxford: Oxford University Press, 2012), 4.

28. Peter Gatrell, *Free World? The Campaign to Save the World's Refugees, 1956–1963* (Cambridge: Cambridge University Press, 2011).

29. Kaye Webb and Ronald Searle, *Refugees 1960: A Report in Words and Drawings* (Harmondsworth, UK: Penguin Books, 1960), 29.

30. Liisa Malkki, "Speechless Emissaries: Refugees, Humanitarianism, and Dehistoricization," *Cultural Anthropology* 3 (1996): 377–404; Heide Fehrenbach, "Children and Other Civilians: Photography and the Politics of Humanitarian Image-Making," in *Humanitarian Photography: A History*, ed. Heide Fehrenbach and Davide Rodogno (Cambridge: Cambridge University Press, 2015), 165–199.

31. Webb and Searle, *Refugees 1960*, 29.

32. Peter Gatrell, "Refugees—What's Wrong with History?," *Journal of Refugee Studies* 30, no. 2 (2016): 178.

33. Matthew Frank and Jessica Reinisch, "Refugees and the Nation-State in Europe, 1919–1959," *Journal of Contemporary History* 49, no. 3 (2014): 478.

34. For a cogent summary of refugee protections as they developed under the League of Nations see Hathaway, *Rights of Refugees under International Law*, 83–91. Hathaway locates the origins of legal protections for refugees in laws concerning aliens and minorities. On the former, 75–81; on the latter, 81–83.

35. G. Daniel Cohen, "Between Relief and Politics: Refugee Humanitarianism in Occupied Germany, 1945–1946," *Journal of Contemporary History* 43 no. 3 (2008): 447. Importantly, however, the 1938 Convention concerning the Status of Refugees Coming from Germany was the first refugee "convention with a clear exclusion clause" for so-called economic migrants. This convention also began to take account of individual motivations for flight. Both issues would become central to the post-1945 regime of protections. Orchard, "Contested Origins of Internal Displacement," 216; see also 217.

36. For a detailed account of this work of repatriation and the so-called "last million" turn to Ben Shephard, *The Long Road Home: The Aftermath of the Second World War* (New York: Alfred A. Knopf, 2011).

37. On USEP refer to Susan Carruthers, *Cold War Captives: Imprisonment, Escape, and Brainwashing* (Berkeley: University of California Press, 2009).

38. Cohen, *In War's Wake*, 79–99.

39. Eva Brems, *Human Rights: Universality and Diversity* (The Hague: Martinus Nijhoff, 2015), 21.

40. Tara Zahra, *The Lost Children: Reconstructing Europe's Families after World War II* (Cambridge, MA: Harvard University Press, 2011). See also Mary Ann Glendon, "The Forgotten Crucible: The Latin American Influence on the Universal Human Rights Idea," *Harvard Human Rights Journal* 16 (2003): 27–40.

41. Cohen, *In War's Wake*, 136.

42. UNRRA, S-520, box 295, Sorieri to Cooley, 31 December 1944.

43. Vito Antonio Leuzzi, "Occupazione Alleata, Ex internati ebrei e slavi in Puglia dopo l'8 settembre 1943," in *La Puglia dell'Accoglienza: Profughi, rifugiati e rimpatriati nel Novecento*, ed. Vito Antonio Leuzzi and Giulio Esposito (Bari: Progedit, 2006), 75–103.

44. This glossed over the tragic story of forced repatriations carried out by the Allies, which prompted the UN agencies' subsequent prohibition on refoulement.

45. Archives du Comité International de la Croix-Rouge (ACICR), Geneva, B AG 280 117–001, Secours à des résidents italiens en Cyrénaïque 31/05/1951–18/04/1952.

46. There exists a sizable literature on return migration of Italy's migrants to third countries. Standard reference works include Betty Boyd Caroli, *Italian Repatriation from the United States, 1900–1914* (New York: Center for Migration Studies, 1973), and Dino Cinel, *The National Integration of Italian Return Migration, 1870–1929* (Cambridge: Cambridge University Press, 2001).

47. On terminology see Ceri Peach, "Postwar Migration to Europe: Reflux, Influx, Refuge," *Social Science Quarterly* 78, no. 2 (1997): 269–283. Smith labels these population movements "reverse migrations of decolonization." Andrea Smith, "Coerced or Free? Considering Post-colonial Returns," in *Removing Peoples: Forced Removal in the Modern World*, ed. R. Bessel and C. B. Haake (Oxford: Oxford University Press, 2009), 414.

48. Rob Skinner and Alan Lester, "Humanitarianism and Empire: New Research Agendas," *Journal of Imperial and Commonwealth History* 40, no. 5 (2012): 731.

49. Dennis Gallagher, "The Evolution of the International Refugee System," *International Migration Review* 23, no. 3 (1989): 583. Similarly, UNHCR, *The 1951 Refugee Convention: Questions and Answers* (Geneva: UNHCR Media Relations and Public Information Service, 2007), 5.

50. Lori Watt, "The 'Disposition of Japanese Civilians': American Wartime Planning for the Colonial Japanese," *Diplomatic History* 41, no. 2 (2017): 399, 413.

51. Colette Dubois, "L'Italie, cas atypique d'une puissance européenne en Afrique: Une colonisation tardive, une decolonisation précoce," *Materiaux pour l'histoire de notre temps* 32–33 (1993): 10–14.

52. Watt, "'Disposition of Japanese Civilians,'" 413.

53. Louise Moor and A. W. Brian Simpson, "Ghosts of Colonialism in the European Convention on Human Rights," *British Yearbook of International Law* 76, no. 1 (2005): 137 fn. 89.

54. Pamela Ballinger, "Entangled or 'Extruded' Histories? Displacement, National Refugees, and Repatriation after the Second World War," *Journal of Refugee Studies* 25, no. 3 (2012): 366–386.

55. In further contrast to the Italian case, the Dutch assumed "the mantle of *liberators* of their colonial subjects rather than merely *liberated* by the Allies." Buettner, *Europe after Empire*, 88.

56. Ibid., 243, 303. The term "emigrant nation" comes from Mark Choate, *Emigrant Nation: The Making of Italy Abroad* (Cambridge, MA: Harvard University Press, 2008).

57. Christopher Seton-Watson, "Italy's Imperial Hangover," *Journal of Contemporary History* 15 (1980): 169–179.

58. Vincent Crapanzano, *Imaginative Horizons: An Essay in Literary-Philosophical Anthropology* (Chicago: University of Chicago Press, 2004), 154.

59. For a sampling of newspaper and magazine articles making the argument for Italy to retain African territories see ASDMAE ASMAI Africa, vol. 4, Fondo Comm. di Studi Economici (Segr. Cerulli), pacco 1, b. 47, fasc. 3, "Libia: Documentazione, articoli vari."

60. Antonio Morone, "Quando è stato archiviato il colonialismo italiano?," *From the European South* 1 (2016): 130.

61. For suggestions on what a "rhythmanalysis" of colonial repatriation might consist of for the case of Italian Libya refer to Pamela Ballinger, "Borders and the

Rhythms of Displacement, Emplacement and Mobility," in *The Blackwell Companion to Border Studies*, ed. Thomas Wilson and Hastings Donnan (Oxford: Blackwell, 2012), 400–402.

62. Vazira Fazila-Yacoobali Zamindar, *The Long Partition and the Making of Modern South Asia: Refugees, Boundaries, Histories* (New York: Columbia University Press, 2007); Nicola Labanca, "The Embarrassment of Libya: History, Memory, and Politics in Contemporary Italy," *California Italian Studies* 1, no. 1 (2010): 15. On a "strange decolonization" go to Nicola Labanca, *Oltremare: Storia dell'espansione coloniale italiana* (Bologna: Mulino, 2002), 428. Emanuele Ertola replicates this language when he deems Italian decolonization a "totally atypical case": Ertola, "Orfani dell'impero: L'assistenza pubblica ai profughi dall'Africa orientale italiana 1942–1956," *Archivio Storico dell'Emigrazione Italiana* 14, no. 18 (2018): 58. Alessandro Pes instead deems it a "missing decolonization": Pes, "Coloni senza colonie: La Democrazia Cristiana e la decolonizzazione mancata (1946–1950)," in *Quel che resta dell'impero: La cultura coloniale degli Italiani*, ed. Valeria Deplano and Alessandro Pes (Milan: Mimesis Edizioni, 2014). For the more helpful understanding of a "long ending of Italian colonialism" see Antonio Morone, "Italiani d'Africa, africani d'Italia: Da coloni a profughi," *Altreitalie* 42 (2011): 23.

63. Akiko Hashimoto, *The Long Defeat: Cultural Trauma, Memory, and Identity in Japan* (Oxford: Oxford University Press, 2015).

64. Jordanna Bailkin, *The Afterlife of Empire* (Berkeley: University of California Press, 2012), 5.

65. W. G. Sebald, *On the Natural History of Destruction*, trans. Anthea Bell (New York: Penguin Books, 2003), ix.

66. Gabriele Proglio has usefully traced out the genealogy of what he calls "the paradigm of memory repression" for the case of Italian colonialism, noting its changing dimensions in the historiography at large and in the work of specific historians like Labanca. Focusing on visual and textual representations in popular magazines like *Epoca* and *Oggi*, Proglio instead argues for the production in the 1950s and 1960s of what he calls a "huge public archive" of memories and images of colonialism that continue to influence understandings in Italy today. Turn to "The Fascist Empire Strikes Back: Reconsidering the Memory of Colonialism after 1945," in *Images of Colonialism and Decolonisation in the Italian Media*, ed. Paola Bertella Farnetti and Cecilia Dau Novelli (Cambridge: Cambridge Scholars, 2017), 240–241.

67. Antonio Morone, "Il vizio coloniale tra storia e memoria," in *Quel che resta dell'impero: La cultura coloniale degli Italiani*, ed. Valeria Deplano and Alessandro Pes (Milan: Mimesis Edizioni, 2014), 368. For a discussion of the reconstruction of the MAI archive after the war refer to ASDMAE ASMAI Africa, vol. 4, Fondo Comm. di Studi Economici (Segr. Cerulli), pacco 1, b. 47, "Relazione sull'attività svolta dal Ministero dell'Africa Italiana fino al 15 ottobre 1948."

68. Gian Paolo Calchi Novati, *L'Africa d'Italia: Una storia coloniale e postcoloniale* (Rome: Carocci, 2011), 41–42.

69. On the recuperation of the UZC documentation refer to Maria Maione, Silvia Re, and Carlotta Cardon, "Ufficio per le zone di confine. L'archivio," *Qualestoria* 38, no. 2 (2010): 7–20. On the history of the Ufficio, Andrea Di Michele, "L'Italia e il governo delle frontiere (1918–1955): Per una storia dell'Ufficio per le Zone di Confine," in *La difesa dell'italianità*, ed. Diego D'Amelio, Andrea Di Michele, and Giorgio

Mezzalira (Bologna: Mulino, 2015). For a good general history of the Istituto Nazionale (Fascista) della Previdenza Sociale that nonetheless omits the story of its work in creating and overseeing colonial villages in Libya turn to Chiara Giorgi, *La previdenza della regime: Storia dell'Inps durante il fascismo* (Bologna: Mulino, 2004).

70. When I consulted the archives of the UNHCR, I was surprised that these too had only recently been cataloged and made available to researchers. One archivist there told me that when UN bureaucrats originally created filing systems for such documents—which jumbled together documents containing personal data (such as medical status) about refugees with interoffice memos and other forms of correspondence—they did not anticipate changes in privacy laws or scholarly ethics that would complicate the task of future archivists.

71. For details see Giulia Barrera, "The Unhappy End of the Italian Institute for Africa and the Orient (IsIAO) and the Uncertain Fate of Its Holdings," *Critical Interventions: Journal of African Art History and Visual Culture* 10, no. 1 (2016): 71–80. See also Costantino di Sante, "Per una 'Nuova Idea Coloniale': Il Museo dell'Africa italiana dal fascismo alla Repubblica," in *Quel che resta dell'impero: La cultura coloniale degli Italiani*, ed. Valeria Deplano and Alessandro Pes (Milan: Mimesis Edizioni, 2014). The IsAIO was itself the product of various mergers of older colonial-era institutions, as discussed in Barrera. Much of the collection of the old Museo Coloniale was given to the Istituto Italo-Africano in 1972 (which later joined with the Istituto per il Medio Oriente to form IsIAO). The Museo Nazionale Etnografico "Luigi Pignorini" acquired many of these materials after IsIAO's closure. In 2017, many of the IsIAO collections became available at the Biblioteca Nazionale Centrale in Rome.

72. Thanks to the tireless efforts of the director Eirini Toliou, the archive has since been transferred to a new site.

73. Jordanna Bailkin, "Where Did the Empire Go? Archives and Decolonization in Britain," *American Historical Review* 120, no. 3 (2015): 885.

74. Ann Laura Stoler, *Along the Archival Grain: Epistemic Anxieties and Colonial Common Sense* (Princeton, NJ: Princeton University Press, 2010), 9.

75. Mia Fuller, "Wherever You Go, There You Are: Fascist Plans for the Colonial City of Addis Ababa and the Colonizing Suburb of EUR '42," *Journal of Contemporary History* 31, no. 2 (1996): 414.

76. On the destruction of archives in Algeria and Kenya see Todd Shepard, "'Of Sovereignty': Disputed Archives, 'Wholly Modern' Archives and the Post-decolonization French and Algerian Republics, 1962–2012," *American Historical Review* 120, no. 3 (2015): 869–883, and Caroline Elkins, "Looking beyond Mau Mau: Archiving Violence in the Era of Decolonization," *American Historical Review* 120, no. 3 (2015): 852–868, respectively.

77. ASDMAE ASMAI Africa, vol. 3, parte 5 (varie), pacco 1911–1970, b. 165, "Scomparsa definitiva dello 'Archivio Storico' dell'Amministrazione Governativa Centrale di Tripoli," 22 August 1955.

78. Filiberto Sabbadin, *I frati minori lombardi in Libia: La missione di Tripoli, 1908–1991* (Milan: Edizioni Biblioteca Francescana, 1991), fn. 5, 67.

79. Nicola Labanca, "Gli studi italiani sul colonialismo italiano in Libia," in *Un colonialismo, due sponde del Mediterraneo*, ed. Nicola Labanca and Pierluigi Venuta

(Pistoia: CRT, 2000), 19–32. The product of a conference of Italian and Libyan specialists held in 2000, this volume represented an important contribution to dialogue between scholars in the former colony and metropole.

80. Michel-Rolph Trouillot, *Silencing the Past: Power and the Production of History* (Boston: Beacon, 1995), 26. This contrasts with those former Italian settlers from Tripolitania who often turned to the parish registers transferred to the Archivio del Segretariato delle Missioni dei Frati Minori lombardi in Milan in order to verify their births or marriages. Sabbadin, *I frati minori lombardi in Libia*, fn. 5, 67.

81. Federico Cresti, *Non desiderare la terra d'altri: La colonizzazione italiana in Libia* (Rome: Carocci Editore, 2011). On the ECL documentation when first recuperated, Federico Cresti, "Documenti per la storia della Libia: L'archivio ritrovato dell'Ente per la Colonizzazione della Libia. Un inventario provvisorio," *Africa* 53, no. 4 (1998): 557–576.

82. For background to the dispute (still ongoing) see Evangelos Raftopoulos, "The Crisis over the Imia Rocks and the Aegean Sea Regime: International Law as a Language of Common Interest," *International Journal of Marine and Coastal Law* 12, no. 4 (1997): 427–446.

83. While the official UNRRA archive is located in New York, useful records from UNRRA can be found in many places, including the countries where UNRRA conducted operations. The personal papers of prominent staff members such as UNRRA directors Herbert Lehmann (located at Columbia University) and Fiorello La Guardia (located at LaGuardia Community College) also provide perspectives on UNRRA different from those offered by its institutional archive.

84. Bailkin, *Afterlife of Empire*; on using local records see Jordanna Bailkin, *Unsettled: Refugee Camps and the Making of Multicultural Britain* (Oxford: Oxford University Press, 2018).

85. Ann Laura Stoler, "Colonial Archives and the Arts of Governance," *Archival Science* 2 (2002): 103.

86. Tony Kushner, *Remembering Refugees: Then and Now* (Manchester: Manchester University Press, 2006), 23.

87. Gatrell, "Refugees," 184. See also the detailed discussion of sources for refugee history in Peter Gatrell, "Population Displacement in the Baltic Region in the Twentieth Century: From 'Refugee Studies' to Refugee History," *Journal of Baltic Studies* 38, no. 1 (2007): 43–60.

88. Serving at war's end as an internment camp for fascists from the Repubblica Sociale Italiana, or RSI, Fossoli then became a camp to which Allied officials sent "undesirable" foreigners, for whom the Italian government had responsibility. Despite the efforts of the American Jewish Joint Distribution Committee to have foreign Jews sent to UNRRA camps, Jews remained at Fossoli until 1946. After the Fossoli camp closed in 1953 with the dispersal of "hard core" refugees to the camps of Fraschette and Farfa Sabina, a settlement for Italian refugees from the eastern Adriatic was created. Costantino Di Sante, *Stranieri indesiderabili. Il campo di Fossoli e i "centri di raccolta profughi" in Italia (1945–1970)* (Verona: Ombre Corte, 2011), 37–39, 51–61, 113. On the Istrians at Fossoli, Maria Luisa Molinari, *Villaggio San Marco, Via Remesina '32 Fossoli di Carpi* (Turin: EGA, 2006).

89. Pamela Ballinger, "A Sea of Difference, a History of Gaps: Migrations between Italy and Albania, 1939–1992," *Comparative Studies in Society and History* 60, no. 1 (2018): 90–118.

90. Stoler, "Colonial Archives and the Arts of Governance," 109.

1. Empire as Prelude

1. On the numbers of Italian migrants see Teresa Fiore, *Pre-occupied Spaces: Remapping Italy's Transnational Migrations and Colonial Legacies* (New York: Fordham University Press, 2017), 4, 8. The most concentrated period of emigration occurred between 1880 and 1915, when some thirteen million Italians departed. Mark Choate, *Emigrant Nation: The Making of Italy Abroad* (Cambridge, MA: Harvard University Press, 2008), 1.

2. Iain Chambers and Lidia Curti, "Migrating Modernities in the Mediterranean," *Postcolonial Studies* 11, no. 4 (2008): 389.

3. Nassima Sahraoui and Caroline Sauter, introduction to *Thinking in Constellations: Walter Benjamin in the Humanities*, ed. Nassima Sahraoui and Caroline Sauter (Newcastle upon Tyne: Cambridge Scholars, 2018), xi.

4. Fiore, *Pre-occupied Spaces*, 13.

5. Ibid., 2.

6. Pamela Ballinger, "Beyond the Italies: Italy as a Mobile Subject?," in *Italian Mobilities*, ed. Ruth Ben-Ghiat and Stephanie Malia Hom (New York: Routledge, 2016).

7. Donna Gabaccia, *Italy's Many Diasporas* (New York: Routledge, 2003), 23.

8. The journal *Altreitalie: Rivista Internazionale di studi sulle migrazioni italiane nel mondo* began publication in 1989. Today, *Altreitalie* serves as the flagship publication for the Centro Altreitalie sulle Migrazioni Italiane. For details go to http://www.altreitalie.it.

9. Gabaccia, *Italy's Many Diasporas*, 11.

10. For an exemplar of the new imperial history refer to Antoinette Burton, *Empire in Question: Reading, Writing, and Teaching British Imperialism* (Durham, NC: Duke University Press, 2011). I heed here Buettner's cautions that in having "taken the 'imperial turn' and then partly transcended it en route to the global, most scholars have bypassed 'Europe' altogether." Buettner, *Europe after Empire*, 12.

11. Dora Marucco, "Le statistiche dell'emigrazione italiana," in *Storia dell'emigrazione italiana*, vol. 1, *Partenze*, ed. Piero Bevilacqua, Andreina de Clementi, and Emilio Franzina (Rome: Donzelli, 2001), 61–64.

12. Federico Ferretti, "Arcangelo Ghisleri and the 'Right to Barbarity': Geography and Anti-colonialism in Italy in the Age of Empire (1875–1914)," *Antipode* 48, no. 3 (2016): 566.

13. Donatella Strangio, *The Reasons for Underdevelopment: The Case of Decolonization in Somaliland* (Heidelberg: Physica Verlag, 2012), 2–3.

14. On French-Italian rivalry over Tunisia turn to Mary Dewhurst Lewis, *Divided Rule: Sovereignty and Empire in French Tunisia, 1881–1938* (Berkeley: University of California Press, 2014), 6.

15. For the broader history of the Società Dante Alighieri refer to Beatrice Pisa, *Nazione e politica nella società "Dante Alighieri"* (Rome: Bonacci, 1995), and Patrizia

Salvetti, *Immagine nazionale ed emigrazione nella società "Dante Alighieri"* (Rome: Bonacci, 1995).

16. Senator Leopoldo Franchetti was entrusted with this project, which saw the arrival of ten peasant families in Eritrea in December 1893. Gian Luca Podestà, "Emigrazione e colonizzazione in Libia e Africa Orientale," *Altreitalie* 42 (2011): 37.

17. Ibid., 39. On the attempts at "civilizing the Southerner [by] taming the African" see Aliza S. Wong, *Race and the Nation in Liberal Italy, 1861–1911* (New York: Palgrave Macmillan, 2006), 79–112.

18. Choate, *Emigrant Nation*, 49–56. Einaudi did not originate this vision of "emigrant colonialism" but rather elaborated ideas first articulated by Leone Carpi in an 1874 publication. In contrast to Carpi, Einaudi valorized diasporic communities as agents who could promote Italian interests. Again, see Choate, 2. At various moments, key figures in the Catholic Church aligned themselves with both models of colonialism. On the tensions created by a vision of an Italian Catholic national identity in service to imperialism in Libya see Eileen Ryan, *Religion as Resistance: Negotiating Authority in Italian Libya* (Oxford: Oxford University Press, 2018).

19. Before World War I, Battisti, a socialist deputy in the Viennese parliament and representative of Trentino's Italian minority, urged the joining of Trento to Italy. He rejected, however, irredentist claims to majority German-speaking Alto Adige / Sud Tyrol, as well as arguments that Italy should acquire formal colonies in Africa. A volunteer in the Italian military during the Great War, Battisti was executed by the Austrians for treason. The fascist regime helped transform him into a nationalist martyr, a process that obscured his particular brand of socialist irredentism. For details see Ferretti, "Arcangelo Ghisleri and the 'Right to Barbarity,'" 575–578. On other critics of the Libyan campaign and Italy's supposed "mission" there, notably the radical parliamentary deputy Leone Caetani, refer to Alessia Maria Di Stefano, "Italian Judges and Judicial Practice in Libya: A Legal Experiment in Multinormativity," *American Journal of Legal History* 58 (2018): 430–434.

20. Pascoli cited in Adriana Baranello, "Giovanni Pascoli's 'La grande proletaria si mossa': A Translation and Critical Introduction," *California Italian Studies* 2, no. 1 (2011): 9.

21. Corradini cited in Michael Miller Topp, *Those without a Country: The Political Culture of Italian American Syndicalists* (Minneapolis: University of Minnesota Press, 2001), 83.

22. Although loud and influential, these interventionist voices did not necessarily represent majority sentiment. David Laven, "Italy: The Idea of the Nation in the Risorgimento and Liberal Eras," in *What Is a Nation? Europe, 1789–1914*, ed. Timothy Baycroft and Mark Hewitson (Oxford: Oxford University Press, 2006), 255–256.

23. For plans to bring Italian settlers to Albania on one-year colonial contracts ("patti colonici") in order to work with Albanian landowners see Giuseppe Scassellati Sforzolini, *Immigrazione di coloni italiani in Albania* (Valona: R. Officina Tipografica Italiana, 1919).

24. Roberta Pergher, *Mussolini's Nation-Empire: Sovereignty and Settlement in Italy's Borderlands, 1922–1943* (Cambridge: Cambridge University Press, 2017).

25. Ruth Ben-Ghiat, *Fascist Modernities: Italy, 1922–1945* (Berkeley: University of California Press, 2001), 4.

26. Gaia Giuliani and Cristina Lombardi-Diop, *Bianco e nero: Storia dell'identità razziale degli italiani* (Milan: Le Monnier, 2013), 47.

27. With the completion of the (re)conquest, the territory officially became Libya (Libia) in 1934. It was occasionally referred to as Africa settentrionale italiana. The Italian regime then created five governmental districts: Tripoli, Benghasi, Derna, Misurata, and Territorio Militario del Sud.

28. Claudio Segrè, *Fourth Shore: The Italian Colonization of Libya* (Chicago: University of Chicago Press, 1974), 161. Refer also to Federico Cresti, *Oasi di italianità: La Libia della colonizzazione agraria tra fascismo, guerra e indipendenza, 1935–1956* (Turin: Società Editrice Internazionale, 1996); Cresti, *Non desiderare la terra d'altri: La colonizzazione italiana in Libia* (Rome: Carocci Editore, 2011). INFPS administered ten of these settlements (comprising some forty-five thousand hectares), all of them in Tripolitania. The ECL instead operated villages in both Tripolitania and Cyrenaica.

29. Clelia Maino, *La Somalia e l'opera del Duca degli Abruzzi* (Rome: Istituto Italiano per l'Africa, 1959); also Robert Hess, *Italian Colonialism in Somalia* (Chicago: University of Chicago Press, 1966), 149–175.

30. Podestà, "Emigrazione e colonizzazione," 42.

31. Mia Fuller, "Wherever You Go, There You Are: Fascist Plans for the Colonial City of Addis Ababa and the Colonizing Suburb of EUR '42," *Journal of Contemporary History* 31, no. 2 (1996): 411.

32. Emanuele Ertola, "The Italian Fascist Settler Empire in Ethiopia, 1936–1941," in *The Routledge Handbook of the History of Settler Colonialism*, ed. Edward Cavanagh and Lorenzo Veracini (New York: Routledge, 2017), 265.

33. Giuliani and Lombardi-Diop, *Bianco e nero*, 42.

34. Philip V. Cannistraro and Gianfausto Rosoli, "Fascist Emigration Policy in the 1920s: An Interpretive Framework," *International Migration Review* 13, no. 4 (1979): 673, 687; Federico Cresti, "'Non emigranti, ma esercito del lavoro': I ventimila in Libia (1938) e la propaganda dell'Italia fascista," in *Da Maestrale e da Scirocco: Le migrazioni attraverso il Mediterraneo*, ed. Federico Cresti and Daniela Melfa (Milan: Dott. A. Giuffrè Editore, 2006), 37–62.

35. Cannistraro and Rosoli, "Fascist Emigration Policy in the 1920s," 673–692; see in particular 675. Also Anna Treves, *Le migrazioni interne nell'Italia fascista: Politica e realtà demografica* (Turin: G. Einaudi, 1976). For a comprehensive view of emigration within broader demographic policy under liberal and fascist Italy see Carl Ipsen, *Dictating Demography: The Problem of Population in Fascist Italy* (Cambridge: Cambridge University Press, 1996). Ipsen's work complicates facile assumptions either that the fascist regime simply condemned emigration or that the call for Italy's colonial "place in the sun" merely followed out of the problems of surplus population.

36. Cited in Mia Fuller, *Moderns Abroad: Architecture, Cities, and Italian Imperialism* (New York: Routledge, 2007), 171.

37. Archivio Centrale dello Stato (ACS), Presidenza del Consiglio dei Ministri (PCM) 1944–47, b. 3423, fasc. 3.2.6/4426, *Italy at Rhodes*, 30.

38. Nicholas Doumanis, *Myth and Memory in the Mediterranean: Remembering Fascism's Empire* (Houndmills, UK: Palgrave Macmillan, 1997), 67–80, 187.

39. Davide Rodogno, *Fascism's European Empire: Italian Occupation during the Second World War*, trans. Adrian Belton (Cambridge: Cambridge University Press, 2006), 47–54.

40. Cited in Roberto Morozzo della Rocca, *Nazione e religione in Albania, 1920–1944* (Bologna: Il Mulino, 1990), 167.

41. Rodogno, *Fascism's European Empire*, 59–60.

42. The description first appeared in Renato Semizzi, "Storia della razza albanese," *Difesa della Razza* 2, no. 9 (5 March 1939). Cited in Valentina Pisany, ed., *La Difesa della Razza: Antologia 1938–1943* (Milan: Bompiani, 2007), 202.

43. On *askari/ascari* see Ruth Ben-Ghiat, *Italian Fascism's Empire Cinema* (Bloomington: Indiana University Press, 2015), 129.

44. Morozzo della Rocca, *Nazione e religione in Albania*, 172.

2. Wartime Repatriations and the Beginnings of Decolonization

1. Grazia Arnese Grimaldi, *I ragazzi della IV Sponda* (Milan: Editrice Nuovi Autori, 1990). Alessandro Rossetto's 2012 documentary *Vacanze di guerra* has reconstructed the story of these *bimbi libici*. Some documents from the time claim a figure closer to fifteen thousand children. See Associazione Nazionale Profughi della Libia, *Memorandum presentato alla Commissione di Indagine delle Quattro Potenze sulle Ex-Colonie Italiane* (Rome, 22 May 1948; held at Istituto Italiano per l'Africa e l'Oriente), 27. This same publication states that on the eve of Italy's entry into the war, the civilian Italian population of Libya numbered at 124,135, with 78,506 in Tripolitania and another 45,629 in Cyrenaica (p. 28).

2. Francesco Prestopino, ed., *Uno dei Ventimila: Diario del colono Giacomo Cason, Libia 1938–1959* (Bologna: Officina grafica di Giorgio Barghiani, 1995), 70–73.

3. Coordinated repatriation of Italians from non-Italian territories, notably France and Tunisia, had occurred as early as 1938. In the context of growing political tensions between Italy and France, Mussolini had called for the establishment of a Commissione permanente per il rimpatrio degli italiani all'estero (CORI). Although CORI sought to send repatriates from French territories to Italy's African colonies (AOI), the largest flows appear to have been to Germany. On the little-studied history of CORI see Romain Rainero, *Le navi bianche: Profughi e rimpatriati dall'estero e dalle colonie dopo la seconda guerra mondiale: Una storia italiana dimenticata (1939–1991)* (Mergozzo: Sedizioni, 2015), 103–131; Carl Ipsen, *Dictating Demography: The Problem of Population in Fascist Italy* (Cambridge: Cambridge University Press, 1996), 136–139.

4. On this, Giulio Esposito, "Profughi e rimpatriati in terra di Bari," in *La Puglia dell'accoglienza: Profughi, rifugiati e rimpatriati nel Novecento*, ed. Vito Antonio Leuzzi and Giulio Esposito (Bari: Progedit, 2006), 114 fn. 49.

5. These movements could nonetheless prove significant in demographic terms. One document from the Ministry of Italian Africa reports that whereas 27,836 Italians migrated to Libya in 1938, another 9,620 Italians repatriated. Similarly, for the following year, 23,122 Italians relocated to the territory, whereas 9,367 left it. By September 1940, only 5,200 Italians had been recorded that year as moving to Libya, versus 5,875 departing migrants. Such numbers do not appear to take account of

the children removed to Italy on their "vacanze di guerra." ASDMAE ASMAI Africa, vol. 4, Fondo Statistica, pacco 3, b. 54, fasc. 9, "Dati vari raccolti per rispondere alla richiesta, 24/9/47"; A. M. Morgantini, "Le migrazioni in Libia," 18 September 1940.

6. Ann Laura Stoler, "Rethinking Colonial Categories: European Communities and the Boundaries of Rule," *Comparative Studies in Society and History* 31, no. 1 (1989): 150. On the "threat" posed by poor Italians to the imperial project in Ethiopia consult Emanuele Ertola, *In terra d'Africa: Gli italiani che colonizzarono l'impero* (Bari-Roma: Laterza, 2017), 99–101.

7. ACS Ente per la colonizzazione Puglia d'Etiopia, b. 6, fasc. 57, A. Trotta, "Famiglie immesse," 20 March 1939; Nuvolari, "Colono Brescia G.," 4 December 1939.

8. Archivio Storico Istituto Nazionale della Previdenza Sociale (AS INPS), Carte della colonizzazione libica, 1933–1968, b. 65, fasc. 278, Alberto Stern, letter, 15 February 1938.

9. Ibid. On the expulsion and repatriation of settlers from Libya during the fascist era refer to AS INPS, Carte della colonizzazione libica, 1933–1968, b. 64, fasc. 273, Alberto Stern, "Immissioni—trasferimenti—rimpatri di famiglie coloniche. Constatazioni patrimoniali del fondo," 4 April 1941. In Eritrea, fascist authorities expelled a number of colonists on the grounds that their behavior threatened "white prestige" in the eyes of the natives. Giulia Barrera, "Mussolini's Colonial Race Laws and State-Settler Relations in Africa Orientale Italiana (1935–41)," *Journal of Modern Italian Studies* 8, no. 3 (2003): 425–443. On the private worries of colonial administrators about the lack of "civilized" behavior on the part of the settlers turn to Charles Burdett, "Journeys to Italian East Africa 1936–1941: Narratives of Settlement," *Journal of Modern Italian Studies* 5, no. 2 (2000): 219.

10. These four ships—the *Duilio*, *Giulio Cesare*, *Saturnia*, and *Vulcania*—were retrofitted in the manner of hospital ships and have often been confused with the twelve actual Italian hospital ships in service during World War II. On the story of the hospital ships refer to Erminio Bagnasco, ed., *Le navi ospedale italiane 1935–1945* (Parma: Albertelli Edizioni Speciali, 2010); David Miller, *Mercy Ships* (London: Continuum, 2008), 63–66. For the role of the *Saturnia* and *Vulcania* refer to Paolo Valenti, *Le quattro sorelle: Storie delle motonavi Saturnia e Vulcania, Neptunia ed Oceania della Cosulich di Trieste* (San Dorligo della Valle: Luglio Editore, 2007). For the "biographies" of these ships see Civico Museo del Mare di Trieste, *Trieste e le 'Navi Bianche'* (Trieste: Museo Civico Storia Naturale, 2007). Important scholarly works on the *navi bianche* include Emanuele Ertola, "Navi bianche. Il rimpatrio dei civili italiani dall'Africa Orientale," *Passato e presente* 31, no. 91 (2013): 127–143, and Rainero, *Le navi bianche*. A number of participants have published memoirs, most notably B. V. Vecchi, *Navi Bianche: Missione di pace in tempo di guerra* (Milan: Gastaldi Editore, 1963). For the perspective of those who were children at the time of events turn to Massimo Zamorani, *Dalle Navi Bianche alla Linea Gotica, 1941–1944* (Milan: Mursia, 2011). For an early scholarly analysis, P. M. Masotti, "Il rimpatrio di donne, bambini, vecchi ed invalidi italiani dall'Etiopia nel 1942–43," *Storia contemporanea* 15, no. 3 (1984): 463–473.

11. Robert L. Hess, *Italian Colonialism in Somalia* (Chicago: University of Chicago Press, 1966), 175.

12. Francis Rennell (Lord Rodd), *British Military Administration of Occupied Territories in Africa during the Years 1941–1947* (London: His Majesty's Stationery Office, 1948), 448.

13. Celso Costantini, *The Secrets of a Vatican Cardinal: Celso Costantini's Wartime Diaries, 1938–1947*, ed. Bruno Fabio Pighin, trans. Laurence B. Mussio (Montreal: McGill–Queen's University Press, 2014), 148.

14. Rennell, *British Military Administration*, 251.

15. Filiberto Sabbadin, *I frati minori lombardi in Libia: La missione di Tripoli, 1908–1991* (Milan: Edizioni Biblioteca Francescana, 1991), 70–71.

16. Ministry of Information, *The First to Be Freed: The Record of British Military Administration in Eritrea and Somalia, 1941–1943* (London: His Majesty's Stationery Office, 1944), 10.

17. Cited ibid., 11.

18. Cited in Philip Boobbyer, "Lord Rennell, Chief of AMGOT: A Study of His Approach to Politics and Military Government (c. 1940–43)," *War in History* 25, no. 3 (2018): 309.

19. Ibid., 326.

20. In particular, article 43 of the 1907 Hague Convention stipulated, "The authority of the legitimate power having in fact passed into the hands of the occupant, the latter shall take all the measures in his power to restore, and ensure, as far as possible, public order and safety, while respecting, unless absolutely prevented, the laws in force in the country." Cited in Adam Roberts, "Transformative Military Occupation: Applying the Laws of War and Human Rights," *American Journal of International Law* 100 (2006): 587. The application of such laws to the former Italian colonies remained a source of debate, however. Writing in 1948, Rennell claimed, "the Legal Advisors [of BMA] were confronted with the serious problem of being supplied, at long last, with text-books on international law, which, compiled by learned writers, dealt with the interpretation and application of a Convention which was inadequate to the existing circumstances." Highlighting the colonial mind-set that guided such administration, Rennell added, "The observations in these learned works dealt with a state of affairs which might have arisen in the territory of a sovereign state in Europe a quarter of a century ago, where homogeneous nations were concerned and where existing law and judicial and executive arrangements were inadequate for the needs of a civilised people. Such was not the picture in the Italian African Empire in 1940 and the ensuing years." Rennell, *British Military Administration*, 345.

21. P. E. Mitchell, "Notes on Policy and Practice in Respect of Occupation of Italian East Africa (8/2/41)," reproduced in *British Military Administration*, 55.

22. There exists a sizable and growing body of literature on the Italian experience in POW camps during World War II. Classic works include Flavio Giovanni Conti, *I prigionieri di guerra italiani 1940–1945* (Bologna: Il Mulino, 1986). On the topic of those in British-administered camps see Bob Moore and Kent Fedorowich, *The British Empire and Its Italian Prisoners of War, 1940–1947* (Houndmills, UK: Palgrave, 2002). The majority of Italian males captured in East Africa were sent to camps in Kenya. Another population instead waited out the war interned in India and South Africa. For a sampling of works go to Lorenzo Carlesso, *Centomila prigionieri italiani in Sud Africa. Il campo di Zonderwater* (Ravenna: Angelo Longo, 2009); Alfredo Gambella,

Ospite di sua maestà britannica. Dalla Cirenaica ai campi di prigionia in India 1940–1943 (Gorizia: Libreria Editrice Goriziana, 2012); Giovanni Marizza, *Diecimila italiani dimenticati in India. La repubblica fascista dell'Himalaya* (Rome: Herald Editore, 2012); and Valeria Isacchini, *Fughe. Dall'India all'Africa, le rocambolesche evasioni dei prigionieri italiani* (Milan: Ugo Mursia, 2014).

23. On Category E go to the National Archives of the United Kingdom (TNA), Kew, England, FO 371/35621, Colonel Mirehouse to MacKereth, 19 October 1943. Details on the color-coded cards come from Alfredo Romiti, *L'evacuazione degli Italiani dall'Etiopia: Il problema dell'alimentazione della popolazione civile europea dell'Harar e dei campi. Donne, bambini, civili, risolto per iniziativa privata* (Parma: S.A. Tipografie Riunite Donati, 1949), 5–6.

24. Thanks to Noelle Turtur for this insight. In the metropole, there instead existed partisan bands fighting the Nazi and fascist forces that included indigenous subjects from AOI. On this, Martina Milone, "25 Aprile, la 'banda Mario': Storia degli africani che si unirono ai partigiani delle Marche. 'L'Empatia vinse sulla paura del diverso,'" *Il Fatto Quotidiano.it* (25 April 2019). For the celebrated case of Italo-Somalian partisan Giorgio Marincola killed by Nazis in the waning days of World War II go to Alessandro Triulzi, *Razza partigiana: Storia di Giorgio Marincola, 1923–1945* (Rome: Iacobelli, 2008).

25. On 3 April 1941 the General Officer Commanding in East Africa had recommended the repatriation of civilians to Italy. By 22 April the War Office had approached the Italian government over the issue of evacuation. Sir Philip Mitchell, chief political officer of the East Africa Command, headed the evacuation operation. Registration of civilians, the first step in the operation, began in June 1941. Rennell, *British Military Administration*, 439–452.

26. ACICR BG 17 06–023 Prisonniers en Afrique Orientale Italienne occupée, 1939–août 1942: correspondance avec les autorités nationales, les SN et les délégations d'Afrique du Sud, Allemagne, AOB, Grande-Bretagne, Égypte, Indes britanniques, Italie 12/10/1939–31/08/1942, Jacques Chenevière, 8 September 1941. Various religious orders in AOI, as well as the bishop of Eritrea, played a role in caring for these civilians. See the National Archives (TNA), London, FO 371/35621, Reid to MacKereth, 2 November 1943; J. G. Marinoni to Bonavia, 22 September 1943.

27. Zamorani, *Dalle Navi Bianche*, 94–98.

28. Romiti, *L'evacuazione degli Italiani dall'Etiopia*, 50. On the assistance work carried out by this Ente, which received high praise from and took place under the supervision of British officials, see Rennell, *British Military Administration*, 79–80. For the highly gendered aspects of what became cast as a humanitarian crisis see Noelle Turtur, "Mothers without Milk: A Humanitarian Crisis in British Occupied Italian East Africa," unpublished paper, 2019.

29. Junod's father, Henri-Alexandre Junod, was similarly a well-known missionary and anthropologist who worked in both South Africa and Mozambique and engaged in important debates with Radcliffe-Brown and Van Gennep, among other anthropologists. Henri-Philippe's cousin, Marcel Junod, also played an important role in the ICRC during the interwar period and Second World War. On these deeply intertwined strands of religious humanitarianism and ethnographic research turn to Patrick Harries, "The Anthropologist as Historian and Liberal: H-A. Junod and the Thonga," *Journal of Southern African Studies* 8, no. 1 (1981): 37–50;

Lorenzo Macagno, "Missionaries and the Ethnographic Imagination: Reflections on the Legacy of Henri-Alexandre Junod (1863–1934)," *Social Sciences and Missions* 22 (2009): 55–88.

30. ACICR BG 17 06–023 Prisonniers en Afrique Orientale Italienne occupée, 1939–août 1942: correspondance avec les autorités nationales, les SN et les délégations d'Afrique du Sud, Allemagne, AOB, Grande-Bretagne, Égypte, Indes britanniques, Italie 12 / 10 / 1939–31 / 08 / 1942, Jacques Chenevière, 8 September 1941.

31. ACICR BG 017 06–22 Prisonniers en Afrique Orientale Italienne occupée, 1939–août 1942: correspondance avec Henri-Philippe Junod, délégué 26 / 11 / 1940–31 / 08 / 1942, "Rapport complémentaire sur la population civile de l'Afrique Orientale Occupée (Écrit à Addis Abeba 22.7.41) par H. P. Junod, délégué honoraire," Henri Junod, 22 July 1941, 1–2. In his history of the BMA in Africa, Rennell highlighted another difference between the different territories that made up AOI, noting that evacuation from Ethiopia (where Italians lived "as recent conquerers of an indigenous population") was compulsory, while it remained largely voluntary for Eritrea and, later, Somalia. Rennell, *British Military Administration*, 448.

32. ACICR BG 017 06–22 Prisonniers en Afrique Orientale Italienne occupée, 1939–août 1942: correspondance avec Henri-Philippe Junod, délégué 26 / 11 / 1940–31 / 08 / 1942, "Rapport complémentaire sur la population civile de l'Afrique Orientale Occupée (Écrit à Addis Abeba 22.7.41) par H. P. Junod, délégué honoraire," Henri Junod, 22 July 1941, 1–2. For a detailed report on the situation of Italian civilians in Mogadishu written a month earlier, in which Junod underlines the hostility of the local population and the "pernicious" climate, see the correspondence of 6 June 1941, "Remarques sur la situation de la population civile de la Somalie Italienne (Mogadiscio)," contained in the same folder. Other ICRC documents testify to acute food shortages in Italian Somalia during this period. On this see ACICR BG 17 06–023 Prisonniers en Afrique Orientale Italienne occupée, 1939–août 1942: correspondance avec les autorités nationales, les SN et les délégations d'Afrique du Sud, Allemagne, AOB, Grande-Bretagne, Égypte, Indes britanniques, Italie 12 / 10 / 1939–31 / 08 / 1942, Jacques Chenevière, 8 September 1941.

33. Luisella Carosio, *Via dall'Etiopia: Diario a due voci* (Genoa: Neos Edizioni, 2014), 107. The CRI in Addis Ababa appeared well equipped, at least in the estimation of Jacques Chenevière of the ICRC. He reported that when Junod visited them in 1941, he found "this section installed in spacious offices and employing a considerable personnel." ACICR BG 17 06–023 Prisonniers en Afrique Orientale Italienne occupée, 1939–août 1942: correspondance avec les autorités nationales, les SN et les délégations d'Afrique du Sud, Allemagne, AOB, Grande-Bretagne, Égypte, Indes britanniques, Italie 12 / 10 / 1939–31 / 08 / 1942, 8 September 1941, Jacques Chenevière, 8 September 1941.

34. The reasons for this were both political and pragmatic. The British did not know whether these territories would be returned to Italy at war's end. In their claim to follow international law, the British also sought to differentiate themselves from their enemies. As a wartime publication put it, "The correct procedure for occupying territory is laid down carefully and clearly by international law." Ministry of Information, *First to Be Freed*, 25. On both the logistical and political challenges (in particular with the local Arab populations) created by adherence to international law and the "continuation of a latent Italian sovereignty" in Libya refer to Rennell, *British Military*

Administration, 252; see also 253, 320–345. Whereas in some parts of the former Italian empire BMA officials largely exercised supervision over or coordination with Italian administration, in other areas—such as Eritrean Asmara and Massawa, and parts of Somalia—BMA eventually adopted fairly direct forms of rule. Boobbyer, "Lord Rennell, Chief of AMGOT," 310.

35. War Office, *British Military Administration of Occupied Territories in Africa during the Years 1941–43* (London: His Majesty's Stationery Office, 1945), 19. Found in ASDMAE AP 1946–50, Italia Ex Possedimenti Parte Generale, b. 4.

36. Carosio, *Via dall'Etiopia*, 53. Other memoirs from Ethiopia by children who traveled on the *navi bianche* express similar mistrust of the British, e.g. Anna Paola Gilioli, *La nostra Africa: Storia di una famiglia modenese nell'Africa Orientale Italiana, 1935–1947* (Modena: Elis Colombini, 2016).

37. Romiti, *L'evacuazione degli Italiani dall'Etiopia*, 38–42. For another memoir that stresses the fear and suffering experienced by Italian women and children civilians in AOI during the initial period of the British occupation see F. G. Piccinni, *Africa senza sole* (Rome: TOSI/Tip. SICCA, 1949). 59–73. Among other things, Piccinni describes how Italian men in Addis Ababa sought to flee or hide (as he did for several months before the English found him and interned him) and how some other "less honorable" Italians turned informers for the British or, in the case of Italian women, became their lovers.

38. TNA, FO 371/37306, H. J. Phillinion to C. M. Weekley, 2 December 1943.

39. TNA, FO 371/35617, Gilbert MacKereth to Major Redvers Taylor, 26 May 1943.

40. Samuel Moyn has gone so far as to claim a "secret history" of Christian human rights in Europe during the interwar and early postwar period. Though the Vatican's humanitarian efforts are not quite secret, they have been overlooked in favor of the story of the UN agencies. Moyn, *Christian Human Rights* (Philadelphia: University of Pennsylvania Press, 2015).

41. On the complex nature of the ICRC's role during the Ethiopian War see the detailed study by Rainer Baudendistel, *Between Bombs and Good Intentions: The International Committee of the Red Cross (ICRC) and the Italo-Ethiopian War, 1935–36* (New York: Berghahn Books, 2006). Baudendistel contends that the Ethiopian War, which led the ICRC to send its first delegation to Africa, played an important role in clarifying the ICRC's role during the subsequent global conflict. The organization asserted its neutrality, particularly vis-à-vis the League of Nations, and stressed the supposedly "apolitical" nature of its work. After World War II, the ICRC's strict adherence to this role would become the source of renewed controversy in light of its actions (and inaction) during the Holocaust.

42. ACICR B G 3 42–4 Missions de Gottfried Senn en Rhodésie du sud, d'E. Grasset dans l'Union sud-africaine, d'André Evalet en Afrique orientale italienne, de Robert Maurice au Congo belge 27/03/1941–14/10/1941, Telegram 8 January 1941, Junod.

43. For his account of the British command's initial failure to provide for communications between those in civilian internment/transit and POW camps and his sense of "duty" in facilitating those communications see Romiti, *L'Evacuazione degli Italiani dall'Etiopia*, 38–40. On Evalet's role in delivering personal letters despite British prohibitions turn to ACICR BG 17 06–024 Prisonniers en Afrique Orientale Italienne

occupée, septembre 1942–1943, 20/02/1942–21/03/1946, C. E. Thibaud, "Note Concernant M. André Evalet," July 1942. For ICRC regulations on the mail refer to ACICR B G 3 42–4 Missions de Gottfried Senn en Rhodésie du sud, d'E. Grasset dans l'Union sud-africaine, d'André Evalet en Afrique orientale italienne, de Robert Maurice au Congo belge 27/03/1941–14/10/1941, "Correspondence between Italian civil internees and their families."

44. ACICR BG 017 06–89 Prisonniers en Ethiopie 15/07/1941–19/02/1948, Dr. A. Liengme, "Rapport confidentiel sur M. André Evalet à Addis-Abeba," n.d. For details on Evalet's life refer to André Evalet, *De Ménélik a Mengistu. Un Suisse en Éthiopie. Témoignage recueilli par Micheline Fontolliet Honoré* (Geneva: Musée d'ethnographie / Association Suisse-Érythrée, 1999).

45. Rennell, *British Military Administration*, 107.

46. BMA documents instead claim to have explicitly decided *against* fostering antifascist movements, at least before the events of September 8, 1943. In Eritrea, for instance, the BMA supported the "ex-fascist majority which must, after all, form the main body of a future Italy." British Military Administration Eritrea, *Annual Report by the Chief Administrator on the British Military Administration of Eritrea Report V for Period 1 January to 31 December, 1943* (Eritrea: BMA, 1943), 5. Another publication similarly stated, "On the whole, therefore, the Administration decided that it was best to regard the Italians in Eritrea and Somalia as neither Fascist nor anti-Fascist, but just Italian; not to attempt to build up an anti-Fascist party, since in so doing one would automatically stimulate a pro-Fascist party; to take the line that would keep the colonies quietest and enable them to be administered with the minimum of fuss." Ministry of Information, *First to Be Freed*, 17.

47. ASDMAE ASMAI Africa, vol. 3, b. 166, Rimpatrio donne, bambini ed invalidi civili dall'Africa Orientale Italiana: Relazione, Allegato. 40 Dichiarazioni, no. 18, Clotilde del Balzo, "Relazione sulla C.R.I. dell'Eritrea dal settembre 1941 al novembre 1942–XXI," 1 January 1943. British documents likewise mention the formation of new CRI committees in former AOI, presumably in light of the need to purge fascist elements. See TNA, FO 371/35621, P. Descouedres, "Seconde Mission à Berbera (Somalie Britannique) (Rapatriement de la population civile italienne d'Éthiopie)," 16 November–22 December 1942, 10. This report describes a new CRI committee constituted in Somalia in June 1942 under the leadership of F. Ravalli. The activities of this group included sending messages in response to Vatican radio transmissions and the transcription and forwarding of radio messages from Radio-Rome, Radio-Vatican, and Radio-Nairobi to POWs in Kenya.

48. Istituto Fascista dell'Africa Italiana, *Guida del rimpatriato d'Africa* (Rome: Arti Grafiche G. Menaglia, 1943), 5. Such materials offered the civilian counterpart to the military dream of return embodied by the postcards and posters vowing revenge upon the British.

49. Emanuele Ertola, "Orfani dell'impero: L'assistenza pubblica ai profughi dall'Africa orientale italiana 1942–1956," *Archivio Storico dell'Emigrazione Italiana* 14, no. 18 (2018): 59.

50. ASDMAE ASMAI Africa, vol. 3, b. 166, Rimpatrio donne, bambini ed invalidi civili dall'Africa Orientale Italiana: Relazione, Achille Saporetti, "Relazione dell'Ufficiale P.A.I Relazione della Seconda Missione Speciale in A.O.I. nave 'Giulio Cesare,'" 30.

51. ASDMAE ASMAI Africa, vol. 3, b. 166, Rimpatrio donne, bambini ed invalidi civili dall'Africa Orientale Italiana: Relazione, Allegato. 40 Dichiarazioni, no. 7, "Ermanno Boffa—imbarcatosi clandestinamente a Massaua e catturato dagli inglesi a Porto Elisabetta."

52. ASDMAE ASMAI Africa, vol. 3, b. 166, Rimpatrio donne, bambini ed invalidi civili dall'Africa Orientale Italiana: Relazione, Achille Saporetti, "Relazione dell'ufficiale P.A.I.," 21. One official even feared that the internment camps had infected repatriates with "the poison of Bolshevism." Cited in Ertola, "Navi bianche," 139. Interestingly, in her diary Maria Carelli uses similar language to convey her frustrations as an upper-class officer's wife being forced to live cheek to jowl with the hoi polloi. Her diary entry for 30–31 December 1941 reads, "We grouped ourselves together in order to avoid contact with women who we don't know and who immediately reveal themselves to be . . . enemies of officials' wives. We are all equal, however, there is neither a general's wife nor a colonel's wife who has any worth, these are the phrases that accompanied us on the trip [to Dire Daua] and afterwards. We are in full Bolshevism! I feel as if I'm living in Russia!!" Carosio, *Via dall'Etiopia*, 32. The similarity of language here suggests that Italian propaganda accused the British (no strangers to class hierarchy themselves) of imposing an unnatural egalitarianism upon Italian civilians.

53. ASDMAE ASMAI Africa, vol. 3, b. 166, Rimpatrio donne, bambini ed invalidi civili dall'Africa Orientale Italiana: Relazione, Achille Saporetti, "Relazione dell'Ufficiale P.A.I," 10.

54. Carosio, *Via dall'Etiopia*, 129, 133.

55. ASDMAE, ASMAI Africa, vol. 4, Fondo Caroselli (1908–1944), pacco 16 (1941–52), b. 83, fasc. 3, "Buon Viaggio," *Il Giornale d'Italia: Edizione di Bordo per i Rimpatriati dall'A.O.I.*, 7 July 1943.

56. TNA, FO 371/35621, "Seconde Mission à Berbera (Somalie Britannique) (Rapatriement de la population civile italienne d'Éthiopie) Visite en Somalie Italieenne (Mogadiscio) Visite au Kenya (Nairobi) faites par le Dr. P. Descouedres du 16 novembre au 22 décembre 1942," 3–4.

57. TNA, FO 371/35621, M. G. Seidl, "Rapport sur l'embarquement a Mogadiscio, a bord du M/V Saturnia, de civils italiens de la Somalie Italienne en vue de leur rapatriement," July (?) 1943.

58. On the negotiations over Ras Imru and the repatriation voyage of 19 Eritreans/Ethiopians, refer to TNA, FO 371/35617, Cypher, 31 May 1943; Cypher, 1 June 1943; Norton, Cypher, 4 June 1943; MacKereth to French, 17 June 1943; and G.M. to Swiss Legation, 24 June 1943. TNA, FO 371/35621 also contains information on the release of Ras Imru.

59. Ertola, "Navi bianche," 139–143. See also ASDMAE ASMAI Africa, vol. 4, Fondo Caroselli (1908–1944), pacco 16 (1941–52), b. 83, fasc. 1, fasc. 2, fasc. 3, fasc. 5.

60. ASDMAE ASMAI Africa, vol. 3, b. 166, Rimpatrio donne, bambini ed invalidi civili dall'Africa Orientale Italiana: Relazione, Achille Saporetti, "Relazione dell'Ufficiale P.A.I," 12. A document from 1942 laid out in great detail the "military training" of such children. See ASDMAE, ASMAI Africa, vol. 4, pacco 16, Fondo Caroselli, b. 83, fasc. 4, F. S. Caroselli, "Inquadramento dei ragazzi rimpatriandi," 28 April 1942.

61. Zamorani, *Dalle Navi Bianche*, 38.

62. Michel Foucault proposed the notion of heterotopia as a counter-site, one where incompatible sites could be juxtaposed as "a kind of effectively enacted utopia in which the real sites, all the other real sites that can be found within the culture, are simultaneously represented, contested, and inverted." Foucault, "Of Other Spaces: Utopias and Heterotopias," *Architecture/Mouvement/Continuité*, trans. Jay Miskowiec (October 1984), 3.

63. Istituto Fascista dell'Africa Italiana, *Guida del rimpatriato d'Africa*, 17, 31–34.

64. For critical reappraisals of the coercive nature of fascism consult Paul Corner, "Italian Fascism: Whatever Happened to Dictatorship?," *Journal of Modern Italian History* 74, no. 2 (2002): 325–351; Michael Ebner, *Ordinary Violence in Mussolini's Italy* (Cambridge: Cambridge University Press, 2011).

65. ASDMAE ASMAI Africa, vol. 3, b. 166, Rimpatrio donne, bambini ed invalidi civili dall'Africa Orientale Italiana: Relazione, Achille Saporetti, "Relazione dell'Ufficiale P.A.I," 34.

66. ASDMAE ASMAI Africa, vol. 3, b. 166, Rimpatrio donne, bambini ed invalidi civili dall'Africa Orientale Italiana: Relazione. Allegato "Segnalazioni riservate (in linea politica e finanziaria)."

67. Martha Branscombe, "The Children of the United Nations: U.N.R.R.A.'s Responsibility for Social Welfare," *Social Service Review* 19, no. 3 (1945): 311.

68. Cited in Tara Zahra, *The Lost Children: Reconstructing Europe's Families after World War II* (Cambridge, MA: Harvard University Press, 2011), 4.

69. TNA, FO 371/35621, Colonel Mirehouse to Mr. MacKereth, 28 September 1943.

70. TNA, FO 371/35621, G. Hartman, 24 August 1943.

71. TNA, FO 371/37306; July 30, 1943, C. M. Ledger wrote, "Relative to arrangements being made in Portuguese East Africa by the German Consul-General and the Italian Consul for the repatriation of their Nationals on the Italian repatriation ships coming from Eritrea and Mogadiscio it may be that the two Axis Consulates were trying by this means to discover which of their nationals were still Nazi or Fascist and therefore willing to return to their home country and those who were indifferent or now opposed to the Axis Governments." On Campini as "completely devoid of scruples" see handwritten notes on the minutes for R7559, 14 August 1943.

72. A series of Schifano's paintings would "return" to Libya in a posthumous 2003 exhibition titled *Deserts*. For details on Schifano's early life see G. Banne, "Mario Schifano . . . crocefissione dell'artista (prima parte)," 29 April 2010 Contemporanea_mente, https://giovanniballetta.wordpress.com/2010/04/29/mario-schifano-crocefissione-dellartista/.

73. Prior to the 1943 armistice, the Ente comunale di assistenza (ECA) had established camps for "bombed out" Italians at Lecce, Brindisi, Venice, and Rome. See Antonio D'Andrea, "Campi profughi, centri di lavoro, di studio e di educazione professionale," in *Atti del convegno per studi di assistenza sociale*, contained in UNRRA, S-520 box 249, 599. Relatively little is known about assistance to colonial repatriates under Salò. Just two months after the armistice of 1943, a Comitato di Assistenza agli Italiani Rimpatriati dall'Estero (CAIRE) was created, but it appears to have achieved few results. On this turn to Rainero, *Le navi bianche*, 17–18, 47. Between 1943 and 1945, two competing Ministries of Italian Africa existed, one in the RSI and one in the Regno del Sud (at Salerno). In both states, repatriates from Africa were excluded

from the category of *profughi di guerra* or war refugees. Alessandra Vigo, *Rimpatriati d'Africa: Assistenza, associazioni e reintegro tra storia e memoria (1939–1952)* (Padua: Scripta Edizioni, 2016), 20–25. By contrast, individuals displaced from the Dodecanese and other Italian territories (occupied by the Germans) could be considered war refugees, at least in the Regno del Sud. Esposito, "Profughi e rimpatriati in terra di Bari," 119.

74. Ministry of Information, *First to Be Freed*, 40–42.

75. Claudio Segrè, *Fourth Shore: The Italian Colonization of Libya* (Chicago: University of Chicago Press, 1974), 167–171. As Rennell recounts, "During the late spring and throughout the summer [of 1943] the interest of every branch of the Administration [of Tripolitania] became focused on grain." Rennell, *British Military Administration*, 279.

76. Rennell, *British Military Administration*, 259.

77. Ibid., 134–135, 164.

78. Ibid., 163.

79. Ibid., 196.

80. A memo within the Stato Maggiore della R. Marina (Italian Royal Navy) dated 8 November 1944, for example, decries the "very tough, almost cruel" treatment of Italian prisoners and internees in Africa and notes the positive changes in Somalia and Eritrea brought about by the arrival of the Americans, who "left our civilians in complete liberty and fittingly assumed them as employees." ACS PCM 48–50, b. 325, fasc. 17.1 / 12491, "Notizie sull'Africa Orientale Italiana," 8 November 1944.

81. In the case of the violence in Greece, novels and films like *Captain Corelli's Mandolin* together with war crimes trials (such as that of Nazi officer Alfred Stork, found guilty in 2013 by an Italian military court for his role in the Cephalonia killings), have shed light on the fate of Italian military personnel. On the tragic fate of Italian military in the Dodecanese Islands, for example, see Isabella Insolvibile, *Kos 1943–1948. La strage, la storia* (Naples: Edizioni Scientifiche Italiane, 2010).

82. Estimates of the *foibe*'s victims range anywhere from four thousand to fifty thousand. On the problems of numbers see Raoul Pupo, "Violenza politica tra guerra e dopoguerra: Il caso delle *foibe* giuliane, 1943–1945," in *Foibe: Il peso del passato*, ed. Giampaolo Valdevit (Venice: Marsilio, 1997), 36–37, and Roberto Spazzali, "Contabilità degli infoibati. Vecchi elenchi e nuove fonti," ibid., 97–127. For a useful English-language summary of debates over the *foibe* go to Gaia Baracetti, "*Foibe*: Nationalism, Revenge and Ideology in Venezia Giulia and Istria, 1943–5," *Journal of Contemporary History* 44, no. 4 (2009): 657–674.

83. ASDMAE AP 1931–34, Dodecanneso, b. 16, fasc. 7, "Trasporti ferroviari di donne e bambini sfollati dall'Egeo," 1 June 1943; "Trasporti ferroviari di donne e bambini rimpatriati dall'Egeo," 12 July 1943.

84. ACICR BG 003 27–26 mai–décembre 1945: correspondance avec Albert Gredinger, correspondance avec la sous-délégation de Rhodes 18–06 / 1945–13 / 12 / 1945. R. Courvoisier, "Dodecanese," 27 July 1945.

85. Ian Gooderson, "Shoestring Strategy: The British Campaign in the Aegean, 1943," *Journal of Strategic Studies* 25, no. 3 (September 2002): 1–36. For an alternative reading of the campaign turn to Matthew Hughes and Matthew Seligmann, "The Battle for the Dodecanese, 1943: A Reassessment," *Imperial War Museum Review* 12 (1999): 109–116. Hoping to exploit possibly declining morale among the Italians and

to bring the neutral Turkish into the conflict on the Allied side, the British had made an earlier and unsuccessful attempt in 1941 to take Kastellorizo / Castellorizo, a small island in the Dodecanese archipelago. S. M. Rose, "Castelorizzo: 24–28 February 1941," *Army Quarterly and Defence Journal* 114, no. 3 (1984): 307–319.

86. Ettore Vittorini, *Isole dimenticate: Il Dodecaneso da Giolitti al massacro del 1943* (Florence: Casa Editrice Le Lettere, 2002), 68.

87. Ester Fintz Menascé, *Buio nell'isola del sole: Rodi 1943–1945. I due volti di una tragedia quasi dimenticata: Il martirio dell'ammiraglio Campioni e dei militari italiani in Egeo, e lo sterminio degli ebrei di Rodi e Coo* (Florence: Editrice La Giuntina, 2005), 85–100; on the fate of other Italian military see 101–121. Refer also to Marco Clementi and Eirini Toliou, *Gli ultimi ebrei di Rodi: Leggi razziali e deportazioni nel Dodecaneso italiano (1938–1948)* (Rome: DeriveApprodi, 2015), 163–174.

88. ASDMAE AP 1931–45, Dodecanneso, b. 16, fasc. 11, Antonio Coccheri, "Al Segretario del Partito Fascista Repubblicano," 4 October 1944. Menascé cites an Italian interned by the Germans who recalls approximately fifteen hundred Italian civilians employed by the Germans in Rhodes: Menascé, *Buio nell'isola del sole*, 104.

89. Clementi and Toliou, *Gli ultimi ebrei di Rodi*, 201–204. In questioning the frequent claim that Faralli was actually an antifascist threatened with dismissal by the Germans on several occasions, they assert, "If it is true that Faralli helped save the life of some Italians interned by the Germans, and the 'if' must be stressed here, it is utterly clear that others, namely the Jewish community, were sacrificed; after which, the complicity of the government of the Aegean Islands in the deportation of the Jews was hidden," 204. Clementi and Toliou's similar skepticism regarding Macchi's role in these events contrasts with the glowing accounts of the work of Macchi in the testimony of Father Giovanni Pellegrini Longobardi, who in October 1945 praised Macchi for helping Italian military personnel escape deportation to Germany, organizing air raid protection, and making secret contact with the Allies. In addition, Longobardi contended that Macchi provided food and assistance to the islands' Jews until the last moment possible, even "when there was nothing more possible to do to help those unfortunates." ASDMAE AP 1946–50, Dodecanneso, b. 2, Padre Giovanni Pellegrini Longobardi, "Stralcio della Relazione del Padre Giovanni Pellegrini Longobardi sull'attività svolta dalla Commissione per la Tutela degli Interessi Italiani nel Dodecanneso costituta in Rodi-Egeo-Dopo l'occupazione Britannica nel Dodecanneso," October 1945. For other positive assessments of Macchi's role see Vittorini, *Isole dimenticate*, 120–123, 156–159, and Menascé, *Buio nell'isola del sole*, 127–129. Luca Pignataro's *Il Dodecaneso Italiano, 1912–1947*, vol. 3, *De Vecchi, guerra, e dopoguerra, 1936–1947/50* (Chieti: Solfanelli, 2018) contains a polemical refutation of the conclusions of Clementi and Toliou (see pp. 36–54; on Macchi and the Jewish deportations, 260–261 fn. 781).

90. Clementi and Toliou, *Gli ultimi ebrei di Rodi*, 27.

91. ASDMAE AP 1931–1945, Dodecanneso, b. 16, fasc. 11, G. Aloisi, "Notizie da Rodi," 13 January 1945.

92. ASDMAE AP 1931–1945, Dodecanneso, b. 16, fasc. 11, G. Aloisi, "Notizie da Rodi," 25 January 1945.

93. Menascé, *Buio nell'isola del sole*, 127. Pignataro's careful reconstruction indicates that it was Faralli who first sought provisioning via Turkey through the services of a commander of the Italian merchant marine. Unsuccessful, he then

appealed to the RSI's Ministry of Foreign Affairs, asking them to request assistance from either the ICRC or the German command. Pignataro, *Il Dodecaneso Italiano*, 3:287–301.

94. ACICR BG 003 60–1 Mission de Raymond Courvoisier en Palestine en août 1944 et dans le Dodécanèse en 1945, 08/08/1944–08/04/1945. This file contains the letter of appeal from the religious heads sent to the president of the ICRC on 3 November 1944. Other relevant details about the mission can be found in ACICR BG 003 27–26 mai–décembre 1945: correspondance avec Albert Gredinger, correspondance avec la sous-délégation de Rhodes, 18/06/1945–13/12/1945. Particularly useful is the ten-page extract of a report by Courvoisier dated 27 July 1945. According to this document, the first relief mission took place between 12 and 28 February 1945 to Rhodes, Leros, Calimnos, Pserimo, and Calemia. The second relief shipments occurred between 11 March and 3 April 1945. On 7 April another shipment of food and medication went to the islands. For a tally of the funds expended and the goods provided in these actions see ACICR Sg. 11, Secours à la Grèce, Secours aux Îles de Dodécanèse et Délé. de Rhodes, 1946–1950, Marc Seidl, "Action de Secours aux Îles du Dodécanèse," 1 October 1946. An Italian consular document instead notes the dates of the three relief missions as 18 February, 16 March, and 20 March 1945. ASDMAE AP 1931–45, Dodecanneso, b. 16, G. Aloisi, "Notizie da Rodi," 6 April 1945. In a request made by the Vatican to the British ambassador to the Holy See and to UNRRA to provide assistance to the Dodecanese, extracts of Courvoisier's report were included, indicating the frequent circulation of such communications. See UNRRA S-0527, box 848, Displaced Persons—Italian Dodecan., S. M. Keeny to Paolo Contini, "Assistance to the Dodecanese Islands," 8 June 1945.

95. ASDMAE AP 1931–45, Dodecanneso, b. 16, fasc. 11, Col. Levesi, "Situazione isole Dodecanneso," 13 April 1945.

96. ASDMAE AP 1931–45, Dodecanneso, b. 16, G. Aloisi, "Notizie da Rodi," 6 April 1945. This presumably referred to the Italian military that had sworn loyalty to the RSI. At war's end, the German general Wagener who oversaw the Isole Egeo was arrested and turned over to the British Military Tribunal. In addition to crimes such as illegal antiquities trafficking and his role in running three internment camps on Rhodes, Wagener was accused of having diverted Red Cross supplies to German troops and for sale on the black market. Handed off to the Italians in January 1947, a year later Wagener received a pardon from the Italian president Luigi Einaudi that permitted him to return to live in Germany. Andrea Villa, *Nelle isole del sole: Gli italiani del Dodecaneso dall'occupazione al rimpatrio (1912–1947)* (Turin: SEB 27, 2016), 277–278.

97. ACICR Sg. 11, Secours à la Grèce, Secours aux Îles de Dodécanèse et Délé. de Rhodes, 1946–1950, Munier to Brigadier Acland (BMA), 26 July 1945; ASDMAE AP 1931–1945, Dodecanneso, b. 16, fasc. 11, Antonio Macchi and Aldo Levi, "Commissione per la Tutela degli interessi italiani nel Dodecanneso. Relazione sull'opera svolta dalla sezione 'Assistenza' nel semestre giugno–novembre 1945."

98. The ambiguous status of the CTIID reflected the fact that until the 1947 Peace Treaty, the islands technically remained Italian and thus there did not exist on the islands an Italian consular or diplomatic office. The Commissione thus stood in for this representation, acting as a de facto section of the Italian Legation in Athens until the opening of the Italian consulate in Rhodes in 1949. Luca Pignataro, "Il tramonto del Dodecaneso italiano (1945–1950)," *Clio* 37, no. 4 (2001): 660–663.

99. ASDMAE AP 1931–1945, Dodecanneso, b. 16, fasc. 11, Antonio Macchi and Aldo Levi, "Commissione per la Tutela degli interessi italiani nel Dodecanneso. Relazione sull'opera svolta dalla sezione 'Assistenza' nel semestre giugno–novembre 1945."

100. ASDMAE AP 1946–50, Dodecanneso, b. 2, Pro Memoria, "Fondi Commissione Italiana di Rodi," 1 August 1946.

101. George Woodbridge, *UNRRA: The History of the United Nations Relief and Rehabilitation Administration*, vol. 1 (New York: Columbia University Press, 1950), 479.

102. For a typical account of those sent to Germany see the diary of the Tuscan sergeant major Silvio Forzieri, who fought against Albanian "rebels" (i.e., partisans) until he was captured by the Germans after Italy's capitulation and interned in Hannover from October 1943 to May 1945. Massimo Borgogni, ed., *Diario di guerra e prigionia del Sergente Maggiore Silvio Forzieri, 1941–1945* (Siena: Edizioni Cantagalli, 2003).

103. On the Perugia and Firenze units see Viscardo Azzi, *I Disobbedienti della 9ª Armata: Albania 1943–1945* (Milan: Mursia, 2010). On the call to arms made by communist leader Enver Hoxha and the Albanian partisans to the Italians see Enzo Misefari, *La Resistenza degli albanesi contro l'imperialismo fascista* (Milan: Edizioni di cultura popolare, 1976).

104. Alessandro Serra, *Albania: 8 settembre 1943–9 marzo 1944* (Milan: Longanesi, 1974), 75, 113–117.

105. Franco Benanti, *La guerra più lunga: Albania, 1943–1948* (Milan: Mursia, 1966), 166–167. Another former Italian soldier recalls this committee helping Italians who had fled to the mountains. According to him, the committee financed its work through donations from wealthier Italians in Albania. Francesco Bonasera, *L'Irreale: Storia di un attesa, Albania 1943–1944–1945* (Jesi: La trucanina, 1986), 63.

106. On Dante Alighieri as a "refuge for soldiers" see Archivio Storico Società Dante Alighieri, Serie Comitati Esteri, 1891–2002 (AS SDA SCE), Tirana 592 E, sf. 8, declaration of 10 October 1947. On the British military estimates, Elena Aga Rossi and Maria Teresa Giusti, *Una guerra a parte: I militari italiani nei Balcani, 1940–1945* (Bologna: Mulino, 2011), 357.

107. Rossi and Giusti, *Una guerra a parte*, 358. The Italian government found itself pressured by its newfound British and American allies to delay or avoid official recognition of the Albanian state under Hoxha, a situation that made Albanians much less sympathetic to Italy's requests for repatriation.

108. Benanti, *La guerra più lunga*, 199–203; Settimio Stallone, *Prove di diplomazia adriatica: Italia e Albania 1944–1949* (Turin: Giappichelli 2006), 144–146. See also ASDMAE AP 1946–50, Albania, b. 10, "Nota Verbale," 11 March 1946. On Italian insistence that Italy and Albania had never officially been at war and thus Albania could not legally request war reparations see Settimio Stallone, "Gli accordi del 14 marzo per il rimpatrio degli italiani dall'Albania," *Clio* 39, no. 4 (2003): 687–701.

109. Stallone, "Gli accordi del 14 marzo," 697–698.

110. "The Italians who were officially to be retained were required to sign a declaration, as a condition of their staying in Ethiopia, absolving the British authorities from responsibility for their protection." Rennell, *British Military Administration*, 196.

111. Settimio Stallone, "La difficile missione del console Ugo Turcato in Albania (29 luglio 1945–21 gennaio 1946)," *Clio* 34, no. 1 (1998): 143–171. Turcato had coordinated repatriation efforts with UNRRA and the British Military Mission.

Turcato's departure further taxed British and UNRRA representatives negotiating with Hoxha's regime in the attempt to repatriate Italians. See UNRRA, S-1012–0005–03 Albania Displaced Persons—Italian Repatriates—Policy and Procedures, Ruby Oakley-Hill, 14 January 1946.

112. UNRRA, S-1012–0005–03 Displaced Persons—Italian Repatriates—Policy and Procedures, Brigadier, British Military Mission in Albania, Cable, Tirana to London, 15 January 1946.

113. UNRRA S-1010, box 8, file 9, Albania—Bureau of Finance and Administration—Personnel-Legal Matters, "Proces Verbal on incidents at house off Rruga Kavaja on the 10th, 11th, and 12th February 1946, and appertaining thereto."

114. AS SDA SCE Tirana 1950–1974 592 E, sf. 7, "L'attività scolastica italiana in Albania negli anni scolastici 43/44 e 44/45." One document states that the Gruppo Democratico Popolare Italiano originated in the days following the liberation of Tirana, when Enrico Danek, Gioacchino Magnoni, and Ugo Merola contacted the command of the Gramsci Battalion. "The men of the Gruppo Democratico Popolare immediately had a notable part to play in the functioning of the Circolo Garibaldi." ASDMAE, AP 1946–50 Albania, b. 8, Verbale, 3 August 1945. Arkivi Qendror Shtetëror (AQSH), Circolo Garibaldi (CG), dosja 14, viti 1944 contains lists of contributions made by Italian companies to both the Comitato Antifascista Italiano and the Circolo Garibaldi in December 1944. Seventy-four companies offered donations, revealing the wide range of Italian commercial interests still present in Albania at that time.

115. For the many communications on this issue refer to UNRRA, S-1012, box 5, file 6. In particular see D. Rielli (president, Circolo Garibaldi) to UNRRA Durazzo, 1 September 1945.

116. AQSH, CG, dosja 1, viti 1944, seduta del 9–12–44.

117. AQSH, CG, dosja 2, viti 1944, Pirrò, 14 December 1944. For an account of the foundation myth of the Circolo's birth in the partisan fight in the mountains see the "Diario Storico Circolo Garibaldi" in AQSH, CG, dosja 52, viti 1945.

118. On the establishment of a canteen restricted to those in need see AQSH, CG, dosja 15, viti 1944, "Conv. Mensa," 30 December 1944. AQSH, CG, dosja 45, viti 1944 contains several documents on a kitchen with rations for transiting soldiers and others who lacked assistance. On aid to an Italian woman married to an Albanian man, AQSH, CG, dosja 16, viti 1944, letter of 27 December 1944.

119. See the letter from the "Comitato Assistenza fra Italiani in Scutari," 9 December 1944 contained in AQSH, CG, dosja 3, viti 1944.

120. AQSH, CG, dosja 68, viti 1945, Magnoni, 2 January 1946. See also AQSH, CG, dosja 95, viti 1945, 3 December 1945; AQSH, CG, dosja 114, viti 1946, 2 January 1946.

121. Maria Rita Bruschi, *Dal Po all'Albania, 1943–1949. Un medico mantovano tra guerra e prigionia* (Verona: Scripta Edizioni, 2013), 40.

122. AQSH, CG, dosja 14, viti 1944 (various lists of contributions). Also AQSH, CG, dosja 28, viti 1944, 29 October 1944, refers to the "help provided on the generous initiative of a woman, well known to many of you, and the generosity of contributors" in making possible recreational outlets for Italian comrades who had returned from the partisan campaign in the mountains. One letter of thanks from Circolo president Gregorio Pirrò (dated 5 January 1945) referenced various items of clothing donated by the Bulgarian vice consul. On this, AQSH, CG, dosja 65, viti 1945.

123. On this see various documents found in ASDMAE AP 1946–50, Albania, b. 3: letter of Gennaro Imondi, 3 April 1946; letter of Eliseo Canavese, 8 August 1946; letter of Gioacchino Magnoni to Ugo Turcato, 5 August 1946; letter of Ugo Turcato to MAE, "Fondi assistenza a disposizione della Missione Italiana in Albania," 16 August 1946. Officials in the MAE nonetheless considered the Circolo "under the direct influence of the Albanian government, with the result that the assistance to Italians is subordinated to discriminatory criteria." ASDMAE AP 1946–50, Albania, b. 2, "Memorandum per l'U.N.R.R.A.," 23 February 1946.

124. See the collection of letters at the Albanian Central State Archives (AQSH), Leterkembimi i qytetareve italianë në Shqipëri, dosjet 39–41/4, viti 1945. For the specific lament about civilians, dosja 41, viti 1945, letter to Calderazzi Sabino, 20 June 1945. In the spring of 2015, the MAXXI (National Museum of Twenty-First Century Art) in Rome featured an installation titled *Sue proprie mani* in which actors read a number of these letters.

125. Gerard Daniel Cohen, *In War's Wake: Europe's Displaced Persons in the Postwar Order* (Oxford: Oxford University Press, 2012), 101–125; Zahra, *Lost Children*, 147.

126. For details turn to Philipp Ther and Ana Siljak, *Redrawing Nations: Ethnic Cleansing in East-Central Europe, 1944–1948* (Lanham, MD: Rowman & Littlefield, 2001); Mark Mazower, "Minorities and the League of Nations in Interwar Europe," *Daedalus* 126, no. 2 (1997): 47–63; Mark Mazower, "The Strange Triumph of Human Rights," *Historical Journal* 47, no. 2 (2004): 379–398; Matthew Frank, *Expelling the Germans: British Opinion and Post-1945 Population Transfer in Context* (Oxford: Oxford University Press, 2008); Philipp Ther, *The Dark Side of Nation-States: Ethnic Cleansing in Modern Europe* (Oxford: Berghahn Books, 2016).

127. In the debates over whether to insert specific minority protection in the 1948 Universal Declaration of Human Rights, only three states proposed special attachments: Denmark, the USSR, and Yugoslavia. These proposals were never voted on. Kristine Midtgaard, "Bodil Begtrup and the Universal Declaration of Human Rights: Individual Agency, Transnationalism and Intergovernmentalism in Early UN Human Rights," *Scandinavian Journal of History* 36, no. 4 (2011): 490–491.

128. At Yalta, the Allies agreed to international supervision of these Italian territories. By the time of Potsdam, the Soviets were demanding that they administer one such trusteeship. As Soviet-American relations deteriorated, these plans disintegrated, opening up a protracted series of negotiations over the individual territories. For more details see Saul Kelly, "Britain, the United States, and the End of Italian Empire in Africa, 1940–52," *Journal of Imperial and Commonwealth History* 28, no. 3 (2000): 52–53.

129. ACICR B G 17 06–088 Prisonniers en Érythrée 25/05/1945–26/08/1946, "Note sur la situation des civils italiens se trouvant actuellement dans des camps en Érythrée," 26 August 1946.

3. Italy's Long Decolonization in the Era of Intergovernmentalism

1. Ana Antic, Johanna Conterio, and Dora Vargha, "Conclusion: Beyond Liberal Internationalism," *Contemporary European History* 25, no. 2 (2016): 359.

2. Steven R. Ratner, "Law Promotion beyond Law Talk: The Red Cross, Persuasion and the Laws of War," *European Journal of International Law* 22, no. 2 (2011): 486.

3. On the Vatican's relief missions to the Western occupied zones of Germany refer to Paul Weindling, "'For the Love of Christ': Strategies of International Catholic Relief and the Allied Occupation of Germany, 1945–1948," *Journal of Contemporary History* 43, no. 3 (2008): 477–492. On the role of Catholic relief in the US National War Fund turn to Bruce Nichols, "Religion, Refugees and the US Government," in *Refugees in the Age of Total War*, ed. Anna C. Bramwell (London: Unwin Hyman, 1988). The Vatican's juridical status within emergent UN intergovernmentalism nonetheless remained a question. In 1946, for example, UNRRA's legal adviser in southeastern Europe weighed in on an aid donation to Italy from the Catholic Communities of the Maritime Provinces of Canada that specified that UNRRA, the Italian state, and the Vatican share its distribution. The legal expert contended that the Vatican satisfied neither the definition of a member state of UNRRA nor that of a "voluntary society within the meaning of this concept as it is used by UNRRA." UNRRA S-0527-0981, Bureau of Relief Services Vatican, Mitchell Franklin to S. M. Keeny, "Participation of the Vatican in UNRRA activities," 13 June 1946.

4. Alan S. Milward, *The European Rescue of the Nation-State* (London: Routledge, 2000 [1992]), 44–45.

5. Tara Zahra, *The Lost Children: Reconstructing Europe's Families after World War II* (Cambridge, MA: Harvard University Press, 2011).

6. Writing of a 1948 film set against the backdrop of an UNRRA camp, Sharif Gemie and Louise Rees note, "If there is a single, unifying theme to the movie, it is the idea of putting people back into their places." Gemie and Rees, "Representing and Reconstructing Identities in the Postwar World: Refugees, UNRRA, and Fred Zinnemann's Film, *The Search* (1948)," *International Review of Social History* 56 (2011): 452.

7. Jessica Reinisch, "'We Shall Rebuild Anew a Powerful Nation': UNRRA, Internationalism and National Reconstruction in Poland," *Journal of Contemporary History* 43, no. 3 (2008): 454.

8. See, for example, Silvia Salvatici, "Between National and International Mandates: Displaced Persons and Refugees in Postwar Italy," *Journal of Contemporary History* 49 (2014): 514–536; Jessica Reinisch, "Internationalism in Relief: The Birth (and Death) of UNRRA," *Past and Present* 210, supplement 6 (2011): 258–289.

9. Reinisch, "'We Shall Rebuild Anew,'" 458–459.

10. Kenneth E. Beer, ed., *UNRRA in Action: United Nations Help One Another* (New York: Interallied, 1945), 52.

11. Reinisch, "'We Shall Rebuild Anew,'" 475–476.

12. For an important exception see Kristine Midtgaard, "Bodil Begtrup and the Universal Declaration of Human Rights: Individual Agency, Transnationalism and Intergovernmentalism in Early UN Human Rights," *Scandinavian Journal of History* 36, no. 4 (2011): 479–499.

13. Jean-Jacques Roche, "Intergovernmentalism," in *International Encyclopedia of Political Science*, ed. Bertrand Badie, Dirk Berg-Schlosser, and Leonardo Morlino (Thousand Oaks, CA: SAGE, 2011), 1232. Much of the scholarly literature on intergovernmentalism (and so-called new intergovernmentalism) discusses it in the context of European integration. Another body of literature focuses on "democratic deficits" within intergovernmental organizations (IGOs), the need for IGO

transparency and accountability (a role often played by NGOs), and the role of IGOs in promoting global democracy. For a review of these debates see Alexandru Grigorescu, *Democratic Intergovernmental Organizations? Normative Pressures and Decision-Making Rules* (Cambridge: Cambridge University Press, 2015), 1–12.

14. Grigorescu, *Democratic Intergovernmental Organizations?*, 189.

15. Susan Pedersen, *The Guardians: The League of Nations and the Crisis of Empire* (Oxford: Oxford University Press, 2015), 398.

16. Ibid., 403. In her masterful study of the League's mandate system, Pedersen details the central unintended consequence of that system. "The League helped make the end of empire imaginable, and normative statehood possible, not because the empires willed it so, or the Covenant prescribed it, but because the dynamic of internationalization changed everything—including how 'dependent peoples' would bid for statehood, what that 'statehood' would henceforth mean, and whether empires would think territorial control essential to the maintenance of global power." Ibid., 406.

17. Sandrine Kott, "Internationalism in Wartime: Introduction," *Journal of Modern European History* 12, no. 3 (2014): 318. Mary McGeachy, the only female director within UNRRA (director of welfare, 1944–1946), came from the League of Nations Secretariat. On this, Mary Kinnear, *Woman of the World: Mary McGeachy and International Cooperation* (Toronto: University of Toronto Press, 2004).

18. Joseph P. Harris, "The Development of an International Civil Service for the Administration of Relief and Rehabilitation of War Devastated Areas," *Iowa Law Review* 31 (1945–1946): 99.

19. Bruce Cronin, "The Two Faces of the United Nations: The Tension between Intergovernmentalism and Transnationalism," *Global Governance* 8 (2002): 64.

20. Midtgaard, "Bodil Begtrup," 493.

21. Cronin, "Two Faces of the United Nations," 68.

22. Matthew Frank and Jessica Reinisch, "Refugees and the Nation-State in Europe, 1919–1959," *Journal of Contemporary History* 49, no. 3 (2014): 490.

23. Ibid., 480.

24. Sharif Gemie and Laure Humbert, "Writing History in the Aftermath of 'Relief': Some Comments on 'Relief in the Aftermath of War,'" *Journal of Contemporary History* 44 (2009): 313.

25. Antic, Conterio, and Vargha, "Conclusion: Beyond Liberal Internationalism," 361.

26. On efforts to contain this violence, Roy Palmer Domenico, *Italian Fascists on Trial, 1943–1948* (Chapel Hill: University of North Carolina Press, 1991), 141, 146–149.

27. Norman Lewis, *Naples '44: A World War II Diary of Occupied Italy* (New York: Carroll & Graf, 2005), 169.

28. The tiny island of Pantelleria actually became the first Italian territory to fall under the administration of the AMGOT (Allied Military Government of Occupied Territories).

29. The negotiation of an Anglo-Ethiopian Agreement signed on 31 January 1942 left the British in control of the "Reserved Areas" in Ethiopia bordering French Somaliland, the Haud area adjacent to British Somaliland, the region of Ogaden in eastern Ethiopia, and the railroad between Addis Ababa and Djibouti. A subsequent 1944 Anglo-Ethiopian Accord reduced British influence; by early 1951, the British

Military Mission in Ethiopia had withdrawn, the United States assuming the role of Ethiopia's "protector." Nonetheless, the efforts to renegotiate the Anglo-Ethiopian Agreement and disagreements between Ethiopia and Great Britain over Somali areas dragged on until 1954, when the United States pressured Britain into agreeing to Ethiopia's terms. Many Somalis were angered by the awarding of Ogaden, Haud, and the Reserved Areas to Ethiopia. Jama Mohamed, "Imperial Policies and Nationalism in the Decolonization of Somaliland, 1954–1960," *English Historical Review* 117, no. 474 (2002): 1181–1183. See also Harold Marcus, *Ethiopia, Great Britain, and the United States, 1941–1974: The Politics of Empire* (Berkeley: University of California Press, 1983), 9–13, 77–78.

30. John Lamberton Harper's *America and the Reconstruction of Italy, 1945–1948* (Cambridge: Cambridge University Press, 1986) provides a valuable account of the diplomatic twists and turns between the fledgling Italian democratic government in the south and the Anglo-Americans, particularly over the vexed question of revising the terms of the armistice and restoring Italy's financial autonomy. See, in particular, pp. 22–36.

31. Combined Arms Research Library, *A Military Encyclopedia Based on Operations in the Italian Campaigns, 1943–1945* (Rome: Headquarters Fifteenth Army Group, 1945), 550. On Rennell's role and the different philosophies of the British and Americans regarding the role of AMGOT turn to Philip Boobbyer, "Lord Rennell, Chief of AMGOT: A Study of His Approach to Politics and Military Government (c. 1940–43)," *War in History* 25, no. 3 (2018): 315–322.

32. Ben Shephard, "'Becoming Planning Minded': The Theory and Practice of Relief, 1940–1945," *Journal of Contemporary History* 43, no. 3 (2008): 415.

33. Ibid.

34. Thomas R. Fisher, "Allied Military Government in Italy," *Annals of the American Academy of Political and Social Science* 267, no. 1 (1950): 122.

35. On this division of labor in the ACC see UNRRA S-0527–1001 PAG-4/3–0/14–3-2–12 UNRRA Subject Files 1944–49, "The Problem of 'Italian Refugees' and 'Displaced Persons' in Liberated Italy," Secret Intelligence Memorandum n. 2, 19 May 1944. See also Costantino di Sante, "I campi profughi in Italia (1943–1947)," in *Naufraghi della pace: Il 1945, I profughi e le memorie divise d'Europa*, ed. Guido Crainz, Raoul Pupo, and Silvia Salvatici (Rome: Donzelli, 2008), 143–144.

36. Combined Arms Research Library, *Military Encyclopedia*, 568. See also Salvatici, "Between National and International Mandates," 522.

37. TNA, WO 204/10077, "Eighth Army Adm Instr. No. 412 Org of refugee control in Eighth Army Area," 11 May 1944.

38. TNA, WO 204/9942, AMG Fifth Army 1943 and 1944 Refugee/DP Reports (Italy); "Weekly Report of Refugee Field Section, October 8th to October 14th (inclusive)," 15 October 1944.

39. Salvatici, "Between National and International Mandates," 522–523. On this initial exception see Francesca Casamassima, "L'assistenza postbellica dal 1943 al 1949: Profughi, reduci e rimpatriati in Terra di Brindisi," in *La Puglia dell'accoglienza: Profughi, rifugiati e rimpatriati nel Novecento*, ed. Vito Antonio Leuzzi and Giulio Esposito (Bari: Progedit, 2006), 297–298.

40. Antonio D'Andrea, "Campi profughi, centri di lavoro, di studio e di educazione professionale," in *Atti del convegno per studi di assistenza sociale*, contained in

UNRRA, S-520, box 249, 600. In May 1945, the Allied Displaced Persons and Repatriation Sub-Commission, Alto Commissariato Profughi, and the BMA Eritrea collaborated on five hundred repatriation cases of Italians from Eritrea on compassionate grounds. Division of responsibilities for displaced and repatriates thus still remained flexible. See ASDMAE AP 1946–50, Italia Ex Possedimenti Eritrea, b. 7, "Minutes of a Meeting in Brigadier Upjohn's office A.C. at 1000 hrs. on Saturday 5 May, 1945"; also "Rimpatri dall'Eritrea," 30 June 1945.

41. Francesca Wilson, *Aftermath: France, Germany, Austria, Yugoslavia: 1945 and 1946* (New York: Penguin Books, 1947), 18.

42. UNRRA, *Out of the Chaos* (Washington, DC: UNRRA, 1945), 1.

43. On planning precedents for UNRRA, including the British Allied Committee on Post-war Requirements, see United Nations, *Helping the People to Help Themselves: The Story of the United Nations Relief and Rehabilitation Administration* (New York: United Nations Information Office, 1944), 1–2. The British had begun planning the future of the Italian colonies in Africa from the moment Italy entered the war. For details, Saul Kelly, "Desert Conquests: Early British Planning on the Future of the Italian Colonies, June 1940–September 1943," *Middle Eastern Studies* 50, no. 6 (2014): 1007.

44. George Woodbridge, *UNRRA: The History of the United Nations Relief and Rehabilitation Administration*, vol. 1 (New York: Columbia University Press, 1950), 456. On the UNRRA-Tessile program, Barbara Curli, "Il programma tessile dell'UNRRA in Italia," in *L'amministrazione per gli aiuti internazionali*, ed. Andrea Ciampani (Milan: FrancoAngeli).

45. UNRRA, *The Story of U.N.R.R.A.* (New York: UNRRA Office of Public Information, 1948), 35.

46. In October 1944, UNRRA and the IGCR divided up responsibility for displaced Yugoslavs, including monarchists/Chetniks, living in camps in the Middle East (primarily Egypt). "UNRRA will assist in the care and repatriation of such of those persons as can, and are willing to, return to their countries of former origin or of former residence. The Inter-Governmental Committee has the function of finding places of settlement for such of them as fall within its competence and as cannot or do not desire to be so repatriated." UNRRA also pledged to help in the care and maintenance of these refugees until the IGCR could move them to "new places of settlement." IRO AJ 43/30, H. R. Emerson, "Memorandum," 23 October 1944. Though not authorized to carry out resettlement, UNRRA was permitted to facilitate it. As a policy directive put it, "The dividing line between 'assisting' or 'facilitating' or 'cooperation,' and 'undertaking' is apt to be somewhat indistinct in practice." UNRRA, S-0517–0119, PAG-4/1.0.1.0.0:34 UNRRA Subject Files 1943–1949, Displaced persons—resettlement, "UNRRA's Responsibility with regard to resettlement of Displaced Persons," 4 December 1946.

47. Philipp Weintraub, "UNRRA: An Experiment in International Welfare Planning," *Journal of Politics* 7, no. 1 (1945): 1–24.

48. On some of the overlaps between the ACC, UNRRA, and Italian state relief to DPs in Italy see Victoria Belco, *War, Massacre, and Recovery in Central Italy, 1943–1948* (Toronto: University of Toronto Press, 2010), 136–141.

49. Martha Branscombe, "The Children of the United Nations: U.N.R.R.A.'s Responsibility for Social Welfare," *Social Service Review* 19, no. 3 (1945): 316, 318.

50. Hoover Archives, Stanford University, Loda Mae Davis Papers, box 1, folder 6, "Italy," Letter to Mikail Menshikov, 30 May 1944.

51. UNRRA, S-520, box 295, E. R. Fryer to George Zanthaky, "Budget for Camps in Italy," 24 August 1944.

52. UNRRA, S-520, box 295, A. A. Sorieri to Thomas Cooley, 31 December 1944, 3.

53. For details on these programs for women and children go to Branscombe, "Children of the United Nations," 318–319.

54. Cited in Savilla Millis Simons, "U.N.R.R.A. on the Threshold of Action," *Social Service Review* 18, no. 4 (1944): 443. On eligibility exceptions, including those for ex-enemy nationals "intruded" in a liberated area, see UNRRA S-0527, box 0475, "Directives on Displaced Persons Operations for the Use of U.N.R.R.A. Missions in Europe and the Middle East," October 1945.

55. Many of these letters are beautifully written and adorned with elaborate artwork, suggesting that teachers, nuns, and priests prepared the missives to which the children then attached their signatures. Some of the letters featured religious imagery such as angels and children genuflecting in prayer and lauded "our beloved protector" La Guardia, whereas others contained drawings of activities such as UNRRA supply distribution. La Guardia and Wagner Archives, LaGuardia Community College, Queens, New York. See the Fiorello H. La Guardia Documents Collection, UNRRA Series, box #26B2, folders #13–20; box #26B3, folders #1–20; box #27B4.

56. On this see Cordell Hull, "840.50 UNRRA/10–444: Telegram the Secretary of State to the American Representative on the Advisory Council for Italy (Kirk)," in *Foreign Relations of the United States: Diplomatic Papers, 1944. General: Economic and Social Matters*, vol. 2, ed. E. Ralph Perkins, S. Everett Gleason, and Frederick Aandahl (Washington, DC: Government Printing Office, 1967), Document 260, 680.

57. Agostino Giovagnoli, "La Pontificia Commissione Assistenza e gli aiuti americani (1945–1948)," *Storia contemporanea* 9, no. 5–6 (1978): 1082.

58. Donato Verrastro, "Lontani dal focolare domestico. La Pontificia Commissione di Assistenza Profughi nell'Italia del secondo dopoguerra," *Archivio Storico dell'Emigrazione Italiana* 14, no. 18 (2018): 54.

59. Primo Mazzolari, *La carità del Papa: Pio XII e la ricostruzione dell'Italia (1943–1953)* (Cinisello Balsamo: Edizioni Paoline, 1991), 71, 107, 127.

60. Carlo Falconi, *L'assistenza italiana sotto bandiera pontificia* (Milan: Feltrinelli, 1957), 12, 44. In his often critical account, Falconi claims that Jesuits and those who had moved in elite fascist circles played a disproportionate role in the founding and expansion of the PCA/POA. Falconi details how the POA shut down one of its key competitors, the Ente Pro Meridione (1954–1956) and created a "totalitarian regime" marked by clericalism and "propagandismo." Falconi, 90; see also 83–90.

61. Eileen Egan, *Catholic Relief Services: The Beginning Years; For the Life of the World* (New York: Catholic Relief Services, 1988), 1–3, 13.

62. For details, including ENDSI's statute, consult UNRRA, S-0527–0981 Bureau of Relief Services UNRRA/ENDSI. See also ACS PCM 48–50, b. 4043, fasc. 19/14.n.13073, sf. 3/12, ENDSI, 16 July 1945.

63. Falconi, *L'assistenza italiana sotto bandiera pontificia*, 97. In terms of funds, the $3 million raised by American Relief for Italy for the CRS between June 1943 and

October 1945 certainly pales by comparison even with initial UNRRA monies for Italy. Egan, *Catholic Relief Services*, 117. For examples of promotional films celebrating the work of the PCA and the POA see "'Caritas' P.C.A." (1953; Cella 98 n. 1967), and "Operazione Carità-POA" (Cella 97 n. 1949) held at the Filmoteca Vaticana.

64. Falconi, *L'assistenza italiana sotto bandiera pontificia*, 55. Predictably, there was a struggle not just between statal and religious entities over assistance but also within the government as to the roles of respective agencies and ministries. In 1951, this division of labor became the subject of an inquiry by a Commissione per il riordinamento dei servizi assistenziali. That same year, Montini wrote to Raffaele Pio Petrilli, "I cannot hide from you that I am amazed to not find a representative of this Administration [AAI] among the components of the Commission. I maintain, in fact, that A.A.I. is among those state administrations that directs one of the largest assistance programs after that of the Ministry of the Interior." See ACS AAI Seg. Presidenza, b. 87, Montini to Petrilli, 11 July 1951. This opens up onto a much broader historiographical debate about how to characterize the nature of the postwar Italian welfare state. For authors putting welfare into the frame of the intersection of national and international postwar assistance in Italy refer to Giacomo Canepa, "Rifare gli Italiani. Profughi e progetti per il welfare (1944–47)," *Meridiana* 86 (2016): 57–78; and Gianpiero Fumi, "L'assistenza nell'Italia del dopoguerra: Un nuovo progetto di lavoro nell'archivio," *Bollettino dell'Archivio per la storia del movimento sociale cattolico in Italia* 37, no. 1 (2002): 11–19. Fumi challenges a commonplace view that the Catholic Church resisted reform of the welfare system in order to maintain its traditional forms of "private" assistance. At the same time, he notes that even while preserving many institutional welfare structures inherited from the previous regime, the leaders of post-1945 Italy rejected the "statism" that had characterized fascism. In terms of the competition over assistance between the PCA / POA and the AAI, both followed similar paths from an initial focus on administering emergency relief to tackling broader questions of welfare in Italy. Lodovico Montini noted that the AAI's work with the impoverished and needy in Italy was a "precedent for the [well-known parliamentary] inquiry, which it stimulated and directly assisted." Montini served as the vice president of the inquiry. Montini, "The Parliamentary Inquiry into Destitution in Italy," *International Labour Review* 71, no. 1 (1955): 63 fn. 1.

65. UNRRA, S-1450-0000-0002, Displaced Persons Division. Correspondence and Working Papers, Standing Technical Committee on Displaced Persons, "Statement on Displaced Persons; Displaced Persons with whom UNRRA is at present authorized to deal," 1 August 1945, 2.

66. Woodbridge, *UNRRA*, 2:265–266, 290–294.

67. "L'UNRRA-CASAS e l'assistenza alle famiglie," *Note Economiche* 69 (9 May 1947). See also Barbara Allason, *UNRRA-CASAS: Contributo alla ricostruzione* (Rome: s.n., 1950), in particular the section titled "il focolare ricostruito." This publication can be found in ACS MI Attività Ass. Italiane ed Internazionale (AAI) Presidenza, b. 90, fasc. 8.

68. UNRRA, S-0527, box 879, Mitchell Franklin, "Destination of Lire Fund," 25 July 1946. See also UNRRA, S-0527, box 869, "Agreement between the Government of Italy and UNRRA on the Use of the Lire Fund," and UNRRA S-0527–0981, D.P. Operations (Italy), Lt. Col. Julian Tomlin, "UNRRA 'Lira Fund,'" 19 December

1946. In 1947, Keeny's demand that Lire Fund monies be put toward the work of the IRO threatened to scuttle the organization's future in Italy. Maria Eleonora Guasconi, "I rapporti dell'AAI con l'IRO e l'assistenza ai profughi in Italia (1947–1956)," in *L'Amministrazione per gli Aiuti Internazionali*, ed. Andrea Ciampani (Milan: FrancoAngeli, 2002), 159.

69. UNRRA, S-0527, box 864, UNRRA Italian Mission Displaced Persons Committee, "Minutes of the First meeting held on 4 July 1946."

70. UNRRA, S-0524–0102, PAG-4/4–2/78 UNRRA-Historian Subject Files Development of Policy on Displaced Persons, London to Washington 2608 of 4.12.46 on WR.8.

71. UNRRA, S-0527, box 880, Martin Germandof to Helen Montgomery, "Collaborationists," 7 March 1946. This confidential memo outlined six categories of collaborationists. After acknowledging the fuzziness of some activities and categories, Germandof nonetheless concluded, "With all apparent difficulties in realty [*sic*] somebody who is acquainted with the European war conditions and the German system of occupation will find easily the moral limits of the definition 'collaborationist.'"

72. UNRRA, S-0527, box 864, UNRRA Italian Mission Displaced Persons Committee, "Minutes of the First meeting held on 4 July 1946."

73. UNRRA, S-0527–0980 PAG 4/3–0-14–3-0–1, UNRRA Subject Files 1944–1949, Helen Montgomery to A. A. Sorieri, "Conference with Col. Fathergill, DPARSC AC HQ," 10 November 1945. On agreements between SACMED and UNRRA for the latter to assume care of non-Italian displaced persons see UNRRA, S-0527–0980 PAG 4/3–0-14–3-0–1, UNRRA Subject Files 1944–1949, S. M. Keeny to De Gasperi, 23 May 1946. Ultimately, the ACC continued to care for a number of refugees until the IRO took over those duties. Many of those found in the ACC camps were Yugoslavs, whereas many of those under UNRRA care were Jewish. IRO AJ 43/26, L. M. Hacking, "Refugee Situation in Italy," 16 August 1946.

74. UNRRA, S-0527–0980 PAG 4/3–0/14–3-0–1 UNRRA Subject Files 1944–1949, Bureau of Relief Services 22 AFHQ Caserta Jan 1946–Dec 1946, S. M. Keeny to AFHQ, 28 June 1946.

75. UNRRA, S-0527–0846 PAG-4/3.0.14.0.2:4, UNRRA Subject Files 1944–1949, Keeny to De Gasperi, 29 July 1946.

76. On the charged debates within the Italian government over responsibility for these UNRRA ineligibles see Salvatici, "Between National and International Mandates," 527–528. Italy would only become a member state of the UN in 1955.

77. UNRRA, S-0527, box 982, "Nota Verbale," 7 October 1946.

78. Ibid. It is worth mentioning that during this period Italian politicians more generally sought to turn their weakness to their advantage. Writing of the early years of the Cold War (1947–1950), for example, Mario Del Pero has argued against a common view of Italy as a mere and passive client of the United States. Del Pero, "Containing Containment: Rethinking Italy's Experience during the Cold War," *Journal of Modern Italian Studies* 8, no. 4 (2003): 532–555.

79. UNRRA, S-0527, box 864, UNRRA Italian Mission Displaced Persons Committee, "Minutes of the First meeting held on 4 July 1946," 6. In 1946, memos between the ACC, UNRRA, and the Italian government transferred responsibility for movements between Italy and its African colonies to the Ministry of Italian Africa,

rather than the Ministry of Foreign Affairs. See ASDMAE AP 1946–50, Italia Ex Possedimenti Parte Generale, b. 4, "Memorandum for the Allied Commission, Memorandum for the U.N.R.R.A.—Italian Mission: Movements of Italian Citizens between Italy and the Italian Colonies," 29 May 1946.

80. Woodbridge, *UNRRA*, 2:479. In applying Resolution 47 about intruded persons to Albania, an UNRRA memo noted, "While Albania is in one sense an ex-enemy area, the draft Agreement with Albania stipulates that U.N.R.R.A. is concluding the agreement on the basis of Resolution 1 (I)(2), which means that we are treating it as a liberated area. In that case Italian displaced persons in Albania will be in the same case as Italian displaced persons in Greece, and we shall have to act under Resolution 47." UNRRA, S-1012–0005–03 Albania Displaced Persons—Italian Repatriates—Policy and Procedures, A. H. Robertson to Delierneux, 25 June 1945. Resolution 47 required the ex-enemy government, in this case Italy, to pay for these repatriation efforts. See A. H. Robertson to Oakley-Hill, 27 June 1945.

81. UNRRA, S-1012, box 5, file 6, Albania—Bureau of Supply, D. R. Oakley-Hill, "*Italian Displaced Persons*," 31 January 1946.

82. UNRRA, S-1011, box 6, file 6, "Minutes of Meeting at the British Military Mission," 30 January 1946.

83. UNRRA, S-1012–0005–03, Cable Tirana to London, 8 February 1946.

84. UNRRA, S-0527, box 848, Cable no. 01787.

85. Cited in D. R. Oakley-Hill, *An Englishman in Albania: Memoirs of a British Officer, 1929–1955*, ed. B. D. Destani (London, 2002), 269.

86. UNRRA, S-1010, box 8, file 7, UNRRA-Albania-Bureau of Finance and Admin-Personnel-Repatriation of DPS—Gerson, Frank J., 31 October 1945–19 December 1946, D. R. Oakley-Hill to J. Halsall, "Italian Passengers and Their Furniture," 21 February 1946.

87. UNRRA, S-1012–0005–03 Albania Displaced Persons—Italian Repatriates—Policy and Procedures, Mihal Prifti to UNRRA Mission in Albania, 18 April 1946.

88. On repatriations carried out on the *Marvia* in April 1946 see AQSH, fondi 490, dosja 204, P. C. Floud to the Prime Ministry, "Repatriation of Italians," 26 April 1946; for repatriations in July 1946 refer to ASDMAE AP 1946–50 Albania, b. 3, "Relazione sull'arrivo a Brindisi, il 11 luglio 1946, di n. 30 connazionali provenienti dall'Albania." For movements on the *Marvia* in September 1946, UNRRA S-1010–0008 UNRRA Albania Mission PAG 4/3.0.0.1: 8, "UNRRA Albania—Bureau of Finance and Administration—Personnel Repatriation of Displaced Persons," Frank Gerson. On repatriations on the *Don Chisciotte* see ASDMAE AP 1946–50, Albania, b. 3, "Repatriation of Italians from Albania," 15 November 1946.

89. UNRRA, S-1012–0005–03 Albania Displaced Persons—Italian Repatriates—Policy and Procedures, L. H. Clemetson, "Repatriation of Italians," 21 June 1947.

90. UNRRA, S-1012–0005–03 Albania Displaced Persons—Italian Repatriates—Policy and Procedures, Cable (Rome to Tirana), 1 [2] March 1946. A representative of the British brigadier in Albania stressed the difficulty of evaluating repatriation lists within Albania. "We also suggest that it be pointed out that should an Albanian pose as an Italian with the approval of the Circolo Garibaldi, it would be almost impossible for you [UNRRA] or BMM to discover his real identity." Major GS to UNRRA Tirana, 4 March 1946. On the acceptance of pre-1939 Italians, P. M. Colburn, Telegram, 19 April 1946 and Cable (London to Rome), 17 [18] April 1946.

91. UNRRA, S-1012–0005–03 Albania; Turcato to Oakley-Hill, 2 September 1945; Turcato, 3 September 1945; Oakley-Hill to E. J. Priddey, 5 September 1945.

92. Woodbridge, *UNRRA*, 2:177.

93. Oakley-Hill, *Englishman in Albania*, 182. The broader history of UNRRA in Albania has generated several studies. See, for instance, Hamit Kaba, *UNRRA në Shqipëri, 1944–1947* (Tirana: Shtëpia botuese "Shkenca," 2000); Settimio Stallone, "Quando la cooperazione andava 'oltrecortina': La Missione dell'Unrra in Albania," in *Cooperazione e relazioni internazionali*, ed. Matteo Pizzigallo (Milan: FrancoAngeli, 2008), 9–29.

94. Rana Mitter, "Imperialism, Transnationalism, and the Reconstruction of Post-war China: UNRRA in China, 1944–7," *Past and Present* 218, no. 8 (2013): 68.

95. Woodbridge, *UNRRA*, 2:140.

96. UNRRA, S-0527–0829 PAG-4/3.0.14.0.0.2 4 UNRRA Subject Files 1944–1949, Venezia Giulia Region, Lehman, Cables, 28 September 1945.

97. UNRRA, S-0527–0853 PAG 4/3.0.14.0.2.:11 UNRRA Subject Files 1944–1949, Fiume- Request for UNRRA Assistance, Miegge (?) to Contini, "Request for Assistance to Fiume," n.d.

98. UNRRA, S-0527–0853 Pag 4/3.0.14.0.2.:11 UNRRA Subject Files 1944–1949, Fiume—Request for UNRRA Assistance, Riccardo Zanella to the Administration of the UNRRA Mission, 4 September 1945, 1.

99. Ibid., 2.

100. In this, UNRRA likely followed the example set by the ICRC and the Red Cross. Zanella's urgent plea for relief in September 1945 acknowledged that Rijeka/Fiume awaited critical supplies from the ICRC. Zanella feared that such supplies, while certainly welcome, would prove insufficient. A few months before Zanella sent out his requests for help, the Vatican had informed the Allied command, the ICRC, and UNRRA of the "grave situation" of food scarcity in the city. UNRRA, S-0527–0853 Pag 4/3.0.14.0.2.:11 UNRRA Subject Files 1944–1949, Fiume— Request for UNRRA Assistance, Secretariat of State of His Holiness to Harold H. Tittmann, "Note Verbale," 28 June 1945.

101. UNRRA, S-0527, box 1174, La Guardia to General Lee, 28 July 1946. On the UNRRA inquiry regarding the accusations of malfeasance made by chief of UNRRA Jugoslav mission regarding Berry White, head of the UNRRA Jugoslav Mission port operation in Trieste, see UNRRA S-0527, box 1173.

102. Woodbridge, *UNRRA*, 2:335–339.

103. Cited in George Padmore, "UNRRA Snubs Ethiopia; Gives Italy 50 Million," *Chicago Defender*, 8 September 1945.

104. UNRRA, S-0527, box 0475, Willard Park to M. Keeny, 6 May 1947. Ethiopia appears to have later relented, allowing a certain number of European refugees to settle in the country under IRO auspices. One document from the Italian governmental representative in Eritrea claimed that 171 refugees were settled in Ethiopia between September and October of 1950. The memo countered reports published in *Il Giornale d'Italia* and other news outlets that Ethiopian "natives" had threatened the refugees and forced them to flee. For both the newspaper account and the memo turn to ASDMAE AP 1950–57, Eritrea, b. 714, "Profughi europei in Etiopia," 24 February 1951.

105. On the repatriation of Ethiopians from Italy turn to UNRRA, S-0527–0475 Pag 4/3.0.8.0:1 UNRRA Subject Files 1944–1949, Willard Park to Ambaye Woldemariam, 30 May 1946. See also UNRRA 410.1 Ethiopia: Repatriation Operations. For requests to facilitate the return of individual Italians to Ethiopia see UNRRA, S-0527–0475 Pag 4/3.0.8.0:1 UNRRA Subject Files 1944–1949, J. P. Bond, "Mrs. Carmela Fonzia in Morgano—Emigration to Ethiopia," 9 January 1947; also, Tullio Fiori to Willard Park, 3 October 1946.

106. Woodbridge, *UNRRA*, 2:323.

107. For details see ibid., 322–331.

108. UNRRA, S-0527, box 848, Displaced Persons—Ital. Dodecan., Paolo Contini to S. M. Keeny, "Assistance to the Dodecanese Islands," 8 June 1945.

109. ACICR, BG 003 27–26, mai–décembre 1945: correspondance avec Albert Gredinger, correspondance avec la sous-délégation de Rhodes, Jean Munier to Brigadier Acland, 26 July 1945.

110. ACICR, BG 003 27–26, mai–décembre 1945: correspondance avec Albert Gredinger, correspondance avec la sous-délégation de Rhodes, Acland to Munier, 30 July 1945. The BMA had been happy, however, to allow the ICRC to fill crucial gaps in relief, as with the forty convoys of assistance sent to the islands in May 1945. For further details on the initial contacts with the BMA see ACICR Sg. 11, Secours à la Grèce. Secours aux Îles de Dodécanèse et Délég. de Rhodes, 1946–1950, G. Ladame, "Rapport Ladame no. 2 sur la Mission de secours aux Îles du Dodécanèse occupées par les Allemands. Situation fin mai 1945," 30 May 1945.

111. The ICRC report of this visit features a number of photographs of the needy children and orphans who received shoes and other items from the ICRC. See ACICR Sg. 11, Secours à la Grèce. Secours aux Îles de Dodécanèse et Délég. de Rhodes, 1946–1950, "Rapport n. 2 de la Délégation du CICR au Dodécanèse Novembre 1945."

112. ACICR Sg. 11, Secours à la Grèce. Secours aux Îles de Dodécanèse et Délég. de Rhodes, 1946–1950, "Te Deum Orthodoxe du 17.2.46. Célébré à Rhodes en reconnaissance de l'arrivée des premiers secours de la CROIX-ROUGE en FÉVRIER 1945," and Jean Munier, "Alla Comunità Cattolica di Rodi," 15 February 1946.

113. ACICR BG 003 27–26, mai–décembre 1945: correspondance avec Albert Gredinger, correspondance avec la sous-délégation de Rhodes 18–06/1945–13/12/1945, D. Michalakis to Délégation du CICR à Rhodes, 28 August 1945.

114. ACICR Sg. 11, Secours à la Grèce. Secours aux Îles de Dodécanèse et Délég. de Rhodes, 1946–1950, Jean Munier, "Note au C.I.C.R.—Genève," 24 September 1945.

115. ACICR Sg. 11, Secours à la Grèce. Secours aux Îles de Dodécanèse et Délég. de Rhodes, 1946–1950, "Rapport Final N. 4 de la Délégation du C.I.C.R. au Dodécanèse Janvier et Février 1946."

116. UNRRA, S-0527, box 848, S. M. Keeny to P. Contini, "Assistance to the Dodecanese Islands," 8 June 1945.

117. UNRRA S-0527–0848 PAG-4/3.0.14.0.2:6 UNRRA Subject Files 1944–1949, Displaced persons—Ital. Dodecanese, Buell F. Maben to Sam Keeny, 5 June 1945.

118. Francis Rennell (Lord Rodd), *British Military Administration of Occupied Territories in Africa during the Years 1941–1947* (London: His Majesty's Stationery Office, 1948), 529.

119. UNRRA S-1242-0000-0066, Subject Files Bureau of Areas—Executive Office, Dodecanese Islands, Ben Eckhaus to Mr. Menshikov, "Subject: Cable n. 1399 from London," 11 June 1945.

120. UNRRA, 410.1 Dodecanese Repatriation Operations, R. J. Youdin, Telegram, 6 August 1945.

121. ACICR Sg. 11, Secours à la Grèce. Secours aux Îles de Dodécanèse et Délég. de Rhodes, 1946–1950, "Minutes of the Meeting of the Central Relief Committee," 14 November 1945.

122. UNRRA, S-0527, box 463, file S-1345–0000–0033, "Introduction to monthly narrative report i.e. for month ending 30th November 1946," 10 December 1946. In a confidential memo sent to Robert Jackson, senior deputy director-general of UNRRA, Wankowicz expressed concern over the ongoing food shortages and the future of relief after UNRRA's departure and the islands' annexation by Greece. He urged that "the skeletal staff which will be active here during the last quarter of this year should be left at their posts at least until the crop of 1947, whatever the organization may be which will take over the general direction of relief." UNRRA S-1534–0000–073 Dodecanese Islands—Greece, Wankowicz to Jackson, 12 September 1946.

123. Greek State Historical Archives of Dodecanese (GSAD), Rhodes, British Military Administration (BMA) of Karpathos CPS 87, C. M. Miles-Bailey, "Entry permits into the Dodecanese from Greece. 1 months visit only, NO permanent residence," 25 June 1946. On unauthorized migrations to the islands see also G. M. Miles-Bailey, "Unauthorised entry Dodecanese (from Greece)," 17 May 1946; also, G. M. Miles-Bailey, "Entry Permits from Greece into Dodecanese," 15 May 1946.

124. GSAD, BMA Karpathos CPS 98 UNRRA General, C. J. Bonington, "U.N.R.R.A. Relief Office," 25 February 1946. While these orders no doubt reflected stereotypes about both emotionally volatile Greeks and erratic refugees, they also drew on previous experiences. When ICRC relief arrived during the winter of February 1945, a desperate crowd launched itself on the packages despite the efforts of German soldiers to beat them back. On this see Andrea Villa, *Nelle isole del sole: Gli italiani del Dodecaneso dall'occupazione al rimpatrio (1912–1947)* (Turin: SEB 27, 2016), 263.

125. UNRRA, S-0527, box 463, file S-1345–0000–0032, "Narrative report for month ending July 1946," 10 August 1946.

126. ASDMAE AP 1946–50, Dodecanneso, b. 1, *Annual Report by the Chief Administrator on the British Military Administration of the Dodecanese Islands for the Period 1 January, 1946, to 31 December, 1946* (Rhodes: Government Press), 11. Prior to UNRRA's arrival in the islands, the BMA had prepared three refugee camps on Kasos in order to house approximately one thousand Greeks and nine hundred Italians and another camp on Karpathos (which, at one point, held four thousand Greeks). BMA staff conducted this work with the help of a Friends Ambulance Unit Relief Detachment. On this, *Annual Report by the Chief Administrator*, 9.

127. UNRRA, S-0527, box 469, file S-1345–0000–0112, W. Wankowicz to J. Munier, 22 December 1945; also Wankowicz, 10 December 1945.

128. UNRRA, S-0527, box 469, file S-1345–0000–0112, R. C. Dagge, "Jewish Refugees," 24 December 1945; W. Wankowicz to Chief of UNRRA Italian Mission, 26 December 1945. On estimates of 204 refugees, see Chief Representative, Dodecanese Mission to Chief of Mission, UNRRA Rome, 29 November 1945, and Valerie Gargett to SCAO and Colonel Toby, 22 November 1945. When the head of the Commissione

per la tutela degli interessi italiani nel Dodecaneso Antonio Macchi visited Italy in January 1946, Wankowicz asked him to inquire into the situation of Jewish refugees there wishing repatriation to Rhodes. Wankowicz to Chief of Italian Mission Rome, 4 January 1946. On Macchi's recommendations to the Italian government regarding the Jews of Rhodes see Villa, *Nelle isole del sole*, 275–276.

129. ASDMAE AP 1946–50 Dodecanneso, b. 1, *Annual Report by the Chief Administrator*, 12. For correspondence between BMA and UNRRA on this issue and the problem of determining who constituted a bona fide Dodecanesian displaced person refer to UNRRA, S-1372–0000–0092 Displaced Persons—Dodecanese Islands.

130. UNRRA, S-0527, box 469, file S-1345–0000–0113, D. Cotzias, 29 April 1946.

131. UNRRA, S-0527, box 469, file S-1345–0000–0113, C. K. Linney, "Re: Vassilios Spirou," 20 March 1946. See also S-0527, box 469, file S-1345–0000–0112, Vassilios Spirou, 26 January 1946.

132. On this see UNRRA, S-0527, box 463, file S-1345–000–0031, "Distribution of Relief in the Dodecanese Islands: General Principles and the Practical Approach," 14 March 1946, 3.

133. ACICR Sg. 11, Secours à la Grèce. Secours aux Îles de Dodécanèse et Délég. de Rhodes, 1946–1950, Jean Munier, "Minutes of a Meeting of the Central Relief Committee," 7 September 1945.

134. On this, ASDMAE AP 1946–50, Dodecanneso, b. 1, *Annual Report by the Chief Administrator*, 9.

135. On temporary visit permits see GSAD, BMA Karpathos CPS 82/A. CPS 83 instead contains requests for permanent transfers from Karpathos, almost always to Rhodes.

136. TNA, FO 371/49830, Western Italy 1945, R. D. H. Arundell to AFHQ / Brig. Henn, 5 June 1945. For details on some of these medical cases refer to GSAD, BMA Karpathos, CPS/112 BMA-GMA Hand-Over.

137. Rennell, *British Military Administration*, 519, 523. Macchi also confirmed the improvement of relationships between Greeks and Italians in the islands after the departure of the most noted fascists. ASDMAE AP 1946–50, Dodecanneso, b. 1, Macchi to Ministero degli Affari Esteri, "Relazione sulla situazione politica del Dodecanneso," 23 December 1945; also Macchi to Ministero degli Affari Esteri, "Situazione politica locale," 14 February 1946.

138. Luca Pignataro, "Il tramonto del Dodecanese italiano (1945–1950)," *Clio* 37, no. 4 (2001): 657–658 fn. 36. A few months after the peace treaty went into effect, a newspaper in Italy (*Il Nuovo Giornale d'Italia*) published an article claiming various acts of violence (including torture and murder) by Greeks against Italians in the islands. The Italian Ministry of Foreign Affairs received testimonies from repatriates, including the architect Mario Paolini, that debunked these accounts. Greek newspapers like *Ethnos* and *Kathimerini* also dismissed (and denounced) the accusations. For the original article, translations of Greek responses, and firsthand testimonies provided to the Ministry of Foreign Affairs turn to ASDMAE AP 1946–50, Dodecanneso, b. 2.

139. These evaluations varied depending on location. Under fascism, Kalymnos remained a center of resistance to infringements on its former tax exemption privileges under the Ottomans. Inhabitants of smaller islands that did not receive the infrastructural investments concentrated in places like Rhodes and Kos also tended

to look less positively on the Italian administration. See Nicholas Doumanis, *Myth and Memory in the Mediterranean: Remembering Fascism's Empire* (Houndmills: Palgrave Macmillan, 1997), 67–80, 187.

140. TNA, FO 371/49830, Western Italy 1945, Telegram from Mr. Hopkinson, ZM 3800 21/22 [14] July 1945.

141. TNA, FO 371/49831, N. Charles (Rome to Foreign Office), 6 September 1945. On this see also TNA, FO 371/49831, Western Italy 1945, N. Charles, "Repatriation of Italians from the Dodecanese," 2[7] September 1945.

142. TNA, FO 371/49831, Western Italy 1945, AFHQ and the War Office to Alcom, Cipher Telegram, 15 October 1945.

143. For the report that the BMA had requested information from each Italian family about its repatriation intentions and "the widespread impression that the English act as if they plan to remain in the Aegean Possessions" see ACS A56 1944–1949, b. 4, Coppini, "Situazione degli Italiani nel Dodecannese," 13 November 1945.

144. The US secretary of war Henry Stimson, for instance, complained that the British Allies sought "to lay a foundation throughout the Mediterranean for their own empire after the war is over." Cited in Patrick J. Hearden, *Architects of Globalism: Building a New World Order during World War II* (Fayetteville: University of Arkansas Press, 2002), 79.

145. ASDMAE AP 1931–45, Dodecanneso, b. 16, fasc. 11, Antonio Macchi and Aldo Levi, "Commissione per la tutela degli interessi italiani nel Dodecanneso: Relazione sull'opera svolta dalla sezione 'assistenza' nel semestre giugno–novembre 1945," 26 November 1945.

146. ASDMAE AP 1946–50, Dodecanneso, b. 1, Comandante A. Agnese, "Richiesta informazioni," 25 November 1946.

147. ASDMAE AP 1946–50, Dodecanneso, b. 1, A. A. Sorieri to Ministero degli Affari Esteri, "Personal property of Italians in DODECANESE," 4 April 1946. This file also contains a number of requests by individuals to obtain property left behind, requests usually forwarded to the Commissione per la tutela degli interessi Italiani nel Dodecaneso. On the advocacy with the Italian government for would-be repatriates by the Commissione per la tutela degli interessi Italiani nel Dodecaneso see in this same file: Macchi, 3 September 1946; Charles Gormley to Brig. Lush, 17 September 1946; and Zoppi, "Comunità italiana dell'Egeo-Rimpatri," 23 September 1946.

148. ASDMAE AP 1946–50, Dodecanneso, b. 1, "Appunto per il Ministero degli Esteri: Estratto da una lettera da Rodi," July 1946.

149. ASDMAE AP 1946–50, Dodecanneso, b. 1, "Appunto per il Ministero degli Esteri: Estratto da una lettera da Rodi," July 1946. On the work of the Ufficio Rodi go to ASDMAE AP 1950–57 Greece, b. 662, Comitato di Gestione Amministrativa del cessato governo delle isole Italiane dell'Egeo: Relazione al bilancio di chiusura della gestione di liquidazione della cessata amministrazione italiana del Dodecaneso, 17 September 1951, 5.

150. ASDMAE AP 1946–50, Dodecanneso, b. 1, *Annual Report by the Chief Administrator*, 13; for the details of the transports see 12–13. Lists of some of the passengers can be found in this same file.

151. GSAD, BMA Karpathos, CPS/107 Displaced Personnel General, C. J. Bonington, "Displaced Persons," 3 August 1946.

152. Alexis Rappas, "The Transnational Formation of Imperial Rule on the Margins of Europe: British Cyprus and the Italian Dodecanese in the Interwar Period," *European History Quarterly* 45, no. 3 (2015): 475–476.

153. ASDMAE AP 1946–50, Dodecanneso, b. 1, Macchi to Italian Ambassador, 12 July 1946. For the case of two Italian brothers, one born in Sardinia and the other in Beirut, requesting UNRRA assistance to join their family in Palestine see UNRRA, S-1345–0000–0117, Natalino and Umbert [*sic*] Piga, 25 September 1946. That same folder contains the request of a widow seeking relocation with her three children to her sister in Alexandria [Domenica Bradicich, 26 September 1946]; and an elderly father at the Old People's Home in Rhodes desiring to join his son in Cairo [A. R. Mills, "Beniamino TRIBUZIO," 12 July 1946]. In UNRRA S-1345–0000–0112 see the letters of J. G. Toby of 24 January 1946 and Carlo Bona of 9 December 1946 regarding an elderly Italian man who sought to move to Alexandria to live with his children there. Carlo Bona had been born in Egypt in 1872 and worked there until moving to Rhodes in 1939 in search of medical treatment; in 1946, he was receiving a small pension from the Egyptian government.

154. UNRRA, S-1345–0000–0117, T. T. Waddington, "DE MARCHI, G.," 16 July 1946. Waddington further suggested that UNRRA might try to persuade the BMA to permit De Marchi's children to join him in Rhodes in transit to Italy on compassionate grounds. For Wankowicz's initially favorable response see UNRRA, S-1345–0000–0112, Wankowicz to Repatriation Division, 26 January 1946. Also Memorandum of 8 January 1946.

155. TNA, FO 371/49864 Western Italy 1945, Major D. W. Logan to J. W. Davidson, 20 October 1945.

156. See various documents on this incident in ASDMAE AP 1946–50, Etiopia, b. 1, b. 2, b. 5, b. 7.

157. For those appeals refer to ASDMAE AP 1946–50, Etiopia, b. 3.

158. UNRRA S-1345–0000–0112, G. M. Miles-Bailey, "Entry Italians into Dodecanese," 14 December 1945.

159. UNRRA S-0527, box 469, file S-1345–0000–0113, G. M. Miles-Bailey, "Repatriation Italian families (through UNRRA) into Dodecanese," 13 April 1946.

160. UNRRA S-0527, box 470, file 1, G. Frampton, "Italians entry into Dodecanese," 24 July 1946.

161. For the petition signed by eight individuals in Bari who claimed "we were born and raised in those lands and believe it is the greatest injustice that we were expelled solely for the fact of our Italian citizenship" see ASDMAE AP 1950–57, Italia, b. 522, "On/le Commissione incaricata per la revisione del trattato di pace," 7 August 1951. The "expulsion" referred to the citizenship articles of the 1947 Peace Treaty that required those opting to retain Italian citizenship to leave the Aegean Islands for Italy.

162. Ultimately, only eighteen of the thirty-eight were classified as eligible for repatriation on "humanitarian grounds." UNRRA S-1345–0000–0116, L. B. Webber, "Repatriation—Italians," 13 December 1946.

163. UNRRA S-1345–0000–0116, J. P. Bond, "FALCONE Children," 19 September 1946; J. P. Bond, "Acceptance in Rhodes of Benedetto VENTURA, aged 16," 16 October 1946.

164. UNRRA S-1315–0000–0116, L. S. J. Nadel, "Repatriation from Italy—PARADISO family," 4 December 1946; S-1345–0000–0117, Giovanni Paradiso to UNRRA Dodecannese, 28 September 1946.

165. See Federico Cresti, "La rinascita dell'attività politica in Tripolitania nel secondo dopoguerra secondo alcuni documenti britannica (dicembre 1945–gennaio 1949)," in *La Libia tra Mediterraneo e mondo islamico*, ed. Federico Cresti (Milan: Giuffré, 2006), 191–194. By contrast, even after the 1947 Peace Treaty, representatives of the Italian community in Tripoli were still submitting petitions to the presidency of the Council of Ministers that claimed "the Arabs, even more than we Italians, have understood well that only Italian rule can create a way of life that promises an economically viable and peaceful future." ASDMAE AP 1946–50, Italian Ex Possedimenti Libia, b. 9, Carlo Buriani, "Promemoria: Come e cosa pensa il coloniale italiano in Tripolitania," 13 February 1947.

166. Filiberto Sabbadin, *I frati minori lombardi in Libia: La missione di Tripoli, 1908–1991* (Milan: Edizioni Biblioteca Francescana, 1991), 65–67. In March 1945, the Italian Ministry of the Navy offered the Allies ships to carry Italian children back to Libya. The ministry recommended that "for reasons of moral character and national prestige," the vessels should fly the Italian flag. ACS PCM 44–47, b. 3543, fasc. 17.4/30208, "Profughi di guerra della Libia," 2 March 1945. This same file contains a letter to Admiral Ellery Stone of the ACC from the minister of foreign affairs Alcide De Gasperi. De Gasperi noted that the Allies had already permitted some Greek and Maltese who had been resident in Libya and were evacuated during the war by the Italian authorities to return. The refusal to permit similar reentries of Italians, continued the letter, "could not but be perceived by all Italians . . . as a serious and deliberate measure directed against them." De Gasperi to Admiral Stone, 15 March 1945.

167. ASDMAE AP 1946–50, Italia Ex Possedimenti Libia, b. 9, "Ritorno in Tripolitania di profughi colà residenti," 14 November 1946. On the voyages, ASDMAE ASMAI Africa, vol. 4, Ufficio per gli Affari del Soppresso Ministero A.I. (1946–1947), pacco 1, b. 42, Rapporto della Missione a Tripoli. Trattative per i rimpatri," 15 November 1946, 7.

168. ASDMAE AP 1946–50, Italia Ex Possedimenti Libia, b. 10, Direz. Gen. Affari Politici to Commissione Alleata, Memorandum, 21 November 1945.

169. ASDMAE ASMAI Africa, vol. 4, Ufficio per gli Affari del Soppresso Ministero A.I. (1946–1947), pacco 1, b. 42, P. J. Sandison, "Minutes of Discussion with Representatives of the Ministero dell'Africa Italiana 16/17 October 1946," 19 October 1946.

170. ASDMAE AP 1946–50, Italia Ex Possedimenti Libia, b. 10, Memorandum, 21 November 1945. See, too, the earlier worries expressed by Italian officials in the Ministero dell'Africa Italiana about the uneven application of the breadwinners' scheme and the unequal flows between Italy and Libya in ACS PCM 1948–50, b. 325, fasc. 17.1/12491, "Rimpatri dalla Tripolitania e rientro nostri connazionali in quella Colonia," 12 November 1945.

171. On head to head (sometimes referred to as "head for head") see ASDMAE AP, 1946–50 Italian Ex Possedimenti Libia, b. 9, "Notes on Dr. Catitti's Memorandum of 6 March 1947." This policy (introduced in June 1946) appears to have been formalized in the negotiations between the BMA and the Italian mission that visited

Tripoli in October 1946. See ASDMAE ASMAI Africa, vol. 4, Ufficio per gli Affari del Soppresso Ministero A.I. (1946–1947), pacco 1, b. 42, P. J. Sandison, "Minutes of Discussion with representatives of the Ministero dell'Africa Italiana 16/17 ottobre 1946," 19 October 1946.

172. On this see ASDMAE AP, 1946–50 Italia Ex Possedimenti Somalia, b. 14, Memorandum from Zoppi, 10 June 1946.

173. Luca Marchi, *Libia: 1911–2011: Gli italiani da colonizzatori a profughi* (Udine: Kappa Vu, 2011). According to a 1948 publication by the Associazione Nazionale Profughi della Libia, a total of 46,883 Italians from Libya were receiving assistance on the peninsula and Sicily. The association claimed a membership of 40,744, with the largest concentration of its adherents in Rome, followed by Catania, Padua, Naples, and Vittoria (in the province of Ragusa). Associazione Nazionale Profughi della Libia, *Memorandum presentato alla Commissione di Indagine delle Quattro Potenze sulle Ex-Colonie Italiane* (Rome, 22 May 1948; contained at IsIAO), 17–25.

174. Rennell, *British Military Administration*, 466–467.

175. UNRRA S-0527, box 864, UNRRA Italian Mission Displaced Persons Committee, "Minutes of the First Meeting," 4 July 1946, 6. On the suspension of returns to Libya see also ACS PCM 1948–50, b. 325, fasc. 17.1/12491, A. A. Sorieri to Pontificia Commissione Assistenza, "Italian Children to Tripolitania," 18 July 1946; also J. P. Bond to Pontificia Commissione Assistenza, "Repatriation to Tripolitania," 12 August 1946.

176. ASDMAE AP 1946–50, Italia Ex Possedimenti Libia, b. 10, Note Verbale, 23 April 1947.

177. ASDMAE AP 1946–50, Italia Ex Possedimenti Libia, b. 10, Note Verbale, 12 April 1947. See also "Espatrio clandestino in Libia," 24 April 1947.

178. ASDMAE AP 1946–50, Italia Ex Possedimenti Libia, b. 9, "Notizie sulla situazione in Tripolitania a tutto settembre 1946," 4 November 1946.

179. ASDMAE AP 1946–50, Italia Ex Possedimenti Libia, b. 9, "Al Signor Brigadiere Generale Blackley Amministratore Capo della B.M.A.," 6 March 1946.

180. Sabbadin, *I frati minori lombardi in Libia*, 77. On Baldelli, ACS PCM 48–50, b. 325, fasc. 17.1/12491, Ferdinando Baldelli to Alcide De Gasperi, 29 August 1946. On PCA/POA aid to Libyan Italian children, Mazzolari, *La carità del Papa*, 136–143.

181. F. Prestopino, ed., *Uno dei Ventimila: Diario del colono Giacomo Cason, Libia 1938–1959* (Bologna: Officina grafica di Giorgio Barghiani, 1995), 70–73.

182. ASDMAE AP 1946–50, Italia Ex Possedimenti Libia, b. 18, Dr. Cibelli, "Gionmaria MALTANA, rientro famigliari," 6 August 1947; Cibelli to Maltana, 11 August 1947; BMA to Cibelli, "Repatriation of Massimo Maltana," 13 August 1947. The role played in this case by Cibelli, head of the local Comitato Consultivo Italiano, points to that committee's important role as intermediary between the colonists and the BMA. For more on the constitution of the Comitato Consultivo Italiano go to ASDMAE AP 1950–57, Libia, b. 761. Other concerns focused on the educational deficits experienced by those children shuttled between institutions on the Italian peninsula during the war years and the need to help children arriving in Libya in clandestine fashion resume their schooling. On this, ASDMAE ASMAI Africa, vol. 4, Ufficio per gli Affari del Soppresso Ministero A.I. (1946–1947), pacco 1, b. 42, "Rapporto della Missione a Tripoli—Ottobre 1946: Scuole," 2.

183. For details see Pamela Ballinger, "Colonial Twilight: Italian Settlers and the Long Decolonization of Libya," *Journal of Contemporary History* 51 no. 4 (2016): 829–830.

184. Fabio Chiodi, *Diario di un profugo* (Pontedera: Tagete Edizioni, 2004), 25–27.

185. ASDMAE ASMAI Africa, vol. 4, Ufficio per gli Affari del Soppresso Ministero A.I. (1946–1947), pacco 1, b. 42, "Rapporto della Missione a Tripoli. Trattative per i rimpatri," 15 November 1946, 2.

186. ASDMAE ASMAI Africa, vol 4, Ufficio per gli Affari del Soppresso Ministero A.I. (1946–1947), pacco 1, b. 42, "Missione a Tripoli—19–29 Novembre 1946: Imbarco dei profughi a Tripoli," 1.

187. ASDMAE ASMAI Africa, vol. 4, Ufficio per gli Affari del Soppresso Ministero A.I. (1946–1947), pacco 1, b. 42, "Missione a Tripoli—19–29 Novembre 1946: Imbarco e viaggio di andata," 4.

188. ASDMAE ASMAI Africa, vol. 4, Ufficio per gli Affari del Soppresso Ministero A.I. (1946–1947), pacco 1, b. 42, "Missione a Tripoli: 19–29 Novembre 1946: Imbarco dei profughi a Tripoli." These complaints were echoed by Marquess Spinola Cattaneo, president of the Auxilium (an ecclesiastical entity based in Genoa and founded in 1931), who reported on the *Vulcania*'s chaotic arrival in Genoa on its first postwar repatriation mission. ASDMAE AP 1946–50, Italia Ex Possedimenti Parte Generale, b. 4, "Rimpatrio profughi italiani sulla M/n 'Vulcania,'" 29 April 1947.

189. ASDMAE AP 1946–50, Italia Ex Possedimenti, b. 27, fasc. 7, "Nota Verbale," 4 March 1948. The BMA complained about the pressures created by the "over-all balance between movements in either direction."

190. ASDMAE AP 1946–50, Italia Ex Possedimenti Libia, b. 90, aide-mémoire, 10 March 1949.

191. ASDMAE AP 1946–50, Italia Ex Possedimenti Eritrea, b. 7, G. Hartman to UNRRA, Italian Mission, "Return of Italians to ERITREA," 6 September 1946.

192. ASDMAE ASMAI Africa, vol. 4, Fondo Bruno Santangelo, pacco 2 (1947), b. 88, fasc. 9, Comitato Italiano della Somalia, "Memorandum affidato alla Missione Diplomatica Italiana per essere presentato in Italia agli organi competenti: Viaggi da e per l'Italia," 16 October 1946. On *Vulcania*'s first postwar journey to AOI see also ACS PCM 48–50, b. 325, fasc. 17.1/12491, "Relazione sul servizio di polizia svolto a bordo della Motonave *Vulcania* durante il primo viaggio di rimpatrio di connazionali dall'A.O.," 4 April 1947. On the second trip see in this same file "Trasporto profughi da e per le colonie italiane," 21 June 1947. For similar arguments for a two-way "repatriation" made by the Associazione Rimpatriandi Italiani dell'Asmara see ASDMAE AP 1946–50, Italia Ex Possedimenti Eritrea, b. 16, "Associazione Rimpatriandi italiani—Asmara," 17 December 1946.

193. ASDMAE ASMAI Africa, vol. 4, Fondo Bruno Santangelo, pacco 2, b. 88, fasc. 12, Relazione primo viaggio m/m Vulcania 25–1-47:27–2, Enrico Olivieri, "Relazione sulla permanenza in Somalia durante il primo viaggio della motonave requisita Vulcania (6–13 febbraio)," 4–5, 8. For an official notice by the BMA's Civil Affairs Office of those Italians granted permits to leave from and return to Somalia see ASDMAE ASMAI Africa, vol. 4, Fondo Bruno Santangelo, pacco 3, b. 89, fasc. 8, Connazionali rientrati temporaneamente dalla Somalia, A. O. Smith, Official Notices. Turn also to ASDMAE AP 1946–50, Italia Ex Possedimenti Somalia, b. 14, Cattani, "Rimpatrio civili dalla Somalia," 19 April 1946.

194. ASDMAE AP 1946–50, Italia Ex Possedimenti Eritrea, b. 16, "Note Verbale," 13 September 1947. "With regard, however, to the proposal in paragraph 2 of the Ministry's Note to the effect that the 1 to 5 ratio should be abandoned, the Embassy feels bound to inform the Ministry that from the information at its disposal there is very little likelihood that the competent British authorities will be prepared to reconsider their decision in this connection; the Embassy fears, indeed, that by making this proposal and by suggesting that Italian nationals who settled in Eritrea after 1935 should in principle be allowed to return, the Italian Government are only courting further delay in bringing about a final settlement of this question, to the inconvenience of all concerned."

195. ASDMAE ASMAI Africa, vol. 4, Fondo Bruno Santangelo, pacco 2 (1947), b. 88, fasc. 12, Relazione primo viaggio M. Vulcania 25–1-47:27–2, Enrico Olivieri, "Relazione sulla permanenza in Somalia durante il primo viaggio della motonave requisita Vulcania (6–13 febbraio)," 1; see also "Relazione sul 1 viaggio del 'Vulcania' (25.1.47–27.2.47)." For various repatriation lists and statistical data see ASDMAE ASMAI Africa, vol. 4, Fondo Bruno Santangelo, pacco 3, b. 89. On the *Vulcania*'s voyages see also ACS PCM 1948–50, b. 325, sf. 12491, "Trasporto profughi da e per le colonie italiane M/n 'Vulcania,'" 21 June 1947.

196. ASDMAE ASMAI Africa, vol. 4, Fondo Bruno Santangelo, pacco 3, b. 89, fasc. 3, Relazione sulla Somalia, Luigi Bruno Santangelo, "Relazione sulla permanenza in Somalia durante il secondo viaggio della motonave requisita 'Vulcania' (28–31 Marzo 1947)," 17. A July 1947 memo from the Ministry of Italian Africa to the Ministry of Foreign Affairs and the PCM claimed over eight hundred settlers (mostly women and children) had obtained permission to return to Eritrea and Somalia. ACS PCM 48–50, b. 325, "Ritorno profughi in A.O.," 30 July 1947.

197. ASDMAE ASMAI Africa, vol. 4, Ufficio per gli Affari del Soppresso Ministero A.I. (1946–1947), pacco 1, b. 42, Mario Franco Rossi, "Relazione sulla permanenza in Eritrea dal 2 al 29 Ottobre 1946," 10 November 1946, 1.

198. ASDMAE AP 1946–50, Italia Ex Possedimenti Eritrea, b. 16, "Note Verbale," 2 September 1946.

199. ASDMAE ASMAI Africa, vol. 4, Ufficio per gli Affari del Soppresso Ministero A.I. (1946–1947), pacco 1, b. 42, Mario Franco Rossi, "Relazione sulla permanenza in Eritrea dal 2 al 29 Ottobre 1946," 10 November 1946, 3; also 2, 11–12.

200. At the Peace Conference, Italian representatives could not request changes to the treaty text but only offer comments or "observations." Giulio Esposito, "Profughi e rimpatriati in terra di Bari," in *La Puglia dell'accoglienza: Profughi, rifugiati e rimpatriati nel Novecento*, ed. Vito Antonio Leuzzi and Giulio Esposito (Bari: Progedit, 2006), 107 fn. 18. Sara Lorenzini maintains, "The history of the 1947 Peace Treaty with Italy demonstrates above all Italy's impotence in the postwar period. . . . The country would not accept the impossibility of changing the situation": Lorenzini, *L'Italia e il trattato di pace del 1947* (Bologna: Mulino, 2007), 147. For publications that present the treaty as a "shameful" act see *Diktat: Il vergognoso "Trattato di Pace" imposto all'Italia dagli Alleati* (Genoa: Effepi, 2005); Anna Borsi De Simone et al., eds., *Testimonianze fotografiche sulle Foibe-Diktat-Esodo* (Milan: Associazione Nazionale Venezia Giulia e Dalmazia, 1992).

201. Norman Kogan, "Revision of the Italian Peace Treaty," *Indiana Law Journal* 28, no. 3 (1953): 348.

202. Lorenzini, *L'Italia e il trattato di pace*, 124–125. These demands would be renewed in 1952, when the USSR vetoed for the fifth time Italy's membership application to the UN. Kogan, "Revision of the Italian Peace Treaty," 334. Other issues of contention revolved around article 76 and war reparation claims against the Italian government. On this see ASDMAE AP 1950–57, Eritrea, b. 877, "Art. 76 del Trattato di pace," 29 October 1952. Also refer to Walter Sterling Surrey, "Problems of the Italian Peace Treaty: Analysis of Claims Provisions and Description of Enforcement," *Law and Contemporary Problems* 16, no. 3 (1951): 436–447, 446; Salvatore Saraceno, *L'applicabilità dell'Art. 76 del Trattato di Pace alle ex-colonie Italiane* (Rome: Ministero degli Affari Esteri, 1952).

203. Lorenzini, *L'Italia e il trattato di pace*, 107.

204. P. J. Philip, "1919 Diplomats Dubious on 1946; Fears of 'Peace by Force' Voiced," *New York Times*, 7 August 1946.

205. Cited in "Obituary: Maria Pasquinelli," *Telegraph*, 8 July 2013. Italy's overseas colonies and recently redeemed ones were intertwined in Pasquinelli's biography. Born in Florence, she was a proud adherent of fascism and in 1940 became a Red Cross volunteer in Italian Libya and North Africa. She then became a teacher in 1942 in the Dalmatian territories Italy occupied during the war and moved to Trieste after Mussolini's ousting in 1943.

206. Lorenzini, *L'Italia e il trattato di pace*, 137. This contrasts with the experience of the Italian community in British Egypt. With much of the community interned during World War II, the horizons of a possible future there rapidly diminished. Joseph John Viscomi, "Mediterranean Futures: Historical Time and the Departure of Italians from Egypt, 1919–1937," *Journal of Modern History* 91, no. 2 (2019): 341–379.

207. Giampaolo Calchi Novati, "Italy in the Triangle of the Horn: Too Many Corners for a Half Power," *Journal of Modern African Studies* 32, no. 3 (September 1994): 371–372. On the entanglement of the colonial question and that of Venezia Giulia at the level of both diplomacy and party politics see Gianluigi Rossi, "Trieste e colonie alla vigilia delle elezioni italiane del 18 aprile 1948," *Rivista di studi politici internazionali* 182, no. 2 (April–June 1979): 205–231.

208. ASDMAE ASMAI Africa, vol. 4, Fondo Comm. di Studi Economici (Segr. Cerulli), pacco 1, b. 47, fasc. 7, "Commissione Profughi Africa a Parigi (1946). Materiale vario." The two-volume publication *Giustizia per il lavoro italiano in Africa* (Rome: Edizioni GEA, 1946) by Corrado Masì, Roberto Rossetti, Angelo Sammarco, and Aethiopicus made similar arguments.

209. See, for example, Mémorandum présenté par le Comité des réfugiés de la Libye, de l'Érythrée et de la Somalie sur la question des Colonies Italiennes / Memorandum presented by the Committee of the refugees from Libya, Eritrea, and Somalia on the Italian Colonial Question. Contained in ASDMAE AP 1946–50, Italia, b. 53, fasc. 1. For the appeal to Byrnes and Macmillan, ASDMAE AP 1946–50, Italia Ex Possedimenti Parte Generale, b. 2, Feliciano Bianchi to De Gasperi, 1 June 1946. Refer to this same file for other declarations and telegrams from groups that include the Associazione Coloni d'Africa e Colonizzatori, the Associazione Nazionale Profughi Libici, the Associazione Nazionale Profughi Africa Orientale, the Unione Profughi, the Unione Nazionale Profughi Africa Orientale, the Comitato Profughi Libici, the Società Africana d'Italia, and the Associazione fra le Imprese Italiane in Africa.

210. Todd Shepard, *The Invention of Decolonization: The Algerian War and the Remaking of France* (Ithaca, NY: Cornell University Press, 2006).

211. Erez Manela, *The Wilsonian Moment: Self-Determination and the International Origins of Anticolonial Nationalism* (Oxford: Oxford University Press, 2007). While the Italian public declared the resulting treaty a diktat in terms that evoked German denunciations of the Versailles settlement of 1919, and while the Paris Peace Conferences of 1919 and 1946 both mobilized a wide range of actors and produced a mountain of propaganda pamphlets, the 1946 conference has received much less scholarly scrutiny than that following World War I. For an account of the atmosphere at the 1946 conference and the tensions over the "combustible" issue of Trieste see the dispatches by Anglo-Irish journalist Elizabeth Bowen collected in *People, Places, Things: Essays by Elizabeth Bowen* (Edinburgh: Edinburgh University Press, 2008), 66–80.

212. Cited in Paolo Radivo, "Il plebiscito negato agli italiani," *L'Arena di Pola*, 20 October 2010. For details on the Julian delegation to the peace conference see Liliana Ferrari, "Trieste 1945–1947: La questione istriana nella stampa," in *Storia di un esodo*, ed. Cristiana Colummi, Liliana Ferrari, Gianna Nassisi, and Germano Trani (Trieste: Istituto Regionale per la Liberazione di Friuli Venezia Giulia, 1980), 271–272. See also Sergio Cella, *La liberazione negata: L'azione del Comitato di liberazione nazionale dell'Istria* (Udine: Del Bianco, 1990), 93–100.

213. Eva Garau, "Italy through British Eyes: Italian Ex-Colonies in British Newspapers (1945–1949)," in *Images of Colonialism and Decolonisation in the Italian Media*, ed. Paola Bertella Farnetti and Cecilia Dau Novelli (Cambridge: Cambridge Scholars, 2017), 215.

214. ASDMAE AP 1946–50, Italia Ex Possedimenti Parte Generale, b. 4, "Promemoria sulla questione delle colonie," 19 June 1945.

215. For details see Richard Pankhurst, "Italian Fascist War Crimes in Ethiopia: A History of Their Discussion from the League of Nations to the United Nations (1936–1949)," *Northeast African Studies* 6, no. 1–2 (1999): 83–140. See the broader discussion in Nicola Labanca, "Colonial Rule, Colonial Repression and War Crimes in the Italian Colonies," *Journal of Modern Italian Studies* 9, no. 3 (2004): 300–313. On Yugoslav efforts to prosecute Italian war crimes and criminals turn to Effie G. H. Pedaliu, "Britain and the 'Hand-Over' of Italian War Criminals to Yugoslavia, 1945–48," *Journal of Contemporary History* 39, no. 4 (2004): 503–529.

216. For a discussion of these publications and the battery of arguments made in favor of either Italian or Yugoslav claims (or those of regional autonomist movements) see Pamela Ballinger, *History in Exile: Memory and Identity at the Borders of the Balkans* (Princeton, NJ: Princeton University Press, 2003), 82–86.

217. For a detailed analysis of the orchestrated efforts to assume "popular power" in Istria turn to Orietta Moscarda Oblak, *Il "potere popolare" in Istria, 1945–1953* (Rovinj: Centro di Ricerche Storiche di Rovigno, 2016).

218. Glenda Sluga, *The Problem of Trieste and the Italo-Yugoslav Border: Difference, Identity, and Sovereignty in Twentieth-Century Europe* (Albany: SUNY Press, 2001), 141; see also 138–142. The "Trieste Question" has been well studied from a diplomatic point of view. For a sampling of key works: Janko Jeri, *Tržaško vprašanje po drugi sveotvni vojni: Tri faze diplomatskega boja* (Ljubljana: Cankarjeva Založba, 1961); Jean Baptiste Duroselle, *Le conflit de Trieste, 1943–1954* (Brussels: Éditions de l'Institut de

sociologie de l'Université libre de Bruxelles, 1966); Bogdan Novak, *Trieste 1941–1954: The Ethnic, Political, and Ideological Struggle* (Chicago: University of Chicago Press, 1970); Diego de Castro, *La questione di Trieste: L'azione politica e diplomatica italiana dal 1943 al 1954* (Trieste: LINT, 1981); Giampaolo Valdevit, *La questione di Trieste 1941–1954: Politica internazionale e contesto locale* (Milan: FrancoAngeli, 1986); Roberto Rabel, *Between East and West: Trieste, the United States, and the Cold War, 1941–1954* (Durham, NC: Duke University Press, 1988). On the structure of the Council of Foreign Ministers, first established at the Potsdam conference, refer to Stephen Kertesz, *The Last European Peace Conference: Paris 1946, Conflict of Values* (Lanham, MD: University Press of America, 1985), 17–18.

219. Cited in Lorenzini, *L'Italia e il trattato di pace*, 93.

220. Tracey Watts, "The British Military Occupation of Cyrenaica, 1947–1949," *Transactions of the Grotius Society* 37 (1951): 74. Watts wondered, "So far as I am aware, a transfer of sovereignty can only take place between sovereign Powers, and neither the Foreign Ministers of the four Allied Powers, nor the Organisation of the United Nations, are sovereign Powers in the eyes of international law."

221. De Gasperi cited in *Diktat: Il vergognoso "Trattato di Pace,"* 39. On the *pace provvisoria*, 43.

222. On the FTT's structure see annexes 6, 7, and 8 of the 1947 Peace Treaty. United Nations, *Treaties and International Agreements Registered or Filed and Recorded with the Secretariat of the United Nations* 49, no. 747 (1950).

223. Rhetorically at least, the FTT also invoked Trieste's longer history as a free port beginning with the Habsburg era. Emperor Charles VI had designated Trieste a free port in 1719, and in 1740 his successor Maria Theresa expanded the borders of the free port and issued an edict of toleration that welcomed to the city ethnically and religiously diverse populations (including Jews, Greek Orthodox, Serb Orthodox, Armenians, Protestants, Croats, and Slovenes). Even today, parts of Trieste's port remain exempt from European Union customs.

224. On the 1954 negotiations see John Campbell, ed., *Successful Negotiation: Trieste 1954* (Princeton, NJ: Princeton University Press, 1976), and Leonard Unger and Kristina Šegulja, *The Trieste Negotiations* (Washington, DC: Foreign Policy Institute, Paul H. Nitze School of Advanced International Studies, no. 16, 1990). For details on Osimo and the debates in the 1990s see Ballinger, *History in Exile*, 52, 93–96.

225. Federico Cresti and Massimiliano Cricco, *Storia della Libia contemporanea* (Rome: Carocci, 2015), 137–138.

226. Angelo Del Boca, *Gli Italiani in Libia*, vol. 2 (Milan: Mondadori, 1997), 345–360, 398–399, 443–445. On the creation of a UN Tribunal in Libya in 1951 and its role in adjudicating property claims by Italians refer to ASDMAE AP 1950–57, Eritrea, b. 756, "UN Tribunal in Libya Formally Installed," 21 August 1951. See also the extensive account by Adrian Pelt, *Libyan Independence and the United Nations: A Case of Planned Decolonization* (New Haven, CT: Yale University Press, 1970). For details on further arbitration by the UN Tribunal see United Nations, *Reports of International Arbitral Awards: The United Nations Tribunal in Libya—Established by Resolution 388 (V) and Adopted on 15 December 1950 by the General Assembly of the United Nations*, vol. 13 (Geneva: United Nations, 2006). For an account by one of its members of the Four Power Commission that first traveled to Eritrea, then to Libya, and finally to Somalia

consult F. E. Stafford, "The Ex-Italian Colonies," *International Affairs* 25, no. 1 (January 1949): 47–55.

227. Fouad Makki, "Subaltern Agency and Nationalist Commitment: The Dialectic of Social and National Emancipation in Colonial Eritrea," *Africa Today* 58, no. 1 (Fall 2011): 42–43.

228. ASDMAE AP 1946–50, Italia Ex Possedimenti Eritrea e Somalia, b. 100, "ERITREA—sicurezza pubblica—incidente del 30 marzo," 23 May 1950. On other incidents see "ERITREA—Sicurezza pubblica," 23 July 1950; "ERITREA: uccisione Maresciallo Carabinieri Semproni Pio," 22 October 1950; "Azioni terroristiche," 3 November 1950; "ERITREA—Uccisione di connazionali," 20 December 1950.

229. ASDMAE AP 1946–50 Italia Ex Possedimenti Eritrea e Somalia, b. 103, fasc. 1 "Status" degli Italiani, "ERITREA: Rimpatrio connazionali," 17 October 1950.

230. Annalisa Urbano, "'That Is Why We Have Troubles': The Pro-Italia Movement's Challenge to Nationalism in British-Occupied Somalia, 1946–49," *Journal of African History* 57, no. 3 (2016): 325.

231. Ibid., 343.

232. Giampaolo Calchi Novati, "Gli incidenti di Mogadiscio del gennaio 1948: Rapporti Italo-Inglesi e Nazionalismo Somalo," *Africa: Notiziario dell'Associazione fra le imprese italiane in Africa* 35, no. 3–4 (December 1980): 327–356.

233. For a summary of events and a discussion of Italian accusations of British complicity refer to Paolo Tripodi, *The Colonial Legacy in Somalia: Rome and Mogadishu from Colonial Administration to Operation Restore Hope* (Houndmills, UK: Macmillan, 1999).

234. Gianluigi Rossi, "Trieste e colonie alla vigilia delle elezioni italiane," 208.

235. ASDMAE ASMAI Africa, vol. 4, Fondo Bruno Santangelo, pacco 4 (1947–19651), b. 90, fasc. 1, Pietro Beritelli, "Relazione del Comitato Rappresentativo Italiano alla Commissione d'investigazione delle Quattro Potenze sul territorio della Somalia," 279.

236. ASDMAE ASMAI Africa, vol. 4, Fondo Comm. di Studi Economici (Segr. Cerulli), pacco 1, b. 47, fasc. 1, Commissione di studi economici. 1948. "Promemoria: Applicazione del Piano E.R.P. alle colonie," 20 July 1046. Marshall Plan aid was extended to Zone A of the Free Territory of Trieste. On the Marshall Plan in Trieste refer to Giampaolo Valdevit, "Trieste e il Piano Marshall," in *United States Information Service di Trieste. Catalogo del fondo cinematografico 1941–1966*, vol. 2, ed. Giulia Barrera and Giovanna Tosatti (Rome: Ministero per i Beni e le Attività culturali—Direzione generale per gli Archivi, 2007), 3–24; Giulio Mellinato and Pier Angelo Toninelli, "Marshall allo specchio: L'Erp nel Territorio Libero di Trieste," in *Il dilemma dell'integrazione: L'inserimento dell'economia italiana nel sistema occidentale (1945–1957)*, ed. Alberto Cova (Milan: FrancoAngeli, 2008), 353–402.

237. In a 1949 article titled "Ritorneremo" published in FeNPIA's official journal, Vittorio Paliotti mocked those who had treated the image of the old man holding up the child with the promise "We will return" as empty propaganda. Blaming Italy's postwar political class, as well as the Anglo-Americans, Paliotti argued that "history doesn't forgive" and that "the prophecy of the old man will come true: the child will return to Africa." Paliotti, "Ritorneremo," *Vergogna* 1, no. 2 (5 November 1949): 2.

238. Mohamed, "Imperial Policies," 1181.

239. ASDMAE AP 1946–50, Ex Possedimenti Eritrea e Somalia, b. 104, fasc. 1, Fornari, "Ingresso in Somalia di connazionali residenti in Etiopia," 9 May 1950. See also ASDMAE AP 1946–50, Italia Ex Possedimenti Eritrea e Somalia, b. 103, fasc. 1 "Status" degli Italiani, Gropello, "Trasferimento in Somalia di connazionali e di ditte italiane," 30 November 1949; see also "Trasferimento mano d'opera dall'Eritrea alla Somalia," 27 November 1949.

240. Gian Paolo Calchi Novati, *L'Africa d'Italia: Una storia coloniale e postcoloniale* (Rome: Carocci editore, 2011), 370. Although the trusteeship had a fixed end point, in 1956 the British raised the question of whether the Italian trusteeship might be extended in the hopes of containing the Somali nationalism that threatened British rule in British Somaliland. This idea was ultimately dropped, as it would have required debate in the UN Assembly. See Mohamed, "Imperial Policies," 1195–1196. See also Antonio Morone, *L'ultima colonia: Come l'Italia è tornata in Africa 1950–1960* (Rome-Bari: Laterza, 2011).

241. ASDMAE AP 1950–57, Libia, b. 765, "Promemoria per il Ministero dell'Africa Italiana: Spese politiche segrete," and "Promemoria per il Sottosegretario di Stato," December 1950.

242. One official Italian document estimated that by March 1949 there remained six hundred "arbitrarily detained" Italians in Albania. See ACS PCM 1944–47, b. 3402 (2.7/14628), Guidotti, 23 March 1949. On the particular question of medical personnel see ASDMAE AP 1946–50, Albania, b. 3, "Sanitari italiani trattenuti in Albania," 4 September 1946; ASDMAE AP 1946–50, Albania, b. 42, letter of Giuseppe De Marchis, 8 November 1949; ACICR BG 017 05.005 Italiens en Albanie 26.03.1945–14.07.1949, letter of 4 February 1948 from Pierre Colombo.

243. ASDMAE AP 1950–57, Albania, b. 517, "Promemoria sulla Situazione in Albania," June 1951.

244. ASDMAE AP 1950–57, Albania, b. 517, Legazione d'Italia in Tirana, "Relazioni sugli avvenimenti maturatisi in Albania durante l'anno 1951."

245. On both Vergarola/Vergarolla and the exodus from Pula/Pola more generally see Raoul Pupo, *Il lungo esodo Istria: Le persecuzioni, le foibe, l'esilio* (Milan: Rizzoli, 2005), 135–141. For recent work on Vergarola/Vergarolla that utilizes previously unavailable Allied documents see Fabio Amodeo and Mario J. Cereghino, *Trieste e il confine orientale tra guerra e dopoguerra, 1946–1951*, vol. 3 (Udine: Editoriale FVG, 2008); Gaetano Dato, *Vergarolla 18 agosto 1946. Gli enigmi di una strage tra conflitto mondiale e guerra fredda* (Gorizia: LEG, 2014).

246. Enrico Miletto, *Istria allo specchio: Storia e voci di una terra di confine* (Milan: FrancoAngeli, 2007).

247. On the role of the *Toscana* see Paolo Valenti, *Toscana: La nave dei due esodi* (San Dorligo della Valle: Luglioeditore, 2009). Valenti does not mention the voyages of the *Toscana* to the AOI in the early postwar period.

248. Sandi Volk maintains that the Italian government did encourage and direct these movements in order to send a powerful message about the impossibility of Italians living under Yugoslav rule. Volk, *Esuli a Trieste: Bonifica nazionale e rafforzamento dell'italianità sul confine orientale* (Udine: Kappa Vu, 2004). It should be noted that the thesis that Istrians were fooled by Italian state propaganda into leaving their homeland was long a staple of pro-Yugoslav rhetoric.

249. US National Archives, box 71, misc. 122.73: 1, Allied Military Government, Trieste, untitled report on Pola, 1947.

250. Ufficio per le Zone di Confine (UZC) PCM Sezione II Profughi (b. 2, vol. 1) 46/3, Micali, Dispaccio Telegrafico to Ufficio Provinciale Assistenza Postbellica & Ministero Interno, 25 July 1947.

251. UZC PCM Sezione II Profughi (b. 2, vol. 1) 46/3, G. Giacomazzi to Gerolamo Luxoro, "Segnalazione di esodo da Pola," 7 December 1946. Also see Ufficio Provinciale Assistenza Postbellica Milano, "Quesito relativo agli esuli di Pola (caso Luxoro Gerolamo)," 13 May 1947.

252. UZC PCM Sezione II Profughi (b. 2, vol. 1) 46/3, Ministro dell'Interno, "Profughi delle Isole del Dodecanneso," 19 June 1947.

253. UZC PCM Sezione II Profughi (b. 1, vol. 2) 46/2, "Promemoria per S. E. Mario Micale Ministero dell'Interno," 3 January 1947; also "Promemoria sulle condizioni degli italiani di Zara," 6 May 1947; Pietro Mimich, "Esodo da Zara," 27 May 1947.

254. UZC PCM Sezione II Profughi (b. 12, vol. 2) 49/4.

4. Displaced Persons and the Borders of Citizenship

1. Nadifa Mohamed, *Black Mamba Boy* (New York: Farrar, Straus and Giroux, 2010), 223.

2. Silvia Salvatici, "Between National and International Mandates: Displaced Persons and Refugees in Postwar Italy," *Journal of Contemporary History* 49 (2014): 523.

3. In comparison to the UN refugee agencies, ICEM/IOM remains understudied. For a critical exception see the work of Jérôme Elie: "The Historical Roots of Cooperation between the UN High Commissioner for Refugees and the International Organization for Migration," *Global Governance: A Review of Multilateralism and International Organizations* 16, no. 3 (July–September 2010): 345–360; and Elie, "Interactions et filiations entre organisations internationales autour de la question des réfugiés (1946–1956)," *Relations Internationales* 4, no. 152 (2012): 39–50.

4. Horng-luen Wang, "Regulating Transnational Flows of People: An Institutional Analysis of Passports and Visas as a Regime of Mobility," *Identities: Global Studies in Culture and Power* 11, no. 3 (2004): 351–376.

5. John Torpey, *The Invention of the Passport: Surveillance, Citizenship and the State* (Cambridge: Cambridge University Press, 2000), 103. In the broader arena of citizenship that those passports usually (but not always) symbolized, however, there also existed competition among states for migrants and attempts by labor-hungry states to woo Europeans with the prospect of dual citizenship. On Argentine efforts to transform Italians and Spanish into Argentine (dual) citizens in the late nineteenth and early twentieth centuries see David Cook-Martín, *The Scramble for Citizens: Dual Nationality and State Competition for Immigrants* (Stanford, CA: Stanford University Press, 2013). During this period, Italy also began to strike bilateral agreements designed to facilitate labor abroad. While pioneering in this regard, the 1904 France-Italy Labor Treaty was merely the first of numerous such arrangements between Italy and France. Go to Caroline Douki, "Accords franco-italiens: Des accommodements d'urgence à l'administration partagée du travail immigré," in *1914–1918.*

Mains-d'oeuvre en guerre, ed. Laure Machu, Isabelle Lespinet-Moret, and Vincent Viet (Paris: La Documentation Française, 2018), 201–225.

6. Sabina Donati, *A Political History of National Citizenship and Identity in Italy, 1861–1950* (Stanford, CA: Stanford University Press, 2013), 29. For a somewhat different take focused on the centrality of the *vincolo di sangue* (blood tie) to Italian identity in both cultural and juridical terms see Nicoletta Poidimani, "Ius sanguinis: Una prospettiva di genere su razzismo e costruzione dell'italianità' tra colonie e madrepatria," in *Quel che resta dell'impero: La cultura coloniale degli italiani*, ed. Valeria Deplano and Alessandro Pes (Milan: Mimesis, 2014), 210.

7. Donati, *Political History*, 84.

8. Nicola Camilleri, "Il discorso sulla cittadinanza coloniale in Italia e Germania," in *Governare l'Oltremare: Istituzioni, funzionari e società nel colonialismo italiano*, ed. Gianni Dore, Chiara Giorgi, Antonio M. Morone, and Massimo Zaccaria (Rome: Carocci editore, 2013), 25. Camilleri discusses the cases of two interpreters in colonial Eritrea who applied for Italian citizenship in 1895. See also Nicola Camilleri, "La cittadinanza negata nella Colonia Eritrea (1882–1941)," *Altreitalie* 57 (2018): 58–59. For the legal reasoning of Judge Ravizza in Eritrea on the reduced status of *piccola cittadinanza* and on the debates over whether such Africans could ever acquire the level of civilization (*grado di civiltà*) that might make it possible to accord them full citizenship rights see Barbara Sòrgoni, *Parole e corpi. Antropologia, discorso giuridico e politiche sessuali interrazziali nella colonia Eritrea (1890–1941)* (Naples: Liguori Editore, 1998), 95–97.

9. Giuseppe Sciortino and Asher Colombo, "The Flows and the Flood: The Public Discourse on Immigration in Italy, 1969–2001," *Journal of Modern Italian Studies* 9, no. 1 (2004): 96.

10. Torpey, *Invention of the Passport*, 114.

11. On "spy fever" go to Daniela L. Caglioti, "Why and How Italy Invented an Enemy Aliens Problem in the First World War," *War in History* 21, no. 2 (2013): 152. On the legislative response, including that of internment, refer to 156–165.

12. On shifting policies toward immigrants, Marij Leenders, "From Inclusion to Exclusion: Refugees and Immigrants in Italy between 1861 and 1943," *Immigrants and Minorities* 14, no. 2 (1995): 115–138. On the restrictions on citizenship for dissident Italians see Luca Bussotti, *La cittadinanza degli italiani: Analisi storica e critica sociologica di una questione irrisolta* (Milan: FrancoAngeli, 2002), 169.

13. Cited in Ferruccio Pastore, "A Community out of Balance: Nationality Law and Migration Politics in the History of Post-Unification Italy," *Journal of Modern Italian Studies* 9, no. 1 (2004): 31; see also 28–29.

14. For the texts of the laws of 1912 and 1992 turn to Giuliano Crifò, *Civis: La cittadinanza tra antico e moderno* (Rome-Bari: Laterza, 2000), 133–141. In regard to naturalization, the 1992 law "instituted a sort of detailed hierarchy between various categories of foreigners, fixing for each of them a different period of legal residence, as [a] necessary condition for presenting a petition for naturalization." Pastore, "Community out of Balance," 38.

15. Valerie McGuire, "Una faccia, una razza: Aegean Citizenship and 'Making' a Fascist Mediterranean in the Dodecanese Islands (1912–43)," unpublished MS, 7.

16. Camilleri, "La cittadinanza negata nella Colonia Eritrea," 55.

17. Donati, *Political History*, 122; see also 11. Refer, as well, to the pioneering work of Ester Capuzzo, "Sudditanza e cittadinanza nell'esperienza coloniale italiana nell'età liberale," *Clio* 31 (1995): 65–95.

18. To some extent, this hierarchy of value also applied to the Italian citizen-settlers. In a 1940 memo to the Commissariat for Migration and Internal Colonization, the Ente di Colonizzazione Puglia d'Etiopia's president Carlo Severini contended that the difficulties presented by the African climate and environment negated the possibility of producing ideal Italian peasant settlers (*contadini perfetti*) in AOI. By contrast, in Albania and other future "Mediterranean" territories, it was "necessary and indeed indispensable to be perfect peasants . . . [whereas] in Africa it is sufficient to be good agricultural laborers [*braccianti d'agricoltura*], provided they have a great love of the land." ACS Ente per la colonizzazione Puglia d'Etiopia, b. 6, fasc. 57, Severini to Giuseppe Lombrassa, 4 July 1940, 2.

19. Alessia Maria Di Stefano, "Italian Judges and Judicial Practice in Libya: A Legal Experiment in Multinormativity," *American Journal of Legal History* 58 (2018): 425–478; see also Roberta Pergher, *Mussolini's Nation-Empire: Sovereignty and Settlement in Italy's Borderlands, 1922–1943* (Cambridge: Cambridge University Press, 2017), 40–44.

20. Camilleri, "La cittadinanza negata nella Colonia Eritrea," 57.

21. Sarah Abrevaya Stein, *Extraterritorial Dreams: European Citizenship, Sephardi Jews, and the Ottoman Twentieth Century* (Chicago: University of Chicago Press, 2016), 73. The concepts of the Levant and Levantines have recently enjoyed a scholarly renaissance. As the editor of the *Journal of Levantine Studies* founded in 2011 put it, "The term 'Levantines' was originally applied to the European inhabitants of the Mediterranean; it later acquired other meanings and was applied to diverse groups. . . . The journal's goal is to reclaim the Levant as a historical and political concept and as a category of identity and classification." Anat Lapido-Firilla, "Editor's Note," *Journal of Levantine Studies* 1, no. 1 (2011): 6. Within the context of Italian studies, authors like Rosetta Giuliani Caponetto have used the term "Levantine" to refer to individuals (in the case she examines, in Egypt) who were "genetically Italian, but culturally 'bastardized.'" The Levantine's ambiguity, however, encoded "murky" racial origins and certainly included Jews and also Turks in Italian possessions like the Dodecanese Islands. Caponetto, *Fascist Hybridities: Representations of Racial Mixing and Diaspora Cultures under Mussolini* (New York: Palgrave Macmillan, 2015), 8.

22. Stein, *Extraterritorial Dreams*, 17.

23. Donati, *Political History*, 199–200.

24. Ibid., 201–202.

25. Camilleri, "Il discorso sulla cittadinanza coloniale," 26. McGuire also uses this term in relation to the specific Dodecanese case. McGuire, "Una faccia, una razza," 22.

26. McGuire, "Una faccia, una razza," 8. Donati notes that both liberal and fascist Italy "used citizenship in the East Mediterranean Sea as a useful instrument of expansionism." Donati, *Political History*, 195.

27. Stein, *Extraterritorial Dreams*, 23.

28. Ibid., 81. For details on the history of Jewish populations in the islands within the wider context of the Sephardic world, go to Esther Benbassa and Aron Rodrigue,

Sephardi Jewry: A History of the Judeo-Spanish Communities in the Modern World, 14th–20th Centuries (Berkeley: University of California Press, 2000).

29. *Treaty of Peace with Turkey, and Other Instruments. Signed at Lausanne on July 24, 1923*, Treaty Series no. 16 (London: His Majesty's Stationery Office, 1923), 27. On the efforts by Italian authorities to deny the right of option to native Orthodox Dodecanese living in Turkey at the time of the treaty and the ultimately negative consequences for Italy see Filippo Espinoza, "Una cittadinanza imperiale basata sul consenso: Il caso delle isole italiane dell'Egeo (1924–1940), in *Sudditi o cittadini? L'evoluzione delle appartenenze imperiali nella Prima guerra mondiale*, ed. Sara Lorenzini e Simone A. Bellezza (Rome: Viella, 2018), 194–196.

30. See McGuire, "Una faccia, una razza," 8.

31. GSAD, 1932 296 1/2.

32. GSAD, 1932 296 2/2, "Rimpatrio di Dodecanesini dal Congo Belga," 26 February 1932.

33. GSAD, 1932 296 2/2, "Rimpatri di dodecannesini disoccupati," 15 June 1932. A memo from the Italian vice consul Grillo in Elizabethville pledged his readiness to examine the passports of "our subjects resident in this Consular District [in Belgian Congo], particularly the Jews." Grillo, 26 May 1932.

34. For details, McGuire, "Una faccia, una razza," 18. See also Espinoza, "Una cittadinanza imperiale," 196.

35. GSAD, 1932 480 1/6, Aloisi, n.d. This missive was authored by Pompeo Aloisi, who was in Ankara between 1929 and 1932 before becoming the MAE cabinet head in July 1932.

36. GSAD, 1932 480 1/6, Lago, "Colonie Italiane in Turchia," 16 June 1932.

37. GSAD, 1932 480 2/6, "Soggiorno degli stranieri nel Possedimento," 30 December 1931. For other rejected requests by Greek subjects either born in the islands or with relatives there to travel/migrate to the Egeo go to GSAD, 1932 480 3/6, "Catracatsos Giovanni—sbarco a Coo," 2 April 1932; "Catracatsos Giovanni—domanda di sbarco," 17 February 1932. An instructive comparison can be made between the request of Catracatsos and that of Luigi de Martino, an Italian who had previously lived on Rhodes and even married an Orthodox Greek woman from Simi. The couple had moved to Italy in 1926, but the wife returned four years later to live with her mother. De Martino's request to return to Rhodes and reside with his wife there was well received. See the relevant documents in the same file.

38. GSAD, 1932 480 1/6, "Colonie Italiane in Turchia," 16 June 1932. An undated translation of an article from a Turkish newspaper contained in this same file reports on a law being debated in Ankara to restrict employment to Turkish citizens. This contextualizes Lago's comment that, once admitted into the islands, these Italian Levantines could not return or be sent back to Turkey. The passage of this law led to fears of "an exodus of Italians from Turkey" toward Rhodes. See "Sbarco nel Possedimento di connazionali di Smirne," n.d.

39. See, for instance, the documentation on the requests by Maria Scagliarini to be joined by her mother and brother's family, then resident in İzmir/Smirne. Contained in GSAD, 1932 480 4/6.

40. GSAD, 1932 480 5/6, "P. Scala—sbarco," 27 June 1932.

41. GSAD, 1932 480 1/6 Lago, "Colonie Italiane in Turchia," 16 June 1932. On the Mancuso case, Crivellari to Italian Consulate (Istanbul), "Sbarchi nel Possedimento," 8 April 1932.

42. Torpey, *Invention of the Passport*, 161.

43. GSAD, 1932 480 1/6, "Visto sui passaporti dei dodecannesini che ritornano dall'America," 22 September 1932.

44. For details see McGuire, "Una faccia, una razza," 12.

45. Pignataro also stresses the "rigidity" with which De Vecchi enforced the laws, even as he also highlights De Vecchi's role in assisting those Central and Eastern European Jews on the *Pentcho* who shipwrecked in the archipelago. Luca Pignataro, *Il Dodecaneso Italiano, 1912–1947*, vol. 3, 212, 423–438. Furthermore, Pignataro emphasizes the distinctiveness of *cittadinanza italiana egea*, often incorrectly lumped together with other forms of "piccola cittadinanza." Pignataro, *Il Dodecaneso Italiano, 1912–1947*, vol. 1, *L'occupazione iniziale 1912–1922* (Chieti: Solfanelli, 2011), 21–29.

46. McGuire, "Una faccia, una razza," 19.

47. Josef Kunz, "Nationality and Option Clauses in the Italian Peace Treaty of 1947," *American Journal of International Law* 41, no. 3 (1947): 627.

48. Nicholas Doumanis, *Myth and Memory in the Mediterranean: Remembering Fascism's Empire* (Houndmills, UK: Palgrave Macmillan, 1997), 2, 7, 146, 166, 184.

49. Ibid., 62–79, 84–85.

50. Cited in Poidimani, "Ius sanguinis," 226.

51. Emanuel Rota, "'We Will Never Leave': The *Reale Accademia d'Italia* and the Invention of a Fascist Africanism," *Fascism* 2, no. 2 (2013): 176–179.

52. Donati, *Political History*, 193.

53. In using the problematic term *meticci* I follow Barrera, Sorgonì, Deplano, and others, who acknowledge its historically derogatory connotations but also recognize that it served as an official category of identity. After stating that she preferred to employ terms such as "Italo-Eritreans," D'Agostino admitted that in contemporary Eritrean society "the term 'meticcio' among meticci is in current use without obvious negative connotations." Gabriella d'Agostino, *Altre storie: Memoria dell'Italia in Eritrea* (Bologna: Archetipolibri, 2012), 13.

54. Donati, *Political History*, 197, 200.

55. Although interracial marriages between Italian women and African men were uncommon, they did occur. According to Deplano, the 1938 census revealed five Libyan men with Italian wives but only one Eritrean married to an Italian. By 1951, five Libyans and three Eritreans (all ex-military based in Italy) had taken Italian wives. Valeria Deplano, *La madrepatria è una terra straniera: Libici, eritrei e somali nell'Italia del dopoguerra (1945–1960)* (Florence: Le Monnier, 2017), 28, 55.

56. Renzo De Felice, preface to Nicola Caracciolo, *Gli ebrei e l'Italia durante la guerra, 1940–45* (Rome: Bonacci, 1986), 7–15.

57. Menachem Shelah, "The Italian Rescue of Yugoslav Jews, 1941–1943," in *The Italian Refuge: Rescue of Jews during the Holocaust*, ed. Ivo Herzer et al. (Washington, DC: Catholic University of America Press, 1989), 205–217; Jonathan Steinberg, *All or Nothing: The Axis and the Holocaust, 1941–43* (London: Routledge, 1990); Susan Zuccotti, *The Italians and the Holocaust* (Lincoln: University of Nebraska Press, 1996). Considerable attention has been paid to the refuge in fascist Italy provided to many foreign Jews, including those fleeing Germany. Until 1943, the fascist regime permitted DELASEM (Delegazione per l'Assistenza degli Emigranti Ebrei) to facilitate emigration for these foreign Jews. Nonetheless, the 1938 Racial Laws prohibited foreign Jews from residing in Italy, Libya, or the Dodecanese and required all non-Italian Jews who had come to Italy after 1918 to leave. For details on DELASEM refer to Settimio

Sorani, Amedeo Tagliacozzo, and Francesco Del Canuto, *L'assistenza ai profughi ebrei in Italia (1933–1947): Contributo alla storia della "Delasem"* (Rome: Carucci, 1983); also Sandro Antonini, *DelAsEm: Storia della più grande organizzazione ebraica italiana di soccorso durante la seconda guerra mondiale* (Genoa: De Ferrari, 2000).

58. See Michele Sarfatti, *The Jews in Mussolini's Italy: From Equality to Persecution*, trans. John Tedeschi and Anne C. Tedeschi (Madison: University of Wisconsin Press, 2007). An important line of argumentation, epitomized by the work of Davide Rodogno, has complicated understanding of what "protection" of Jews in Italian territories meant and the motivations for such assistance. In unpacking the self-exculpating myth of Italians as good people (*Italiani, brava gente*) Rodogno writes of Italian operations in the Balkans, "'Good Italians' did rescue Jewish victims of persecution, as well as those of other faiths and nationalities, but the claim that 'the Italians' as a people did not betray the Jews to the Germans for humanitarian reasons simply cannot be sustained. Nor is it defensible to highlight individual actions in order to prove that humanitarianism is inherent in the Italian national character or to assert *a priori* that the fact of being Italian precluded anti-Semitic acts." Davide Rodogno, "*Italiani brava gente*? Fascist Italy's Policy towards the Jews in the Balkans, April 1941–July 1943," *European History Quarterly* 35, no. 2 (2005): 234–235.

59. For a small sampling of works on Italian racial theory and practice: Alberto Burgio, ed., *Nel nome della razza: Il razzismo nella storia d'Italia, 1870–1945* (Bologna: Mulino, 1999); Aaron Gillette, *Racial Theories in Fascist Italy* (London: Routledge, 2002); Claudia Mantovani, *Rigenerare la società: L'eugenetica in Italia dalle origini ottocentesche agli anni Trenta* (Soveria Manelli: Rubbettino, 2004); Francesco Cassata, *Molti, sani e forti: L'eugenetica in Italia* (Turin: Bollati Boringhieri, 2006); Marius Turda and Aaron Gillette, *Latin Eugenics in Comparative Perspective* (London: Bloomsbury Academic, 2014).

60. For a summary of some of these debates see "Three Documents on Race: *The Manifesto of Race* (1938), Critique of *The Manifesto of Race* (1941–42), and New Revised Draft of *The Manifesto of Race* (1942)," in *A Primer of Italian Fascism*, ed. Jeffrey Schnapp (Lincoln: University of Nebraska Press, 2000), 172–184.

61. Olindo de Napoli, *La prova della razza: Cultura giuridica e razzismo in Italia negli anni trenta* (Florence: Le Monnier, 2009). Barbara Sòrgoni's pioneering research, for instance, evidences the degree to which colonial jurists and administrators in Italian Africa were in dialogue with broader anthropological theories of race prevalent in the nineteenth and early twentieth centuries. See Sòrgoni, *Parole e corpi*; also, *Etnografia e colonialismo. L'Eritrea e l'Etiopia di Alberto Pollera (1873–1939)* (Turin: Bollati Boringhieri, 2001).

62. In using this phrasing, I have in mind Mary Lewis's helpful distinction between social/cultural strangeness and legal/technical foreignness. Mary Lewis, "The Strangeness of Foreigners: Policing Migration and Nation in Interwar Marseille," *French Politics, Culture & Society* 20, no. 3 (2002): 65–96.

63. For some key texts see Gaia Giuliani and Cristina Lombardi-Diop, *Bianco e nero: Storia dell'identità razziale degli italiani* (Florence: Le Monnier, 2013); Pergher, *Mussolini's Nation-Empire*.

64. Elio Apih, *Italia: Fascismo e antifascismo nella Venezia Giulia (1918–1943)* (Bari: Laterza, 1966), 276.

65. Pergher, *Mussolini's Nation-Empire*, 22.

66. Cited in Glenda Sluga, *The Problem of Trieste and the Italo-Yugoslav Border: Difference, Identity, and Sovereignty in Twentieth-Century Europe* (Albany: SUNY Press, 2001), 54.

67. GSAD, 1936 231 1/2. This file contains considerable documentation on these migrants from Calese and Merano to the colonial village of Campochiaro on Rhodes. A *pro memoria* defined these individuals as being "elementi allogeni," even as it noted that the selection of families was made "without regard to whether they were of Italian or German language." See "Promemoria per il R. Consolato Generale d'Italia in Innsbruck," 10 November 1936. The presence of monolingual German speakers appears to have created problems in practice, however.

68. For the original scholarly formulation of the "myth of the good Italian" turn to Davide Bidussa, *Il mito del bravo italiano* (Milan: Il Saggiatore, 1994); see also D. Bidussa, "Razzismo e antisemitismo in Italia: Ontologia e fenomenologia del 'bravo italiano,'" *La Rassegna Mensile di Israele* 58, no. 3 (1992): 1–36. Historian Angelo del Boca has proven the most prominent critic of the notion of Italians as humane colonizers. For a summary of his arguments go to Del Boca, *Italiani, brava gente? Un mito duro a morire* (Vicenza: Neri Pozza, 2005).

69. Camilleri, "La cittadinanza negata nella Colonia Eritrea," 60.

70. Luciano Martone, *Diritto d'Oltremare: Legge e ordine per le colonie del Regno d'Italia* (Milan: Dott. A. Giuffrè, 2008), 67. On the Libyan case see Donati, *Political History*, 191.

71. Martone, *Diritto d'Oltremare*, 67.

72. Nonetheless, whereas most Italian women lost their citizenship when they married a foreign spouse, in the rare cases of marriage between an Italian woman and an African man, the Italian woman retained her citizenship in recognition of her supposed racial superiority. Sòrgoni, *Parole e corpi*, 110. As in other colonial societies, settler women within Italian colonies bore a heavy symbolic and practical role. Fascism overlaid these notions of gender with its particular vision of women as mothers of the nation whose very bodies constituted "the border between purity and impurity, morality and immorality, racial regeneration and degeneration." Giuliani and Lombardi-Diop, *Bianco e nero*, 47. For the role assigned to Italian women as protectors of respectability and race in AOI and the paradoxical situation of Italian women imported by the regime for prostitution in service to respectability (through the avoidance of miscegenation) see also Emanuele Ertola, *In terra d'Africa: Gli italiani che colonizzarono l'impero* (Bari-Roma: Laterza, 2017), 102–115.

73. Giulia Barrera, "Patrilinearity, Race, and Identity: The Upbringing of Italo-Eritreans during Italian Colonialism," in *Italian Colonialism*, ed. Mia Fuller and Ruth Ben-Ghiat (New York: Palgrave Macmillan, 2005), 98. That said, from the early twentieth century there did exist colonial legislation prohibiting miscegenation. Sarfatti has argued that Italian laws in the pre-fascist colonies were very much in keeping with broader trends in European colonies at the time. What differed was the selective application of this legislation. Sarfatti, *Jews in Mussolini's Italy*, 53–54.

74. Sòrgoni, *Parole e corpi*, 146. In reality, colonial administrators in Eritrea monitored both *madamato* and *demoz*, another type of union approximating marriage that most Italian men nonetheless treated as "ephemeral." See pp. 120, 127–138.

75. Deplano, *La madrepatria è una terra straniera*, 92–93.

76. Eric Salerno, *"Uccideteli tutti": Libia 1943. Gli ebrei nel campo di concentramento fascista di Giado. Una storia italiana* (Milan: Il Saggiatore, 2008).

77. Federico Cresti and Massimiliano Cricco, *Storia della Libia contemporanea* (Rome: Carocci, 2015), 132–135.

78. Between the Armistice of 1943 and the war's end there existed another system of "dual tracks": that constituted by the citizenship codes of the Italian monarchy in the south and the RSI in the north. The former would usher in female suffrage and would increasingly link citizenship with antifascism. Donati, *Political History*, 231–233.

79. ACS PCM 51–54 (Certificati di Cittadinanza), b. 509, fasc. 19.17/ 13659 sf. 40. Circolare n. 31, "Oggetto: Territori Ceduti alla Francia: Opzioni," 15 July 1948, 2.

80. ACS PCM 51–54 (Certificati di Cittadinanza), b. 509, fasc. 19.17/13659, sf. 40, Consiglio di Stato, "Trieste: cittadinanza del Territorio Libero di Trieste," 23 March 1948. At the same time, the treaty required that within three months of its coming into effect, Italy and the other respective states (France, Yugoslavia, and Greece) must enact legislation concerning the specifics of the option process. Kunz, "Nationality and Option Clauses," 626. On the interpretation of the term "country of former habitual residence" contained in the 1951 Refugee Convention refer to Atle Grahl-Madsen, *The Status of Refugees in International Law*, vol. 1 (Leyden: A. W. Sijthoff, 1966), 160–163.

81. Nonetheless, the French situation required respecting a French law that the territories in question hold a referendum on such annexation. On 12 October 1947, a large majority of residents in Briga and Tenda voted to join France. See Andrea Gandolfo, "La 'dolorosa' cessione di Briga e Tenda alla Francia, il racconto dettagliato dello storico Gandolfo," *Sanremo News*, 25 August 2013.

82. Kunz, "Nationality and Option Clauses," 625.

83. Ibid., 630.

84. ACS PCM 51–54 (Certificati di Cittadinanza), b. 509, fasc. 19.17/13659 sf. 40, letter from Perassi for Segretaria Generale (Commiss. Confini) e la Direzione Generale Affari Politici, 15 September 1947.

85. ASDMAE AP 1950–57, Jugoslavia, b. 533, "Oggetto: Ammissione Scuole Slovene figli di optanti per la cittadinanza italiana," 4 August 1950.

86. Alessandra Algostino, "Profughi e profuganze: Note sullo *status* giuridico dei profughi dal confine orientale," in *Dall'Impero Austro-Ungarico alle foibe: Conflitti nell'area alto-adriatico*, ed. Alessandra Algostino et al. (Turin: Bollati Boringhieri, 2009), 231.

87. Deplano, *La madrepatria è una terra straniera*, 89–91.

88. ACS PCM 51–54 (Certificati di Cittadinanza), b. 509, fasc. 19.17/13659 sf. 40, CLN di Gorizia, "Riacquisto della cittadinanza italiana perduta a seguito del trattato di pace," 24 September 1947.

89. ACS PCM 51–54 (Certificati di Cittadinanza), b. 509, fasc. 19.17/13659 sf. 40, Prefettura di Udine, "Oggetto: Optanti jugoslavi per la cittadinanza jugoslava—KRANIEC Andrea fu Andrea," 18 August 1953.

90. IRO officials did not always possess reliable information as to these citizenship statuses. When asked whether the Yugoslav authorities provided information

about the option, chief eligibility officer Gesner recalled in 1952, "We had to be satisfied with a certificate from the Venezia Giulian Committee. These were not reliable as it was not a completely valid document. In the Communes they knew which people had opted. In some communes they issued certificates which are normally valid. When it came time to register for IRO, the refugee went to the Venezia Giulian Committee and made a statement as to the date he opted." AN IRO AJ 43/140, "Interview between Mr. R. L. Gesner, Chief Eligibility Officer, Italian Office and Mr. J. Mandel on Thursday, 10th January 1952," 6.

91. AN IRO AJ 43, 1038, Willard B. Cowles, 17 June 1947, 1–2. On the narrowing of eligibility with the transition from UNRRA to the IRO see Phil Orchard, "The Contested Origins of Internal Displacement," *International Journal of Refugee Law* 28, no. 2 (2016): 219.

92. AN IRO AJ 43/476, "Memorandum on the question of Refugees from Venezia Giulia," 11 March 1949.

93. AN IRO AJ 43/1036, P. Jacobsen to G. F. Mentz, 5 November 1948.

94. AN IRO AJ 43/1036, G. I. Mentz to W. Hallam Tuck, 5 November 1948.

95. AN IRO AJ 43/1036, Letter from M. W. Royse, Eligibility Adviser, to Chief of Mission, PCIRO, Italy, 27 May 1948.

96. AN IRO AJ 43/1053, Michael Sedmak, "Criteria and Instructions to Interviewers," 26 September 1949.

97. AN IRO AJ 43/1036, G. F. Mentz to W. Hallam Tuck, "Treatment of Refugees of Italian Customary Language," 9 June 1949.

98. AN IRO AJ 43/1038, J. H. D. Whigham, "Report on the Operations of the Eligibility Division in Italy Covering the 3 Months period September–October–November 1948," 3.

99. Ibid.

100. AN IRO AJ 43/1036, G. F. Mentz to W. Hallam Tuck, 5 November 1948.

101. One IRO document states that the IRO never ran camps for the "Italian" Venezia Giulians, although some did come through the transit center run in Trieste out of the old Casa dell'Emigrante. After an IRO area office was established in Trieste in 1950, approximately two thousand Venezia Giulians came under IRO "legal protection and care." A much smaller population (initially two hundred and then increased to five hundred) actually received "IRO assistance." In April 1950, another three thousand such DPs became eligible for IRO assistance. AN IRO AJ 43/140, "Background notes on Trieste and the Venezia-Giulian Refugee Situation," 7 October 1951.

102. ACS PCM 51–54 (Certificati di Cittadinanza), b. 509, fasc. 19.17/13659 sf. 40, "Regolamento opzioni nel territorio ceduto alla Jugoslavia," 20 February 1949. For examples of individuals whose options the Yugoslav government refused (sometimes more than once), and the reasons given, consult ASDMAE AP 1946–50, Jugoslavia, b. 61, fasc. 2, "Opzioni: Fascicoli per lettere alfabetiche."

103. UNRRA 0527-469-S-1345-0000-0116, "Displaced Persons classified as of undetermined nationality," 26 October 1946. As UNRRA was winding down operations in 1947, a memo from S. K. Jacobs noted, "The topic of displaced persons classified as of 'undetermined nationality' has been the subject of a number of cables to and from London. Originally, the Central Committee raised the question as to why there were so many displaced persons listed under 'undetermined nationality.'"

Instructions discussed the application of this label to certain categories of Jews, persons of "Ukrainian extraction who had previously lived in areas now ceded to the USSR," and Nansen passport holders, among others. See UNRRA S-0520–0179 PAG-4/1.3.1.1.0.:11, "Categories of D.P.'s Eligible for UNRRA Aid," S. K. Jacobs, "Undetermined Nationality," 3 February 1947.

104. AN IRO AJ 43/140, "Interview between Mr. R. L. Gesner, Chief Eligibility Officer, Italian Office and Mr. J. Mandel on Thursday, 10th January 1952," 5.

105. "The statistical reporting on Venezia Giulia refugees in camps or Intake Centers and the recording of their nationality on IRO forms and other documentation should uniformly be done by classifying them as: '*Undetermined Venezia Giulia.*'" AN IRO AJ 43/1036, A. A. Simpson to Camp Directors, "Classification of Venezia Giulians," 3 October 1949.

106. AN IRO AJ 43/1036, Malfatti to Mentz and Lapenna, "Assistance to Giulian Refugees," 4 April 1950.

107. AN IRO AJ 43/476, V. A. Temnomeroff, "Venezia Giulia Refugees with Italian provisional passports," 4 October 1950. This echoed the exasperation expressed in an earlier 1946 UNRRA memo: "It is also important to take cognizance of the fact that an exhaustive study of the nationality of each individual displaced person, from the legal point of view, would impose a tremendous burden on staff . . . and goes far beyond the present practical administrative possibilities. Beyond this, of course, the ultimate determination of nationality in a legal sense is not a matter for which UNRRA has either final authority or final responsibility." UNRRA 0527–469-S-1345–0000–0116, "Displaced Persons classified as of undetermined nationality," 26 October 1946, 2.

108. AN IRO AJ 43/303, To the Director-General from Giulian Refugees, IRO Camp, Carinaro d'Aversa, 31 October 1950.

109. GSAD, BMA Karpathos CPS 66, "Transactions in land," 5 May 1945.

110. AN IRO AJ 43/417, Inter-Office Memorandum, Myer Cohen to Donald Kingsley, "Refugees from the Dodecanese," 13 January 1950.

111. AN IRO AJ 43/457, Teleprinter message from Inorefug Rome to Inorefug Geneva 963, 11 October 1949.

112. Ibid.

113. AN IRO AJ 43/457, L. M. Hacking to G. G. Kullman, "Refugees from the Aegean," 14 October 1949.

114. Ibid.

115. AN IRO AJ/417, Del Drago to Chiavari, 10 December 1949.

116. AN IRO AJ/417, Cohen to Kingsley, "Refugees from the Dodecanese," 13 January 1950.

117. AN IRO AJ/417, Del Drago to Chiavari, 10 December 1949.

118. Ibid.

119. AN IRO AJ 43/417, Cohen to Kingsley, "Refugees from the Dodecanese," 13 January 1950.

120. GSAD, BMA Karpathos CPS 69, C. J. Denington, "Repatriation to Italy," 26 June 1946.

121. UNRRA S-0527, box 848, Agostino Cecchi (Swiss Legation in Athens, Foreign Interests Section) to UNRRA, Greece Mission, 7 December 1945.

122. UNRRA S-0527–0846 PAG-4/3.0.14. 0.2:4, UNRRA Subject Files 1944–1949, A. A. Sorieri to Gov. R. L. Cochran, "Agreement with Greek Government for repatriation of Greeks and Italians," 30 July 1945.

123. UNRRA S-0527–0987 PAG 4/3–0-14–3-0–8, UNRAA Subject Files 1944–1949, DP Operations (Italy) SG1 Greece, letter from N. F. Kerr, 23 July 1946.

124. GSAD, BMA Karpathos CPS 69, L. B. Webber, "Repatriation of Italians: Greek women married to Italians," 31 July 1946.

125. GSAD, BMA Karpathos CPS 69, L. B. Webber, "Repatriation Italians: Negri Virginia," 19 June 1946.

126. GSAD, BMA Karpathos CPS 69, P. A. Mason Pay, "Italian-Greek Marriages," 18 November 1946. This file contains many requests for proof of matrimony, including by Italian husbands already repatriated to Italy who wished their wives to join them.

127. Bussotti, *La cittadinanza degli italiani*, 208. For various aspects of the option process consult ASDMAE AP 1950–57, Jugoslavia, b. 533.

128. Kunz, "Nationality and Option Clauses," 628.

129. ASDMAE AP 1946–50, Jugoslavia, b. 30, fasc. 2, Consolato Generale d'Italia, "Jugoslave che desiderano raggiungere il marito residente in Italia," 22[?] October 1948; ASDMAE AP 1946–50, Albania, b. 42, "Italiani non rimpatriati dall'Albania con l'ultimo scaglione," 28 January 1950.

130. ASDMAE AP 1950–57, Albania, b. 586, G. Palutan, "Luku Abdul: Cittadinanza," 7 May 1952.

131. ASDMAE AP 1950–57, Albania, b. 586, Servizio Stranieri, "Luku Abdul: Cittadinanza," 6 October 1952.

132. ASDMAE AP 1950–57, Grecia, b. 522, Consolato Generale d'Italia, "Comunità ebraica rodiota al Congo Belga," 4 December 1947.

133. R. E. Ovalle-Bahamoń, "The Wrinkles of Decolonization and Nationness: White Angolans as Retornados in Portugal," in *Europe's Invisible Migrants*, ed. Andrea Smith (Amsterdam: Amsterdam University Press, 2003), 156.

134. Ann Stoler, "Making Empire Respectable: The Politics of Race and Sexual Morality in 20th Century Colonial Culture," *American Ethnologist* 16, no. 4 (1989): 635.

135. Charles Burdett, *Journeys through Fascism: Italian Travel Writing between the Wars* (New York: Berghahn, 2007), 134–136.

136. Cited in Giulietta Stefani, *Colonia per maschi: Italiani in Africa Orientale: una storia di genere* (Verona: Ombre Corte, 2007), 161.

137. ASDMAE ASMAI Africa, vol. 4, Fondo Statistica (1), pacco 3, b. 54, fasc. 3, "Popolaz. A.O.I. Meticci per nazioni e razza della madre e il sesso per territorio," 1 October 1938.

138. Deplano, *La madrepatria è una terra straniera*, 98.

139. Ibid., 115–117.

140. For details on this see ibid., 117–118. According to a publication of the Italian Consulate in Asmara, however, the British had permitted notaries to put down the name of Italian fathers of mixed-race children, in effect allowing them to be recognized. See Gino Cerbella, *Eritrea 1959: La Collettività Italiana nelle sue attività economiche sociali e culturali* (Asmara: Consolato Generale d'Italia, 1960), 9–10.

141. D'Agostino, *Altre storie*, 67–68; for the entire testimony, 55–68.

142. Barrera, "Patrilinearity, Race, and Identity," 105–106.

143. D'Agostino, *Altre storie*, 75, 69–78. On the phenomenon from the 1970s on of Italo-Eritrean meticci with legal recognition "selling" their name to Eritreans desperate to obtain Italian citizenship refer to Valentina Fusari, "Mobilità umana e acquisizione della cittadinanza italiana nel caso degli italo-eritrei," in *La fine del colonialismo italiano*, ed. Antonio Morone (Florence: Le Monnier, 2019), 239–240.

144. D'Agostino, *Altre storie*, 64.

145. Within this federation, Eritrea was to exercise autonomy. In reality, however, Ethiopian leaders treated the federation as a full union. In 1962, Eritrea became merely another province within Ethiopia. After decades of violent resistance to Eritrea's absorption into Ethiopia, Eritrea achieved independence in 1993.

146. On the recognitions see ASDMAE AP 1950–57, Etiopia, b. 102, "Collettività italiana in Etiopia," Smergani, 16 March 1955, 8. On citizenship and the "option" see ASDMAE AP 1950–57, Eritrea, b. 878, "'Opzioni' degli italo-eritrei," 22 March 1953; also Consolato Generale d'Italia, Asmara, "Meticci eritrei di cittadinanza italiana. Rinuncia alla cittadinanza federale," 8 June 1953. See also the many documents on the Ethiopian and Eritrean laws of citizenship contained in ASDMAE AP 1950–57, Eritrea, b. 801. Because Italian documents sometimes refer to Eritrea alone or to Ethiopia as presumably including Eritrea, it can prove confusing to parse out whether population figures refer to the entire federation or just one of its entities.

147. ASDMAE AP 1950–57, Eritrea, b. 878, "Meticci eritrei di nazionalità italiana. Rinuncia alla cittadinanza federale," 10 March 1953.

148. See Giulia Barrera, "Colonial Affairs: Italian Men, Eritrean Women, and the Construction of Racial Hierarchies in Colonial Eritrea (1885–1941)" (PhD diss., Northwestern University, 2002), 21–22. Also Barrera, "Patrilinearity, Race, and Identity," 103.

149. ASDMAE AP 1950–57, Eritrea, b. 878, "Rifiuto visti per l'Etiopia ad Italiani," 9 October 1953. The issue of entry permits for Italians had also troubled relations between the Italian government and the BMA in Eritrea but had apparently been resolved in 1951–1952. See ASDMAE AP 1950–57, Eritrea, b. 801, "Autorizzazioni per l'entrata in Eritrea di Italiani," 20 October 1951; Frank Stafford to Capomazza, 15 May 1952.

150. ASDMAE AP 1950–57, Eritrea, b. 878, "Meticci eritrei di nazionalità italiana. Rinuncia alla cittadinanza federale," 10 March 1953.

151. Silvana Patriarca, "Fear of Small Numbers: 'Brown Babies' in Postwar Italy," *Contemporanea* 4 (2015): 537–568.

152. On the biracial children in Italy (often referred to as "mulattoes") and for analyses of these two films turn to Patriarca, "Fear of Small Numbers," 552–554. On the constitution of meticci as a postwar problem refer to Deplano, *La madrepatria è una terra straniera*, 111–114, 120. On the CRI of Eritrea and "colonie estive" see ASDMAE AP 1950–57, Eritrea, b. 801, "Croce Rossa Italiana in Eritrea," 21 September 1951.

153. ASDMAE AP 1950–57, Etiopia, b. 102, "Collettività italiana in Etiopia," Smergani, 16 March 1955, 5.

154. ASDMAE AP 1950–57, Etiopia, b. 102, "Collettività italiana in Etiopia," Smergani, 16 March 1955, 5.

155. Vittorio Longhi, "Eritrea, due generazioni di 'meticci' con sangue italiano senza riconoscimento di paternità," *L'Espresso*, 22 April 2014. On the discussions of the 1990s go to Deplano, *La madrepatria è una terra straniera*, 124–125. On debates

over and obstacles to Italian citizenship in contemporary Eritrea see Valentina Fusari, "La cittadinanza come lascito coloniale: Gli italoeritrei," *Altreitalie* 57 (2018): 34–51.

156. Gianni Mari, "Le tristi conseguenze della politica italiana coloniale e post-coloniale: Intervista a Gianni Mari, presidente dell'ANCIS, Associazione Nazionale Comunità Italo-Somala, con Barbara Faedda," http://www.diritto.it./articoli/antropologia/faedda16.html, 2001, 8.

157. Gianni Mari, interview with the author, 11 May 2011; Francesca Caferri, "I bimbi italiani strappati alla Somalia," *La Repubblica*, 17 June 2008.

158. Guido Tintori, "Italian mobilities and the Demos," in *Italian Mobilities*, ed. Ruth Ben-Ghiat and Stephanie Malia Hom (New York: Routledge, 2016), 119–123.

5. Reclaiming Fascism, Housing the Nation

1. To offer just one example, a headline in *Vergogna* (the journal of FeNPIA, Federazione Nazionale dei Profughi Italiani d'Africa) trumpeted, "According to the bully Senator Conti, 'We are the residue of a nationalist mentality lodged in the past.'" *Vergogna* 3 (20 November 1949).

2. Ruth Ben-Ghiat, *Fascist Modernities: Italy, 1922–1945* (Berkeley: University of California Press, 2001), 4.

3. Ann Stoler, "Imperial Debris: Reflections on Ruins and Ruination," *Cultural Anthropology* 23, no. 2 (2008): 197.

4. Noa Steimatsky, *Italian Locations: Reinhabiting the Past in Postwar Cinema* (Minneapolis: University of Minnesota Press, 2008), 48. See also N. Steimatsky, "The Cinecittà Refugee Camp (1944–1950)," *October* 128 (2009): 23–50.

5. Steimatsky, "Cinecittà Refugee Camp," 29.

6. Ibid., 50. See also the film by Marco Bertozzi and Noa Steimatsky, *Profughi a Cinecittà* (Rome: Istituto Luce, 2012).

7. A 1957 memo to INPS president Angelo Corsi diagnosed a "true and proper 'psychosis'" of exodus from the farms of Tripolitania. See AS INPS, Carte della colonizzazione libica, 1933–1968, b. 130, fasc. 515, Raccomandata, 15 February 1957. Other observers, including colonial expert Armando Maugini, feared the effects of mass repatriations. "Such a repatriation," he mused, "would give rise to political speculation; the colonists would find defenders in the unions and political realms and could easily fall prey to subversive propaganda." AS INPS, Carte della colonizzazione libica, 1933–1968, b. 62, fasc. 259, A. Maugini, "Relazione sulla colonizzazione contadina della Tripolitania," May 1953, 17.

8. Giovanni Spagnolli, "Il problema della casa e l'opera di recupero sociale dell'UNRRA-CASAS," *Assistenza d'oggi* 4, no. 3 (June 1953): 7–8.

9. Paola Bonifazio, *Schooling in Modernity: The Politics of Sponsored Films in Postwar Italy* (Toronto: University of Toronto Press, 2014), 246 fn. 9. On financing see also ACS MI AAI Presidenza, b. 89, fasc. 2, Lodovico Montini to Oscar Sinigaglia, 19 July 1951. On INA-CASA see Paola Di Biagi, ed., *La grande ricostruzione: Il piano Ina-Casa e l'Italia degli anni cinquanta* (Rome: Donzelli, 2010).

10. UNRRA-CASAS, *Realizzazioni edilizie per gli esuli adriatici* (Rome: UNRRA-CASAS, 1957), 17. On complaints in 1950–1951 by the Opera per l'Assistenza ai Profughi Giuliani e Dalmati that the housing units promised by UNRRA-CASAS for

esuli had been reduced see the testy exchanges between Lodovico Montini of the AAI, various other officials, and Oscar Sinigaglia contained in ACS MI AAI Presidenza, b. 89, fasc. 2.

11. Spagnolli, "Il problema della casa e l'opera di recupero sociale dell'UNRRA-CASAS," 22–23.

12. Paolo Scrivano, "Signs of Americanization in Italian Domestic Life: Italy's Postwar Conversion to Consumerism," *Journal of Contemporary History* 40, no. 2 (2005): 322.

13. On new notions of citizenship and the impact of American ideas see Scrivano, "Signs of Americanization in Italian Domestic Life," 323–324. For the program of ERP-CASE turn to the publication by Gli Stati Uniti d'America per la Ricostruzione Europea, *Ad ogni famiglia la sua casa* (Rome: SET Apollon, n.d.) contained in ACS MI AAI Presidenza, b. 89, fasc. 2.

14. Olivetti remains best known for his experiment in transforming the town of Ivrea (the headquarters of his typewriter company) into an urban utopia. Olivetti outlined his vision in his *Città dell'uomo* (Milan: Edizioni di comunità, 1960). For details on the Council of European Municipalities formed in 1951 and which conceived of an internationalism at a very different scale from that associated with the UN and other intergovernmental bodies see Oscar Gaspari, "Cities against States? Hopes, Dreams and Shortcomings of the European Municipal Movement, 1900–1960," *Contemporary European History* 11, no. 4 (2002): 597–621.

15. Paul Betts and David Crowley, introduction to *Journal of Contemporary History* 40, no. 2 (2005): 214, 215.

16. For a summary of Italy's efforts to cope with housing shortages in the first decade and a half after the war see Paul F. Wendt, "Post World War II Housing Policies in Italy," *Land Economics* 38, no. 2 (1962), 113–133.

17. David Maraniss, *Rome 1960: The Olympics That Changed the World* (New York: Simon & Schuster, 2008), 71.

18. T. Corey Brennan, "The 1960 Rome Olympics: Spaces and Spectacle," in *Rethinking Matters Olympic: Investigations into the Socio-Cultural Study of the Modern Olympic Movement*, ed. Robert Knight Barney, Janice Evelyn Forsyth, and Michael K. Heine (London, ON: University of Western Ontario, 2010), 26.

19. Karen Pinkus, "Empty Spaces: Decolonization in Italy," in *A Place in the Sun: Africa in Italian Colonial Culture from Post-Unification to the Present*, ed. Patrizia Palumbo (Berkeley: University of California Press, 2003), 300.

20. Mia Fuller, "Wherever You Go, There You Are: Fascist Plans for the Colonial City of Addis Ababa and the Colonizing Suburb of EUR '42," *Journal of Contemporary History* 31, no. 2 (1996): 397.

21. The Villaggio Giuliano Dalmata was the only sizable OAPGD project built for Adriatic national refugees outside the Italo-Yugoslav border region. The OAPGD instead concentrated its housing in the area around Trieste: Chiarbola-Trieste, Opicina, S. Croce, Sistiana, Prosecco, Muggia, Servola, Monfalcone, Gorizia, and Udine. UNRRA-CASAS, *Realizzazioni edilizie per gli esuli adriatici*, 39–97.

22. Giuliano Gresleri, "Ordine e destino della città fondata," in *Città di fondazione e plantatio ecclesiae*, ed. Pasquale Culotta, Giuliano Gresleri, and Glauco Gresleri (Bologna: Editrice Compositori, 2007), 14–43. A 1923 law on *bonifica integrale* went beyond earlier legislation on reclamation, introducing not just the requirement to

clean up unhealthy marsh areas but also render them productive for both agriculture and human habitation. The Serpieri law passed the following year. The 1928 Legge Mussolini provided extensive funding for *bonifica*, and the following year a new agricultural ministry came into existence. Turn to Federico Caprotti, *Mussolini's Cities: Internal Colonialism in Italy, 1930–1939* (Amherst, NY: Cambria, 2007), 83. For details on Serpieri's role in shaping fascist agricultural policies refer to Fabrizio Marasti, *Il fascismo rurale: Arrigo Serpieri e la bonifica integrale* (Rome: Edizioni settimo sigillo, 2001). Refer also to Dario Gaggio, *The Shaping of Tuscany: Landscape and Society between Tradition and Modernity* (Cambridge: Cambridge University Press, 2017), 27–29.

23. Caprotti, *Mussolini's Cities*. For a study of these intertwined processes of internal and external colonization go to Roberta Pergher, *Mussolini's Nation-Empire: Sovereignty and Settlement in Italy's Borderlands, 1922–1943* (Cambridge: Cambridge University Press, 2017).

24. Lucio Caracciolo, "Presentazione," in Antonio Pennacchi, *Fascio e martello* (Rome-Bari: Laterza, 2008), x.

25. On this broader cultural turn refer to Roger Griffin, "The Reclamation of Fascist Culture," *European History Quarterly* 31, no. 4 (2001): 609–620. For examples of studies of fascist new towns that focus on plans and/or planners, as opposed to their residents, see Pasquale Culotta, Giuliano Gresleri, and Glauco Gresleri, eds., *Città di fondazione e plantatio ecclesiae* (Bologna: Editrice Compositori, 2007); Carlo Cresti, Benedetto Gravagnuolo, and Francesco Gurrieri, eds., *Architettura e città negli anni del fascismo in Italia e nelle colonie* (Florence: Angelo Pontecorboli Editore, 2005). Similar approaches characterize studies of specific towns, like those in Sardinia: Giorgio Peghin and Antonella Sanna, *Carbonia: Città del Novecento* (Milan: Skira, 2009); Eugenio Cocco, *Fertilia* (Albano Laziale: Associazione Culturale Novecento, 2007).

26. Suzanne Stewart-Steinberg, "Grounds for Reclamation: Fascism and Postfascism in the Pontine Marshes," *differences* 27, no. 1 (2016): 109–110. For another example of an approach that reads these spaces in utopian terms turn to Charles Burdett, "Journeys to the Other Spaces of Fascist Italy," *Modern Italy* 5, no. 1 (2000): 7–23.

27. Mia Fuller, "Tradition as a Means to the End of Tradition: Farmers' Houses in Italy's Fascist-Era New Towns," in *The End of Tradition?*, ed. Nezar AlSayyad (London: Routledge, 2004), 171–186; Joshua Samuels, "Of Other Scapes: Archaeology, Landscape, and Heterotopia in Fascist Sicily," *Archaeologies: Journal of the World Archaeological Congress* 6, no. 1 (2010): 62–81.

28. Frank Biess, introduction to *Histories of the Aftermath: The Legacies of the Second World War in Europe*, ed. Frank Biess and Robert G. Moeller (New York: Berghahn, 2010), 3.

29. Pennacchi, *Fascio e martello*, 287–297. For his discussion of the contested definition of a new town versus a settlement (*borgo*), 276–286.

30. Sandi Volk, *Esuli a Trieste: Bonifica nazionale e rafforzamento dell'italianità sul confine orientale* (Udine: Kappa Vu, 2004), 101–106.

31. Though the OAPGD eventually became the Opera per l'Assistenza ai Profughi Giuliani Dalmati e Rimpatriati, including in its remit repatriates from other former possessions, it remains best known for its work with Adriatic displacees (particularly its census of refugees). Sandi Volk notes that in 1948 the Associazione nazionale

profughi dalla Libia encompassed 127 provincial committees and proposed the creation of an assistance entity for refugees from Africa, the Opera per l'assistenza ai profughi d'Africa, modeled on the OAPGD. This was never realized. Volk, *Esuli a Trieste: Bonifica nazionale e rafforzamento dell'italianità sul confine orientale* (Udine: Kappa Vu, 2004), 87 fn. 60.

32. Ibid., 298–312.

33. Ibid., 299.

34. Enrico Valsecchi, *Da Alghero a Fertilia* (Alghero: Rotary Club, 2016), 124. In trying to resettle its former colonists from Libya, for example, the INPS contacted the entity involved in reclamation of the once malarial and sparsely populated Maremma region (in Tuscany). On this, AS INPS, Carte della colonizzazione libica, 1933–1968, b. 64, fasc. 269, "Disponibilità coloni ex residenti in Libia per Enti di colonizzazione in Italia," 8 November 1954; fasc. 271, "Contatti con l'Ente Maremma per il riperimento di terreni per le famiglie coloniche rimpatriande dalla Libia," 15 October 1956. The departure of peasant sharecroppers for cities in places like Tuscany also created spaces for repatriates, especially those from Libya and Tunisia, welcomed for their presumed political conservatism in contrast to restive Tuscan peasants who voted for leftist parties. On this, turn to Gaggio, *Shaping of Tuscany*, 141, 146–147.

35. Ufficio Propaganda della S.A.C.I.D.A., ed., *Gebelia: Il miracolo del Gebel cirenaico rinnovato da settecento profughi d'Africa in una boscaglia alle porte di Roma* (Rome: Tip. A. Tambone, 1955), 20.

36. Here we see another example of the entwined processes of internal and external colonialism, as the INFPS also oversaw and administered ten villages created ex novo for Italian settlers in Tripolitania, Libya. More directly, the governor of Libya (and former *ras* or boss of Ferrara) Italo Balbo promoted the EFC and became the major shareholder of a canning factory intended to handle agricultural products from the reclaimed Nurra territory. The reclamation of the Nurra built on the earlier efforts undertaken to drain the area around Calik interrupted by Italy's entry into World War I. The French government sent representatives to visit the Nurra project, expressing interest in using this as a model for its own colonies. Valsecchi, *Da Alghero a Fertilia*, 49–55, 64.

37. This stood for the architects' names: Petrucci, Paolini (the 2 Ps), Silenzi, and Tufaroli. For a detailed discussion of these architectural plans see Cocco, *Fertilia*, 13, 37.

38. On the life of the colonists from Ferrara and their experience of the Allied bombings see the testimony of Agnese Cecconello contained in State School Alghero 2 & Fertilia, *Ischida: The History within the Stories* (Alghero: La Poligrafica Peana, 2007), 76–78.

39. Cited in Marina Nardozzi, ed., *Ricordi di Fertilia, 1947–1997* (Comitato Provinciale di Sassari dell'ANVGD, 1997), 10. For a more prosaic account of the commission's visit and its findings see UZC 5, PCM Sezione II (b. 26, vol. 1) Profughi 53/1, "Relazione della commissione tecnica istriana sulla possibilità immediata di sistemare parte della popolazione istriana in Sardegna."

40. State School Alghero 2 & Fertilia, *Ischida*, 82–83. For details of the commission sent to Sardinia to evaluate both Fertilia and Castiadas (a former penal colony) refer to UZC 5, PCM Sezione II (b. 26, vol. 1), Profughi 53/1, "Sardegna. Fertilia e

Castiadas. Sopraluogo di una commissione tecnica istriana per esaminare la possibilità di sistemare parte della popolazione istriana in Sardegna."

41. Cited in State School Alghero 2 & Fertilia, *Ischida*, 85. Compare Dapiran's description to the strikingly similar one in Gino Rovesti's 1936 Luce documentary, *Fertilia di Sardegna*: "The picture is that of the most authentic desolation: very few inhabitants and all of them cowherds or shepherds, the only activities the region affords. All around, in that inertia that corrodes the spirits, in that monotonous passage of time that saps any energy, the only companions men have are the vast stretches of wild palm groves and marshes with their noxious vapors." Cited in Silvio Carta, "Sardinia in Fascist Documentary Films (1922–1945)," *Journal of Italian Cinema and Media Studies* 1, no. 2 (2013): 181.

42. A memo from Fausto Cella noted that in 1946 in his capacity as mayor of Alghero he had drawn up a proposal for Fertilia to accommodate those in Alghero who had lost their homes in the war. He worried about the delays in drawing up a new plan, given that refugees had already arrived in Alghero. UZC 5, PCM Sezione II (b. 26, vol. 1), Profughi 53 / 1, "Sistemazione della Borgata di Fertilia per ricoverarvi i profughi Istriani," 9 February 1947. A note sent in March 1947 to Giovanni Carignani, a member of the Constituent Assembly, also mentions refugees from Pola who had made their way to Alghero "to this point completely on their own initiative." UZC 5, PCM Sezione II (b. 26, vol. 1), Profughi 53 / 1, Letter to Carignani, 18 March 1947. There did exist an association formed by and for such refugees in Alghero, which apparently was in contact with prospective and newly arrived settlers in Sardinia. Letter from Francesco Chieffi to Cappa, 24 February 1947. On the temporary housing of refugees from Pola at the airport, "Profughi giuliani," 11 February 1947. On the refugees sent by the CLN refer to Valsecchi, *Da Alghero a Fertilia*, 125–126; also Marialuisa Manfredini Gasparetto, "Aspetti geografici dello sviluppo di Fertilia," *L'Universo* 42, no. 3 (1962): 406.

43. Valsecchi, *Da Alghero a Fertilia*, 94–95. See also UZC 5, PCM Sezione II (b. 30), Profughi 53 / 6, Dapiran, "Breve relazione sulla borgata di Fertilia circa la possibilità di sistemarvi pel momento 120 famiglie di pescatori Giuliani," 22 November 1947. UNRRA also provided the first refugee families with clothing, linens, and bedding. On this, UZC 5, PCM Sezione II (b. 26, vol. 1), Profughi 53 / 1, "Interrogazione On. Corsi" and "Risposta all'Interrogazione dell'On. Corsi," 18 November 1947. The local UNRRA committee initially sponsored the running of the day nursery and offered the children there snacks. See also "Situazione profughi giuliani in Fertilia," 12 November 1947; also the letters from Salvatore of 19 July 1947 and 10 November 1947. Another "new town" that became home to many Italian refugees from the eastern Adriatic was Latina (formerly Littoria). For details go to Angelo Francesco Orsini, *L'esodo a Latina: La storia dimenticata dei Giuliano-Dalmati* (Rome: Aracne, 2007).

44. For details consult Frank Snowden, "Latina Province, 1944–1950," *Journal of Contemporary History* 43, no. 3 (2008): 509–526. On Sardinia specifically, go to Marcus Hall, "Today Sardinia, Tomorrow the World: Malaria, the Rockefeller Foundation, and Mosquito Eradication," *Bardpolitik* 5 (2004): 21–28; Eugenia Tognotti, "Program to Eradicate Malaria in Sardinia, 1946–1950," *Emerging Infectious Diseases* 15, no. 9 (2009): 1460–1466.

45. UZC 5, PCM Sezione II (b. 26, vol. 1), Profughi 53/1, "Relazione della commissione tecnica istriana sulla possibilità immediata di sistemare parte della popolazione istriana in Sardegna," 10 December 1946, 2. A 1947 memo likewise cautioned that the Ente Sardo di Colonizazzione had determined that the "bonifica of Fertilia did not offer the possibilities for a definitive settlement of families of agricultural workers but only their provisional housing until they could be sent on to Castiadas. Instead, in Fertilia there can be settled permanently a certain number of fishermen." "Sistemazione famiglie istriane," 25 March 1947.

46. Enrico Moretti, "Giuliani in Sardegna / Fertilia dei Giuliani," 1949, Archivio Storico Istituto Luce D034807, http://www.archivioluce.com/archivio/ (accessed 4 June 2015). This Luce film is heir to a tradition of documentaries about Sardinia made under fascism, the most significant of which, "*Mussolini di Sardegna* [1933], *Carbonia* [1941], and *Fertilia* [1942] address the themes of progress of the agrarian civilization and the urban spaces of the *città di fondazione*." Silvio Carta, "Documentary Film, Observational Style and Postmodern Anthropology in Sardinia," *Visual Anthropology* 28, no. 3 (2015): 228–229.

47. UZC 5, PCM Sezione II (b. 26, vol. 1), Profughi 53/1, "Trasferimento profughi giuliani residenti a Fertilia in Continente," 17 July 1947.

48. Interview with Lidia M., 4 June 2012. See also UZC 5, PCM Sezione II (b. 29), Profughi 53/5, "Partenza di profughi giuliani," 7 January 1950. Refer as well to Biblioteca dell'Associazione E.GI.S., Ente Giuliano di Sardegna, "Don Francesco Dapiran," Fertilia, Sardinia, Documenti vari (E.GI.S.), "Rientrate in Continente."

49. State School Alghero 2 & Fertilia, *Ischida*, 94. A 1974 article on Fertilia also noted that the common practice in Sardinia of dynamite fishing had "impoverished" the seas. This description seems at odds with the testimony of Massarotto and other refugees about the plenitude of the waters off Fertilia, though it may reflect changes over the intervening decades. See Gasparetto, "Aspetti geografici dello sviluppo di Fertilia," 409–10 fn. 8.

50. UZC 5, PCM Sezione II (b. 30), Profughi 53/6, "Bilucaglia Sergio—Esposto," 23 April 1952. For the complaints of the refugees themselves refer to "Appunto," 22 August 1951. A counter-version of events defending the actions of the Unione and, in particular, its founder Sergio Bilucaglia can be found at "Promemoria," 27 August 1951. For Andreotti's official denunciation of the Unione, Andreotti, "Unione Pescatori Giuliani, x Venezia," 11 March 1953.

51. UZC 5, PCM Sezione II (b. 29), Profughi 53/5, EGAS Comitato Esecutivo, 14 October 1948. For the more positive position on EGAS's accomplishments go to Valsecchi, *Da Alghero a Fertilia*, 149–155. Marina Pinna and Marina Nardozzi, *Orfeo: The Archives of the Memory of the Exiles from Istria, Fiume and Dalmazia* (Alghero: La Poligrafica Peana, 2007), 32–40, offer a critical account.

52. UZC 5, PCM Sezione II (b. 29), Profughi 53/5, "Appello degli esuli giuliani e dalmati di Fertilia," 20 April 1958.

53. Dario Manni, interview with the author, 23 June 2013, Fertilia.

54. Dario Manni, interview with the author, 22 June 2013, Fertilia. The figures Manni provided me differ from those found in a 1958 document, which lists 54 refugees in accommodations provided by UNRRA-CASAS and another 139 non-refugees in such housing. It proves difficult to determine from that document whether those numbers map onto actual housing units or merely indicate the number of residents

of those units. Biblioteca dell'Associazione E.GI.S., "Don Francesco Dapiran," Fertilia, Sardinia, Documenti vari (E.GI.S.), Posta in arrivo, "Relazione," 1958.

55. Gasparetto, "Aspetti geografici dello sviluppo di Fertilia," 418. The Ente di Trasformazione Fondiaria della Sardegna made available five hundred hectares in the area of Lazzaretto. UZC 5, PCM Sezione II (b. 29), Profughi 53/5, "Relazione sulla colonia profughi giuliani di Fertilia: Situazione dell'Ente giuliano al 30 settembre 1952," 18 October 1952, 2.

56. Istrian Maria Anna Santin described similar disapproval on the part of southern Italians when she and her fellow *esuli* in the camp of Altamura forwent stockings or, even more scandalous, donned pants. Anna Gervasio, "Il Centro Raccolta Profughi di Altamura," in *La Puglia dell'Accoglienza: Profughi, rifugiati e rimpatriati nel Novecento*, ed. Vito Antonio Leuzzi and Giulio Esposito (Bari: Progedit, 2006), 212–213.

57. Lodovico Montini, "The Parliamentary Inquiry into Destitution in Italy," *International Labour Review* 71, no. 1 (1955): 72.

58. Bodleian Library, Special Collections, Oxford, UK; Papers of the United Nations Career Records Project; Papers of John Alexander-Sinclair, Ms.Eng.C 4658, folios 186–362.

59. Lodovico Montini, *Giorno per giorno tra i protagonisti di un'epoca 1944/1970: Scritti e appunti di Lodovico Montini*, ed. Giorgio Mingoni and Claudio Del Vico (Florence: Fallecchi Editore, 1971), 21–22; see also 19–26.

60. Eileen Egan, *Catholic Relief Services: The Beginning Years; For the Life of the World* (New York: Catholic Relief Services, 1988), 126.

61. Ibid. Without a doubt, many Italians—whether refugees or not—continued to emigrate abroad in search of work during the early postwar period. On the clandestine movements of Italians within Europe, especially to France, refer to Sandro Rinauro, *Il cammino della speranza: L'emigrazione clandestina degli italiani nel secondo dopoguerra* (Turin: Einaudi, 2009). In part to curb such movements and protect its migrants, in the 1950s and 1960s the Italian government pushed for the right of free movement of laborers within the emerging European Community. For details, see Giuliana Laschi, "L'Europa comunitaria e le migrazioni: Elementi di rottura e continuità, dal secondo dopoguerra ai nostri giorni," in *Europa in movimento: Mobilità e migrazioni tra integrazione europea e decolonizzazione, 1945–1992*, ed. Giuliana Laschi, Valeria Deplano, and Alessandro Pes (Bologna: Mulino, 2017), 23–70.

62. Montini, "Parliamentary Inquiry into Destitution," 69.

63. Pandolfi cited in Nicola Mai, "The Cultural Construction of Italy in Albania and Vice Versa: Migration Dynamics, Strategies of Resistance and Politics of Mutual Self-Definition across Colonialism and Post-colonialism," *Modern Italy* 8, no. 1 (2003): 84. Caponetto similarly argues, "Colonialism seemed to offer a way of bridging the gap between the North and the South by means of the larger contrast between Italians and Africans; the Italy/Africa and North/South dichotomies were appropriated, as the real Africa provided a stronger point of contrast in post-unified Italian society." Rosetta Giuliani Caponetto, *Fascist Hybridities: Representations of Racial Mixing and Diaspora Cultures under Mussolini* (New York: Palgrave Macmillan, 2015), 2. For the role played by Sardinians in colonization projects in Africa refer to Valeria Deplano, ed., *Sardegna d'Oltremare: L'emigrazione coloniale tra esperienza e memoria* (Rome: Donzelli, 2017).

64. Bonifazio, *Schooling in Modernity*, 137.

65. Ibid., 139–140.

66. Spagnolli, "Il problema della casa e l'opera di recupero sociale dell'UNRRA-CASAS," 20.

67. Tracey Heatherington, *Wild Sardinia: Indigeneity and the Global Dreamtimes of Environmentalism* (Seattle: University of Washington Press, 2010). Most of the documentaries on Sardinia made in the 1950s by mainland and foreign directors (including the Disney short, *Sardinia*) replicated tropes of Sardinian backwardness and failed to offer Sards themselves any voice. Carta, "Documentary Film," 229–230.

68. Gaggio, *Shaping of Tuscany*, 172. In the early postwar period, Sardinian shepherds had begun to migrate to mainland Italy, creating yet more "empty spaces" to be filled on the island. They often went to the same desolate spaces targeted for resettlement by colonial repatriates, such as the Tuscan Maremma. The linkage in the popular imagination of these shepherds with banditry, kidnapping, and arson made them particularly unpopular migrants with local Tuscans. See Gaggio, 176–193.

69. Bodleian, Papers of John Alexander-Sinclair, Ms.Eng.C 4658, folios 186–362, E. A. Bayne, "Everybody here is for Sardinia," 25 July 1955, 2.

70. Bodleian, Papers of John Alexander-Sinclair, Ms. Eng.C. 4657, folios 1–179; Alexander-Sinclair to Mr. Wynham-White, 24 April 1953. Those working with international refugees in Italy also worried about the Italian police's use of the "compulsory movement order" to confine so-called undesirable refugees to what amounted to internment camps. Ms.Eng.C 4658, John Alexander-Sinclair to James Read, 22 March 1955.

71. Bodleian, Papers of John Alexander-Sinclair, Ms.Eng.C 4658, folios 186–362, letter to George Warren, 24 February 1953.

72. Bodleian, Papers of John Alexander-Sinclair, Ms.Eng.C 4658, folios 186–362, Alexander-Sinclair to James Read, 22 March 1955.

73. UZC 5, PCM Sezione II (b. 26, vol. 1), Profughi 53/1, "Sardegna. Fertilia e Castiadas. Sopraluogo di una commissione tecnica istriana per esaminare la possibilità di sistemare parte della popolazione istriana in Sardegna." For Corsi's specific proposal to create resettlement areas for INPS colonists in Sardinia refer to AS INPS, Carte della colonizzazione libica, 1933–1968, b. 130, fasc. 515, "Sistemazione in Italia dei coloni della Libia," 16 February 1957, 4.

74. Bodleian, Papers of John Alexander-Sinclair, Ms.Eng.C 4658, folios 186–362, Alexander-Sinclair to J. Colmar, 21 June 1954.

75. Bodleian, Papers of Alexander-Sinclair, Ms.Eng.C 4659, folios 1–190, Alexander-Sinclair to Benvenuti, 15 April 1958.

76. Bodleian, Papers of Alexander-Sinclair, Ms.Eng.C 4658, folios 186–362, Alexander-Sinclair to Paolo Canali, 30 March 1957. Alexander-Sinclair suggested that "the Sardinia scheme would provide a very useful outlet for some of your [Italian] refugees from Egypt."

77. Bodleian, Papers of Alexander-Sinclair, Ms.Eng.C 4659, folios 1–190; Council for Europe Consultative Assembly, "Motion for a Resolution presented by M. de la Vallée Poussin and a number of his colleagues," 28 April 1958.

78. Bodleian, Papers of John Alexander-Sinclair, Ms.Eng.C 4658, folios 186–362, "A note on the possible application of M. Schneiter's plan submitted to the Council of Europe as Doc. 331 of 10.2.55," 6 November 1955, 3.

79. Bodleian, Papers of John Alexander-Sinclair, Ms.Eng.C 4659, folios 1–190, Egon Glesinger to Frank Kerr, 8 January 1958.

80. Bodleian Library, Papers of John Alexander-Sinclair, Ms.Eng.C 4658, folios 186–362, Memo to A.B.D., 20 May 1957. Segni believed the project should focus more on industrial, rather than agricultural, development.

81. Bodleian, Papers of Alexander-Sinclair, Ms.Eng.C 4659, folios 1–190, Alexander-Sinclair to Anna Matson, "Sardinia Project," 14 January 1958.

82. Bodleian, Papers of Alexander-Sinclair, Ms.Eng.C 4658, folios 186–362, International Rescue Committee [author's name illegible] to Alexander-Sinclair, 5 September 1957.

83. Bodleian, Papers of Alexander-Sinclair, Ms.Eng.C 4659, folios 1–190, letter to Migone, 8 July 1958. By this point, Migone had assumed the position of Italian ambassador to the Holy See.

84. Bodleian, Papers of Alexander-Sinclair, Ms.Eng.C 4659, folios 1–190, Alexander-Sinclair to Vassallo, 8 September 1958. The actual note sent by Alexander-Sinclair, on which he also hand wrote, "This makes me very sad. Triste," can be found in the files of ACS MI AAI Segr. Presidenza, b. 84. This file also contains a copy of the proposed Sardinia project.

85. Bodleian, Papers of Alexander-Sinclair, Ms.Eng.C 4659, folios 1–190, letter to Migone, 31 October 1958. See also the confidential letter of Alexander-Sinclair to Benvenuti at the Council of Europe of 8 September 1958 contained in the same file.

86. See ACS AAI Seg. Presidenza, b. 84, Benvenuti to Montini, 12 July 1958; Montini to Benvenuti, 31 July 1958.

87. The only aspect that appealed to Pescatori was the provision that were this Sardinia plan put into place, it would not house Yugoslav refugees and that other European countries would be required to step up and take Yugoslav migrants in Italy (arriving, according to Pescatori, at a rate of approximately one thousand persons each month). ACS AAI Seg. Presidenza, b. 84, Pescatori, "Appunto," 20 June 1958.

88. ACS AAI Seg. Presidenza, b. 84, Vassallo to Montini, 17 July 1958.

89. This did not stop Alexander-Sinclair from vaunting his experience on the Sardinia project and realizing his ambitions of simultaneous resettlement and development schemes elsewhere, in this case on a UN mission to Iran. This actually resulted in the downsizing of workers in the Iranian oil industry. For details, Eva-Maria Muschik, "'A Pretty Kettle of Fish': United Nations Assistance and the Mass Dismissal of Labor in the Iranian Oil Industry, 1959–1960," *Labor History* 60, no. 1 (2019): 8–23.

90. In a letter to Alexander-Sinclair, Auguste Lindt of the UNHCR commented, "As you know, there is a record in Sardinia of some successful small and medium-scaled projects of a similar nature to yours. I will cite only the Don Murray project as an example of a new small one." Bodleian, Papers of Alexander-Sinclair, Ms.Eng.C 4659, folios 1–190, Lindt to Alexander-Sinclair, n.d. Alexander-Sinclair's papers also include copies of HELP publications and an invitation to HELP's inauguration. Paulson to Alexander-Sinclair, 18 July 1958.

91. ACS AAI Seg. Presidenza, b. 84, Pescatori, "Appunto," 20 June 1958.

92. Belden Paulson, *Odyssey of a Practical Visionary* (Plymouth, WI: Thistlefield Books, 2009), 101.

93. Ibid., 121.

94. Cited ibid., 141. Paulson later promoted HELP as a model for refugees in the Middle East, particularly Palestinians displaced by the Six Day War.

95. Bodleian Library, Papers of John Alexander-Sinclair, Ms.Eng.C 4658, folios 186–362, letter to James Head, 22 March 1955.

96. Paulson, *Odyssey of a Practical Visionary*, 121.

97. Cited ibid., 140.

98. Interview with widows and children of HELP refugees, Simaxis, Italy, 30 June 2015.

99. Bodleian, Papers of John Alexander-Sinclair, Ms.Eng.C 4659, Paulson, "Refugee Attitudes," 7.

100. Ibid., 9–10.

101. Bodleian, Papers of John Alexander-Sinclair, Ms.Eng.C 4659, folios 1–190, Alexander-Sinclair to Migone, 20 June 1958.

102. Bodleian, Papers of John Alexander-Sinclair, Ms.Eng.C 4659, folios 1–190, C. Balmelli to John Alexander [Sinclair], 20 January 1958. In a slightly different vein, both Belden and Lisa Paulson also described their work in Sardinia as that of "pioneers," pointing to how such a metaphor operated on numerous levels and cultural registers. See Paulson, *Odyssey of a Practical Visionary*, 99–100.

103. Ufficio Propaganda della S.A.C.I.D.A., *Gebelia*, 2–3.

104. Ibid., 3.

105. Ibid.

106. For more details on the Italian cooperative movement, which predated fascism but really took off after 1945, see the materials of the Italian Documentation Centre on Cooperatives and Social Economy at http://www.cooperazione.net/eng/pagina.asp?pid=383&uid=361 (accessed 28 May 2015).

107. Bodleian, Papers of John Alexander-Sinclair, Ms.Eng.C 4659, folios 1–190, C. Balmelli to John Alexander [Sinclair], 20 January 1958.

108. On the desire of Italian officials to end the passive life of refugee camps and turn their residents into "pioneers" see Giacomo Canepa, "Rifare gli Italiani. Profughi e progetti per il welfare (1944–47)," *Meridiana* 86 (2016): 76.

109. AS INPS, Carte della colonizzazione libica, 1933–1968, b. 64, fasc. 272, Palatiello, "Sistemazione in Patria dei coloni rimpatriandi dalla Libia," 15 January 1957. On Barra's requests to INPS for funds and assistance see AS INPS, Carte della colonizzazione libica, b. 64, fasc. 272, DeAnna, Pro-memoria, 12 July 1956.

110. AS INPS, Carte della colonizzazione libica, 1933–1968, b. 64, fasc. 272, Enrico Barra, "Soc. Coop. Agricola fra i colonizzatori italiani d'Africa: Contributo per la sistemazione di famiglie d'esuli," 14 March 1956. It should be noted, however, that the request to INPS came after SACIDA's founding in order to acquire more land and thus settle additional families from Libya.

111. AS INPS, Carte della colonizzazione libica, 1933–1968, b. 64, fasc. 272, Enrico Barra, "Assegnazione poderi agli ex coloni dell'I.N.P.S. in Libia," 5 December 1956.

112. Another man I interviewed had instead migrated to Venezuela in 1958, returned to Italy in 1965, and moved back to Gebelia in 1967 (interviews conducted 16 and 23 May 2011).

113. Bodleian, Papers of John Alexander-Sinclair, Ms.Eng.C 4659, C. Balmelli to John Alexander [Sinclair], 20 January 1958; Enrico Barra, "Relazione di massima per

la costruzione in Italia di un centro per la definitiva sistemazione di lavoro e di vita dei profughi," 16 January 1958.

114. Nick Yablon, *Untimely Ruins: An Archaeology of American Urban Modernity, 1819–1919* (Chicago: University of Chicago Press, 2009), 3–7; Tim Edensor, *Industrial Ruins: Space, Aesthetics and Materiality* (Oxford: Berg, 2005), 11–14.

115. Julia Hell and Andreas Schönle, introduction to *Ruins of Modernity*, ed. Julia Hell and Andreas Schönle (Durham, NC: Duke University Press, 2010), 1. Hell and Schönle argue that since 9/11, what was essentially a European story of imperial ruins has also become an American one. For a counter-view, see the discussion of the untimeliness and sui generis nature of American ruins in Yablon, *Untimely Ruins*, 10–12.

116. Stoler, "Imperial Debris," 194.

117. It should not surprise readers to learn that in recent years another group of mobile and marginalized subjects—Romani—have moved from the outskirts into the largely abandoned center of Fertilia, given that many of the *esuli* and their families long ago relocated to nearby Maristella and Alghero. When in 2013 I visited the elementary school in Fertilia (its architecture as pure an expression of fascist rationalism as one might hope for), I saw Romani mothers anxiously waiting to speak with the administrators there. On a return visit to Fertilia in the summer of 2016, opinions were divided over the use of the defunct Hotel Bellavista to house African migrants and refugees. See "Profughi all'Hotel Bellavista di Fertilia, cresce la protesta dei residenti," *La Nuova Sardegna*, 26 June 2015.

118. My use of this term differs from that of Alexander Regier, who employs it to capture the importance of the event of the Lisbon earthquake to articulations of the sublime. See Regier, "Foundational Ruins: The Lisbon Earthquake and the Sublime," in Hell and Schönle, *Ruins of Modernity*, 357–374. In using this phrasing I also gesture toward the ways in which the new towns have been seen as (seemingly) paradoxical projects: as zones of "destructive creation" and "tradition as a means to the end of tradition." On the former refer to Federico Caprotti, "Destructive Creation: Fascist Urban Planning, Architecture and New Towns in the Pontine Marshes," *Journal of Historical Geography* 33, no. 3 (2007): 651–679. On the latter see Fuller, "Tradition as a Means to the End of Tradition."

119. Edensor, *Industrial Ruins*, 141.

Conclusion

1. If anything, this tendency to pathologize refugees—already so marked in the aftermaths of the First and Second World Wars—has only become more pronounced over time. "In any report on conflict today," notes Vanessa Pupavac, "refugees are invariably presented as being 'traumatized,' 'psychologically scarred,' 'indelibly marked,' 'emotionally damaged,' 'hopeless,' 'overwhelmed by grief,' and so forth." Vanessa Pupavac, "Pathologizing Populations and Colonizing Minds: International Psychosocial Programs in Kosovo," *Alternatives: Global, Local, Political* 27, no. 4 (2002): 489.

2. The law of 4 March 1952, n. 137, laid out assistance to Italian refugees from Libya, Eritrea, Ethiopia, Somalia, and from territories ceded by the 1947 Peace

Treaty, as well as Italian refugees from foreign countries (such as Tunisia) and from those within Italy impacted by World War II.

3. Tonino Mirabella, *Sospesi: Racconto fotografico del 'Rossi Longhi' da Campo Profughi a Campus Universitario* (Rome: Gangemi Editore, 2015), 4–5. See also Giovanni Ferrari, "Rifugiati in Italia. Excursus storico-statistico dal 1945 al 1995," https://www.unhcr.it/wp-content/uploads/2015/12/Excursus_storico-statistico_dal_1945_al_1995.pdf.

4. Ruth Ben-Ghiat, *Italian Fascism's Empire Cinema* (Bloomington: Indiana University Press, 2015), 305. Patrizia Manduchi instead takes Goffredo Alessandrini's *Giarabub*, a film made the same year as *Bengasi* and which features a heroic but unsuccessful last stand against British forces by an Italian garrison in Libya, as marking the end of this imperial film genre. See Manduchi, "The Warm Sand of the Desert: Italian Colonial Cinema and the Image of Islam," in *Images of Colonialism and Decolonisation in the Italian Media*, ed. Paola Bertella Farnetti and Cecilia Dau Novelli (Cambridge: Cambridge Scholars, 2017), 38.

5. Daniela Baratieri, "*Bengasi-Bengasi anno '41*: The Evidence of Silences in the Transmission of Memory," in *Italian Colonialism: Legacy and Memory*, ed. Jacqueline Andall and Derek Duncan (New York: Peter Lang, 2005), 75–98. See also Baratieri, *Memories and Silences Haunted by Fascism, MCMXXX–MCMLX* (Bern: Peter Lang, 2010).

6. Baratieri, "*Bengasi-Bengasi anno '41*," 83.

7. E.g., Francesca Di Giulio and Federico Cresti, eds., *Rovesci della Fortuna: La minoranza italiana in Libia dalla seconda guerra mondiale all'espulsione (1940–1970)* (Ariccia: Aracne Editrice, 2016).

8. Maurice Roumani, *The Jews of Libya: Coexistence, Persecution, Resettlement* (Eastbourne: Sussex Academic Press, 2009), 89.

9. Renzo De Felice, *Jews in an Arab Land: Libya, 1835–1970*, trans. Judith Roumani (College Station: University of Texas Press, 1985). De Felice offers an extensive account of the debates over Libya's "minorities"; in particular see 234–257.

10. AQSH, CG, dosja 58, viti 1944, letter of Magnoni, 12 November 1945.

11. For further details see Pamela Ballinger, "A Sea of Difference, a History of Gaps: Migrations between Italy and Albania, 1939–1992," *Comparative Studies in Society and History* 60, no. 1 (2018): 90–118.

12. It appears that some "Italians from Libya" were asked to meet with Gadhafi. Giovanna Ortu, the longtime president of the Associazione Italiani Rimpatriati dalla Libia (AIRL), claimed she was invited in a nonofficial capacity but then never heard anything further. See "Giovanni Ortu: La visita di Ghedaffi? Una burla," *Politicamente Corretta*, 25 June 2009, http://www.politicamentecorretto.com/index.php?news=13925.

13. This brings to mind partition and Muslim migrants from India to Pakistan who were discouraged from settling and told "Karachi is full." Vazira Fazila-Yacoobali Zamindar, *The Long Partition and the Making of Modern South Asia: Refugees, Boundaries, Histories* (New York: Columbia University Press, 2007), 171.

14. For details on historians' efforts to situate the Istrian exodus into the frame of East European population movements see Pamela Ballinger, "Remapping the Istrian Exodus: New Interpretive Frameworks," in *At Home but Foreigners: Population Transfers in 20th Century Istria*, ed. Katja Hrobat Virloget, Catherine Gousseff,

and Gustavo Corni (Koper: Univerziteta zalozba Annales, 2016), 69–90. The volume *Naufraghi della pace: Il 1945, I profughi e le memorie divise d'Europa*, ed. Guido Crainz, Raoul Pupo, and Silvia Salvatici (Rome: Donzelli, 2008) represents a pioneering work for its insertion of the history of refugee flows from Italy's eastern border into broader refugee histories. Addressing both the origins and consequences of postwar European displacements, the contributions locate Istrian migrants in the wider migration trajectories of European displaced persons and debates about relief and assistance. Historian Romain Rainero's study *Le navi bianche* links various migration histories, although it leaves several key archival sources for such histories untouched. In the context of memory studies, Patrizia Audenino has compared the recollections of Istrian displacement with those of Italians repatriated from Africa, as well as German expellees and French *pieds-noirs*. For the important work by Audenino see *La casa perduta: La memoria dei profughi nell'Europa del Novecento* (Rome: Carocci, 2015).

15. Rebecca Bryant, "History's Remainders: On Time and Objects after Conflict in Cyprus," *American Ethnologist* 41, no. 4 (2014): 684.

Archives and Collections Consulted

Archives Nationales, Paris, International Refugee Organization Papers
Archivio Centrale dello Stato, Rome
Archivio di Stato, Trieste
Archivio Storico dell'Istituto Nazionale della Previdenza Sociale, Rome
Archivio Storico Diplomatico del Ministero degli Affari Esteri, Rome
Archivio Storico Istituto Luce, Rome
Archivio Storico Società Dante Alighieri, Rome, Comitati Esteri
Arkivi Qendror Shtetëror (Central State Archives of Albania), Tirana
Arthur and Elizabeth Schlesinger Library on the History of Women in America, Radcliffe Institute, Cambridge, Massachusettes, Louise W. Holborn Papers, 1989–1975
Biblioteca dell'Associazione E.GI.S. Ente Giuliano di Sardegna "Don Francesco Dapiran." Documenti vari, Fertilia, Italy
Biblioteca Nazionale, Florence
Bodleian Library, Special Collections, Oxford, Papers of the United Nations Career Records Project
Centro Studi Emigrazione, Rome
Columbia University, Herbert H. Lehman Collections, New York, UNRRA papers of Hugh R. Jackson, Robert G. A. Jackson, Marshal McDuffie, and Richard B. Scandrett
General State Archives, Regional Archives of Dodecanese, Rhodes, Greece
Hoover Institution Library and Archive, Palo Alto, California
Intergovernmental Committee for European Migration/International Organization for Migration, Geneva
International Committee of the Red Cross Archive, Geneva
Istituto Agronomico per l'Oltremare, Florence, Documenti Inediti
Istituto italiano per l'Africa e l'Oriente, Rome
La Guardia and Wagner Archives, LaGuardia Community College, Queens, New York
National Archives and Records Administration, College Park, Maryland
National Archives of the United Kingdom, Kew
Oberlin College Library, Oberlin, Ohio, Special Collections, Belden and Lisa Paulson Papers, 1937–2012
Presidenza del Consiglio dei Ministri, Rome, Ufficio per le Zone di Confine
Refugee Studies Programme, Oxford University, Oxford, Weis Archive
United Nations Archives, New York, UNRRA Papers
United Nations High Commissioner for Refugees Archive, Geneva
United States National Archives, College Park, Maryland
Vatican Film Library, Vatican City
World Council of Churches Archive, Geneva

Index

Acland, Brigadier, 100
Addis Ababa
British occupation of, 232n37, 243n29
building plan comparison, 180
conquest of (1936), 61
CRI in, 54, 231n33
Italian consulate in, 170
mass evacuation to Asmara, 49
wartime "safe zones," 48
Aegean Islands. *See* Dodecanese Islands
African migrants, *clandestini*, 29–30
Africa Orientale Italiana (AOI)
British control, 47
definition of, 2
Italian empire, 38
Italian farmers in place during WWII, 62
military collapse in World War II, 46
natives and Italian agricultural activities during WWII, 63
profughi di guerra (war refugees), 14, 121
repatriation to Italy, 118
wartime evacuation, 45–46, 49–50
See also AOI refugees; Eritrea; Ethiopia; Somalia
Aide Suisse, 194–95, 200–203
Albania, 239n107
British administration, 94
citizenship in, 140
civilians return to Italy, 68–69
decolonization of, 18
discretional citizenship, 140
effects of armistice in, 64, 73
expulsion of Italians, 94–95
Gramsci Battalion, 68–69
imperial racial hierarchy, 40
internationalism in, 96
Italian repatriation from, 130, 248nn79–80, 248n90
Italian soldiers in, 68, 239n102
lack of cooperation with UNRRA, 95–96
protectorate status, 40
quinta sponda (fifth shore), 40
repatriation negotiations, 69–70, 239n107
repatriation of soldiers and civilians, 72
treatment of Italians and property, 70–71, 209
UNRRA and, 87, 93–95
"When we were the Albanians," 30
See also Circolo Garibaldi, Albania
Alexander-Sinclair, John, 191, 194–98, 200, 206, 285n84, 285n89
Alfieri, Dino, 40
Alghero, 184–85, 187, 281n42, 287n117
See also Fertilia, Sardinian "new town"
Allied Control Commission (ACC), 83–84, 86–87, 91, 248n73
Allied Military Government (AMG), 83–84, 92, 96, 98, 130–31
Allied Military Government of Occupied Territories (AMGOT), 82–83, 243n28
Alto Commissariato Profughi (High Commission on Refugees), 84, 245n40
American Joint Distribution Committee, 90
American Relief for Italy, 88
Amministrazione per gli Aiuti Internazionali (AAI), 4, 89, 194, 197, 200, 216n6, 247n64
Andreotti, Giulio, 189
Angeli, Umberto, 146
"anno zero," 176
antimiscegenation laws, 40, 146–49, 168, 269n53, 269n55, 271n73
Antonioni, Michelangelo, 180
AOI refugees
after Mussolini's fall, 62, 235n71
Fasci Femminile in, 58
moral improprieties and, 55, 57–58, 60
suspicion of British, 50–51
wolf children, 60
Arab Spring and asylum seekers, 212
archives, Italian, 20–26, 222nn70–71, 223n80
Arnese (Grimaldi), Grazia and family, 43–44
Arundell, Brigadier, 104–5
Askari / ascari, 40, 126, 227n43
Associazione Nazionale Cittadini Italiani e Familiari Rimpatriati dall'Albania (ANCIFRA), 210

Associazione Nazionale Comunità Italo-Somala (ANCIS), 172, 210
Associazione Nazionale Profughi della Libia, 257n173
Associazione Nazionale Venezia Giulia e Dalmazia (ANVGD), 189
Audenino, Patrizia, 289n14

Badoglio, Pietro, 61, 63, 69, 76, 82
Bailey, Alice, 60
Bailkin, Jordanna, 20–21, 25
Baldelli, Ferdinando, 88–89, 115
Balli Kombëtar (National Front) movement, 68
Balmelli, C., 200–203
Baratieri, Daniela, 207–8
Barra, Enrico, 202–3
Barrera, Giulia, 149, 169–70
Battisti, Cesare, 34, 225n19
Belgian Congo, 142
Bengasi/Bengasi anno '41 (Genina), 207
Ben-Ghiat, Ruth, 28, 36, 176, 207
Benjamin, Walter, 29
Beritelli, Pietro, 128
Bertellini, Maria, 169
Bevin-Sforza Plan (1949), 75
Biess, Frank, 182
bigamy, 164–65, 169, 171
bimbi libici (Italian children from Libya), 44, 78, 115, 117, 227n1
biracial children (meticci). See Eritrea; Ethiopia; Italy, citizenship and; Somalia
Blackley, Travers Robert, 115
Black Mamba Boy (Mohamed), 134
Bonifazio, Paola, 193
bonifica integrale (reclamation)
  bonifica post-imperiale, 183
  ethnic Slavs and, 184
  and fascism, 36, 176, 203–4
  foreign refugees in Sardinia, 194, 198
  national reclamation, 148
  new towns, 180–83
  on peninsula and colonies, 181, 278n22
  post-imperial reclamation, 183–84, 204–5, 280n36
  racial reclamation, 37
  "Southern Question," 34, 192–93
  See also Cinecittà; Fertilia, Sardinian "new town"; Gebelia; Homeless European Land Program (HELP); Latina (former Littoria), "new town"; Simaxis
Bonomi, Ivanoe, 88, 122
Borghese, Donna Elena Dusmet, 202
Branscombe, Martha, 60
British Military Administration (BMA)
  AOI wartime management, 53–54, 232nn36–37, 233n46, 236n80
  "breadwinner's scheme," 111, 113–14, 148, 256n170
  empire building, 254n144
  family reunification issues, 75, 104, 112–13, 115–16
  "Hill Farms Scheme," 62
  internment, co-optation, and repatriation in AOI, 47–48, 229n22, 230n25
  Italian government agreements, 116–17
  Italian police in territories, 50, 231n34
  Italian territories government, 18
  Italy's antimiscegenation laws enforced, 168
  Red Cross wartime issues, 53–54, 67, 232n43
  transit camps for women and children, 48
  Vatican issues, 52
  See also Africa Orientale Italiana (AOI); Dodecanese Islands; Eritrea; Libya
Bruschi, Vittorio, 72
Byrnes, James, 122–23

Calchi Novati, Giampaolo, 121, 129
Calvino, Italo, 29–30
Camilleri, Nicola, 140, 266n8
Campioni, Inigo, 65
camps, post-war
  Aversa, 135, 159, 202–3
  Bagnoli, 188
  Cinecittà, 62, 135, 177, 179, 182, 188
  comparison to Indian partition, 288n13
  complaints about Allied administration, 92, 234n52
  displaced persons on Italian peninsula, 83, 86
  Ente comunale di assistenza (ECA), 235n73
  Fossoli, 26, 223n88
  Miramare Transit Camp, 104
  Padriciano, 26
  Pagano, 188
  Risiera di San Sabba, 9, 26, 135, 177
  "Rossi Longhi" camp, 207
  See also AOI refugees
Cancellieri, Edmondo, 192
Captain Corelli's Mandolin (film), 236n81
Caracciolo, Lucio, 181
Carelli, Maria and family, 48–51, 54, 58, 234n52
Caroselli, Saverio, 55

Carosio, Luisella (née Carelli), 50–51, 58
Cason, Giacomo, 44, 115
Castiadas, 194, 280n40, 282n45
Catholic Association for International Peace, 88
Catholic Church and Catholic organizations
  bimbi libici (Italian children in Libya), 78
  blurred categories of refugees, 175–76
  collaboration with American Catholic institutions, 88
  and Italian POW repatriation, 52
  relief efforts in Italy, 87–88, 246n55, 247n64
  wartime and post-war assistance, 78
Catholic Relief Services (CRS), 88–89, 175, 246n63
Celona, Antonino, 1–2
Censimento degli Italiani all'estero (census), 32
Chambers, Iain, 29
Chiavari, Marquis, 160–61
China, Italian concession, 33
Choate, Mark, 34, 220n56
Cinecittà, 62, 135, 177, 179, 182
Circolo Garibaldi, Albania, 71–72, 93, 95, 107, 209–10, 240n114, 240n122, 241n123
citizenship question, 4, 132, 135–36
  See also Italy, citizenship and
Clementi, Marco, 66, 237n89
Cohen, Gerard Daniel, 12, 78, 218n27
Cohen, Myer, 160, 163
collaborationists, 90, 248n71
coloni (colonist)
  anxiety of, 115–16
  British and, 63
  definition of, 28
  fascist view of, 39
  in Fertilia, 186
  in Gebelia, 201
  Peace Treaty effect, 120
  repatriation of, 44, 49
  See also bonifica integrale (reclamation); decolonization; Unione Coloni Italiani (d') Africa
Comitato Amministrativo Soccorso ai Senzatetto (CASAS), 89–90, 178–79, 190, 193–94, 200, 277n10
Comitato d'assistenza tra gli italiani, 69, 239n105
Comitato di assistenza agli italiani rimpatriati dall'estero (CAIRE), 235n73
Comitato di Gestione Amministrativa delle Isole Italiane dell'Egeo, 107
Comitato Nazionale per i Rifugiati Italiani (CNRI), 14
Comitato per la Documentazione dell'Opera dell'Italia in Africa, 20
Commissione per la tutela degli interessi italiani nel Dodecan(n)eso (CTIID), 106–7, 238n98
Commissione permanente per il rimpatrio degli italiani all'estero (CORI), 227n3
concentration camps
  Fossoli, 26, 223n88
  Risiera di San Sabba, 9, 26
  Schokken, 65
Contini, Paolo, 97
Convention concerning the Status of Refugees Coming from Germany (1938), 219n35
Convention on Refugees (1933), 11
Corradini, Enrico, 35
Corsi, Angelo, 184, 194, 277n7
Costantini, Celso, 46
Courvoisier, Raymond, 64, 66–67
Cresti, Federico, 24, 223n81
Crispi, Francesco, 34
Croce Rossa Italiana (CRI), 45, 50, 53–54, 58, 113, 231n33, 233n47, 246n63, 247n64
Cronin, Bruce, 80–81
Curti, Lidia, 29
Cyrenaica, Libya, 1, 7, 14, 35, 37, 39, 46

D'Agostino, Gabrielle, 168
D'Annunzio, Gabriele, 35–36
Dapiran, Francesco, 186–87, 190, 194, 281n41
Davis, Loda Mae, 86
De Berti, Antonio, 184, 194
"Declaration on the Granting of Independence to Colonial Countries" (1960), 15
decolonization
  in Dutch possessions, 16–17, 220n55
  French, 6, 15, 207, 222n76
  Japanese, post World War II, 5–6, 16–17, 20, 217n14
  Portuguese, 6, 17, 167
  and refugees, 3, 15
  statist principle of UN, 80
decolonization, Italian
  cultural and social reverberations, 20, 221n62
  documentation of, 20–21, 221n66, 222n70
  long process of, 17–19
  rights codified in Italy, 7
De Felice, Renzo, 147, 209

De Gasperi, Alcide, 91, 120, 123, 186, 256n166
Del Balzo, Clotilde, 53–54
Del Boca, Angelo, 271n68
Del Drago (Prince), 161–63
Del Pero, Mario, 248n78
Democrazia Cristiana (DC), 3
De Napoli, Olindo, 147–48
Deplano, Valeria, 168, 269n53, 269n55
De Vecchi, Cesare Maria, 37, 39–40, 105, 144, 146, 150, 269n45
De Winton, Robert, 121
Difesa della Razza (journal), 40, 146
Direzione di Pubblica Sicurezza, 4
displaced persons, 79
  definition, 9, 218n27
  ethno-national categories, 108–9
  foreign and Italian refugees status and treatment, 84
  ineligible for UNRRA question, 91–92
  national and international intersections, 79
  reasons for, 207
Displaced Persons and Repatriation Subcommission (ACC DP), 83
Di Stefano, Alessia Maria, 139
Dodecanese Islands
  acquisition of, 34–35
  administrative battles over relief, 101
  appeal to ICRC for food and supplies, 66–67, 238n93
  armistice and confusion, 64
  BMA in, 6, 67–68, 73, 99, 102, 104–7, 236n85, 253n137
  citizenship in, 139–40
  demand for assistance to refugees, 132
  fascism and, 39–40, 253n139
  Greek administration, 101–2
  Greek and Italian relations, 105–6, 253n138
  Greek annexation, 100
  head-to-head scheme, 118
  ICRC relief efforts, 99–101, 104, 251nn110–11, 252n124
  Italian fascist collaborators, 65–66
  Italian loss of control, 18
  Italian soldiers become German POWs, 65
  Jewish community, 65–66, 103, 140–42, 144–46, 269n45, 269n57
  Jewish 'protégé Italians,' 141
  movement of people to and from, 142
  non-Italian repatriates to Turkey, 64
  outmigration during WWII, 66
  repatriation tasks, 102–3
  similarity to Venezia Giulia, 161–63
  SS *Gaetano Donizetti* sunk by British, 65
  SS *Orion* shipwrecked, 65
  starvation at end of war, 100
  territorial status as possession, 2, 39
  transit camps of, 104, 106–7
  Turkish requests to emigrate, 142–43
  UNRRA and BMA cooperation, 102, 252n124, 252n126
  UNRRA in, 87, 99–104, 110–12, 252n122
  wartime repatriation to Venice, 64
Dodecanese Islands, citizenship and citizenship in, 269n45
  complicated claims, 142
  Greek law and, 161–63
  Levantines and, 140–41, 143–44, 267n21, 268n37, 268n38
  naturalization requests, 164–65
  undetermined nationality, 145–46, 151, 158–64, 173, 273n103, 273n105
Dodecanese Welfare Association, 101
Donati, Sabina, 136, 139–40, 150, 267n26
Don Murray Project. *See* Homeless European Land Program (HELP)
Doumanis, Nicholas, 105
Duilio, 58, 228n10

Edensor, Tim, 205
Egan, Eileen, 191–92
Einaudi, Luigi, 34, 225n18, 238n96
Ente colonizzazione Puglia d'Etiopa, 39, 267n18
Ente comunale di assistenza (ECA), 235n73
Ente di Trasformazione Fondiaria e Agraria in Sardegna (EFTAS), 187, 197, 200, 283n55
Ente Ferrarese di Colonizzazione (EFC), 184–85, 280n36
Ente Giuliano Autonomo di Sardegna (EGAS), 187, 189–90
Ente Nazionale per la Distribuzione dei Soccorsi (ENDSI), 88
Ente per la Colonizzazione della Libia (ECL). *See* Libya
Eritrea
  Adwa, Italian military defeat, 34, 36
  agriculture in, 63
  archives of, 223n80
  Bevin-Sforza Plan (1949), 75
  British administration, 18, 47, 118–19
  colonial citizenship, 139, 266n8
  colonists and refugees, 49
  Dogali, battle of (1887), 34

and Ethiopian federation, 169–70, 276n145
fascist expulsion of some colonists, 228n9
first Italian colony, 32–33
Four Power Commission of Inquiry on, 126
Italian civilians in evacuation camps, 75
Italian colony in, 32, 225n16
Italian women and children evacuation, 45
mixed race children (*meticci*), 149–50, 167, 169–72, 269n53, 275n140, 276n143
numbers of repatriates to and from, 114
parliamentary plan for settler colony, 33
Red Cross and, 53
repatriation to and from, 118–19, 259n194
trusteeship plan, 129
See also Africa Orientale Italiana (AOI)
Ertola, Emanuele, 55, 59, 221n62, 271n72
Esposizione Universale di Roma (EUR), 23, 38, 179–80, 182
Ethiopia
BMA in, 73, 243n29
fascist invasion, 38
fear of locals retaliation to colonists, 48–49
ICRC role, 232n41
identity and refugee status, 2
Italian industrialists expelled, 110
Italy's chemical weapons attack, 52–53
mixed race children (*meticci*), 169–72
post-WWII European refugees in, 98–99, 250n104
refugee camps, 50–51
refusal to issue visas to Italians, 170
rejection of Italian DPs, 99
UNRRA, lack of trust for, 98
war crimes prosecution, 122–23
See also Africa Orientale Italiana (AOI)
ethnographic colonies, 34, 36, 38, 196, 225n18
European Recovery Plan (ERP), 3, 78, 129, 178–79, 263n236
Evalet, André, 51–53
Everybody Here Is for Sardinia, 193

Facchinetti, Camillo Vittorino, 46, 112, 115, 117
Falconi, Carlo, 88, 246n60
Fanfani Plan (1950), 177
Faralli, Iginio, 65–66, 237n89, 237n93
fascism, Italian
antimiscegenation laws and *madamismo*, 149
and Aryan race, 40
bonifica integrale (reclamation), 36, 181, 176, 184
bonifica nazionale, 148, 183–84
legacy of and resettlement projects post-war, 180
"mutilated victory" (*la vittoria mutilata*), 36
policies on emigration, 38–39, 226n35
racial reclamation, 37
refugees, view of, 176, 277n1
response to fall of, 61–62
See also Africa Orientale Italiana (AOI); Ethiopia; Libya; Somalia
Fascist Party (PNF), 36, 48, 58, 65, 233n46
Fertilia, Sardinian "new town"
Alghero, help for, 281n42
development of agriculture, 190, 282n54
fascist architecture, 180, 185, 287n117
foreign refugees in, 194
foundational ruins, 204
founding with Ferrara colonists, 184–85
malaria problem, 187, 193
resettlement of Istrian-Julian-Dalmatian refugees, 186, 281n41
Romani in, 287n117
transformation into fishing village, 187–89, 282n45, 282n50
See also Ente Giuliano Autonomo di Sardegna (EGAS)
Fertilia dei Giuliani (film), 187–89
film industry, Italian postwar, 177, 180
See also Bengasi (Genina); *Germania anno zero* (Rossellini)
Fiore, Teresa, 29–30
foibe killings, 64, 211, 214, 236n82
foreign spouses, 147, 151, 164–66, 175
Foucault, Michel, 235n62
Frank, Matthew, 10, 78, 81
Franklin, Mitchell, 89–90
Fryer, E. R., 86
Fuller, Mia, 23, 180, 182

Gabaccia, Donna, 31
Gadhafi, Muammar, 31, 209–10, 288n12
Gaggio, Dario, 193
Gallagher, Dennis, 15
Gatrell, Peter, 10, 26, 78
Gebelia, 184, 201–5, 287n118
General Commissariat for Migration and Internal Colonization, 181

Geneva Convention on Refugees (1951)
Algerian *pieds-noirs*, 6
con-national refugees, 216n11, 217n16
consolidation of categories, 12
country of habitual residence question, 152, 272n80
exclusions, 6, 8
international refugees, 4–5, 206
territorial and geographic clauses, 5, 16, 206, 216n10
Genina, Augusto, 207
Germania anno zero (Rossellini), 177
Germany
citizenship, descent-based, 136
Volksdeutsche communities expulsion, 5, 11, 74, 155, 217n16, 217n18, 289n14
Giarabub (film), 288n4
Giorno del Ricordo (Day of Remembrance), 211, 214
Giulio Cesare, 53, 228n10
Great Depression, 142
Grisologo Fabi, Pier, 67
Gruppo Democratico Popolare Italiano, 71, 240n114
Guida del rimpatriato d'Africa (Guide for the repatriate from Africa), 55, 233n48

Hacking, L. M., 160–61
Hague Convention (1907), 229n20
Hashimoto, Akiko, 20
Heatherington, Tracey, 193
Hell, Julia, 204, 287n115
Hodgson, Edward, 94
Holian, Anna, 78
Homeless European Land Program (HELP) or Don Murray Project, 196–99, 285n90, 286n94
housing and population postwar, 89, 177–80, 277n7
Hoxha, Enver, 69, 73, 94–96, 130, 166, 209, 239n107
Hoxha-Palermo Accord, 69–70, 72
humanitarianism, imperialism and, 15
human rights, 12–13, 77, 80, 217n19, 232n40, 241n127

Imru, Ras, 59
Intergovernmental Committee on European Migration (ICEM), 4, 8, 135, 175, 265n3
Intergovernmental Committee on Refugees (IGCR), 4, 85, 108, 135
displaced Yugoslavs, 245n46
intergovernmentalism, 242n13
definition of, 79
and transnationalism, 80–81
internally displaced persons (IDPS), 1–2, 6, 13, 154, 217nn18–19
See also refugees, national
International Committee of the Red Cross (ICRC)
Dodecanese Jews and, 103
food shortages in AOI, 231n31
interwar period and, 230n29
legal international personality, 77–78
mass evacuation in AOI, 49
partiality complaints, 52–53
records of, 25, 64
relief efforts, 250n100
and repatriates, 14
return migration encouraged, 75
supplies for Albania, 250n100
wartime humanitarian repatriation, 45
International Conference on Refugee Problems Today and Tomorrow, 195
International Labor Organization (ILO), 80
International Refugee Organization (IRO)
citizenship and international refugees, 153–54, 157–58, 272n90
eligibility denials, 208
ethnonational categories, 108–9
five year mandate, 12
focus on children, 60
goal of new homes, 11–12
help for Italian refugees, 191, 248n73
international refugees, 3, 216n5
Italian threat to withdraw, 7
liberal internationalism of, 77
Lire Fund usage, 248n68
negotiations with UNRRA, 7
refugees and displaced persons definition, 154–56, 273n101
undetermined nationality, 5, 132, 158–64, 173, 175, 273n103
See also Dodecanese Islands; United Nations Relief and Rehabilitation Administration (UNRRA)
irredentism
Italy's "lost" territories, 33, 225n19
post-WWII fears about kin states, 74
socialist variant, 34–35
See also Lega Nazionale; Società Dante Alighieri
Istituto Italiano per l'Africa e l'Oriente/ Italian Institute for Africa and the Orient (IsIAO), 21–22, 222n71
Istituto Nazionale della Previdenza Sociale (INPS), 116, 194, 202, 280n36
Istituto Nazionale Fascista della Previdenza Sociale (INFPS), 37, 39, 44, 226n28

Istrian-Julian-Dalmatians, 26, 142, 180, 183, 186, 189–90, 202, 210–12, 283n56
Italian armistice (1943), World War II
 consequences for Albania, 68–69
 consequences for Dodecanese, 64–65
 division of Italian peninsula, 3, 82, 244n30
 "Dual tracks" (relief and citizenship) in northern and southern Italy, 235n73, 272n78
 impact on migrations on *navi bianche*, 45, 61
 in Venezia Giulia, 63–64, 73
Italian Passport Law (1901), 136, 265n5
Italian POWs
 British and, 47–48, 52
 and CRI, 54
 Dodecanese Islands and, 106
 experiences of, 229n22
 to Germany, 65
 Italian arrangements for, 117
 radio transmissions to, 233n47
 Vulcania voyages and, 119
 wives of, 165
Italian Red Cross (CRI), 50–51, 53–54, 58, 83, 88, 107, 113, 171
Italian repatriates
 analogy to current migrants, 30–31
 citizenship of, 16
 fascism and, 17
Italia Oltremare (Italian overseas territories), 75
 civilian situation at war's end, 73
 under fascism, 31
 hope for continued role, 73–74
 post-World War I acquisitions, 35–36
 See also rimpatriato (return migrants)
Italy, citizenship and
 allogeni (ethnic Slovenes), 146–48, 271n67
 binary citizenship regime, 135
 Central Registration Bureau for Aliens, 137–38
 cittadinanza italiana in Tripolitania e Cirenaica, 139
 cittadini (citizens) or *sudditi* (subjects), 138–39, 267n18
 history of, 136–38
 language criteria, 152–53
 madamismo, 149, 167–68, 271n72, 271n74
 mixed race children (*meticci*), 146, 149–50, 167–69, 171–72, 269n53
 naturalization, local or full, 137, 144
 postwar determination, 173–74
 postwar status, 151, 272n78
 racial hierarchies of territories, 145–47
 revised citizenship law (1912), 138
 "vincolo di sangue" (blood tie), 145, 266n6
 "white Slavs," 153
 See also Yugoslavia and Yugoslavs
Italy, state of
 African repatriates, view of, 119–20
 Albania as *quinta sponda* (fifth shore), 40
 border issues and citizenship, 153–54
 census and registration of aliens, 7, 192, 218n20, 283n63
 complaints about undesirables, 92, 248n78
 declaration of empire, 38
 diminished sovereign capacity, 78
 eastern border, 91
 legacies and memories of colonialism, 17, 20–21, 221n66
 meridionalismo and southern Italy, 148, 192, 270n62
 models of colonialism, 32–42, 225n18, 280n36
 myth of "good" Italian, 149, 270n58, 271n68
 postwar situation, 82, 247n64
 repatriation of POWs within peninsula, 83
 repatriation slowdown, 7, 176
 responsibility for displaced persons, 206, 287n2
 right to regulate flow of displaced persons, 190–91
 Risorgimento, 36

Jacobsen, P., 154–55, 160
Japan and Japanese people, 2, 5, 16–17, 217n14
Jaquinet, Luigi, 66
Jewish people
 Belgian Congo communities and links to Italian territories, 103, 141–43, 166
 citizenship issue and antisemitism, 141, 144, 146–47, 269n57
 clandestine passage to Palestine, 13
 deported from Libya, 150
 deported from Rhodes to Auschwitz, 65–66, 237n89
 displaced in Europe, 11
 of Dodecanese Islands, 103
 protection in Italian territories, 147, 269n58
 UNRRA help for, 90
 See also Racial Laws

Julian March
exodus of Italians after Peace Treaty, 130
postwar demonstrations by pro-Italian and Yugoslav groups, 123
Treaty of Osimo (1975), 73, 125
See also Venezia Giulia
Junod, Henri-Alexandre, 230n29
Junod, Henri-Philippe, 49, 53, 231n32

Keeny, Spurgeon Milton, 86, 91, 101, 247n68
Kellett, J. A., 130–31
Kunz, Josef, 145, 152, 165
Kushner, Tony, 25

Labanca, Nicola, 19–20, 221n66
Lago, Mario, 39, 105, 142–44, 146, 268n38
La Guardia, Fiorello, 87, 223n83, 246n55
Landi, Andrew Paul, 88
Latina (former Littoria), "new town," 181–83, 207, 281n43
League of Nations, 11, 80, 124, 219n35, 243n16
L'eclisse (Antonioni), 180
Lega Nazionale, 33, 130
Lehman, Herbert, 96–97, 223n83
Lester, Alan, 15
Levant or levantine, 140, 143, 148, 175, 267n21, 268n38
Levi, Aldo, 106
Lewis, Norman, 83
Libya
agriculture in, 62, 226n28, 236n75
Bevin-Sforza Plan (1949), 75
BMI suspends Italian immigration, 30
citizenship in, 139
clandestine immigration, 30–31, 112, 114–15, 256n165, 257n182
colonists view of, 39
Ente per la Colonizzazione della Libia (ECL), 24, 37, 62, 226n28
flow of migrants before WWII, 227n5
Four Power Commission of Inquiry on, 125–26
head-to-head scheme, 113–14, 116, 118, 256n171
Istituto Nazionale Fascista della Previdenza Sociale (INFPS), 37, 39, 44
Libyan opposition to Italian returns, 112, 256n165
mass evacuation of Italian children and return, 43–44, 112–13, 115, 227n1
minorities and citizenship, 209
nominal control by Italy prior to World War I, 35
quarta sponda (fourth shore), 40, 112
"reconquest" (*riconquista*), 37, 226n27
territory of, 2
UNRRA applications for repatriates return, 114–15
See also bimbi libici (Italian children from Libya); Cyrenaica, Libya; Tripolitania
Libyan Nationalist Party, 112
Lire Fund (Fondo Lire), 89, 178
L'ora del Sud (Cancellieri), 192
L'Orda (Stella), 30
Luce Institute, 187, 189, 282n46
Luku, Abdu, 166

Macchi, Antonio, 65–67, 106–8, 111, 165, 237n89, 253n128, 253n137
malaria, 36, 181, 183, 185, 187–88, 193, 200, 280n34
Manni, Dario, 189, 282n54
Mari, Gianni, 172
Maristella, 190, 287n117
Marshall Plan. *See* European Recovery Plan (ERP)
Martelli Law (1990), 5, 216n9
Martone, Luciano, 149
Mascherpa, Luigi, 65
Massarotto, Piero, 188, 282n49
Mauro, Salvatore, 169
Mazzola, Giovanni, 168–69
McGeachy, Mary, 243n17
McGuire, Valerie, 138, 144
Mentz, George Francis, 155, 157–58
metropolitan Italians, 17–18, 105, 107–8, 143, 176, 208
Migone, Bartolomeo, 194–95, 198, 200, 285n83
Miles-Bailey, Major, 110
Miletto, Enrico, 131
Milward, Alan, 78
Ministero degli Affari Esteri (MAE), 1, 21, 23, 140, 142, 144, 196, 241n123
Ministero dell'Africa Italiana (MAI), 20, 38
Ministero dell'Assistenza Post-Bellica (Ministry of Postwar Assistance), 84
Ministero dell'Interno, 4
Miraglia (SS), 107, 117
Miraglia, Arturo, 185
Mirehouse, Colonel, 61
Mitchell, Philip, 47, 230n25
mixed race children (*meticci*). *See* Italy, citizenship and
Mohamed, Nadifa, 134
Montini, Giovanni Battista (Pope Paul VI), 87

Montini, Lodovico, 87, 89, 190–92, 195–96, 247n64
Munier, Jean, 100
Murray, Don, 197–98
Mussolini, Benito
 antimiscegenation laws, 40
 camp for traitors, 65
 CORI and, 227n3
 deposition of, 3
 fascist empire, 36, 38
 Jews from Belgian Congo, 142
 mass emigration, view of, 34
 meticci and, 167
 navi bianche (white ships) of, 59, 61

Nansen, Fridtjof, 11
National Catholic War Council (NCWC), 88
National Catholic Welfare Council (NCWC), 195
naturalization
 foreign partners, 164–66
 Islam and, 166
 naturalization, local or full, 137, 144
 post-World War II, 30
navi bianche (white ships)
 ambivalence of evacuees, 54–55
 fascist insignia removed, 61
 fascist political reeducation, 59, 61, 235n62
 Italian police on, 50
 Italian ships with British escort, 58
 mass evacuation use, 45, 228n10
 navigation in dangerous waters, 59
 non-Italian repatriates on, 58
 onboard surveillance, 60
 postwar repatriations on, 75, 118–19
Netherlands, 16, 220n55
"New imperial history," 31, 224n10
Novati, Giampaolo Calci, 121, 129
Nurra, 184, 186, 194, 280n36

Oakley-Hill, Dayrell R., 93–94, 96
Oakley-Hill, Ruby, 94
Occupied Enemy Territories Administration (OETA). *See* British Military Administration (BMA)
Olivetti, Adriano, 179, 278n14
Olivieri, Enrico, 118
oltreitalie, 31–32
Opera Nazionale Combattenti (ONC), 181
Opera Nazionale di Assistenza Religiosa e Morale degli Operai (ONARMO), 88
Opera per l'Assistenza ai Profughi Giuliani e Dalmati (OAPGD), 14, 180, 183, 189–90, 211, 277n10, 278n21, 279n31
Operazione CORA, 210
Option. *See* Peace Treaty with Italy (1947)
outmigration, Italian, 10, 18, 29, 32, 224n1, 283n61
Ovalle-Bahamon, R. E., 167

Palermo, Mario, 69
Pandolfi, Mariella, 192
Pantelleria, 243n28
Paris Peace Conference (1919), 35, 122, 152, 261n211
Park, Willard, 98
Partito Comunista Italiano (PCI), 3, 128, 198
Pascoli, Giovanni, 34
Pasquinelli, Maria, 121, 260n205
Patriarca, Silvana, 170
Paulson, Belden, 197–99, 286n94, 286n102
Peace Conference (1946)
 arguments to retain colonies, 121–22
 Julian territorial dispute, 123
Peace Treaty with Italy (1947)
 border issues unresolved, 123
 ceded territories of, 2
 citizenship option clause, 108
 Dodecanese Islands to Greece, 100
 Italian citizenship issues, 151, 161–64
 Italian national refugees, 7
 Italians leave areas ceded to Yugoslavia, 186
 Italy renounces colonies, 14, 18, 73
 Italy's right to colonies, 121–22
 language instead of race criteria, 145, 151–52, 272n81
 legal and political issues unresolved, 129–30, 262n220
 new borders, 3
 request for trusteeships, 260n206
 response in Italy, 120–21, 260n202
 territorial details of, 124
 territory ceded to Yugoslavia, 121
Pedersen, Susan, 243n16
Pelt, Adrian, 126, 209
Pennacchi, Antonio, 175, 182
Pergher, Roberta, 148
Piccini, Gino, 69
pieds-noirs (Algerian refugees), 6, 15, 289n14
Pignataro, Luca, 237n93, 269n45
Pinkus, Karen, 180, 182
Pius XII (pope), 112
Polizia Africa Italiana (PAI), 50, 53, 60
Pollera, Alberto, 167

Pontificia Commissione di Assistenza/ Pontificia Opera di Assistenza (PCA/ POA), 88–89, 113, 176, 246n60, 247n64
Portugal and Portuguese people, 17
Portuguese Angola, 167
Proglio, Gabriele, 221n66
Protocol Relating to the Status of Refugees (1967), 6
Puglia, 13, 29, 177, 181, 183, 192
Pula/Pola
 assassination of General de Winton, 121
 inclusion in Zone A (1945–1947), 130
 mass migration from, 130–32, 186, 264n245, 264n248
 refugees in Sardinia, 281n42
Pupo, Raoul, 289n14

race and racism, 40, 148, 270nn60–61, 271n72
 See also antimiscegenation laws
Racial Laws, 144, 146, 150, 269n45, 269n57
Radossi, Raffaele, 186
Ragusin-Righi, Livio, 148
Rainero, Romain, 289n14
refettori del papa (pope's dining halls), 88
refugees
 Central and Eastern Europe, 212, 288n14
 codification of categories, 10–11
 confinement of undesirables, 284n70
 definition of, 4–5, 12
 distinctions among, 3, 12, 135, 212–14
 "economic migrants" and, 6
 group status, 13
 inclusion or exclusion, 12
 inconsistent classification, 3, 13–14, 219n44
 mixed groups in camps, 135–36
 "Nansen passport," 11, 274n103
 responsibility for, 135, 206
refugees, international
 Italian resistance to residency, 7–8
 rifugiati stranieri (foreign refugees), 13–14, 200, 207
refugees, national
 con-national terminology, 216n11, 217n16
 exclusion from Geneva Convention, 4–5
 newly decolonized states and, 8, 215n4
 profughi di guerra (war refugees), 13
 rapatrié (French Algerians), 15
 sinistrati ("bomb-damaged" persons), 13
 unequal treatment of, 1, 7, 191–92, 207
 See also rimpatriato (return migrants)
refugees, non-European, 5–6, 217n13
Refugees 1960 (Webb and Searle), 9
Reinisch, Jessica, 10, 78–79, 81
Rennell, Francis James (Lord Rodd), 46–47, 63, 82, 101, 105, 114, 229n20, 231n31
repatriates. *See rimpatriato* (return migrants)
repatriation, humanitarian, 45
repatriation, involuntary
 by Allies, 219n44
 from Ethiopia, 44
 from Libya, 44–45
repatriation to (former) Italian territories, 109–10, 114–17
Repubblica Sociale Italiana (RSI), 62, 65, 82, 147, 223n88, 235n73
Republic of Salò. *See* Repubblica Sociale Italiana (RSI)
Rhodes
 agricultural villages, 39
 British in, 67, 99–100, 102, 165
 Germans in, 65–67, 237n88, 238n96
 infrastructure investments under fascism, 253n139
 Italian citizenship in, 160
 Italian consulate, 238n98
 Italian refugee requests, 103–4, 111–12
 Italian refugees to Fertilia, 190
 Italian repatriation from, 107–9
 Italians in Turkey claims, 143
 Jewish population of, 65, 103, 141, 150, 166
 Jewish refugees repatriation, 253n128
 refugee requests, 255n154, 268n37, 271n67
 relief missions, 238n94
 temporary visit permits to, 253n135
rifugiati stranieri (foreign refugees), 13–14
rimpatriato (return migrants), 14–15, 28, 208
 ambiguity of, 16
 effect on foreign refugees, 28–29
 from Italian colonies, 215n4, 227n3
Rockefeller Foundation, 187, 190, 200
Rodogno, Davide, 270n58
Rome, 24
 Allied Control Commission (ACC) in, 83, 88, 106, 112
 archives, Italian, 22–23, 64
 Associazione Nazionale Profughi della Libia, 257n173
 British Embassy, 118
 center of Italian power, 146
 CRI goods to Mogadishu, 58
 ECA camps in, 235n73
 EUR zone, 179–80
 Four Power Commission of Inquiry on, 126

Gadhafi visit, 210
IRO Eligibility Office, 155
Italian refugees to, 62
Ministry of Africa's Assistance Office, 59
reclamation of towns near, 179, 183, 203
UNRRA in, 97, 103
Rome Olympics (1960), 179–80
Romiti, Alfredo, 48, 51–53
Rossellini, Roberto, 177
Rossi, Mario Franco, 119
Rovesti, Gino, 281n41

Sabaudia, "new town," 183
Sabbadin, Filiberto, 24
Salvatici, Silvia, 78, 84, 135
Samuels, Joshua, 182
Santangelo, Bruno, 119
Sardinia
documentaries on, 187–89, 193, 281n41, 282n46, 284n67
exodus of shepherds to Tuscany, 284n68
foreign refugees in, 194–95
HELP project, 196–99
national refugees in, 195
refugee resettlement in, 191, 193
"Sardinia plan," 195–96, 203, 206–7, 284n76, 285n87
See also bonifica integrale (reclamation); Fertilia, Sardinian "new town"
Sarfatti, Michele, 147, 271n73
Saturnia, 43, 45, 51, 58, 228n10
Schifano, Mario, 62, 235n72
Schlatter, Ernest, 8, 197–98
Schönle, Andreas, 204, 287n115
Search, The (Zinnemann), 242n6
Searle, Ronald, 9
Sedmak, Michael, 155
Segni, Antonio, 195, 285n80
Selassie, Haile, 52–53, 58, 70, 73, 82, 110, 172
sfollati or *profughi* (displaced from territories), 13–14, 179, 207, 257n173
Shelah, Menachem, 147
Shepard, Todd, 122
Shephard, Ben, 83
Sicily, 61, 82–83, 114, 181, 193, 257n173
Simaxis, 196, 199, 201
Simpson, Alva, 158
sinistrati ("bomb-damaged" persons), 13, 179, 195
Skinner, Rob, 15
Sluga, Glenda, 123
Smergani, Francesco, 171–72
Società Agricola Cooperativa fra i Colonizzatori Italiani d'Africa (SACIDA), 201–4, 286n102, 286n110
Società Agricola Italo-Somala (SAIS), 37
Società Dante Alighieri, 24, 33, 69
Somalia
agriculture in, 62
Anglo-Ethiopian Agreement, 243n29
archives of, 223n80
Bevin-Sforza Plan (1949), 75
breadwinner argument, 118
fascist "pacification," 37
few Italian colonists, 39
food shortages, 231n32
Four Power Commission of Inquiry on, 126–28
free movement request, 118
independence of, 15–16
Italian-administered UN trusteeship, 2, 15, 18, 73, 75, 80, 128–29, 172, 207, 264n240
Italian delegation on one-way repatriation, 118
Italo-Somalis, 172, 210
mixed race children (*meticci*), 172
repatriation to and from, 114, 118–19
territory divided with French and British, 32–33
See also Africa Orientale Italiana (AOI)
Soriano, Elia, 103
Sorieri, Antonio, 86, 90, 92
South Asian refugee regime, 217n13
Spagnolli, Giovanni, 193
Spellman, Francis, 88
Steimatsky, Noa, 177
Stein, Sarah, 141
Steinberg, Jonathan, 147
Stella, Gian Antonio, 30
Stern, Alberto, 44–45
Stewart-Steinberg, Suzanne, 182
Stimson, Henry, 254n144
Stoler, Ann Laura, 21, 23, 27, 44, 167, 176
Syracuse, Sicily, 30, 114

Taylor, Myron, 88
Temnomeroff, V. A., 159
Tirana, Albania, 69–72, 94, 210
Tito, Josip Broz, 123, 153, 157, 198, 210
Toliou, Eirini, 25, 66, 222n72, 237n89
Torpey, John, 136–38, 144
Toscana, 115, 118, 131, 264n247
Treaty of Lausanne (1923), 11, 35, 141–42, 145
Treaty of London (1915), 35–36

Trieste
  Free Territory of Trieste (FTT), 124–25, 129, 262n223
  history of, 33, 35
  UNRRA relief through, 97–98
  Zone A and Zone B, 125
  See also foibe killings; Julian March; Venezia Giulia
Tripoli, 24, 43–46, 112–13, 115–17, 143, 175, 203, 256n165, 257n171
Tripolitania
  BMA in, 73, 116–17
  clandestine immigration, 30, 112, 114
  incorporated as province of Italy, 39
  Italian settlers in, 35, 37
  repatriation to and from, 44, 110–11, 113, 116–17
  trusteeship plan, 75, 241n128
Tuck, W. Hallam, 155
Tunisia
  early repatriation from, 227n3
  Italian irredentism, 33
  Italian repatriation from, 121
  Italians to Castiadas, 194
  refugees to metropole, 207
  repatriation to Tuscany, 280n34
Turcato, Ugo, 70, 72, 95, 240n111

Ufficio per le Zone di Confine, 21, 91, 132, 187, 189, 222n69
Ufficio Rodi, 107, 254
Unione Coloni Italiani (d') Africa, 1–2, 7, 21, 46
Unione Pescatori Giuliani, 189
United Nations High Commissioner on Refugees (UNHCR)
  after IRO, 5, 12, 216n5
  archives of, 222n70
  citizenship questions and, 173
  "durable solutions," 207
  economic migrants and, 116
  and foreign refugees, 7–8, 191, 194, 197
  international refugees, 3
  statute of, 80, 216n11
  work with other groups, 175
United Nations Relief and Rehabilitation Administration (UNRRA)
  aid to Italy and ex-enemy states, 82, 85–86, 89
  archives of, 223n83
  citizenship and international refugees, 153–54
  civilian control, 84–85
  contention over DP's, 90, 248n71, 248n76
  critical relief to Italian refugees, 12
  Displaced Persons Operation, 85
  displaced Yugoslavs, 245n46
  "Helping people to help themselves," 60
  international refugee assistance, 3
  liberal internationalism of, 77
  limited relief to Italy, 87
  loyalty oath of League of Nations, 80
  mission in Italy, 86
  misunderstandings with Italian officials, 91
  national and international intersections, 79
  period of operation, 216n5
  pilfering and armed guards, 98
  repatriation of ex-enemy Italians, 87, 93
  repatriation progress, 90–91
  return of intruded enemy nationals, 93
  supplies for Albania, 250n100
  worldwide humanitarian needs, 85
Universal Declaration of Human Rights (UDHR), 13, 80, 241n127
UNRRA-CASAS (Administrative Committee for Assistance to the Homeless). *See* Comitato Amministrativo Soccorso ai Senzatetto (CASAS)
UN trusteeship
  history of, 80, 243n16
  Italy request for former colonies, 121–22
UN War Crimes Commission, 122–23
Urbano, Annalisa, 126
US Special Committee on Migration and Displacement, 16
US State Department, 16, 87

Vacanze di guerra (Rossetto), 227n1
Vanoni Plan (1955), 178
Vassallo, Giovanni, 196
Vatican, 52, 232n40, 242n3
  See also Catholic Church and Catholic organizations
Vecchi, Bernardo, 55
Venezia Giulia
  areas ceded to Yugoslavia, 2, 9, 182
  bonifica nazionale, 148, 154, 183, 189
  civilian post-war decisions, 73
  comparison to other areas, 155
  dispute over territory with Yugoslavia, 96–98, 123–25, 130
  nationality question, 156–58, 166, 211, 274n107
  Ufficio Venezia Giulia, 91

undetermined nationality, 151–53, 159, 173
Zone B of Istria, 121
Venice, 64, 131, 140, 189, 235n73
Victor Emmanuel III, 61, 82, 140
Villaggio Giuliano Dalmata, 180
Vulcania, 59, 118, 228n10, 258n188, 258n192

Waddington, T. T., 109, 255n154
Wagener, Otto, 238n96
Wang, Horng-luen, 136
Wankowicz, Witold, 101, 109, 252n122, 253n128
war crimes prosecution, 122–23, 236n81, 238n96
Watt, Lori, 16
Watts, Tracey, 123, 262n220
Webb, Kaye, 9
Whigham, I. H. D., 156–57
Wilson, Francesca, 84
Wilson, Woodrow, 35, 261n211
World Council of Churches, 175
World Refugee Year (WRY), 8–9, 15
World War I, 35–36

"Year of Africa," 15
Yugoslavia and Yugoslavs
displaced persons of, 245n46
Italians who remained, 208–9
Peace treaty of 1947, 73
Pula / Pola evacuation, 130–32, 264n248
residence and citizenship decision, 152–53, 155–59, 272n90
territories from Peace Treaty, 124–25

Zahra, Tara, 78
Zamindar, Vazira Fazila-Yacoobali, 19
Zamorani, Massimo, 55
Zanella, Riccardo, 97, 250n100
Zuccotti, Susan, 147

Milton Keynes UK
Ingram Content Group UK Ltd.
UKHW010141121023
430419UK00006BA/396